EARLY PRAISE FOR *BEAVER'S FIRE*

"As *Beaver's Fire* makes clear, for more than forty years now, George Venn—writer, editor, critic, and cultural documentarian—has contributed to and worked tirelessly to define, deepen and preserve a northwest literary tradition. Having served as general editor of *The Oregon Literature Series*—for that alone he already deserves our fullest esteem and gratitude. Venn's own words about poet John Haislip could as easily apply to Venn himself: he has 'held to his art by finding and holding his ground.' Gathered here, George Venn's wide-ranging work is at once foundational and essential."

—LEX RUNCIMAN, Author, *One Hour That Morning, Luck, The Admirations* (Oregon Book Award), *Out of Town,* and *Starting from Anywhere*

. . .

"I have loved George Venn's work since I first read the draft manuscript of *Marking the Magic Circle* in 1986. *Beaver's Fire* is a fine anthology, beautifully illustrated."

—JO ALEXANDER, Editor Emerita, Oregon State University Press

. . .

"For decades George Venn has been among the preeminent editors, scholars, and advocates of Pacific Northwest literature. *Beaver's Fire* is, for me, a long-awaited distillate of Venn's contributions in this field. Eclectic, at times strident, and deeply insightful, this is a carefully vetted collection of work gleaned from that span of decades, and an encapsulation of his life's work. It will enrich, and likely alter, any reader's understanding of the region and its literature."

—ROB WHITBECK, Author, *Writing Home Notes on the History* and *Literature of the Northern West*

. . .

"George Venn's collection *Beaver's Fire* usefully covers a lot of important ground—not just his own long and indispensable career as a Northwest writer and editor, but also the whole subject of Northwest history, literature, and lore. These are wise markings to travel our region by, and it is a welcome gift to have them done up handsomely in a book."

—JAROLD RAMSEY, Author, *Thinking Like a Canyon, Coyote Was Going There,* and *Reading the Fire*

. . .

"*Beaver's Fire* is an inside look at the tremendous, mind-boggling variety of Pacific Northwest literature. Venn is both practitioner (poet, essayist, teacher) and cool critic. He calls up a whole, mysteriously vibrant, growing region. His inner world, revealed in his own poems and little introductions to each writer, brings a sharp sense of place."

—THOMAS J. LYON, Editor, *The Literary West: An Anthology of Western American Literature* (1998); Editor, "Western American Literature" (1974 –1997); Editor-in-Chief, *Updating the Literary West* (1997)

"George Venn's *Beaver's Fire* is much more than a valuable compendium of his life-long work to describe and promote the literature of our region. He understands the importance of place and has been its champion. He ranges over it, giving us context and honest assessment without sentimentalism. In his many roles—historian, writer, teacher, husband, friend, and colleague—George is a passionate champion of the power of stories to teach us and unite us, even in our differences. He has blazed trails, not of tears but of celebration, connecting our past to our future. It's been a delight to follow them."

—DENNIS STOVALL, Publisher, Writer, Educator, and Literary Activist

"*Beaver's Fire* brings together in a single volume the gems of George Venn's writings over thirty-plus years in academia. Teaching in a fairly small college in a small town in sparsely populated eastern Oregon, George lived what he taught and wrote about: the local, the regional. These varied essays/poems/interviews/reviews are held together by a core perception: region is seen as microcosm, not as province. 'Place' takes on philosophical import that yields meaning through the particular and speaks to an audience far beyond the bounds of subject matter. I enjoyed my journey through this book, especially learning about C. E. S. Wood's transition from soldier to advocate through his role in the pursuit of Chief Joseph's fated Nez Perce tribe. Other highlights were his interactions with writers whose works he discussed—William Stafford, Wallace Stegner, and many others. This volume is a multifaceted book that is at once personal, literary, and eclectic."

—BARBARA HOWARD MELDRUM, Professor Emerita, University of Idaho;
Past President, Western Literature Association;
Editor, *Old West-New West; Centennial Essays* (1993)

"George Venn is *iconic*, a Lewis and Clark of northwest literature. *Beaver's Fire* exemplifies his unflagging quest to explore, share, encourage and contribute to the region's rich literature. Here we perceive Venn's scholarly appreciation for the Northwest's complex history and outstanding literary figures which, combined with his broad cultural vision and personal generosity, have created a lasting and productive regional fellowship of students, editors and fellow writers."

—LOIS BARRY, Professor Emerita, Eastern Oregon University;
Author, *Always First Class: The Pleasure of Personal Letters* (2009)

"George Venn uncovers many hidden histories of the Pacific Northwest, a region he cares about deeply. Between these covers, you will encounter stories you didn't know and counter stories for the ones you thought you knew. You need to know these other histories."

—NANCY COOK, Professor of English, University of Montana

"Like the myth of its title, *Beaver's Fire* works its magic by carrying the warmth of wisdom to the seeker in us all. The breadth and depth of this collection/anthology/portfolio of literary biographies, interviews, reviews, lectures, poetry, translations, and essays (personal, textual, critical, historical) is stunning and illuminating—offering a penetrating coherence that marks it as a distinct and invaluable work. The selections in *Beaver's Fire* span almost half a century in their publication dates and scan a great swath of Northwest literature in their contents. Poet, scholar, essayist, historian, and teacher, Venn has an original and essential grasp of Northwest literary history and a profound awareness of the play of place in its making. To read this *wonderful miscellany* is to feel Northwest culture and literature animate overlapping circles. The roads and rivers, fields and forests, neighborhoods and towns—where you live—might never be the same."

—Tim Barnes Author, *Definitions for a Lost Language* (2010)
and *Everyone Out Here Knows: A Big Foot Tale* (2014)

"*Beaver's Fire* is an amazing piece of work! George Venn is one of our best writers and observers."

—Shannon Applegate, Author, *Skookum: A Pioneer Family's History and Lore* and *Living Among Headstones: Life in a Country Cemetery*; Co-editor, *Talking on Paper: An Anthology of Oregon Letters and Diaries* and *Minus Tides*, an unpublished novel

"*Beaver's Fire* combines George Venn's passion, scholarship, and artistry by collecting in one volume legacy material and contemporary work. Venn proves that stories are not metaphors, symbols, or documents, but entities entirely unto their own, providing sustenance, solace, and seed, enriching our individual and collective lives. In *Marking the Magic Circle* we share and experience a snowbound evening simultaneously looking out into the world and deeply into ourselves. This is but one example of Venn focusing intently on the world at hand, and placing it in a complex, unique, and illuminating context. His gift is proving this close attention to our immediate physical and cultural surroundings renders us less provincial and more human and humane as citizens and selves.

We encounter Stafford, Kizer, and Hugo considering and creating the work that has become so important and vital to the larger Northwest. History encountered in these pages is neither placid nor past. We learn from soldiers, writers, activists, and witness examples in how to speak and act out against inhumane wars, the exploitation of workers, to shatter the dullness and conformity that can encase and isolate. *Beaver's Fire* demonstrates Venn's value to our region as a teacher, scholar, activist, and artist. I place *Beaver's Fire* upon my bookshelf knowing I will return to the pages again and again for knowledge, inspiration, and sheer pleasure."

—Robert Stubblefield, Author, University of Montana

PRAISE FOR OTHER WORKS BY GEORGE VENN

"For several years I have known George Venn, and have come to admire his poetry and criticism. I have read and listened to him in the company of other writers and scholars: we agreed on our assessments: high quality. There is a special quality about these writings— they are direct, clear, cogent. They flourish in the language, too. In particular, I have realized George's background and scope in his criticisms; he is a self-motivated scholar with great ability and authority."

—WILLIAM STAFFORD (1976)

* * *

"[*Marking the Magic Circle*] is the kind of book that makes one wish more writers had the interest and ability to explore their worlds of consciousness in different literary forms and that publishers would make them available. The pieces collected here fit together well, forming a natural habitat."

—NATHAN DOUTHIT (1987)

* * *

"Few people know as much about our region and its values as George Venn*** The Oregon Institute of Literary Arts and the Oregon Book Awards were created not only to recognize writers but to encourage Oregonians and others to learn about our rich literary heritage and its history. The *Oregon Literature Series* does just that. On behalf of Literary Arts, Inc., it is my great pleasure to present to George Venn the 1994 Stewart Holbrook Award for outstanding contributions to Oregon's literary life."

—BRIAN BOOTH (1994)

* * *

"Running like Blake's "Golden Thread" throughout all of George Venn's extraordinary career is a single, humbling, and unifying idea: whatever is close at hand, whatever is local, possesses all the qualities of excellence, or the possibilities for excellence that we are forever seeking in some other distant place. George Venn always reassures us that this very place is good enough, no apologies necessary. And we are all capable and sufficient for the hard task ahead of us: making something that is equally beautiful and enduring from whatever we've been fortunate enough to be given."

—DAVID AXELROD (1995)

* * *

"Professor Venn's work as General Editor of the *Oregon Literature Series* changed the way Oregonians think about their cultural traditions. His service to the region has been incalculable. He is an acknowledged scholar, poet, and teacher whose work has already made a difference to the cultural and historical literature of the region."

—MARIANNE KEDDINGTON-LANG (2002)

Selected Works by George Venn

Fred Hill: A Photographer's Life

Keeping the Swarm: New and Selected Essays

*Darkroom Soldier: Photographs and Letters from the
South Pacific Theater World War II. With Frederick H. Hill*

Soldier to Advocate: C. E. S. Wood's 1877 Legacy

West of Paradise: New Poems

The Oregon Literature Series, Vols. 1-6

Marking the Magic Circle: An Intimate Geography

Off the Main Road

Sunday Afternoon: Grande Ronde

Beaver's Fire

A Regional Portfolio (1970–2010)

GEORGE VENN

redbat books
2016

Printed in the United States of America

ISBN: 978-0-9971549-4-8
Library of Congress Control Number: 2016951263

First Trade Paperback Edition: September 2016

Published by
redbat books
2901 Gekeler Lane
La Grande, OR 97850
www.redbatbooks.com

Cover Art: "Mask 2" (1984) Water Color by Stephani Stephenson | www.revivaltileworks.com

Cover & Book Design: Kristin Summers | redbat design | www.redbatdesign.com

Author Photo: Stephani Stephenson

0916: clr+sGray

CONTENTS

Beaver's Fire

A Regional Portfolio (1970–2010)

INTRODUCTION

Like other regions in the United States—New England, South, Midland, Southwest—the Northwest literary ecosystem is complex, dynamic, and vast: innumerable poets, writers, readings, small presses, workshops, classes, conferences, MFAs, organizations, awards, contests, magazines, scholars, historians, bookstores, libraries, publishers, anthologies, readers, teachers, students, archives. Between 1970 and 2010, I contributed over one hundred non-fiction texts to enrich that regional literary culture—sometimes as critic or editor, other times as historian or scholar, still other times as translator or reviewer. Looking back at that lifetime of work, I realized that probably no one would ever find or even remember such a dispersed and eclectic body of writing created when Northwest literati invited me to contribute to publications, workshops, and other occasions.

So, this collection, which alludes directly or indirectly to the work of over 700 other writers, offers general readers, students, teachers, and literati—anywhere—a portfolio documenting over four decades in the Northwest literary community. Interviews, reviews, introductions, essays, symposia, translations, lectures, radio series, photos—these twenty-six texts provide a rich sample of grass roots literary life in the territory where—along with many brilliant, memorable, and generous contemporaries—I've lived, worked, studied, taught, written, edited, and published. Someday, maybe someone will write a comprehensive literary history of Oregon, Washington, Idaho, and Montana. Until that time, this portfolio will bear witness to selected occasions in these four decades.

To identify these pieces, I first reduced my choices to fifty-six, then commissioned a jury to formally evaluate those works. From fifteen invitations, sev-

en northwest literati accepted: Eric Muller, poet, author of *Steps*, editor of *Fire-weed* and Traprock Books, Eugene; Tim Barnes, co-editor of *Wood Works*, poet, professor, and C. E. S. Wood scholar, Portland; Robert Stubblefield, fiction writer and professor, University of Montana, Missoula; Nancy Cook, critic and professor of English, University of Montana, Missoula; Lois Barry, author of *Always First Class*, Professor of English emerita, Eastern Oregon University, La Grande; Rob Whitbeck, poet, historian, author of *Writing Home*, Fossil; Andy Meyer, historian, scholar, and humanist, The Northwest School, Seattle. (Here, I thank them for their stellar and enlightening work.)

Beginning in summer, 2013, I sorted those fifty-six pieces by three personae—"Historian," "Critic," and "Editor"—then mailed hard copies to all seven jurors. (Some texts were edited or revised, but all were substantially the same as published.) Working independently, jurors were asked to rate all fifty-six pieces to identify which might be most worthy of reprinting. No quotas implied or expected. By December, 2014, all jurors sent me their ratings which, added together, showed a surprising convergence on twenty-two of the pieces published here. With jurors' approval, I added four pieces to enrich and extend the record: (1) my 1984 essay on the Chinese poet Ai Qing; (2) Brian Attebery's 1980 "Northwest Poetry and the Land Symposium;" (3) Ronald H. Bayes' 1965 interview with Richard Hugo; (4) my 1993 speech from the Wallace Stegner Memorial Service.

To organize those combined choices, I have used reverse chronological order, expecting that if readers first encounter the "Symposium on Northwest Literature" from *Northwest Review* (2007), they may better engage some of the recurring issues and terms and questions in the Northwest literary forum: regional identity, stereotypes, literary merit, expanded canon, boundaries, and appropriate terms. For example, contrary to some contemporary exclusivity that identifies coastal sub-regions as "The Northwest," or lumps Washington and Oregon and Nevada into one region called "The Far West," I use "The Northwest" to include its sub-regions and their naturally occurring contiguous territories. That choice is consistent with cultural historians using the relationships between "Coast" and "Plateau," and regional editors such as H. G. Merriam and scholars such as

Raymond Gastil who have used "Northwest" or "Pacific Northwest" to name the bioregion of the Columbia River watershed and contiguous geography for over one hundred years.

All twenty-six texts included here would likely appear on any thoughtful literary map. In fact, each piece may enjoy a distinctive appeal, insight, and locale. Some texts, for example, would engage the entire region: the 1996 *StoryLines Northwest* programs reached over 676,000 listeners in Montana, Oregon, Washington; the 2007 *Northwest Review* "Symposium on Northwest Literature" published commentaries from writers across the entire region; the 1980 "Northwest Poetry and the Land" symposium based in Idaho included poets and writers from multiple subregions, Canada, and the Northeast. Other texts might be better understood as appealing to the universal via a particular subregion: the 2011 *Where the Crooked River Rises* by Ellen Waterston illuminates Oregon East; the 2004 "Rider in the Wilderness: Minor White in La Grande" reveals Oregon North. Still other texts combine a broad regional, national, and universal appeal: the 1971 "Elizabeth Gurley Flynn: Bringing Down Missoula" is grounded in Montana Rockies, but the successful 1909 free speech fight there influenced the entire American labor movement; the 1981 "Carolyn Kizer at Cannon Beach: An Interview with Tim Barnes" locates in Oregon West, but Barnes and Kizer's work and influence now clearly appeal beyond the site of origin; the 1993 "Remembering Wallace Stegner" tribute held in Portland alludes to his entire career and writing in various Western and Northwestern states.

For readers to perhaps gain some insight into the vast and transitory regional literary ecosystem, I added a brief "Preface" to each piece that describes original audience, purpose, message, persona, and occasion, and to enhance research and easy progress from piece to piece, most original footnotes and extended bibliography have been moved to the *Notes and Sources* section at the end of the book. To further enrich this record, I also include over fifty photos and images that generally identify some of the individuals and occasions contributing to the wealth of Northwest literature. To all those not included due to page limits, I apologize.

Finally, I want to offer an omnibus acknowledgment and a fire bundle of gratitude to these editors and publishers who were directly instrumental in first publishing the texts reprinted here: David Memmott, Elizabeth Canty-Jones, Marianne Keddington-Lang, John Witte, David Axelrod, Jodi Varon, Ulrich Hardt, David Milholland, Lowell Jaeger, Paul Zalis, Peter Sears, Anita Helle, John Daniel, Dennis Stovall, Linny Stovall, Tom Lyon, Robert Frank, Jo Alexander, Frank Walsh, Brian Attebery, Victor Trelawny, Vivian Paladin, David Wagoner, Vi Gale, Ron Ragsdale, and renewed thanks to my dedicated, patient, and skilled publisher Kristin Summers.

In the Nez Perce myth of the title, the elite pines are plainly selfish. They will not share their life-preserving and enhancing fire. So Beaver must steal that hoarded light, then escape down river, shaping our world, demonstrating survival strategy, and distributing illuminating force to the commonplace trees along the water. Because of Beaver's theft and gift, everyone now enjoys the freedom to live. Just as Beaver gives that integrity, complexity, and diversity to life downstream, so each writer offers the possibilities of discovering, illuminating, and extending Northwest literature—the voices and complexities of the place. So, wherever they are, let the elite of this world be selfish; let them hoard their power. Northwest writers still steal that coal of hope, escape downstream, find ways to spread the gift of revelation to us all.

George Venn
La Grande
October 2015

"Lower Grande Ronde River." *Courtesy Dave Jensen, April 2008.*

CHAPTER 1 | Farewell Speech / Nez Perce Myth (2002)

Preface to

BEAVER (Tàxcpol) AND THE GRANDE RONDE RIVER (Welíwe)

During graduate school in Missoula, I first read the story of In-Who-Lise, Nez Perce wife of Andrew Garcia in *Tough Trip Through Paradise*. Awakened by Garcia, by Jim Welch, and by *Black Elk Speaks*, I moved to the Grande Ronde Valley to teach at Eastern Oregon University where—early on—I collaborated on "Indian Elders Speak," the first and only interdisciplinary course to invite tribal elders—Umatilla, Warm Springs, Nez Perce, Walla Walla, and Cayuse—to address our class. Enlightened by elders, students, and colleagues, I served on the Indian Education Institute board, attended root feasts on the reservation and on campus, learned to round dance to beautiful drums, helped the tribe successfully oppose a local dam. Assigning Native American works in my Western and Northwestern literature courses, I became the first professor east of the Oregon Cascades to regularly teach indigenous texts such as those in Jarold Ramsey's *Coyote Was Going There*. After thirty years of teaching (1970–2002), Eastern Oregon University honored me with the "Distinguished Faculty Teaching Award." Invited to give a short speech, I read the following address to a packed campus theater on October 1, 2002, a text made possible by discovering and valuing universal motifs in indigenous local narratives. In a later revision, I incorporated local Nez Perce nouns from the tribal lexicon.

Sources: Nez Perce Tribe. *Indian Legends of the Pacific Northwest.* Ella Clark(ed). Berkeley: U. of California 1953. The following text incorporates minor revisions of the 2002 speech as well as revisions in *Ronde Dance* 1.1 (2006): 9-11.

BEAVER (Tàxcpol) AND THE
GRANDE RONDE RIVER (Welíwe)

At the end of my teaching career this October afternoon, I don't want to say too much. Teaching writing and literature at this university for thirty years, I've probably done that already. So, to bring you—in my allotted ten minutes— something about teaching and learning, about the universal and the particular, the native and the immigrant, present and past, myth and reality, let me tell you the oldest story I learned about the valley where we live today—a Nez Perce (Ni-Mi-Pu) myth first transcribed in 1891, but probably told around Wallowa band winter fires along the Snake and Imnaha Rivers for thousands of years—until the United States stole the Wallowa Valley in 1863 and drove out the Nez Perce in 1877. During the story, I'll interrupt twice to comment on the phases of the quest—departure, initiation, return—the quest being the most universal story of the search for a place, object, person, identity, essence, condition, truth.

PROLOGUE

> *Before there were any people in the world, animals and trees moved about and talked together just like human beings. At that time, only Pine Trees knew how to make fire. The Pines were selfish and would not tell anyone what they knew. The other trees did not know the secret of fire. The animal people did not know the secret of fire. No matter how cold the winters, no people but the Pine Trees could warm themselves.*

> *One winter it was very, very cold—so cold that the animal people feared they would freeze to death. They begged the Pine Trees to warm them or to tell them their secret of fire. But the Pines would not tell. Again and again the animal people tried to find out the secret, but they could not.*

At last Beaver had an idea. Beaver said to the other animal people, "I have a plan. I believe it will work. I believe I can get fire from the Pine Trees." Beaver knew the Pine Trees were planning a great council in the Grande Ronde Valley. Beaver decided to go to that council.

DEPARTURE (SEPARATION)

In the first phase of the quest, Beaver answers the "Call to Adventure." Leaving the commonplace, the every day, the freezing, the vulnerable, the fearful, the inner suffering, Beaver voluntarily proceeds to the threshold of adventure. Destiny has summoned Beaver, transferred Beaver's spiritual center of gravity from the known social world to an unknown zone... a place of strange and dangerous amorphous beings. There is no guide, no threshold guardian, no shadow guarding the route. Trusting only in vision, dream, idea, Beaver must now go into the kingdom of the dark unknown to perform a heroic task.

On the bank of the Grande Ronde River, the Pine Trees built a big fire, so they could warm themselves after bathing in the cold water. Guards stood all around the fire and the camp. They kept away all the other trees and animals. No one was allowed to learn the Pine Trees' secret.

Before those guards took their places, Beaver hid under the overhanging bank—the way all beavers do. There, the wise one waited and watched the Pine Trees warm themselves around their big fire. After a while, a live coal came rolling down the bank—right toward where Beaver was hiding. The wise one grabbed that coal, hid it under one armpit, and swam away—across the valley—as fast as beavers can go.

INITIATION (Road of Trials, Tests, Meeting the Goddess, Atonement with the Father, Apotheosis, the Boon Gained)

In this middle phase of the quest, the hero/heroine must survive a series of miraculous tests and ordeals and gain a boon—some physical or spiritual gift. In this strange place ruled by the powerful, selfish, and unfriendly Pine Trees, The River becomes Beaver's helper. At the moment of greatest test—that coal of fire rolling down the bank—Beaver triumphs because of position, patience, receptivity, courage, self-control, self-discipline. When Beaver reaches out, tucks away that coal of fire, and starts to flee, we all recognize a selfless heroic act. We all feel some kind of triumph. We grimace at the implied pain. The impossible becomes possible. Wonder, mystery, freedom, hope, courage, understanding—all these expand.

RETURN

Now, the final phase of the universal pattern can begin—the return. If the Pine Trees had blessed Beaver, they would protect the wise one now, but those selfish trees are still angry. What will happen to Beaver and this stolen and life-transforming gift?

> *The Pine Trees started chasing Beaver. When they got too close, Beaver swam in big curves from one bank of the river to the other, and when the Pine Trees stopped for breath, Beaver swam in a straight line. That's why the Grande Ronde River (Welíwe) today meanders back and forth in some places and flows straight in other places. The river follows the route Beaver (Tàxcpol) took when stealing the coal of fire.*
>
> *After a while, most of the Pine Trees were out of breath and gave up the chase. They stopped above the Grande Ronde River, where they still stand in a forest so thick hunters can't walk through it. A few trees kept on chasing Beaver, but—a few at a time or one at a time—even those Pine Trees got tired and gave up—and they're still there today in the canyon along the Grande Ronde River.*
>
> *One Cedar Tree (Talàtat) had been running along with the Pine Trees. When he too gave up chasing Beaver, Cedar said to his friends, "We can't catch Beaver now, but I'll see where the wise one goes." So, Cedar Tree climbed a high ridge and watched as Beaver—far below—swam down the Grande Ronde River until he entered the Snake. Then, the Pine Trees knew Beaver had escaped. (This is where Beaver crosses the return threshold—the site of the Wallowa band's permanent winter camp at the confluence of the Grande Ronde and Snake Rivers.)*
>
> *As Cedar Tree watched Beaver swim down the Snake River, he told the Pine Trees below what Beaver was doing: "Now Beaver is giving some fire to the Willow Trees on the west bank," Cedar called down. Then, he watched Beaver swim across the river. "Now, Beaver is giving some fire to the Birch Trees on the east bank," called Cedar. "Now he is giving*

some fire to the Cottonwoods." Beaver was sharing the fire with many other trees, and now, they have fire in them too—if you rub their woods together in the right way.

On a ridge where the Grande Ronde River joins the Snake, Cedar Tree still stands alone. He is very old and his top is dead. Ni-Mi-Pu point to him and say to their children, "There's Old Cedar. He still stands where he stopped chasing Beaver, the wise one who gave our people fire."

EPILOGUE

Beaver's return shapes the world we live. The gift of fire brings life and light and renews the people. When the pursuing Pine Trees come too close, Beaver shows us symbolically how to evade: move in deceptive curves. Whenever we see the meandering channel of the Grande Ronde River, we remember that life-preserving advice—to avoid the rigidity of straight lines. We see what human success means. We also see how The River, Beaver's helper, sustains this heroic return. At the return threshold, the Pine Trees must remain behind; only Cedar Tree can see Beaver now as the wise one comes back alive from the unknown. Now, bearing the power of a superhuman gift, Beaver must confront the problems of heroic return: being overwhelmed with banality, being rejected, being cold-shouldered with indifference. To solve these crises of bearing mysterious gifts into the common world, Beaver freely gives away that otherworldly fire—the stolen boon—to other trees. With that gift, Beaver symbolically makes life accessible and possible in the world of suffering people and animals, and so the wise one becomes the vehicle of illumination. Universal mystery is reconciled with individual consciousness, the infinite becomes the local, the abstract concrete. Now, there is freedom to live.

So, there is the quest—the most universal literary pattern—departure, initiation, return—and there is its oldest local manifestation, perhaps known for 10,000 years in this valley where we live today. In ten minutes, you now know—in summary—everything we attempt—in multitudinous ways—to learn and teach and live. I wish you all the best. May Beaver and The River be with you on your journey. *Wisteqné mise! Adios! Zai Jian!*

Preface to

WHERE THE CROOKED RIVER RISES: A HIGH DESERT HOME

February, 2011, *Oregon Historical Quarterly (OHQ)* editor Eliza E. Canty-Jones asked me to review *Where the Crooked River Rises*, Ellen Waterston's essay collection. I had served on the *OHQ* editorial board, a respected journal for scholars and general readers in the Pacific Northwest with circulation around 3,500. The editors had previously published both my reviews and articles. So, I accepted the Waterston assignment—gratis—as usual. For years, I'd known Waterston as an ambitious, talented, rising Central Oregon writer and poet. Back in 1980, she sent me her poems to critique. We presented poetry readings together. She attended my C. E. S. Wood lecture. She invited me to present a workshop at The Nature of Words—her Bend writer's conference. So, in eight weeks I read the 140 pages, read her other three books, then drafted 600 words that addressed the five assigned topics: (1) a brief summary of the book; (2) a critique of the reliability and readability of the book; (3) a recommendation about audience and utility; (4) a critical reflection on the quality of scholarship; (5) an explanation of the basic arguments of the book. After a second reading of her essays, I revised: made more complete references to all of Waterston's writing; made more specific references to events and names Waterston had obscured or omitted; made the text more canonical by briefly placing Waterston in the company of other high desert authors. Responding by email on April 18, Canty-Jones wrote, "I want to thank you for being so conscientious about the review (this will only result in your being asked to do more, I hope you know)."

Sources: *Oregon Historical Quarterly* 112, No. 2 (Summer 2011): 268-269; Photo courtesy Ellen Waterston.

WHERE THE CROOKED RIVER RISES:
A HIGH DESERT HOME
by Ellen Waterston

From Sarah Winnemucca to Julia Gillis, Dorothy Lawson McCall to C. E. S. Wood, Ada Hastings Hedges to Jarold Ramsey, and William Kittredge to Eileen McVicker, Oregon's high desert has inspired nearly 150 years of literary revelation. With this fourth book, Ellen Waterston adds to those revelations. Nine published and seven unpublished works predominate—non-fiction essays that can mix autobiography, biography, history, anecdote, journalism, and folklore. Three pieces derive from Waterston's acclaimed 2003 memoir *Then There Was No Mountain: A Parallel Odyssey of a Mother and Daughter through Addiction* (Rowman Littlefield). Two poems and at least nine photographers enhance the work with twenty-six black-and-white photographs—four by Waterston herself.

Where the Crooked River Rises seems grounded in two personal epochs. New England native, 1968 Harvard B.A., University of Madagascar M.A., stringer for *Time*, Waterston was suitably married to Samuel J. Bartow. As readers of *Then There Was No Mountain* know, the newlyweds first ranched in Montana, then came to Oregon in 1973 and bought a remote spread on the Crooked River. For seventeen years, the couple ranched. While raising three children, Waterston learned to love the desert, but Bartow became a drug addict. Their paradise became hell. In 1985, Ellen Bartow and her three young children evacuated "our desert ranch to town in the family station wagon" (*Then There Was No Mountain*, xiii).

Single mother and divorced, Bartow adopted her maiden name again. As Ellen Waterston, she found refuge in booming Bend, where she became a suc-

cessful strategic planner and communications specialist. As journalist, writer, and poet, she founded a literary retreat, published her 2003 memoir, and won the 2005 national WILLA award in poetry for *I Am Madagascar* (2004). Since 2005, she has been the impresario of The Nature of Words, an ambitious and successful literary organization. Among her recent honors is a second WILLA award for *Between Desert Seasons* (2009, Wordcraft of Oregon).

Many of these essays tacitly contrast those two personal epochs. In "Pau-Mau," she celebrates ranch women at their Christmas party, then in "What One Thing," she describes a Bend dinner party of new peers—non-profit schmoozers and shakers. In "That's Deep," she describes "Jack," a nonagenerian rancher and his "settin in the saddle" theories (p. 48). "Main Thing," in contrast, sketches the urban advocacy of Don Kerr, founder of the High Desert Museum, and documents his theory: we must shift from "user to steward or all will be lost" (p. 63). In "Two Alices," Waterston describes homesteader Alice Day Pratt (1872–1963) and rancher Alice DeLore. Sketching those single women living alone, Waterston explores the differences between her own flight and those who refused to marry or leave. Her poems continue these tacit contrasts: in 2000, she published "Trapping Coyotes," a folkloristic monologue of Van Houston, a character documented during her ranching past in *Then There Was No Mountain*; in 2005, Waterston was commissioned to write and perform "Take a River," a pop history of Bend, for the city centennial. Finally, she contrasts her "homes." In "The Old Hackleman Place..." she "takes a sentimental journey...to that beloved, dusty ranch where I once lived...as a newlywed, carried three children, raised a family, and watched a husband become invisible to himself..." (p. 29–30). In "Looking Up to Low," she describes her new urban home "on the banks of the Deschutes River as it flows through downtown Bend" and fifty-some pages later mentions her failing second marriage to David Bong (p. 67).

Some readers may find Waterston unreliable: in "Cows Kill Salmon," "Last Log," and "Morally Certain," the author avoids stating how and why capitalism degrades and destroys ecosystems, begins and ends industries, attracts and subjugates populations. Other readers may want fewer inaccuracies, more credits, and larger, sharper photographs. Nevertheless, Waterston delivers: perched on an empty barn wall, coiled riata in hand, black Stetson on her head, she stares out—a rider ready for whatever revelation comes next. Sometime she lives in hard country, sometimes she lives in boom town. Winnemucca to McVicker, her desert ancestors understand and applaud.

Chapter 2 ▪ WHERE THE CROOKED RIVER RISES: A HIGH DESERT HOME

DARKROOM SOLDIER

PHOTOGRAPHS AND LETTERS FROM THE SOUTH PACIFIC THEATER WORLD WAR II

By **Frederick H. Hill** with **George Venn**

CHAPTER 3 | Editorial Introduction (2007)

Preface to

THEY ALSO SERVED:
A SOLDIER'S PACIFIC THEATER ALBUM, WW II

On May 12, 2004, while researching the internationally-distinguished photographer Minor White, I scheduled an interview with Fred Hill, a nonagenarian photographer living just a few blocks from my home in La Grande. I'd been told that Fred Hill knew Minor White. I knew nothing about Hill or his work. In his basement studio that afternoon, Hill showed me his original photo archive—over 13,000 negatives—and a box of 315 of his World War II letters to his first wife Martha Simonson (at left). At that point, serendipity took over. After I finished the Minor White essay (see Ch. 6), Hill and I spent the next two years collaborating on a book-length manuscript of his World War II experience. Jan Boles, The College of Idaho, selected the photographs. Union County Cultural Trust, Lyle Schwarz, Hill family, Verna Hill, and Marie Balaban supported that process. (My task was researching, drafting, and revising captions to convert the 250 original images from artifacts to documents.) Eventually, Timothy Lucas of Bushwhack Graphics digitized Hill's images, and formatted the manuscript that became *Darkroom Soldier*. Rejected by publishers, I queried *Oregon Historical Quarterly* editor Marianne Keddington-Lang. She replied that "the *Quarterly* would be enriched by a piece that introduces [Hill] to readers through his photographs and letters…If you have an interest in putting together a piece for *OHQ*, I would be delighted…." By October, 2007, *Darkroom Soldier* was released to national and regional reviews. Both hardback and paper sold out; the Caxton reprint still sells. In 2008, National Best Books honored the volume as a Finalist in Military History. Hill's entire WW II collection is now online in two libraries: Pierce Library, Eastern Oregon University (pierce.eou. edu/home/collections); McDermott Library, US Air Force Academy (afac.sdp. sirsi.net/client/cadet).

Source: *Oregon Historical Quarterly* 108.2 (2007): 294-316.

THEY ALSO SERVED:
A SOLDIER'S PACIFIC THEATER ALBUM,
WORLD WAR II

by Frederick H. Hill with George Venn and Jan Boles

Born in 1920 in Elgin, Oregon, photographer Fred Hill grew up in a family that loved cameras, darkrooms, and black-and-white prints. His grandfather had worked with glass-plate negatives, and he had taught Fred's mother how to develop and print her own pictures. By the time Fred turned eleven, his father Lynn, who ran the local hardware store, and his mother Etha, a teacher and homemaker, had cleared a space in their cellar, and their boy was making contact prints. Down in that darkroom one day, Fred mustered the courage to develop his first roll of personal film, and that process launched his seventy-year quest for memorable, useful, and beautiful images.[1]

Attending Eastern Oregon University in La Grande between 1938 and 1940, the novice photographer carried his camera everywhere. During the summer of 1940, Hill met and befriended Minor White—later an internationally famous fine-art photographer—who was then teaching his first photography classes at the Works Progress Administration Art Center in La Grande. Using the Hill family car, White and Hill photographed northeast Oregon together—more as fellow freelance photographers than as teacher and student. After White left La Grande in November 1941, he continued to correspond with Etha Hill, Fred's mother, and in February 1945, the two young photographers met again on Mindoro, the Philippine island where now Sergeant White was serving in Army 24th Infantry Intelligence and Sergeant Hill was working in 5th Air Force Photo Reconnaissance. At

Fred Hill included this photograph of the 17th Photo Section posing on their foxhole cover in Dulag, Leyte, in his January 10, 1945, letter to his wife: (From left) Sgt. Van Reimer, Cpl. Dick Baxter, Pvt. A. J. Countryman, Pvt. Walt Peters (medic), Sgt. Fred Hill, and Sgt. Ed Bernardo.

their February 1945 meeting, they discussed photography, took photographs of orchids, and talked about enrolling in a California art school after the war.[2]

In July 1940, Hill joined the 41st Division National Guard unit in La Grande. Once a week, his infantry unit drilled at the armory for three hours until, on September 16, 1940, everything changed. National Guard units were federalized, and Private Hill became a full-time soldier in the U.S. Army. Though he insisted he was a photographer, the army placed Hill in an infantry mortar squad and shipped him to Fort Lewis, Washington, for training. After asserting for fifteen months that he was, in fact, a photographer, in November 1941 a month before the Japanese attack on Pearl Harbor, the army finally transferred Hill to the new Oregon National Guard 123rd Observation Squadron at the fort's Gray Airfield.[3]

In May 1942, Hill married his sweetheart Martha Simonson at her parents' home in Tacoma. For the next seven months, he flew as an observer on coastal submarine patrol, photographed the camouflage of Coast Guard units, worked in various offices, and—as always—recorded the world around him with his camera. In December, Private Hill was transferred to a base in Salinas, California, where the army assigned him to the 17th Tactical Reconnaissance Squadron, 5th Air Force. Eventually, the squadron got its orders, and the men moved to training bases in Louisiana and Mississippi.

On October 6, 1943, they boarded the SS *General John Pope* in Newport News, Virginia, and sailed for the South Pacific front. For some time, offi-

Fred and Martha Simonson were photographed on their wedding day in Tacoma, Washington.

cial opinion had generally agreed that "the military organization with the most efficient photographic reconnaissance would win the war."[4] Fred Hill would contribute to that victory.

Hill served as an aerial photo reconnaissance lab chief in the Pacific Theater. Like the men in other such squadrons, he and his crew set up and operated darkrooms to process the photographs brought back by squadron planes that flew over Japanese-held territory. Sometimes, if American anti-aircraft guns fired three red warning flares over their tents, they ran for their foxholes, but if these darkroom soldiers were to provide critical target and topographic photographs to commanders and pilots, they had to be removed from combat.

Like thousands of other support troops who survived World War II, Sgt. Fred Hill never fired a shot in combat.[5] His only weapon was accurate, clear aerial photographs; his front line the darkroom tent; his enemies dust, heat, fatigue, sickness, loneliness, insects, boredom, faulty equipment, military life, KP. To survive that perpetual chaos, Hill found a way to share, preserve, and order his inner life. He wrote regularly to Martha—sometimes, twice a day.

On November 4, 1943, the day he landed at Milne Bay to the heat, sweat, native drums, mud, papaya, mosquitoes, and malaria of tropical New Guinea, he sent his first letter to Martha. Over the next two years, he sent some 315 more, letters always censored by the army, letters Martha still read, responded to, and saved. After the war, she sorted and tied them with string and, leaving most in their original envelopes, stored them in a plywood box with other war memorabilia. Now, sixty years later, the letters have been transcribed and edited, and excerpts appear for the first time in the following pages. They constitute one part of Hill's Pacific Theater album—a rich, personal, and intimate correspondence from an Oregon soldier to his wife.

Hill's album is also rich with the many photographs he collected during his time in the Pacific Theater.[6] As he and his lab crew moved north from Milne Bay toward Japan, they processed up to thousands of aerial photographs per day. During their all-night shifts, they watched for compelling images, which they sometimes copied and saved: bombing runs, enemy fortifications, bomb damage, and significant events such as the February 16, 1945, landing on Corregidor of the 503rd Parachute Infantry. Copies of these official images make up another part of Hill's Pacific Theater album.

Sometimes, other soldiers or photographers asked Hill's darkroom crew to develop personal film for them. If Hill saw an intriguing or potentially compelling image, he saved an extra print or two for his collection. Sometimes, he asked other photo lab workers, visitors, or Filipinos to take pictures with his camera—pictures of groups, of individuals, and of Fred himself. In his published work, Hill refers to all these photographs as the "Fred Hill Collection."

Throughout his two-year deployment with the 17th Tactical Reconnaissance Squadron, Hill also regularly sent Martha another part of the Pacific Theater album—his own black-and-white photographs. While stationed on New Guinea for eight months, Hill and his fellow soldiers frequently used their days off to make personal photo expeditions: on bases, in local towns and villages, around the countryside. From Japanese wreckage to beautiful ammunition, from native dancers to army fishermen, Hill recorded both military and civilian life. Moving to the island of Biak, he photographed warplanes, drilling wells, blasting la-

Fred Hill (above) works with his 3-A camera, purchased from Bass Camera in Chicago. Using unexposed ends of K-17 film, Hill could make 3×5" photos.
Sgt. Roy Wolford (left) holds a K-17 Fairchild aerial reconnaissance camera without the film magazine attached.

trines, Bob Hope, Frances Langford, darkroom set-up and tear-down, beautiful WACS, Queen Wilhelmina's birthday dancers. Arriving on Leyte in October 1944, he shot photographs of Philippine *carabao*, cockfights, outriggers, native women, folk art. By war's end, Hill had accumulated over six hundred black-and-white photos.[7]

Many of those images were made possible by an unlikely source—aerial reconnaissance film for the K-17 camera. This film came in rolls ten inches wide by up to two hundred feet long. After a mission, Hill's crew brought the magazine of exposed film to the photo lab, and in total darkness, they cut off the exposed portion of the film to be developed, printed, annotated, and delivered to commanders. When there were only ten exposures left on a roll, they discarded that tag end and installed a new two-hundred-foot roll to be loaded in the plane for the next mission. Wasting that end of unexposed film—perhaps ten feet long by ten inches wide—"tore our hearts out," Hill remembered.[8] So he and four other men invented a slitter, cut the aerial film into three and one quarter inch strips, wound those strips onto film spools, and installed the salvaged film in Kodak 3-A

Eight .50 caliber machine guns were mounted in the bombardier's compartment in this B-25J. With two packet guns mounted on sides of the fuselage and the top turret gun locked in forward position, this photo reconnaissance plane could also engage in effective strafing attacks.

cameras (postcard cameras) ordered from the States. Blocking out the red window on the back of the camera, they calibrated and recorded the number of turns required to advance the film to the next exposure.[9]

⸱ ⸱ ⸱

Hill's Pacific Theater collection—letters, official aerial photos, copied photos, personal photos, movies, artifacts—may be most readily appreciated by focusing on his three months on Mindoro, the Philippine island where he served from January 7 to April 4, 1945. On workdays, he photographed mechanics, weapons, planes, and pilots. On days off, he and his friends found a jeep and left the base to capture local civilian life—fishing, farming, landscapes—and visited locals such as James Aubi, who invited Hill to his home on Ambulong Island. Frequently, he used three cameras on a single outing: a Zeiss Super Nettel, an 8mm Revere movie camera, and a Kodak 3-A. He also planned a photo

Fred Hill's print crew works in the darkroom: (front to back) Sgt. Earl Powers at the contact printer, Pvt. A. J. Countryman at the developer tray (the "Souper"), and Corp. Oakley Scott at the fixer tray (the "Splasher").

marketing project and joined the Photographic Society of America. During a wildcat leave in Manila, he delivered canned milk to a Filipino family with a baby and talked with journalist Roberto Villanueva about opening a studio there after the war.[10]

During those three months, Martha Hill found ways to sustain her distant husband. After working on the construction of war planes all day at Boeing in Seattle, she bought, packed, and shipped nine used Kodak cameras that Hill re-sold to soldiers. She mailed orange juice, newspapers, maps, sunglasses, cookies, and, most important, cans of movie film for his Revere and rolls of 35mm color film.

When Hill returned from his wildcat leave in Manila, his cot was stacked: eleven letters and a pile of packages—all from Martha. In his thirty-eight letters from Mindoro, he professed his love, dreamed of houses, bathrooms, children, and clean water. He sent Martha money orders from the used camera sales, a Philippine newspaper, a risqué cartoon, and many black-and-white prints with a list of enclosures. An army censor removed his photo of Major Shomo, a famous fighter pilot doing a "Victory Roll"—one complete rotation before landing to signal the shooting down of a Japanese plane. In early March, he sent her a box of souvenirs, his negatives file, and all his slides and prints. Martha saved everything. After the atomic destruction of Hiroshima and Nagasaki on August 6 and 9 and the Japanese surrender on August 15, Hill sailed home to Seattle and Martha.

These selections from Hill's Pacific Theater album have been taken from *Darkroom Soldier*, a book-length manuscript in progress. Excerpted from Hill's letters and selected from over a hundred black-and-white prints, these largely unknown Mindoro and Manila images and texts provide an important and rich personal record of endurance and humane understanding in a time of war.

Hill recorded the U.S. Navy miscalculation at Leyte that might have saved his life. Preparing to load this LST, the navy captain beached 626 too high. After being loaded, not even a navy tug and other LSTs could pull the ship off the sand. Hill and the 71st Group soldiers watched their assigned convoy sail for Mindoro, then camped on San Pedro Beach and began to unload the boat. While Hill's squadron spent a hot week unloading, refloating, relanding, and reloading LST 626, Japanese planes attacked their convoy, bombed and sank several LSTs, and blew up an ammunition ship. When they sailed for Mindoro on January 3, the convoy was watched by only one Japanese observation plane.

December 30, 1944: San Pedro Bay Beach, Leyte Gulf

Hello Darling—

We're about one hundred yards from the beach. Black sand everywhere in shoes, clothes, barracks bags, blankets, even mess kits. Any breeze picks up light sand and deposits it everywhere. There are three Filipino homes about thirty feet from here. We are camped in their front yard—so to speak. We go swimming in the surf.

We were told that we could say we were at sea on an LST, but we aren't. However, LSTs are very nice. I always thought they were just empty shells, but no, they are very complete ships. Nice quarters and facilities. First ice water I've had since Finschhaven and the first lavatories and good lighted mirrors since the USS John Pope. And the toilets were the first land-type jobs with levers to pull since we left Virginia. Good meals too. Risdon and I spent a couple of nights on deck, and it rained both nights, but we were well-sheltered.

This episode of ours [grounding and reloading LST 626] is humorous—now that we look back on it. While we're here, I'm going to try to get some shots of local people at home with my telephoto lenses. Today, I got them washing clothes with well water. Also, a woman bathing. They put on sort of a heavy slip with no straps and wash right through it. They soap it up, rub themselves with it, and then pour water over their heads to rinse off. Put a dress on, drop the slip, and step out of it.

Some of these people are just as nice as any you'd meet back in the States. They wear wooden sandals with carved, built-up heels. Many white dresses. Don't know how they keep them so snowy white, but they are spotless. So are their homes.

Honey, this is the end of this year and I had figured only eleven more months, but with Germany still holding out so vigorously, I'm beginning to wonder if "Golden Gate in '48" isn't a more logical slogan. I'd hate to only come home for twenty one days, then have to come back overseas again.

January 10, 1945: San Jose, Mindoro

Hello Sweetheart—

Whew! It's hot. This place is matted dry grass and scattered trees that look like scrub oaks. Our camp is on top of a hill; there are valleys on three sides

McGuire Airdrome outside San Jose was a temporary base for the B-25s of Hill's 17ᵗʰ Tactical Reconnaissance Squadron. To build these bright runways and taxi strips, army engineers crushed, spread, and compacted tons of white coral. Mindoro Strait is in the background.

about fifty feet below. Not a tree in our area, but there does seem to always be a breeze. Drinking water isn't bad, and it cools off pretty much at night. Humidity isn't very high, and evaporation is good. Rather discouraged about getting our Section set up. No tents or tent poles. We have big tarps, but no lumber or poles to build frames. Practically no bamboo. Practically no bananas.

Our tent has the same occupants as before: Ugly Bernardo, Second Ugly Baxter, and Third Ugliest—me. Useless Pete the Medic, *Carabao Eyes* (Elsie) Reimer, and *the* AJ Countryman. What an assortment. You have the pix I sent of all of us on our foxhole cover at Dulag (*p. 31*). That should show you the horrors of war!

Down in the valley to the east is a pasture and swamp where *carabao* and Brahma steers graze. There is a white heron that feeds right beside the animals—even flies up and rides on the backs of the *carabao*. Could have gotten it with the long telephoto, but the light was no good, and I don't have a tripod unpacked.

Sergeant Hill copied and saved this aerial photograph of Allied bombing during the Philippines campaign.

No showers yet. The boys are digging a well. They took three trucks and took us three miles to the river for a swim and wash. Thigh-deep river and unsuccessful swimming. Had some strong cheap soap at the time, and as I bent over to submerge and rinse my hair, some soap ran into my right nostril. So irritated those delicate membranes that my nostril has dripped clear water for the last two days and my head aches right above the bridge of my nose.

January 11, 1945: San Jose, Mindoro (same envelope)

Am marked "Quarters" today. Last night, had fever of 102.2. This a.m., it was 99.6. Now, it is sub-normal. Will probably be up towards night. Dengue fever. Will last three days at most. Probably go back to work tomorrow. Been taking aspirin and codeine.

They are digging a well. Down eighteen feet through red and blue clay by noon. I've heard three blasts since then, and they still haven't hit water. If they ever do hit a vein of sand or gravel, there will be more water than we can use.

January 14-15, 1945: San Jose, Mindoro

Hello My Precious—

Have been playing chess much of late. We have a heavy board and some of those neat molded plastic chess men. I have whopped Bernardo, Gertz, and

Fred Hill (center) watches 17th Photo Section men play chess. Waiting for their planes to return, the soldiers had time to read, take pictures, and play games. Once they had unloaded film from the planes, they often worked all night.

Robbins pretty consistently. Robbins continually tries to pull "Scholar's Mate" on me! Tsk! Tsk! Do I know some blocks for that one.

I had to go help Bernardo get cameras ready for tomorrow's mission, and when I got back the lights were out. Oh well. I was nearly through writing anyway.

Not much happened today. We got the lab a little nearer ready for operation. Got the print dryer assembled and the command post tent, which serves us as a make-shift printing room, is practically ready to go. We still have to use the little one-man igloo developing room with zipper opening. Not high enough to stand up in and mercilessly hot. I guess I told you about those igloos before—when we were forced to use them at Finschhaven.

Van and Price took today's film over to the 82nd to get processed. They have one of the fancy new portable labs. There are quite a number of them around, but we'd never get one. We've had one on requisition since last April, renewed each month.

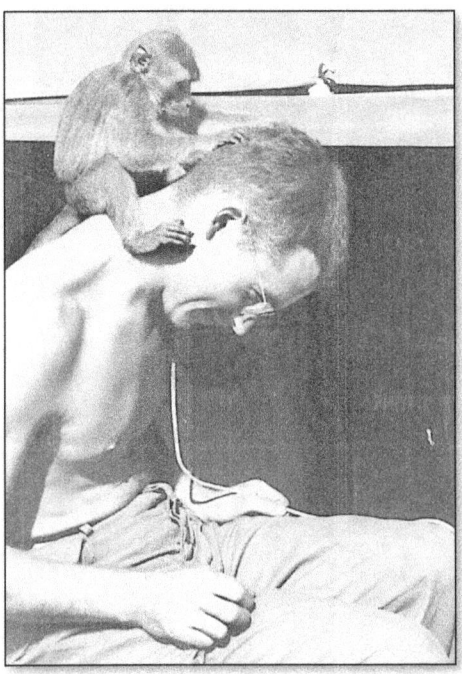

Jocko, Baxter's new pet monkey, searches Fred's hair for any delicacy.

You know, we've never had a lab that would take care of any production. These igloos are from airborne units designed to operate in a flying plane, so you can imagine their output capacity. We have turned out over 2,000 prints in one night on several occasions, but always from labs we've built—never from any prefabricated set up that we could take with us. It's always the same story: build, build, build, then tear down and move, then build, build, build. Of course, it does add variety: never the same layout twice.

Beat Bernardo to a bloody pulp at noon today with chess. Honey girl, I dream only of the days I'll be with you again and for the happy times there will be eating ice in lemon Cokes, sherbet, iced tea, and lots and lots of loving. Then, an after-dinner mint or two and some swimming.

January 29, 1945: San Jose, Mindoro

Hello My Darling—

Baxter bought a monkey today for $35.00. Tame friendly fellow. Likes to throw the local dogs for a loop. Right now, he's lonesome and raising a hell of a fuss trying to get me to come and play with him. Everyone else has gone to the show, "Guy Named Joe." The monkey was asleep when Baxter left. Now he wants to play, and I'm much too busy writing to you.

Darn monkey is just like a baby. I just put him to sleep like I did Marjorie lots of times. Held him until he quieted down, then gradually shifted him to a folded blanket. Kept rubbing him and talking to him until I could get completely away from him. Surely an affectionate critter. Gets mighty lonesome for companionship.

Maj. Gen. Ennis Whitehead (center) visited the camp to award medals to flight crews for distinguished past service. Whitehead talks here with Master Sgt. Robert Lincoln Barlow (left), a twenty-eight-year veteran. Maj. Joel C. Wise, commander of the newly decorated 17th Reconnaissance Squadron and Hill's immediate supervisor, stands and listens.

Here are four pix: the orderly room at 72 with bulletin board; our present operations tent; our shower, showing the valley to the east; and women washing clothes in the river.

February 5, 1945: San Jose, Mindoro

Hello Sweetheart—

Mosquitoes are plenty thick tonight. Khakis aren't thick enough—they bite right through it. Seems good to have Bob back again. Have missed his superb line of bullshit. It's good even when you know it's stretched. There is a small rat snooping around under Baxter's sack. He watches me from behind a box and occasionally ventures out in the open.

Today was an outstanding day. Major General Whitehead presented awards and medals to members of flight crews of this squadron. Think

I have some good shots of it. Took eight slides and half a roll of Koda-chrome—the last and only roll of Kodachrome I have. Took the roll out and put the black and white back in the camera. So, I am sweating out packages of film—from any source.

Those three lenses began paying for themselves today. From one point, I shot all the staff and a man being decorated and a couple of still photographs. Then, changing lenses, I got just the General and one of our crew members. Changing again, I got just the upper part of the two men showing the General shaking hands with the man he decorated. Later, I got head and shoulders only of General Whitehead as he gave the entire squadron a congratulatory talk. Then, some very informal shots. All in all, an event worthy of the color film and a day well-spent. The General drives his own jeep, and I got him climbing in and driving away. Sure do like this Revere camera.

February 8, 1945: San Jose, Mindoro, The Philippines

Hello Sweetheart—

Today has been a very red-colored one for me. Back at Finschhaven and henceforth, the Wing's crash boat has been taking men fishing. Each day, so many men are taken—a different squadron every time. I've missed it every time. This time, Sergeant Orlando won the privilege for Photo Section. Late last night, Orlando asked me if I wanted to go in his place. He was too tired, and it required arising at 5:00 a.m. Sure thing! I leapt at the chance. So, after lights out, I got ready. Reloaded the 3-A and threw in an extra roll of Kodachrome.

We got to the crash boat about day break. Nice boat—about a thirty-five foot job. Four men at a time could troll off the stern. About two miles out, they slowed down to trolling speed. No luck. I really didn't intend to do any fishing—unless they were really biting—rather do it with cameras. Later, we headed for a coral reef and an island. I took a couple of shots (35mm) from the boat showing beach and palms and sky. Near a small barrio, we dropped anchor to fish with drop lines. A couple of civilians paddled out to talk to us. I got one of them to take me ashore.

Bonanza! He—James Aubi—took me to his home, offered me cigarettes, showed me his album. Before the war, he had a camera and has nice pix. I met his wife and daughter, took their pix. Took pix around the house with 3-A and color. Got some beautiful flowering vines in color. At a neighbor-

James Aubi's sister bathes her daughter on Ambulong Island, Mindoro Strait.

ing house, his brother-in-law and the kids were taking baths. Have a shot of Mother bathing a little girl just big enough to walk. So cute. Then a little boy, bawling his eyes loose. Pix around canoes, other houses, old people, boy bathing, house with pigs around, etc. Then back to Aubi's house where he gave me some pretty shells. I tried my best to buy them—but no. The only thing I could give him was a package of gum. Then, he rowed me back out to the crash boat. Very well-spent time.

February 17, 1945: San Jose, Mindoro

Hello My Precious Darling—

Tuesday was a day off and I went on a trip toward the mountains. Ehrman, Billy Cox (mess sgt.), a guide, and Clara Cohen of the local Red Cross took off with a picnic lunch and ten cameras. There is certainly a lot of gorgeous mountain and prairie scenery here. Little hills—half a mile long, two-hundred feet high and perhaps two-hundred feet thick—rise almost vertically out of a level, kunai grass-covered plain. Some high and extremely rugged saw-toothed mountains stick up midst old round-topped, worn-down hills.

I hoped we would run onto a village of some of the real natives—but no. However, we did see four men walking along the road. Wore the scantiest

Mangyan tribesmen (possibly Hanunoo) wear traditional dress (above)—a bahag (loin-cloth), a bayong (bag for knife, comb, and so forth), and a panyo (head-band for long hair). Hill and his friends traded buns for the watermelon carried by the man on the right. Fred Hill (third from left, below) enjoys a picnic lunch with an unidentified soldier; Clara Cohen, a Red Cross Nurse; and Charles Ehrman, a soldier with the 49th Fighter Group.

Billy Cox, photographer

of breech clouts and chewed betel nut just like the New Guinea people. We traded them some buns for a watermelon. Clara and I ate part of the melon. Others were scared to try it. It was small and round—maybe eight inches in diameter. Meat was white but seeds were real and the taste was sort of there. (Damn these fluctuating lights. Makes my head ache. Alternates bright to dim about every three seconds. Very disgusting.)

We ate our lunch on the bank of the river in the shade of some juniper type trees. We were far enough up to be away from GIs. Nothing military around except our jeep and the uniforms we wore. Had boned-chicken sandwiches and strawberry jam sandwiches, fresh buns, an unfrosted chocolate cake, fresh butter, and I had a can of Mother's watermelon rind preserves. Cox brought along the little gas stove and a little white enameled percolator. What a war! Up in the high timber with a swell bunch, an American girl, and for the day, at least, not a care in the world.

In 1940, Fred Hill and Minor White met as civilians in La Grande, Oregon, where White was teaching photography at the local WPA Art Center. The two men became friends, photographed the region together, and then both went to war. Hill took this photo of White when they visited on February 25, 1945. After the war, White's eastern Oregon images launched his career as a fine arts photographer.

February 25, 1945:
San Jose, Mindoro

Hello My Darling—

This morning I mailed you a letter with a couple of money orders, then I got shaved and rode to town with Clara of the Red Cross. She took me over to see Minor. Nice of her, but it was only a hundred yards out of her way.

Minor is like a good dose of Carter's little pills—leaves you refreshed and changed. We had a long bull session. His is a rare

form of humor. Thoroughly enjoyed my visit with him. Had dinner—Vienna sausage, green beans, and pears and bread. Sat in the dust to eat. Pears looked like I'd peppered them, so I turned them over. Ha!

Took in an orientation lecture on today's war moves on all fronts. Not bad, but sweetheart, if I see you by Christmas this year, it will probably be on a furlough—not at home for keeps.

Found—thanks to Minor—a tiny orchid in a tree and Minor helped me shoot a pic of it. Fear it will be blurred, for I was standing on tiptoe to reach and shooting at 10 and 3/4ths. Minor is thinking about taking a night course at the Art Center after this mess is cleared up. Thinks he's too old for GI bill of rights.

March 4, 1945: San Jose, Mindoro

Hi Sweetheart—

This morning Casey and Powers got me out of the sack to go out sightseeing with cameras. No, I went to church, thanks to them getting me up. But at 10:15 we took off. Bob with the Nettel. Stuck gum and fruit bars (from K Rations) in our pockets and prepared to be gone all day. Hitched a ride to the air strip, took a pic or two, then took out for the high kunai grass [and] some farms.

Had to cross the river and Bob and Powers took off their shoes. Not me. It's a waste of time, so I plowed off through the stream. Others sort of hobbled across two branches of the stream, so they dried their feet and put on their shoes. Just over a rise was another fork of the stream, and then another. Casey said, "To hell with it," and waded in with me, but not Powers. Off came his shoes again. We took some *carabao* shots, then some of a farm house, then the three women put on their best dresses and came out for a picture. Gad, such finery. A couple of American style dresses that made me homesick.

En route home, we stopped at the deep part of the river for a swim. Couple of dozen men swimming. Sign downstream reads, "No Nude Bathing." I saw one pair of shorts. Two hundred yards down the river, the Filipino women do GI laundry. AJ told his Mrs. about that place, and she is sending him some shorts. Says she doesn't want all those Filipino hussies eyeing all she possesses....

A mother and her children cross a slough at Dulag, Leyte, passing a log (lower left) that Philippine women used for washing GI and personal laundry. Hill sent many such photographs to Martha, knowing that they would be passed along by army.

Sending you a pic of Ehrman (the nose) and Lois at a corn feed they had at 49th one evening. (Ehrman is a nosey so and so to boot.) Also a Filipino trio crossing the slough by our camp at Dulag. Skein of hemp on her head. And the latest of Countryman-Hill shots. Taken with Baxter's camera southeast corner of our tent. Surprising how homey a tent can become after a few months. Oh boy, oh boy—I'm waiting for that real home complete with all the fixtures and you to share it with me. What a wonderful invention a bathroom is. It will probably take me some time to get house broken again.

March 7, 1945: San Jose, Mindoro

Hello Sweetheart—

Music—GI Jive coming over our headset speaker. Plenty nice. Oh how it helps our morale for a quick-made speaker job. Bernardo did himself up proud. We've decided to make our tent a little more like home. As long as we have to live here. So, we'll probably have to leave now that we've decided to fix up our abode.

Understand that the officers are beginning construction of an Officers' Club. Guess they don't feel right about coming to the Red Cross Blue Room, although some of them do. Mostly flight officers come; they don't feel the distinction between the officers and enlisted men quite as sharply as our older ground officers. We, at least, feel more at ease over there if it is all enlisted people. But back to the original thought: At Finschhaven, the officers got a nice club built, had a couple of dances, invited the local contingent of nurses, and we pulled out of there immediately.

Ed just took an inventory of our set up: we have a drop parachute canopy to keep the tent cool and light; two stoves for cooking; the radio extension; a switch on our lights; two water cans; and a collection of characters to provide the floor show. Chess players drift in and out. And—the monkey.

Granted a three-day, unofficial "wildcat" leave from Mindoro, Fred Hill and Dick Baxter hitched rides in planes and trucks to photograph post-liberation Manila. Standing in an upper window of an empty building, Hill took this photograph of Filipinos as they bathed, washed, and cleaned up at a hydrant that had escaped the bombing and still flowed clean water.

Hill took photographs of local people that he became friendly with in the Philippines, including Corazon and Roberto Villanueva (left). He and Baxter met the couple through Captain Price of the 49th Fighters and an AP photographer. As a gift, the soldiers brought the baby canned milk, and Roberto's brother, Rudolph, showed the visitors the city. The two soldiers later met Alberto Abaya and his wife (right).

Today came your four letters of February 15, 18, 19, and 22. I too am surprised that the picture I sent you of Major Bong was removed from my letter by the censor. Please honey, any time anything is missing from my letters, note if the envelope has been cut open and resealed with tape. It should also have an extra censor's stamp—if it has been opened. That would indicate a spot check by some base censor. Have any of my letters been so resealed? They wouldn't necessarily remove any enclosures to spot check it.

March 18-19, 1945: Manila, Luzon

Hello Sweetheart—

The Villanuevas are a very wealthy Filipino family. The elder, Mr. Manuel H. Villanueva, was ten years the equivalent of a district attorney. Two of his sons (and a cousin), Roberto and Rudolph, are writers on the *Post* staff.

Daughters Manuelita and Estralita are stenographers at present working in General Headquarters offices. They are both skilled pianists and there are two pianos in the house. The Abayas are living at the house too. Mrs. Abaya and Mrs. Roberto Villanueva are sisters.

Mr. Abaya is a civil engineer and was my choice of friends there. Such an interesting and understanding conversationalist. I was discussing with him post-war business opportunities here. Seems to be the finest situation I've yet considered. So, I discussed price of land, building material, food, labor, commodities. At the Villanueva estate, they have several gas refrigerators, three radios, a phonograph—any and all American facilities. Streetcar fare was around three cents to downtown Manila. Gasoline was twenty six cents a gallon. Good theatres. Nicer than the Roxy. Practically the entire population speaks English.

Mr. Abaya tells me that American families usually have a combination cook and houseboy who is provided with room and meals and is paid seven to ten pesos a month—if the family is thrifty. But separate cook, maid, houseboy, and chauffeur are also common.

Hill's collection includes many photographs of Philippine towns and activities, including this one of women selling their wares at the Dagupan public market.

After I get out of Art Center and if competition in the photo business on the west coast is no different than it was, well, getting a job with Eastman would be worth looking into. There is a big Kodak store maintained in Manila. These people are great supporters for a portrait studio, but that requires a lot of fixtures. I'm wondering about a commercial photographer set up here.

March 22, 1945: San Jose, Mindoro

Hello My Precious—

Best pictures we got were at the public market at a small town in one of the provinces. Rows and rows of little booths where outlying farmers come in and sell their wares. All kinds of vegetables—Bermuda onions at two pesos a bunch or turnips at five centavos a bunch. Dried corn, rice, flour, bananas, peppers, mangoes, clothing, cloth, wooden shoes, thread, buttons, snaps, needles, and fish—dried or alive—crabs, shrimp, etc. Ready-to-eat meals, pastries, sugar.

Women sell molasses at the Dagupan public market.

Now this was a lulu: the sugar is boiled down molasses—brown and very thick. It was displayed in open-topped five gallon containers. Customers stuck their fingers in to sample it and test for viscosity. Customers brought their own containers—no dipper. The dealer filled the can by handfuls....

Then, out in the open and away from the booths, Hindus were bargaining off remnants of printed cloth, baskets, wicker wear, and pottery. Dick Baxter bought a water jug—fifty centavos. Pigs, chickens, horse and *carabao* shoes, horse shoe nails, and related hardware. Dick bought a knife—bargained from fifteen pesos down to nine. I got a pair of carved shoes for Marjorie, two linen tablecloths for us.

Chapter 3 ▪ THEY ALSO SERVED: A SOLDIER'S PACIFIC THEATER ALBUM, WWII

Preface to
ONCE MORE: A REPORT ON THE LITERARY ELEPHANT

The published symposium can offer discoveries—topics, writers, critics—a richness of Northwest literary discourse. Sometimes written out and focused on a single issue, sometimes a ramble of extemporaneous comments, those forums may be held face to face and leave no trace, while other times they're extended by transcription and publication in literary magazines. In the following text, John Witte (above), the editor of the 50th Anniversary issue of *Northwest Review*—one of the leading literary magazines in the territory—sent me a letter. At the top of his June 7, 2007 missive, Witte quoted a recent article by Seattle historian John M. Findlay:

Authors such as Theodore Roethke, David Wagoner, Jonathan Raban and Tess Gallagher have all served as sources of regional pride; in bookstores their titles fill shelves marked "Pacific Northwest." Curiously, though, the writers themselves—when asked directly— have not proven eager to be pigeonholed as regional, likely because in their profession the label can connote provinciality.... What value resides in being defined by a single place when one's audience, one's subject, perhaps most of all one's talent and ambition are not necessarily place-bound? ("Something In The Soil..." *Pacific Northwest Quarterly*, Fall, 2006:188.)

Below that bolded quotation Witte wrote: "Dear George—If you had 500–1000 words on the subject (as I suspect you might) they'd be most welcome. But soon—by 15 June or so! Best to you, John Witte." As it turned out, Witte had wisely invited fourteen different writers and poets from across the region to submit written responses to Findlay's quotation for publication: Ursula Le Guin, Tess Gallagher, Vern Rutsala, Lawson Fusao Inada, Christopher Howell, George Venn, Kathleen Dean Moore, Katrina Roberts, John Keeble, Colleen McElroy, Lucia Perillo, Marvin Bell, William Kittredge, and Jarold Ramsey. To further enrich the forum, all writers wrote blind—no one saw other writers' texts before publication. In my contribution below, I offered arguments against the clichéd and stereotypical use of "region" and "regional" as a means of dismissing writing and/or writers associated with a given geography.

Sources: "Literature of the Northwest Symposium." *Northwest Review* 45.3 (2007):30-35; Photo courtesy John Witte.

ONCE MORE: A REPORT ON THE LITERARY ELEPHANT

Reading John Findlay's 2006 article, "Something in the Soil?: Literature and Regional Identity in the 20th-Century Pacific Northwest" reminded me of a story I heard at a Pacific Northwest History Conference. At dinner, I was seated across from a Seattle book dealer who had been in charge of assembling the Centennial Booklist for the entire state of Washington. "Before I started the list," he said, "I was told that I must have a novel, a book of poems, a book of literary essays, and a book of short stories on the Centennial List, but I left all of them off." "Did anyone complain about their absence?" the woman next to him asked. "There were no complaints," he quipped.

So, I first want to commend Findlay for taking on this kind of blatant and ignorant prejudice. That book dealer is not alone. Northwest regional literature has attracted only a handful of trustworthy scholars. No literary historians have explained why national literary maps and most American school anthologies between 1917 and 1957 did not include northwest writers who had achieved national recognition: H. L. Davis, D'Arcy McNickle, John Reed, C. E. S. Wood, Opal Whiteley, Stewart Holbrook, Vardis Fisher, Betty McDonald, Nard Jones. Instead, national map makers filled the blank northwest corner with neat little icons—Conestoga wagon, fir tree, salmon, mountain, river, desert, and the national anthologists only published "Man with the Hoe" and chunks of Paul Bunyan.

Nevertheless, as Findlay begins to explain, over a hundred years of northwest literature and literary activity forms an abundant and complex web: all kinds of writers, innumerable literary periodicals, multiple state and regional anthologies, some insightful reviewers, large and small publishers, all levels of theater and film, active writing groups, reading tours and series, extensive prizes, libraries with literary archives, teaching writers and poets, a glut of degrees, government and private literary and folklore programs, writers' conferences, literary festivals, aesthetic feuds, uncountable readers, and—would you believe—almost no critics.

In that clash between an ignored but abundant literature, consider Findlay's statement: "Authors such as Roethke, Wagoner, Raban, and Gallagher have all served as sources of regional pride; in bookstores their titles fill shelves marked "Pacific Northwest." Curiously, however, the writers themselves—when asked directly—have not proven eager to be pigeonholed as regional, likely because in their profession the label can connote provinciality." Pigeonholed? Provincial? Shelf labels? For critical purposes, these clichés are archaic and useless. Using them, Findlay falls for the popular delusion that "local," "provincial," "regional," "national," and "universal" form some mutually exclusive hierarchy of significance or merit. Well, they don't—not for the serious critic. All those terms might be used to describe the complex relationships implicit in any single literary work.

Twenty years ago I criticized such terms in my award-winning book, *Marking the Magic Circle* (1987):

> A region is a microcosm—a magic circle centered on home. The values generated by that circle are many, but I have limited myself here to three— confidence, wholeness, and intimacy. For me, the authentic map of the universe is composed of these microcosms—a mosaic of specific human constructs crossing all abstract political, geographic, economic, and racial boundaries. This view of region as *microcosm* stands in contrast to the more dangerous metrocentric fantasy of region as *province*. When defined as *province*, region becomes an edge in a far remote place, a fragment of some empire with a far-away center. When the magic circle is defined as *province*, local life can be drained of significance, since only those who live at The Center are real. Thus, local intimacy, confidence, and wholeness are threatened. In contrast, region as *microcosm* enables an artist living anywhere—including the Northwest—to get work done, to achieve character, belief, aesthetic, purpose, and style. Region as *province* imposes a centralizing political

and demographic metaphor which can artificially elevate the significance of artists who live in political or population centers, and artificially dismiss significant artistic achievements that are not centralized
by non-artistic forces. An artist who chooses not to live in political or
population centers, who chooses not to become an alien to the oldest
and most immediate sources of human nurture, who chooses not to
become a victim of nationalism—such an artist must assert the region
as *microcosm*—this locust flowering, that hive by the Columbia—and
where do you live? (19-20)

If Findlay intends to describe the complex relationships among a writer's
imagination, the cosmos, a social system, and the mystery and wonder of all those
forces combined, he might have better used other non-colonial terms that don't
disconnect the universal from the particular.

Again, in that clash between an ignored but abundant literature, consider
another of Findlay's questions: "What value resides in being defined by a single
place when one's audience, one's subject, perhaps most of all one's talent and ambition are not necessarily place-bound?"

Well, this value is obvious. Findlay's article itself provides ample evidence of
these four values he names:

Value of a Placed Audience: When Findlay delivered this address to the Book
Club of Washington annual holiday dinner in Seattle, December, 2005, he benefitted from the invitation; he benefitted from access to an immediate and friendly
audience. When he submitted his revised version to *Pacific Northwest Quarterly*
(PNQ), local editors and referees gave him comments, which might have made
his sources more inclusive. When his paper was published in the 2006 issue of
PNQ, he benefitted from the staff, editors, and subscribers' investment of time,
money, and energy, as well as free outreach to a larger audience. When his research appeared on the University of Washington website under History and
Literature, a potentially indefinite and universal audience became eligible to read
and/or respond.

Applied to the larger northwest literary culture, these benefits of a placed audience—acceptance, invitation, motivation, dialogue, criticism, investment, en-
hancement, visibility, interest, funding, affirmation—are also visible and available
in varying degrees, as they are anywhere that literacy and literature are valued.

Value of a Placed Subject. In the University of Washington libraries, on campus, or in his office, Findlay could count on immediate free access to most—if not all—the information he required to discover and evaluate the literature of northwest immigrant culture. The Seattle area offered quite a few immediate and significant sources: archived papers of Theodore Roethke and Richard Hugo; books by scholars Nicholas O'Connell and Harold Simonson; books and interviews of poets and writers such as David Wagoner and Jonathan Raban. Findlay could even paraphrase without credit some stellar University of Washington Press books such as *Northwest Perspectives: Essays on the Culture of the Pacific Northwest*. To find all of these, and more—an easy walk, maybe a short drive?

Applied to the larger northwest literary culture, the benefits of a placed subject seem obvious: established interest, a community of practicing writers, collaborative congenial colleagues and elders, free access to primary documents and places, unlimited secondary resources, large and networked libraries and archives, a university press invested in regional literature, cross-disciplinary expertise. Given these advantages, and the opportunity to test his insights by observing daily life in place, Findlay can work something like an archeologist: he lives close to or on his research site and spends his days digging. For writers placed elsewhere, those benefits may or may not be available in the same degree, though the basic creative process may be the same: wonder, inquire, research, read, evaluate, draft, revise, edit, proof, test, mail, wait, start over.

Value of a Placed Talent: Invoking another contemporary cliché, "being place-bound," Findlay wants readers to ask if "talent" is somehow constrained by "place." Applied to Findlay's own essay, this seems contradictory, since his talents as a cultural historian seem to be enabled by focusing on a specific cultural record. While Findlay's "northwest" essay criticizes a self-serving regional jury for failing to be inclusive, his own essay seems weakened by the same problem—too much dependence on university and Seattle literati. Nevertheless, there is no evidence that he feels constrained by teaching at the University of Washington, editing a regional history quarterly, or writing, delivering, or publishing essays about the Pacific Northwest.

Instead, it might be argued that, as a placed historian, Findlay enjoys advantages similar to those of an ecologist studying the structure and function of a particular ecosystem. Limiting and focusing on the specifics of one immigrant cultural record enables critical zoom—discoveries of texts and writers unseen and unknown by more distant, grandiose, pretentious historians. This limiting and focusing also provides the opportunity to be inclusive and detailed, an approach found, at present, in only one northwest anthology, the six-volume *Oregon Literature Series*. In his essay, Findlay shows some of the specific advantages of a placed talent using his historical imagination: selecting and evaluating the texts and insights of insiders; criticizing status quo metaphors; constructing new more inclusive metaphors; selecting events for context and sequence; identifying and interpreting long-term change; distinguishing literal from figurative language; synthesizing multiple and divergent sources, maintaining a persona.

Applied to the larger northwest literary culture, those benefits of a placed talent can be found everywhere. Wherever they live, writers participate—more or less—in a universal imaginative process: they live, observe, and internalize local images, which become psyche, microcosm, narrative, metaphor. Those acts of imagination generate community, macrocosm, order, illumination, discourse, insight, art.

Value of a Placed Ambition: At first glance, it seems reasonable to agree that "place" limits the self-promoting pursuit of fame, money, prizes, status. In Findlay's case, this may be true: his essay on northwest literary culture may not attract much audience, attention, or reward beyond the immediate territory. A prize, a promotion, tenure—those hopes might be realized within the University, Seattle, historical society, or state, but probably not outside the region.

That outline of mere regional rewards for a single historical essay cannot, however, be applied to the one hundred years of northwest literary culture. In *Contemporary Northwest Writing* (1979), for example, Roy Carlson published pages of facts proving that regional writers and poets had won every national literary award ever offered to American writers. The awards are listed. As any study of the record will show, that level of ambition and reward has not changed. So much for the cliché: "place" necessarily limits ambition. More likely, place empowers ambition, or, as Stegner once said, "You can't high jump from a pan of jello."

So, I welcome Findlay's cultural history assignment: to describe and evaluate over one hundred years of literary activity in a regional immigrant culture. While we await the reports of other blind men to give us the whole elephant, Findlay offers an important model for discussing the value of placed writers and writing, and, more important, he gives a cogent rejoinder to the arrogant and ignorant who arbitrarily dismiss the abundance and significance of northwest literary practice.

CHAPTER 5 | Literary Biography (2005)

Preface to

SOLDIER TO ADVOCATE: C. E. S. WOOD'S 1877 DIARY OF ALASKA AND THE NEZ PERCE CONFLICT

Between 1989 and 1994, while serving as General Editor of the *Oregon Literature Series*, I learned that at least four current historians writing about the nationally-famous "Chief Joseph Surrender Speech" denounced the poet C. E. S. Wood for "prostituting the truth," for being "unreliable," for "composing the famous speech himself," for not "being particular about the truth." That attack on the integrity of this poet, soldier, attorney, anarchist—perhaps the most complex literary figure in the 19ᵗʰ century Northwest—raised a cloud of fascinating questions. So, for the next ten years, I tracked down over ninety sources from national, regional, and local archives while also transcribing, editing, and annotating Wood's unpublished 1877 Nez Perce war diary. First presented at the Oregon Cultural Heritage Commission C. E. S. Wood Symposium in Portland on October 17, 1998, my search was dramatically rewarded in 1999 when the Chicago Research Library sent me the bound original 1877 New York newspapers in lieu of microfilm. In those pages, I discovered eighteen of Wood's 1877 drawings and numerous articles leaked to the eastern press. After recovering from subdural hematoma surgery during most of 2003, I queried Marianne Keddington-Lang, veteran editor of *Oregon Historical Quarterly*, about publication of the Wood diary. On January 3, 2004, she replied, "I love the idea of putting this kind of document in the journal: it is the kind of primary document that will inform and intrigue readers and...it will layer new ideas and images into people's knowledge of the war." Over the next year, thoughtful, comprehensive, and encouraging responses from both Marianne and her historian husband Bill Lang, and assistance from innumerable archivists, librarians, historians, and photographers shaped the annotated and illustrated diary below. By October, 2006, this article became the precursor for *Soldier to Advocate: C. E. S. Wood's 1877 Legacy*—a widely reviewed monograph featuring archival photos of Joseph and Wood on the cover.

Sources: *Oregon Historical Quarterly* 106.1 (2005): 34-75; Photos courtesy Huntington Library (Wood 1878) and Washington State Historical Society (Joseph 1877).

SOLDIER TO ADVOCATE
C. E. S. Wood's 1877 Diary of Alaska and the Nez Perce Conflict

I.

Close to graduating from the United States Military Academy in spring 1874, Charles Erskine Scott Wood strongly disliked the idea of becoming an army officer. The cadet who later became the "one officer [who] rejected the fundamental assumption of American civilization's superiority," the cadet who composed the most famous poem in nineteenth-century western American literature, the cadet who became a Portland lawyer and civic leader, Erskine Wood disliked all that military math and physical science.[1] He disliked military discipline—"work, work, work from reveille to taps" left him no free time for reading novelists and poets. He disliked military routine and piled up "all sorts of petty infractions: inattention at drill, not turning his head and eyes to the left, a soiled collar at guard mounting, shoes not properly blackened at reveille and inspection, swinging his arms as he marched from dinner." He disliked military punishment—being "confined to West Point for six months and forced to stand guard duty every alternate Saturday." He disliked military stoicism—no whistling in the hallways. He disliked being humiliated and hazed and oppressed. Discontent, literate, sociable, and imaginative, Erskine wrote his father Dr. Wood that he wanted freedom—to become a writer, or maybe a mercenary, or maybe an orange grower: anyone except a military officer. Every night before bed at West Point, he was secretly writing passionate letters in his new diary to his new love, Nannie Smith.[2]

His father thought Erskine was crazy. A retired surgeon general of the Navy, Civil War veteran, absentee parent, author, and world sailor, Dr. William Max-

Lt. C. E. S. Wood, 1878. Taken June 6, 1878, the day before he and General O. O. Howard boarded the steamer Wide West *in Portland for Umatilla, Boise, and the Paiute Bannock War, this portrait shows Wood's personal evolution from an innocent West Point infantry lieutenant in 1874, to General Howard's new aide-de-camp in 1877, to the veteran field officer here: derringer in hand, pistol on hip, leather cavalry boots, canvas greatcoat, silk scarf, campaign hat, and sensitive, fearless stare. Concealed inside that coat is his next diary—all blank pages again—along with pens and pencils.*

Photo reproduced by permission of The Huntington Library, San Marino, California well Wood lectured his son: "abandon all feverish and restless desire after change and address yourself with honest and unceasing vigilance to the labor, the claims and obligations of the present around you—and the place and position to which you are called."[3] When his father heard about Erskine's secret lover's diary, he told his son to quit writing such private trash. As any son might, Erskine seemed willing to be oppressed by his father's expectations, and in spring 1874, West Point commissioned him 2nd Lieutenant Wood—though his dress uniform would conceal Erskine's passion for the freedom to be a writer and artist and his passion to be the lover and husband of Nannie Smith.

On furlough after graduation, the reluctant new lieutenant returned to the idyllic family estate and farm outside Owings Mills, Maryland. During that green and growing summer, Erskine saw his mother Rose Wood, a pious and strict Presbyterian, still struggling to "manage the household and keep up appearances in spite of the damage her husband's spending [and drinking] habits wrought on the family economy." In the home of his innocent childhood, he also saw his retired father, "reduced to alcoholism, bitter and powerless...[,] abuse his mother with ferocious eruptions of temper...." Later, he would say of that summer at Rosewood Glen: "Our home became a wretched place." After courting Nannie all summer, Erskine—at twenty-two—was ripe with passion. He asked permission to marry the "beautiful, histrionic, and coquettish" belle whose "thick chestnut hair...came down to her knees," but Miss Smith's stepfather rejected him. New second lieutenants earned a meager $115 per month, barely enough to cover living expenses.[4]

Alienated from family, frustrated in love, inspired by the arts, conflicted with militarism, Erskine kissed Nannie Smith farewell, boarded the train in Washington, D.C., and escaped to the mythic west in California. Clattering day and night for three thousand miles on that transcontinental train, he appeared to be a dashing young officer, an innocent "with resolute chiseled features, curly black hair, and keen, penetrating eyes...cultured, self-assured, immensely charming...[with] high connections and impeccable lineage."[5] As Lieutenant Wood, he seemed dutiful, obedient, official, and honorable, but beneath that uniformed military surface he was also Erskine, the young artist on a private and personal quest for

Lt. C. E. S. Wood, West Point graduation, 1874. Wood's biographer Robert Hamburger explains that Wood "stood apart from his classmates in only two areas: he was one of the top four or five students in drawing; and his four-year total of disciplinary demerits was surpassed by only three other cadets" (p. 30).

Reproduced by permission of The Huntington Library, San Marino, California

freedom, love, new life, discovery, expression, adventure. As Erskine, he was sub-versive, mischievous, anarchistic, vulnerable. This division made him human, complex, and potentially literary, for, as William Faulkner said, "the problems of the human heart in conflict with itself...alone can make good writing...."[6]

When he arrived at Camp Bidwell, his assigned army post in northern California, a love letter from Nannie Smith was waiting for him. "Of course, that letter made me very happy," he would say years later.[7] As Nannie's impecunious lover, Erskine wrote regularly to her, the "most sought-after belle in Washington D.C."[8] Ignoring his father's attempt to quash a young writer's dreams, Erskine wrote and mailed "a manuscript to his brother Maxwell at the Navy department in Washington, D.C., requesting that Max try to place it with *Harpers* or *Scribners*." When Max reported that Erskine's manuscript had been rejected for "being 'too deep for the reading public,'" he also "encourage[d] his younger brother to turn to lighter, more attractive subjects growing out of experiences and materials close at hand...[such as] 'little sketches...of some of the *funnier ports*..., [with] a little mirth, a little love, etc. and a good deal of fiction.... Do this. Don't write trash.... Cultivate a style of your own—concise free and simple.'..."[9]

Now, three thousand miles from West Point, the Lieutenant Wood who disliked militarism did his duty: "I took my company allotment of recruits and drilled them into shape and my captain [Robert Pollock] said he wouldn't want anything better than that...and that's about all they gave me to do...."[10] For Captain Pollock, the new lieutenant also "took over the company's record keeping and report writing," a duty that allowed him some freedom to write and explore and map the surrounding country and to meet and camp and live with a Paiute Indian family.[11]

By August 1875, these multiple personae and their conflicting commitments—military, literary, and romantic—had not changed. When Lieutenant Wood's company was transferred to Vancouver Barracks, across the Columbia River from Portland, he marched these complex personae across the Great Basin from Fort Bidwell to The Dalles. En route, he filled a personal diary with his delight at the wild world of waterbirds and rimrock and sage, the beauty of high desert stars and coyotes and owls, the wonders of the Malheur oasis, Blitzen River, Alvord Desert, upthrust Steens. Years later, Erskine's most private and important poems and paintings would arise from this remote Oregon region, and eventually he would be described as "the only distinguished poet" in the Pacific Northwest between 1880 and 1920.[12]

Early in the winter of 1876, his commanding officer at Fort Vancouver sent Lieutenant Wood to army headquarters in Portland, a mission that would permanently change his life. As he later recalled,

The Columbia was full of running ice and no one would take me across...finally I found a flat bottom skiff—appropriated it and set out pushing my way through the ice as openings came and of course going slowly down with the current.... Just before I got even with... Hayden Island I found the seams of my boat had been plugged with ice frozen in them which had now melted. The skiff was filling with water and I hardly got to where I could get ashore when she sank. I let her go, walked across the island—only a couple of hundred yards or so—then...some wood choppers got me across to the mainland...then I walked a muddy road through dense fir forest...and delivered my dispatches to General Howard. I rather think that was our first meeting. Anyway he took a fancy to me...."[13]

The general's "fancy" was both personal and military. Both Brig. Gen. Oliver O. Howard and his wife, Elizabeth Howard, welcomed the sociable and handsome young man as a family member. At the Howard home—the present Tenth and Morrison in Portland—Erskine would frequently take his meals, stay overnight, and visit with the general, Mrs. Howard, the young Howard children, and "Howard's daughter Grace [who] had recently graduated from Vassar College and found her father's post grievously lacking in suitable companions."[14] In 1879, when the Howards moved to their new home at Fort Vancouver, they provided Erskine with a room of his own.[15] In a letter to Howard some eight years later, Erskine summarized the evolution of their relationship: "I came to you a boy, I lived at your house, loved your family. Mrs. Howard was a mother to me. I loved Grace as my own sister.... I married from your house, you stood sponsor for our first home, my father died and I felt the sympathy of all of you."[16]

In General Howard, Erskine found not only a benign father but also a supportive literary mentor. To supplement his Army income, Howard was already publishing in religious papers and eastern magazines. So, when the young writer couldn't cross the icy Columbia, he and the general began corresponding about writing—a commonplace in literary life. On January 11, 1876, for instance, Erskine sent Howard a manuscript with the following note: "I ought to mention that I made no attempt at any broad humor or burlesque except twice and I tried to cover under a smile many points that are worth while thinking of seriously; for I wouldn't waste my time in trying to make people smile and *only* smile." In another letter to the general, he wrote, "Here's a description of the detail of a battle. A sort of microscopical view in which the minutiae are made visible to the exclusion of the vast and important objects. It may possibly be of some service to you tho' I think not. I would like to have it again if you will kindly keep it for me." Two weeks later, General Howard responded: "Dear Wood: I send back these slips. The writer gives graphic incidents. I do not forget scenes as trying & exciting & plaintive.... Yours gratefully, O. O. Howard."[17] Simultaneous with these literary exchanges, "Erskine wrote regularly to Nannie—lengthy letters, almost comically conventional, gushing with the ardent spirit of young love."[18]

In addition to this personal and private writing, Lieutenant Wood took up an official military role as Howard's judge advocate, a roaming and privileged position that required him to settle and write up "legal and jurisdictional disputes as well as questions involving military discipline and criminal acts" throughout the Department of the Columbia.[19] As Erskine later explained, he was "ordered around rather promiscuously[:] to Puget Sound...in a rather important case... [;] to the mouth of the Columbia to attend to some matters of government rights...[;] to Fort Walla Walla to get material for confidential reports." All this region-wide travel and work as judge advocate "gave [him] a black eye in the regiment," so he asked Captain Pollock to "find some real company or regimental duties." When General Howard received this request, he refused to reassign his favored and literary lieutenant, who was "doing him and the government more service in faithfully administering those [judge advocate] offices and duties... [than those] he [Pollock] allotted me."[20]

By April 1877, Lieutenant Wood was well known to General Howard as family friend, young writer, budding artist, and judge advocate. So, as freedom-seeking Erskine later explained, "when Charles Taylor, with a letter from the War Department in Washington applied for a military companion and escort on his expedition to climb Mt. St. Elias, Alaska,... Gen. Howard sent for me at Vancouver Barracks and asked if I wanted to go. In 24 hours I was on the [steamer] *California* bound for Sitka."[21] Heading north to explore wild Alaska, Lieutenant Wood carried a thin, brown, leather-bound five-by-eight-inch vest pocket notebook—thirty unnumbered, lined blank pages ready to be filled by the exploring mind—a

commonplace for beginning writers. Erskine probably intended to use this private "diary of situation" as a literary "source book that might be mined for materials to be used in [later]...public writing"—poem, article, essay, autobiography.[22]

After five weeks escorting Charles Taylor's expedition—not recorded in this diary—Lieutenant Wood returned to rainy Sitka, and Charles Taylor sailed for Portland. On May 16, Erskine wrote General Howard an eleven-hundred-word letter describing Taylor's adventure, asking for permission to stay longer, then announcing his own exploring party and signing off as "your friend."[23] Without waiting for Howard's reply, Erskine set off on his own expedition into the wild beauty of Alaskan landscape and Tlingit culture—shamans, stories, totem poles, ceremonies, cedars, masks, salmon, hunts, canoes, glaciers, icebergs, bays, seals—and a night of love with a Chilcat woman.[24] Returning to Sitka in early June, Lieutenant Wood "received word that the army had granted him the three-year leave he requested" but he also learned that "the Nez Perce Indians had attacked settlers...[and] his Twenty-first Regiment had been called to the front."[25] To further complicate Erskine's quest for freedom and adventure, he was out of money and all his fellow soldiers were withdrawing from Sitka. Now he had to choose: should he stay in the north alone and dare more unfunded exploring? Should he go south with his comrades on the monthly steamer? By June 11, he decided: though Erskine had just enjoyed the freedom of a cross-cultural adventure among the Tlingit, as Lieutenant Wood he now conformed, fell in, and sailed for war.

How much Lieutenant Wood knew about the causes of the Nez Perce-U.S. Army conflict when he boarded that steamer to leave Alaska on June 11, 1877, is an open question. If he had read Colonel Clay Wood's 1875–1876 report, *Status of Young Joseph and His Band of Nez Perce Indians,...* he might well have been disturbed. It was widely known that, "because Joseph's band had never signed the 1863 agreement [treaty],...the band could not be forced to move...[and that] Howard was so impressed...he wrote to the War Department, 'I think it a great mistake to take from Joseph and his band of Nez Perces Indians that valley [the Wallowa].' "[26] Since saving the lives of the members of the Lewis and Clark Expedition in 1805, the Nez Perces had maintained peaceful and friendly relations for over sixty years with white missionaries, soldiers, and government agents, and in 1855 they signed a treaty with the United States that apportioned 6.4 million acres to the five Nez Perce bands living in Oregon, Washington, and Idaho. In 1863, the federal government made a dubious new treaty that reduced the 1855 Nez Perce lands to 784,996 acres in Idaho alone—about one-tenth of their former holdings. The government agent who negotiated that 1863 treaty "secured the signature or the agreement of every headman whose lands the new treaty would not affect, *but did not secure the signatures of Joseph, White Bird, or any leader, save Timothy and Jason, who lived outside the borders of the new reservation*" [emphasis added]. "By the [new] treaty's terms, all of the [non-treaty] bands were required to move on the reservation [in Idaho] within one year after the document was ratified."[27] Erskine would have known that Joseph and his Wallowa Valley band had not signed the 1863 treaty, and that they and other non-treaty bands rightfully refused to leave homelands legally agreed to be theirs in 1855. He may also have known about the failures of various commissions and councils to right the obvious injustices—murder, trespass, and theft—committed against the non-treaty bands by invading white settlers, miners, and headmen of the Christianized treaty bands.

Lieutenant Wood could not have known, however, the chief reason his Twenty-first Infantry battalion had now been called to war. When the Lapwai Council concluded on May 15, Erskine had been exploring Alaska and learning Chilcat culture. No telegram, letter, or messenger from Lapwai could have reached him with the ominous news: General Howard had turned the peaceful Lapwai council from a legitimate treaty rights forum into a bellicose, ethnocentric, and racist assault. Failing to grant the validity of non-treaty rights, becoming intolerant of cultural and religious differences, trusting force to intimidate the parties in a legal dispute, and knowing he had the approval of racist Indian agents, settlers, and state and federal agencies, General Howard had imprisoned the chief Nez Perce orator and proclaimed his militarist ultimatum: all non-treaty Nez Perces had thirty days to "remove" from their legally held homelands or they would face the threat of "removal" by his forces. Wanting to avoid the bloodshed Howard threatened, the Wallowa band had, in fact, crossed the Snake River and were moving to the Idaho reservation when four drunk young men from White Bird's band—shamed by years of white greed, invasion, murder, and theft—retaliated against settlers along the Salmon River. In the U.S. military imagination, this retribution became "the outbreak of war." Re-imagining the tribe that saved the lives of Lewis and Clark as "the enemy," General Howard then ordered around a hundred cavalry to attack "the hostiles" camped on White Bird Creek. In that battle, Nez Perce warriors—outnumbered two to one—killed thirty-four soldiers and forced the survivors to panic and retreat. Sailing south on the Inside Passage the afternoon of June 17, Lieutenant Wood had no idea that ten days later—on the afternoon of June 27—he would record in his diary the unforgettable burial of those thirty-four dead soldiers.[28]

Sailing down the rainy Northwest coast that June, Lieutenant Wood could never have imagined that for the next four months—actually, for the rest of his life—he would play a part in what historians generally agree was the "meanest, most contemptible, least justifiable thing that the United States was ever guilty of "—the U.S. Army's eviction and seventeen-hundred-mile pursuit of around eight hundred fleeing and fighting non-treaty Nez Perce men, women, and children with their baggage and horse herd.[29] After confronting, defeating, or eluding General Howard's forces in battles and skirmishes in Idaho, the Nez Perce refugees and their two thousand head of horses fled across rugged Lolo Pass into western Montana. Assuming General Howard's troops would not follow, the Nez Perces made a non-aggression pact with Montana settlers and traveled south to camp at Big Hole, where they were attacked at dawn on August 9 by more federal troops and local civilians. After intense fighting and numerous casualties on both sides, the Nez Perces escaped from Big Hole, and for the next two months they successfully fought off or eluded the three different armies sent to capture them, including Howard's foot-weary men and his Lieutenant Wood. Riding north to seek peace and asylum in Canada, the non-treaty bands stopped to rest at Bear's Paw on September 29, a day's ride from freedom over the border. There, on the afternoon of September 30, they were attacked and besieged by soldiers under Col. Nelson A. Miles and, promised they could return to Idaho in the spring, Chief Joseph—the only present non-treaty band leader—surrendered to Miles and General Howard on October 5, 1877.

II.

One of Wood's few surviving original texts from that summer of 1877, the diary transcribed below has two distinct sections. Part 1 is Alaska entries written between April and June 17, 1877, and confirmed by Erskine himself as incomplete: "When I set out to explore Alaska, I began a journal and kept it faithfully for three days while I was on the steamer."[30] Wood's most recent biographer notes that "[These] fragments...from his Sitka journal suggest that he [Wood] wished to produce...a humorous anecdotal account of frontier life, its roguish characters, and colorful speech" in the manner of Bret Harte and Mark Twain.[31] They may also reflect his brother Max's earlier advice to write "little sketches...of some of the *funnier ports,*...[with] a little mirth, a little love, and a good deal of fiction." Part 2 of Wood's diary records his first five weeks in the U.S. Army–Nez Perce conflict in Oregon and Idaho—entries written between June 19 and July 23, 1877. Like the first section from his Alaska exploration, this section is incomplete. Another commonplace of young writers called to adventure appears: the novice buys a blank diary and starts to write daily entries, but life—action, excitement, exhaustion, weather—takes over. Art disappears. Blank pages march on and on. Erskine did not intend this text as a complete, official, or exact historical record. In fact, he argued against making "history from the diaries of soldiers."[32]

Here, in the second section, cited by numerous historians and Wood's biographer, are the rough notes of a young and undifferentiated writer in his multiplicity of personae. Erskine cryptically and tacitly records his initiation by conflict and complexity into racism, injustice, militarism, identity—some of the same forces he first encountered as a West Point cadet. In these pages, he also faces unknowns—cultural differences, ethnicity, terrain, self-destruction, mortality. All these encounters made that summer and fall of 1877 unforgettable. Converting these thirty diary pages into publishable postwar texts would present numerous problems. For one, Erskine wrote his diary rapidly and briefly in pencil, mixing military and private diction in an idiosyncratic shorthand—fragments, abbreviations, dashes, symbols, numbers, quotations, allusions, lowercase letters, no

months, few place-names. Reading his own writing here might have been difficult, and the original text shows that—sometime later—he added dates and details. After the war, he also had to decide what he should censor and what he could publish based on these entries. Clearly, he could not betray General Howard, who had trusted him sufficiently to promote him to aide-de-camp on July 22. He also had to decide how to portray the non-treaty Nez Perces, whom he came to respect and admire during this summer. Finally, he had to decide whether or not to expand on, further reveal, or suppress his personal responses, his inner life, his own observations. He addressed these questions for the rest of his career, and his answers—both published and unpublished—make his life and work both important and contemporary.

C. E. S. Wood's diary, showing the entry for June 27, 1877
Reproduced by permission of The Huntington Library, San Marino, California

C. E. S. Wood's Diary, 1877:
Alaska and the Nez Perce War

{+ *Sitka 1877 May ?*}

Phillipson's account of the "old times" under the Russian government: "They was the most happiest people I ever see.* Come draw their rations same as at the Commissary, go to the store and get all kinds of things. Best quality.

"Soup kitchen: this was the soup kitchen for the poor. All come at three o'clock and get their bowl of soup. A bowl had to be sent in every day to the Master of the Port for inspection. Prince often sent down for his bowl of soup.† Pig roasted whole on Sundays. Market and trade room for the Indians.

"They was the most virtuous people I ever see in a seaport."

Contrast now: the poor old loafing clerk with nothing to do; the old musician. Day off. Drunkenness, squalor, debauchery, prostitution, stagnation, filth and all uncleanness. Unreliability of the men for work. Prostitution a necessity.

Berry's discussion on drunkenness: "I've got no use for drunkard around me.‡

Published here by permission, the original diary is housed in the C. E. S. Wood Collection, WD Box 26(1), Huntington Library, San Marino, California [hereafter Wood Collection], where it was deposited by Sara Bard Field with Wood's other papers sometime after 1947. To decode Erskine's shorthand, I've done the following: (1) standardized spelling and mechanics; (2) added [in brackets] month and place names, Army campsites, headings, and occasional clarifications; (3) added paragraph breaks in longer passages; (4) noted indecipherable words with [illegible] and arbitrary choices with [lost? last?]. When Erskine underlined, I retained the underlining. All of Erskine's postwar additions in ink—dates, overstrikes, additions, marginalia, interlineations— are enclosed in {+*italics*}, as is his major 1878 revision. All of Erskine's deletions are enclosed in {−*italics*}.

* William Phillipson was a Sitka trader and schooner captain. He told Wood that "his schooner will return about the 15th of June and that he [Phillipson] is going to trade with the Chilcat chief at his village and that he will take me [Wood] along." C. E. S. Wood, letter to General Howard, May 16, 1877, Oliver Otis Howard Papers, Bowdoin College Library, Brunswick, Maine [hereafter Howard Papers]. Appointed postmaster in Sitka on August 14, 1871, Phillipson died July 18, 1924. Karen Meizner, email to author, March 4, 2004.

† Prince Dmitry Maksutov was chief manager for the Russian government from December 1863 to October 1867. C. L. Andrews, *Sitka: The Chief Factory of the Russian American Company*, 3rd ed. (Caldwell, Idaho: Caxton Printers, 1945), 88.

‡ Probably Maj. M. P. Berry, a veteran of the Civil War and Mexican War, who served as U.S. collector of customs in Sitka in 1877. Andrews, *Sitka, 112n10*; Hubert Howe Bancroft, *History of*

Been a millionaire if I hadn't had twice on four drunkards for partners. Good fellows too. Couldn't shake 'em.

"There's old Smith. Baldy Smith we used to call him because he was bald. Made some $15,000, left ranching came to town, started saloon keeping, married a woman fit for no man's wife. She wasn't a <u>bad</u> woman. Had a baby every three or four hours. And a filthy dirty slovenly slut. Perfect bitch about the house. Smith drank himself to death, left his wife and six children, three of 'em his, went down to Astoria the other day and drowned himself."*

"There's Dr. Wilcox. Perfect gentleman, good friend of mine, fine gentleman he was too. Committed suicide in Portland the other day. He'd carry that thing full of whisky inside of him and you'd meet him on the street and think him perfectly sober, but he couldn't stand it you know. Killed him."†

"Damn the stuff. No man of happiness can afford to drink whisky. An occasional tear is bad enough for any man but an habitual drinker will never die rich."

Lewis having his horse stolen, offered $2.50 for his saddle, and drops it in the Deschutes in disgust.

Walker: "Injuns likes [*sic*] to catch the 'erring.' [*herring*]."

June 11th [Sitka—begin dated/post-dated entries]

Monday. Steamer [*California*] arrives.‡

June {+*12th -13*} [Sitka]

Rush of preparation to evacuate. Sale of goods and government stores.

Alaska (San Francisco: History Company, 1886), 619.

  * Possibly a reference to Capt. Harry M. Smith, Company G, Twenty-first Infantry, who "Died at Fort Lapwai, Idaho Territory April 23, 1877 of inflammation of the stomach and bowels." Trevor K. Plante, National Archives and Records Administration, letter to author, April 14, 2004. In his next letter to General Howard, Wood wrote: "[Major Canby] says too that Smith of the 21st killed himself." Wood to Howard, May 16, 1877, Howard Papers. These frank diary notes show Erskine's uncensored writing for himself about taboo subjects, and the letter shows his self-censorship as Lieutenant Wood when writing to Howard.

  † Dr. Ralph Wilcox was a native of Ontario County, New York, who came to Oregon in 1845. He shot himself April 18, 1877, at age 58. Biography Card File, Oregon Historical Society Research Library, Portland [hereafter OHS Research Library].

  ‡ The private ocean steamer that made monthly trips between Portland and Alaska.

Mule sale.§

Conversation at the priest's house. Fright of the wretched women. Madame Metropolsky's offer of subsistence for the troops. Her fears of attack and murder.¶

June 14ᵗʰ [Sitka to Wrangel]

The leave taking. Mistresses and sweethearts. Soldier's parting with his child. The old Russian woman praying to be taken to portland {+*P*}. The tearful group on the wharf. Bring {+ *ing* } in the drunks. Farewell to Sitka.

June 15ᵗʰ

Wrangel. Scenes in Wrangel. Slavery in U.S. Slave difficulty on the ship. Sacrificing slaves & etc. Small Siwash smoking his meerschaum, old blind Paul. His opinion of the manufacturing of whisky: "Bad—fooling mighty bad, damn bad...."

June 16ᵗʰ [Inside Passage]

Fair weather in morning, foggy rainy at night. Pass Metlakatla—Church and settlement—run through Grenville Channel.** { - *Did you see her looking for gloves under the cattle when she first came in? Hadn't lost her gloves at all.*}

June 17 { - *& 18*} [Inside Passage to Port Townsend]

Still progressing southward. Pass through Seymour Narrows morning of 18ᵗʰ

---

§ After ten years of responsibility for Alaskan affairs—except customs, commerce, and navigation—the Army was withdrawing completely from this remote and expensive post. Wood probably knew men in Company M, Twenty-first Infantry, who were selling everything and boarding the southbound steamer. Paul T. Scheips, "Darkness and Light: The Interwar Years 1865–1898," in *American Military History* (Washington, D.C.: U.S. Army Center of Military History, 1989), 296–7; R. N. DeArmond, email to author, February 27, 2004.

¶ "The priest's house" refers to the residence of the Russian Orthodox priest Father Nicholas G. Metropolsky, who "presided over the church [Cathedral of St. Michael] for many years" and later helped to organize a local government and Sitka city charter. Madame Metropolsky, like many Sitka residents, feared that U.S. military withdrawal would leave them vulnerable to a Tlingit attack similar to the one that had driven out the Russians. There was no Tlingit attack. Andrews, *Sitka*, 70; Dr. Charles Coate, email to author, February 21, 2004; Meizner, email to author, March 4, 2004.

** "Church and settlement" refer to Father Duncan's Tsimshian mission. Duncan believed Native peoples needed to be isolated from white civilization and degeneracy until they could be prepared for assimilation. He pushed prohibition, adoption of the English language, and abandonment of Native culture. He later moved his settlement to New Metlakatla near Ketchikan. Coate, email to author, February 21, 2004.

{ - *17th*} about 3:30 o'clock. Hard wind. Party around smoke stack in cruel glee over the sufferings of the seasick doctors. Baker's exasperation: "Why don't the old scoundrel take her out of the trough of the sea?" Arrive at Fort Townsend in evening. Visit Dr. Alden and Scrubby and go to bed.*

June 19ᵗʰ { - *20ᵗʰ*} [Port Townsend to Columbia River]

Put Bancroft and his Company ashore at Townsend and take Burton and his Company aboard.† Rumors of war. Touch at Townsend, sound Flattery light and put to sea.

June 20 { - *21ˢᵗ*} [Astoria to Portland]

Cross the bar, touch at Canby's.‡ The telegram. Stirring news. No companies to disembark. All under orders for the front. Discharge the baggage and sick. Farewell to [Fort] Canby. Touch at Astoria and { - *all we*} hear reports of Perry's massacre with his command.§ Growing excitement. Cheering remarks from citizens of, "Go in and kill 'em all boys. Don't spare the bloody savages." Confound these curses. Wish they were going to fight them instead of standing on a wharf and put us on the track.¶ Arrive in Portland at about 2 o'clock at night. Round up

---

* Baker may be an Army surgeon who had arrived on March 19, 1876, and was returning to the lower states. See Emily Fitzgerald, *An Army Doctor's Wife on the Frontier*, ed. Abe Laufe (Pittsburgh: University of Pittsburgh Press, 1962), 179. Dr. Charles H. Alden was a U.S. Army surgeon assigned to Fort Townsend. The 1877 Territorial Census listed "Mrs. Alden 37, and four children 10-2." Scrubby may be the nickname of Lt. Ebenezer W. Stone, Twenty-first Infantry, who served as post commander. Plante, letter to author, April 7, 2004; Victoria Davis, email to author, March 23, 2004.

† Capt. Eugene A. Bancroft, Company M, Fourth Artillery, was stationed at Fort Townsend; Capt. George H. Burton, Company C, Twenty-first Infantry, at Fort Vancouver.

‡ Fort Canby, Washington, at the mouth of the Columbia River. See Lewis A. MacArthur and Lewis L. MacArthur, *Oregon Geographic Names*, 7th ed. (Portland: Oregon Historical Society Press, 2003), 155. In his work as judge advocate, Wood had been here before.

§ Capt. David L. Perry was stationed at Fort Lapwai. On June 17, Perry led 103 men of the First Cavalry into battle against a force of 60–70 Nez Perce warriors. Ignorant of terrain and unskilled in war, Perry's men were routed by veteran Nez Perces, who were superior horsemen, marksmen, and tacticians. Perry's command panicked and retreated, leaving behind 34 dead soldiers—though Perry himself survived the so-called Battle of White Bird Canyon. Jerome Greene, *Nez Perce Summer, 1877* (Helena: Montana Historical Society Press, 2000), 25–48.

¶ This is the first explicit evidence of Wood's ambivalence toward aggression.

{*+Col. Adjut*} Wood [*sic*] and get news and orders.** I visit Mrs. Howard.†† General well. Perry not killed. Theller of mine {*+21ˢᵗ*} killed.‡‡ Volunteers called for. All troops ordered up.

June {*+21ˢᵗ*} [Portland to Celilo]

Off for the front. Bancroft's Company on board with us—once more.§§ Meet the [steamer] *Canby* and pick up Throckmorton and Rodney with his Company. Now we have five Companies in all.¶¶ Touch at Vancouver. Say howdy do and goodbye in a breath. Take on some of the munitions of war—field pieces and gatlings and howitzers.

Cascades at noon. Party of admiring damsels gaze on the defenders of the country. Wainwright in desperation.*** Paddock's advice to him: "Come along and telegraph for permission, and if permission is refused at that end, begin to tele-

---

** Col. Henry Clay Woods, assistant adjutant general, stationed at Fort Vancouver. In 1875–1876, he had researched and written the definitive report on the non-treaty bands' status, arguing that "because Joseph's band had never signed the 1863 agreement [treaty]...the band could not be forced to move.... Howard was so impressed...that he wrote to the War Department, 'I think it a great mistake to take from Joseph and his band of Nez Perces Indians that valley [the Wallowa].' " Bruce Hampton, *Children of Grace* (New York: Henry Holt, 1994), 42; U.S. Army, Dept. of the Columbia, The *Status of Young Joseph and His Band of Nez-Perce Indians*...(Portland, Ore.: Assistant Adjutant General's Office, Dept. of the Columbia, 1876).

†† Elizabeth Anne Waite married Oliver Otis Howard in 1855, a year after he graduated from West Point. She welcomed and treated Wood as a family member—evidenced here by his visit to her.

‡‡ 1st Lt. Edward R. Theller, Twenty-first Infantry, stationed at Fort Lapwai. Killed on June 17 at White Bird, he had been Perry's subordinate officer.

§§ "When the *California* left the posts in Alaska on the 16ᵗʰ of June, she had on board 'A,' 'G,' and 'M' companies of the Fourth Artillery. Three days laters [*sic*], she stopped at Fort Townsend, near the mouth of Puget Sound, to discharge 'M' Company and take on 'C' Company of the 21ˢᵗ Infantry. The boat was hardly out of sight before Captain Eugene A. Bancroft, commanding 'M' company, received his orders. Taking a boat to Tacoma, and a train thence to Kaloma [*sic*] on the Columbia River, 'M' Company rejoined their comrades at Portland." Mark H. Brown, *The Flight of the Nez Perce* (New York: Putnam, 1967), 145.

¶¶ Capt. Charles B. Throckmorton, Fourth Artillery, and Capt. George B. Rodney, Company D, Fourth Artillery.

*** 2ⁿᵈ Lt. Robert P. Page Wainwright, Company K, First Cavalry, stationed at The Dalles. In September 1877, Wainwright participated in the reburial of soldiers killed at White Bird. In 1879, he was stationed at Fort Walla Walla. *Roster of Troops Serving in the Department of the Columbia* (Vancouver: U.S. Army, August, 1879), 5; Greene, *Nez Perce Summer*, 390n48.

graph to the General at Lewiston."* Anything to gain time and keep moving to the front.

Arrive at Dalles in evening. Feel { - *Felt feell*} very much like staying in Dalles and keeping some of the pretty girls that look so favorably upon us from any sadness or anxiety on my account.† Buy a hat in Dalles. First opportunity to purchase anything whatever since I left Sitka. Everything I own, blankets and clothes are all in my boxes in hold of *California*.

Through to Celilo. The poor Indians on the rocks of The Dalles wave encouraging signals to us to go on and kill and be killed. Hard to tell which they prefer. Leave Celilo about seven o'clock in the evening and at last are on a boat where we remain for two days and two nights and can take a rest. One week from Sitka to Celilo. Whoopla!

{+ *June 1877*} [**in left margin**]

{+ *June '77*} [**in top margin**]

June 22ⁿᵈ [Celilo to Snake River]

En route aboard the [steamer] *Almota*. Touch at Umatilla. News—sixty men missing. Troops camped near Lewiston. Lapwai said to be abandoned. Heard that at Dalles yesterday. Don't believe it.

June 23ʳᵈ {+3} [Snake River to Lewiston]

Nearing the field. Peculiar nervous feeling of going to death. Shrinking from the exposure. Want desire to be out of the expedition. Old soldiers the same way. Each fight more dreaded than the last. The desire to investigate immortality. Thoughts of death, inability to change the mood and tenor of life and thoughts. Each one's expectation that <u>he</u> will escape.‡

---

* 1st Lt. George H. Paddock, Fourth Artillery, later involved in a "friendly fire" death. See July 6 entry and accompanying note.

† These and later paragraphs further reveal Wood's ambivalence about aggression.

‡ Greene notes that this entry provides "rare contemporary insight into the emotions of soldiers bound for the front during an Indian campaign..." (*Nez Perce Summer*, 389). Greene deciphers Wood's handwriting somewhat differently than given here.

June 24th

Arrival at Lewiston. Bustle of preparation. Lapwai.§

June 25th [Fort Lapwai to Norton's Ranch/Cottonwood]

Arrival of pack trains. Incidents in packing, comic and serio comic. 25th. Troops start for the front. Mrs. F's description of her Indian scare—in the cellar.¶

June 26th [Norton's Ranch to White Bird Creek]

A new pack train. On the road. Rodney's camp. The nest of officers in one tent. Pouring rain. Night ride in cold drenching rain. Hail. Camp at Norton's. Norton's pup. Deserted houses, flowers and chickens uncared for. Milk pails left on the fence. Evidence of a hurried flight.**

{+ *June 27th* } [Whitebird Battlefield to Camp Theller on Salmon River]††

---

§ Wood may have sketched Fort Lapwai while passing through. Here, he may also have been issued the standard forty pounds or so of infantryman's equipment. As an officer, Wood was required to purchase a Springfield rifle, ammunition belt, and canteen. For a heroic depiction of uniformed infantry marching as Wood probably marched, see the Vincent Colyer drawing "In Pursuit of Joseph," *Harpers*, August 18, 1877, 641.

¶ Mrs. F. is Emily FitzGerald, the wife of Army surgeon Dr. Jenkins FitzGerald. She apparently told Wood how, four "days after the rout at White Bird[,] some white ruffians chased and fired on two friendly Indians who promptly whipped their ponies to top speed and dashed to the post [Fort Lapwai.] Before their excited remarks could be properly interpreted, the cry spread that the hostiles were coming; the troops took up defensive positions, and the wives of enlisted men and their children 'came running, wild with fear, to the officers' line of houses' where 'a block house had been established,...and casks of water and provisions were kept in the cellar. Cord wood had been stacked around the house to protect it from shot and all the women and children had been instructed in case of attack to take shelter there.' " Brown, *Flight of the Nez Perce*, 141.

** The ranch was established on Nez Perce land in 1862 by some of the twenty thousand invading gold miners. Originally called "Cottonwood House" and later "Norton's Ranch" after then-owner Benjamin B. Norton, the ranch straddled the Lewiston–Mount Idaho road and included barns, stables, and corrals, as well as a "store, saloon, hotel, and stage station." The Norton family and others had fled the ranch for Grangeville on the night of June 14. Alvin Josephy, *The Nez Perce Indians and the Opening of the Northwest* (New Haven: Yale University Press, 1965), 386–442; Greene, *Nez Perce Summer*, 32, 59; Brown quotes from but does not credit this diary entry (*Flight of the Nez Perce*, 157).

†† Brown quotes this entire day's entry as providing "an intimate picture of this camp" and credits Wood anonymously (*Flight of the Nez Perce*, 159–61). See also Robert Hamburger, *Two Rooms: The Life of Charles Erskine Scott Wood.* (Lincoln: University of Nebraska Press, 1998), 46; Greene, *Nez Perce Summer*, 45–6; and Hampton, *Children of Grace*, 90: all quote excerpts and give in-text credit. Greene deciphers Wood's handwriting somewhat differently than given here.

Graves by the wayside. Overtaking the main column. Gentlemanly officers looking like herders. Rough aspect of everyone. Business—not holiday —costumes.*

Burying the dead {+*in White Bird Canyon*}.† Horrible stench. Arms and cheeks gone. Bellies swollen. Blackened faces. Mutilations.‡ Heads gone. Tragic fate of the bugler. Indian atrocities. Ravishing and burning women. The man of 14 days—gooseberry his ⌊illegible⌋.

Camp. Singing, storytelling and swearing. Profanity—carelessness—accepting things—horrible at other times. As a matter of course, each as mutilated corpses and death in ghastly forms, strewn on every side. Again there is the necessary leaving of last messages for sweethearts, mothers, and wives, telling of { - *mementoes*} jokes about being killed, about not looking for "my body" and etc. Firing expected tomorrow. The nerve it takes to face the probabilities by writing these last letters and leaving mementoes for loved ones is wonderful—and one feels demoralized by such acts as these.

Rain—eternal rain—veal and no veal. Supper in camp. Visiting at the different messes. Youngsters with neither bedding nor shelter. Roughing it jokingly. Night duty. Posting the pickets. Rough times all night standing in the rain. No fire. No talking. No bedding. No sleeping. Up at two o'clock for fear of Indian habits of attack. Roll call at six. (The alarm shot at midnight. One of our own pickets shot by one of our men.)§ Breakfast.

---

* Wood's Company D, Twenty-first Infantry, and the four other companies from the *Almota* joined General Howard's other forces on this day, the second day of burials. Brown, *Flight of the Nez Perce*, 160–1; John D. McDermott, *Forlorn Hope* (Boise: Idaho State Historical Society, 1978), 123–4.

† Wood's unpublished poem "Ballad of the Burials" and passages published in *The Poet in the Desert* arise from this burial detail at White Bird Canyon. The soldiers' naked bodies had lain unburied for ten days.

‡ Wood records Army misperception here. Citing Lucullus V. McWhorter, *Hear Me, My Chiefs: Nez Perce Legend and History* (Caldwell, Idaho: Caxton Printers, 1952), 256–9, Alvin Josephy states the prevailing view: "Despite stories that circulated to the contrary, none of the bodies...were discovered to have been mutilated." Josephy, *Nez Perce Indians*, 531.

§ Jerome Greene explains that "During the movement of Howard's forces to and below the Salmon River, two inadvertent army shootings occurred that, because of the limited information available about them, have caused considerable confusion. The first was the accidental wounding of Private Henry Reed, Company E, First Cavalry.... Reed was mistakenly shot in the

"In Pursuit of Joseph" *by Vincent Colyer. In contrast with Wood's journal, Colyer here idealizes infantry power, order, and confidence in the vicinity of Fort Lapwai—probably before the White Bird defeat. A former Board of Indian Commissioners member, active artist, YMCA activist, and zealous Christian assimilationist, Colyer was touring northwest Indian reservations that summer.* Harper's Weekly, *August 18, 1877, Library of Congress photograph*

{+ *June 28th* } [Camp Theller at Salmon River (East Bank)]

The advance. More ruins. Indians speckling the hills like ants. Firing. ¶ Sudden feeling of interaction on hearing the shots. Nervous eagerness for the fight. Desire to be at the front. All thoughts of the future vanishing. Only want a crack at an Indian** and feel no disposition to show any quarter. Advance to river. Planted batteries and left picket lines commanding the crossing. Rodney encamps at Camp Theller.†† Artillery remains in position. E and I Companies return with

---

shoulder by an infantry picket [unidentified] and was taken to the post hospital at Fort Lapwai, where he was recuperating as of July 30, 1877." Greene, "Appendix B, Two Army Shootings at the Salmon River, June 30 and July 7, 1877," unpublished manuscript, 702–10; Greene, *Nez Perce Summer*, 391n1.

¶ The fleeing non-treaty bands—over six hundred men, women, children and around fifteen hundred horses—had crossed the Salmon on June 19. The gunfire Wood reports here came from rearguard scouts who "rode out from the canyons and from behind buttes and came charging down the slope. They pulled up opposite the soldiers.... Some of the soldiers began shooting, and the Indians fired back. None of the bullets found a mark, and a few moments later, when the Nez Perces saw Howard's artillerymen coming down the bluff with the howitzer, they broke off the fight" and rejoined the main non-treaty camp in the mountains. Josephy, *Nez Perce Indians*, 532.

** Robert Hamburger uses this phrase to title his chapter on Wood's Nez Perce War experience (*Two Rooms*, 41–58). Coming immediately after his recent traumatic burying of fellow soldiers at White Bird, it seems doubtful that Wood "hurried exuberantly" to the war or that he felt "mounting anticipation at the prospect of seeing his first combat," as Hamburger claims (*Two Rooms*, 39). Wood's phrase may be better understood as reactionary bravado rather than bellicose passion.

†† General Howard's campsite a "mile or two above the mouth of White Bird Creek" was named for 1st Lt. Edward Theller, whose body Wood and other soldiers had found and buried

"U.S. Troops Crossing Salmon River Rapids." *Wood originally printed this caption in the lower left corner. Sometime later, he wrote in longhand a second caption in the upper right sky. Wood spent June 29 through July 1 at White Bird Crossing and returned to cross again on July 8 and 9. Because the sketch depicts Army delay, he didn't send it to the eastern press.*

Reproduced by permission of The Huntington Library, San Marino, California, WD Box 293

Cavalry to camp.

{+ *June 29th* } [Salmon River at White Bird Crossing]

Entire command moves to river. Attempt to cross the river.*

{+ *June 30th*} [Salmon River at White Bird Crossing]

Still constructing the ferry.† Cavalry leave us for Looking Glass. My fare-

---

earlier that day. Brown, *Flight of the Nez Perce*, 160.

* At spring flood stage, the river created a formidable obstacle to Howard's pursuit. Securing three boats, "a 'practical ferryman' attempted to rig a rope ferry." Brown, *Flight of the Nez Perce*, 163.

† Wood omits many complications: inadequate pulley, improvised shackles, breaking rope, spliced rope, exhausting rowing. This three-day delay was one reason the Nez Perces would eventually name General Howard "General Day After Tomorrow." During these three days, Wood

well to Rains.‡ Wilkinson and Mason come up.§ D, E, I, and part of Artillery cross this day.

July 1ˢᵗ [Salmon River at White Bird Crossing]

(Sunday). Remainder of troops cross this day.

July 2ⁿᵈ [West Bank, Salmon River to Deer Creek Canyon]

Moved to point 3/4ᵗʰ way to summit of Snake river mountains.¶ Rain. Mud. Forty five degree ascent. {- *Show*} Bombarded with pack mules. Dead Mule Trail.** Return to pack trains. Camp Misery. Sleeping in water. [illegible].

July 3ʳᵈ [Deer Creek Canyon to Brown's Mountain (Camp Mountain)]††

Mountain camp finally reached after long toil over Dead Mule Trail.‡‡

---

completed a pen-and-ink sketch of the scene: "Troops Crossing the Salmon River," C. E. S. Wood Collection, WD Box 293 (2), Huntington Library. About nine by twelve inches, the drawing is currently Wood's only extant and signed original from 1877 and the only depiction of this activity. This drawing also suggests Wood carried or obtained pad, pencils, ink, and pens.

‡ Rains is 2nd Lt. Sevier M. Rains, probably Wood's contemporary at West Point. Wood graduated in 1874 and Rains in 1876. Four years after the war, General Howard described Rains as "prompt, loyal, able, without fear, and without reproach." Oliver Otis Howard, *Nez Perce Joseph* (Boston: Lee and Shepard, 1881), 151.

§ 1ˢᵗ Lt. Melville C. Wilkinson, Third Infantry, an artilleryman serving as an aide-de-camp to General Howard; Maj. Edwin C. Mason, Twenty-first Infantry, stationed at Fort Vancouver and General Howard's chief of staff "supervising the placement of troops." Greene, *Nez Perce Summer*, 81. For Mason's letters from this conflict, see Stanley R. Davison, "A Century Ago: The Tortuous Pursuit," *Montana, the Magazine of Western History* 27:4 (1977): 3–29.

¶ These mountains are now commonly demonized as "The Seven Devils" or "Seven Devil Range."

** This place-name—apparently Wood's unique, non-military appellation—seems to have been used only by Wood in this diary and in the caption, "Dead Mule Trail, Idaho—From a Sketch by an Army Officer," for a drawing published on the cover of *Harpers*, September 20, 1877. Brown cites this entry and uses Wood's term, "Camp Misery" (*Flight of the Nez Perce*, 170).

†† Referred to as "Brown's Mountain" or "Camp Howard Ridge." Cheryl Wilfong, *Following the Nez Perce Trail* (Corvallis: Oregon State University Press, 1990), 100. A Portland journalist adds, "The place of our camp was extremely cold, the entire command being overcoated and huddled around immense pine wood camp fires during our entire stay." Thomas Sutherland, *Portland Daily Standard*, July 16, 1877.

‡‡ Two drawings—both associated with Wood—depict the Army's wet, muddy, ten-mile uphill climb out of Deer Creek and the death of four pack mules. Wood's sketch was likely revised for heroic effect by a *Harpers* staff artist before it was published on the cover of *Harpers* and widely reprinted. Recent expert analysis concluded that this cover drawing is not characteristic of

July 4 [Brown's Mountain to Camp Rains* on Johns Creek]

March fifteen miles. We camp in sight of Mount Idaho. News of Rains disaster.† Duncan and Eltonhead fighting.‡ Camp. Rains.

July 5 [Johns Creek to Salmon River at Craig Billy Crossing]§

Move to Camp Otis on Salmon. Twelve miles below Camp Haughey. Raft.¶ Alarm by Lear[y ?].** Arrival of "Ruben" {+*friendly Nez Perce*}.†† On Picket.‡‡ { - *"Crusoe Otis"*}

Wood's art. Henry Sayre, interview by author, Eastern Oregon University, May 19, 2002

   * "On the Fourth of July…we reached a campground in a pine forest which General Howard named after Lieutenant Rains, who was killed while performing perilous scout duty in the neighborhood of Camas Prairie." Sutherland, *Portland Daily Standard*, July 16, 1877.

   † Rains and his scouting party of ten soldiers were killed on July 3 at Cottonwood. The fleeing "Nez Perces were about to launch a surprise attack against the main soldier body, when they… sight[ed] the smaller troop riding out from the command[, so] they pursued the scouting party… and eventually all were dispatched" by Strong Eagle, Yellow Wolf, Two Moons, Five Wounds, Rainbow, and other Nez Perce warriors. Merrill D. Beal, *I Will Fight No More Forever* (Seattle: University of Washington Press, 1963), 68; McWhorter, *Hear Me*, 282–6.

   ‡ Lt. Joseph W. Duncan and Lt. Francis E. Eltonhead, both Twenty-first Infantry, stationed at Fort Walla Walla.

   § "This crossing, at the mouth of Billy Creek, had once been the home of the Nez Perce Indian known as Salmon River Billy. His son, Luke Billy, now lived there in a cabin. A ferry had also existed at the site during the gold rush, and a good trail still led from the crossing toward Craig Mountain and the main road between Lewiston and Camas Prairie. Hence the name of the place, which was also called Craig's Ferry." Josephy, *Nez Perce Indians*, 535n10. Attempting to avoid violence, the fleeing non-treaty bands and their livestock had crossed here on July 2—three days earlier.

   ¶ Refers to the Army's dismantling of Luke Billy's cabin to build a raft for crossing the Salmon. "Its timbers were a foot thick and thirty or forty feet long. Twenty-three years after the war, Luke Billy was still trying to collect from the government for its loss." Bill Gulick, *Chief Joseph Country* (Caldwell: Caxtons, 1981), 212.

   ** Possible reference to an unidentified action by Lt. Peter Leary, Howard's "purchasing agent for commissary supplies." Brown, *Flight of the Nez Perce*, 303.

   †† James Ruben, a bilingual, Christianized treaty Nez Perce, was "the son of old Ruben, who had operated a ferry and grown wealthy during the gold rush, and of Joseph's sister." An interpreter and messenger prior to the conflict, he became a scout, adviser, and interpreter for General Howard. On this day at Craig's Ferry, Ruben demonstrated how to cross the Salmon River with his horse—a feat Howard's troops could not accomplish. Josephy, *Nez Perce Indians*, 486; Howard, *Nez Perce Joseph*, 150.

   ‡‡ A letter by Wood's commanding officer describes the situation: "The company along with Lt. Woods [sic], three Indian scouts and myself have been on picket duty last night on the side of

July 6 [Craig Billy Crossing to Salmon River Mountains (Camp Parnell)]

"Crusoe Otis."§§ Arrival of pack train from Haughey Horrible retrograde march. Camp at head of canyon. Soldier shot [by] {+ *Lieutenant Paddock. Solemnity of the silent corpse, the simple grave, the soldier's burial clothes. The lonely mound under the mournful pines, and all the pathos of death in loneliness. How all things earthly sink into nothingness before the dread silence of the dead one.*}¶¶ "False Alarm."***

July 7 [Camp Parnell at Salmon River Mountains]

Long weary dragging march to mountain camp.††† Cavalry and Headquarters

---

the mountain overlooking the vicious Salmon River.... Our duty is to see that no Indians steal on us or surprise the camp or command in a scalping bee while in the act of preparing our crossing of the river." Robert W. Pollock, *Grandfather, Chief Joseph, and Psychodynamics* (Caldwell: Caxton Printers, 1964), 57–8.

§§ Wood records the nickname—alluding to Defoe's novel *Robinson Crusoe*—given to Lt. Harrison Otis after his log raft "and the lariat ropes of the cavalry—all went down the river three or four miles. When the impromptu sailors returned, the shavetail [newly commissioned West Point officer] was dubbed, quite appropriately, 'Crusoe Otis.'" Brown, *Flight of the Nez Perce*, 185.

¶¶ According to a published postwar "Court of Inquiry," Wood refers here to the second "friendly fire" incident—a fatal shooting that occurred the night of July 7. The soldier killed was Pvt. Michael Cassidy, Battery D, Fourth Artillery. That night, Cassidy had been posted as a camp guard and "wrapped himself in a blanket," which looked like "the ordinary costume of the hostile Indians." Cassidy "went outside the camp limits, and...while returning to the camp he attracted Lieutenant [George H.] Paddock's notice, excited his suspicions by the stealthy and unusual manner of his approach, and that Lieutenant Paddock fired upon him under the impression that he was an Indian, with the result of killing Private Cassidy." Paddock was found to have "acted in good faith and that his action was warranted under the circumstances." *General Orders No. 8,* Headquarters Department of the Columbia, Portland, Oregon, February 9, 1878.

Wood moved his additional reflection on Cassidy's death from this 1877 Nez Perce War diary to an 1878 "literary notebook,"—which he completed after the 1878 Bannock conflict. To show some of his revising, I have added—in italics—part of his July 9, 1878, entry to this 1877 entry. For the complete and previously unidentified revision, see "C. E. S. Wood Private Journal, 1878" *Oregon Historical Quarterly* (March 1969): 26–7.

*** "[We] have just had an Indian scare. A man cam [sic] doubling down the trail crying The Indians are coming! The Indians are coming! I [illegible] this into [illegible] and commenced giving orders—in a few moments it was discovered to be a false alarm and with a hearty laugh everybody settled down again—" Maj. Edwin Mason to his wife, July 5, 1877, pp. 3–4, Mason Correspondence, Microfilm 80, Montana Historical Society, Helena, Montana.

††† The march back to White Bird Crossing from Billy Craig Crossing is one of the most avoided accounts in Army narratives. General Howard abstracted all three days into one (*Nez Perce Joseph*, 155) and Thomas Sutherland, a Portland journalist and one of General Howard's postwar

leave us for Grangeville. Stragglers. Hard march.

July 8th [Salmon River Mountains to Salmon River at White Bird Crossing (Camp Haughey)]

March to river by shorter route. Avoid Dead Mule Trail. Overtake Cavalry and Headquarters. Put Cavalry over river and ferry our Infantry Battalion over. Cavalry and Headquarters and Haughey push on.

July 9th [West Bank, Salmon River, to East Bank and White Bird Canyon]

Artillery crosses. Command camps at "Theller." Hunting berries. Camp struck and {+we} push for the front. Night's march and our wretched "bivowk" [sic] at head of White Bird Canyon. No food. No anything.

July 10th [White Bird Canyon to Walls at South Clearwater (East Bank)]

Take wagons for Grangeville. Arrive and breakfast. Our hostess Madame Crooks.* She cun [sic] talk. Proceed to General Howard's camp about six miles in rear of Indians. Crossing the Clearwater on the bridge. Wild flowers, tulips & etc. Duncan's [horse? house?].

July 11 [Walls to South Clearwater Battlefield (East Bank)]

Advance on Indians. Engage them at about 11:30 am. We occupying a rolling broken plateau. They the rocks and wooded ravines. Howitzers open fire. Skirmishing. Sharpshooting.

Famous hat. The Sergeant and McNally shot. Charge by line in front of me. Firing till after dark. Indians in the ravines after horses. Caring for the wounded. No food no drink no clothing. All day without water. Night in the trenches. Preparing for an attack at dawn. Anxious times. Sound of Indians dancing and

---

apologists, did much the same. Sutherland also rebutted Howard's critics by rationalizing the Army's inability to cross the Salmon as a tactical move: "They [the Nez Perce] had to be driven out [of the mountains] and they were." Thomas Sutherland, *Howard's Campaign against the Nez Perce Indians, 1877* (Portland: A. G. Walling, 1878), 4.

* Passing through Grangeville again, Wood has now marched an oval of around ninety miles. Martha Crooks was the fifty-five-year-old wife of "J. W. Crooks, cattle king and Grangeville promoter" and mother of eight children. McDermott, *Forlorn Hope*, 38–75; 1870 Census, Nez Perce County, Idaho.

wailing. Williams and Bancroft shot.† I, [lost? last?] on the picket line. Incidents.

July 12 [East Bank, South Clearwater Battlefield]‡

Morning firing reopened. Jackson appearing.§ Artillery withdrawn. Extending our line. The charge. Rapid firing. Indian works. Their camp captured. Preparing to follow. Our camp with the wounded. The Command camp [*sic*] on the river.¶

July 13 [West Bank, South Clearwater, to Kamiah]

The pursuit. Hampered with howitzer ammunition. Crossing the river. The Indian camp.** Left behind with the howitzer ammunition. Losing the trail. Hear-

---

† Wood accurately describes the terrain where the semicircular battle line formed that afternoon. About 100 non-treaty warriors and 350 Army troops—cavalry, infantry, and artillery—fought through the hot afternoon without either side gaining decisive advantage. Pvt. David McNally, Company E, Twenty-first Infantry, was one of eight soldiers killed; 2nd Lt. Charles A. Williams, Company C, Twenty-first Infantry, and Capt. Eugene A. Bancroft, Company A, Fourth Artillery, were two of twenty soldiers wounded. No exact number of Nez Perce casualties for this day is known. Greene, *Nez Perce Summer*, 77–88, 361–2.

‡ During the second day of the battle, the non-treaty warriors attacked and retreated intermittently until artillerymen under Capt. Marcus J. Miller charged "double time across the plateau straight toward the warriors in the ravine." Cavalry and infantry—including Wood—followed Miller's charge, and the warriors retreated on horseback to the South Fork of the Clearwater, swam the river, and "raced their ponies up Cottonwood Creek and into the hills after their families." Known Nez Perce casualties for both July 11 and 12 were four warriors killed and six wounded. Greene, *Nez Perce Summer*, 88–96.

§ Capt. James Jackson, Company B, First Cavalry, who was escorting a "pack train of 120 mules and twenty Nez Perce scouts and Captain Birney B. Keeler, General McDowell's aide-de-camp" from Fort Lapwai. Brown, *Flight of the Nez Perce*, 193.

¶ Wood may have sketched four different events of this battle. On August 3, 1877, these four sketches, General Howard's studio portrait, and six other drawings made up the entire front page of the *Daily Graphic* in New York. For Wood's published account of this two-day "Battle of the Clearwater," see "Chief Joseph, The Nez Perce," *Century Magazine* 28 (1884): 135–42.

** Writing to an Idaho historian forty some years after the war, Wood described the plundering of the Nez Perce camp: "There were valuable buffalo-robes and beaded garments lying about in the teepees and meat cooking at the fire. I, myself, picked up a buffalo-horn drinking-cup hanging on a stick at the door of a teepee as we ran through the camp." Wood to C. J. Brosnan, January, 7, 1918, Special Collections and Archives, University of Idaho Library, Moscow, Idaho. After the war, he had that buffalo horn mounted in silver at Tiffany's with this inscription: "Taken from Chief Joseph's camp at the Battle of the Clear Water, July 13, 1877, by Lieut. C. E. S. Wood." Mary Rose, *C. E. S. Wood and Chief Joseph*... (Vancouver, Wash.: Celebrate Freedom Project, 1991–92), 14; see also Erskine Wood, *Life of Charles Erskine Scott Wood* (Vancouver, Wash.: Rose

"Indian Chief." *One of the ten C. E. S. Wood sketches published August 3 in the New York press, this traditional Nez Perce leader remains unidentified by tribal officials and historians. He may be Red Heart, chief of the wrongfully imprisoned non-combatants. If so, Wood may have interviewed him and sketched him while serving as officer of the day on July 17.*

Daily Graphic, *August 3, 1877, Chicago Research Library*

ing the firing. View from the hills.* Our doubts as to our position. Coming into camp. Indians across [east of] the river.

July 14th [Kamiah (Camp Macbeth)]†

Still in camp. Indians across the river.

Wind Press, 1978), 14.

* Wood's unpublished poem "Ballad of the Flight across the Salmon River" memorializes Nez Perce skills at river crossing. "Ballads of the Nez Perce War," WD Box 8 (16), Wood Collection.

† Deciding to escape over Lolo Pass to Montana, the fleeing non-treaty bands were passing through the Indian agency and settlement when the soldiers attacked them again. After exchanging long-distance and mostly ineffectual gunfire across the river, both forces withdrew. Camp Macbeth was named by General Howard for Presbyterian missionary Kate Macbeth, who fled to Lapwai at the outbreak of hostilities. [Author unknown], *Journal of Expedition against Hostile Nez Perce Indians, from Lewiston, I.T. to Henry's Lake, I.T.*, July 13, 1877, WD Box 26 (2), Wood Collection [hereafter Adjutant Journal].

July 15 [Sunday, Kamiah]

Day off. Resting. Joseph wants to talk.‡ Wait all day. No talk. Begin to cross river in afternoon.

July 16 [Kamiah to East Bank, Clearwater River]

Finish crossing the river. Go into a hot camp after being recalled from a march about a mile and a half. Prisoners begin to come in.§ "Joseph *halo* come in," {+ *no come in*}. Clatawa Lolo Trail." {+ *gone away by Lolo Trail*}.¶ Cavalry start in pursuit. Rest for the weary sole.**

July 17 [East Bank, Clearwater River at Kamiah]

Military commission formed to try prisoners.†† Still they come. {- *18th*}. Officer of the day.‡‡ Night with the prisoners. Musings on the unhappy people and the

---

‡ Kulkulsuitim, a messenger from Joseph, was talking with General Howard and Major Mason about terms of surrender near the river when shots were fired at the officers. The parley ended. Joseph never appeared. Later, Howard imagined that this meeting was actually "a ruse designed to further impede the army while allowing the tribesmen time to move their noncombatants and livestock toward Lolo trail." Greene, *Nez Perce Summer,* 99–100.

§ Wood echoes official diction here in using "prisoners" to name Nez Perce noncombatants caught in "one of the most unjust episodes of the Nez Perce War." Lucullus McWhorter, *Yellow Wolf* (Caldwell, Idaho: Caxton Printers, 1940), 310. "Renown for their law-abiding and peaceful proclivities," Red Heart's band of thirty-five noncombatants—just returning from buffalo hunting in Montana—were designated "hostile" when they voluntarily surrendered, so General Howard had the group arrested as "prisoners of war." Among these noncombatants were Chief Red Heart and Red Heart, Jr., who were present when Captain Whipple and Companies E and L, First Cavalry, and twenty volunteers attacked—without provocation—Looking Glass's camp on Sunday morning, July 1. Josephy, *Nez Perce Indians,* 554–5; McWhorter, *Yellow Wolf,* 310–12; Brown, *Flight of the Nez Perce,* 204–5; McWhorter, *Hear Me,* 331–4; Greene, *Nez Perce Summer,* 100, 408–9.

¶ Wood quotes his translator's Chinook jargon, which he—sometime later—translated to English in his diary.

** This pun exemplifies Wood's sense of humor, a rare trait in 1877 Army diaries.

†† "Day was spent in forming commission which met 1 PM & adjourned for want of witnesses. Fenn & Brown of Mt. Idaho asked for as complete a list of witnesses as possible in order to identify Indian murders." Adjutant Journal, July 17, 1877. Since none of the "prisoners" were even present in Idaho at the outbreak of war, Captain Throckmorton had clearly convened a kangaroo court. Such an obvious injustice to known noncombatants would cause Wood, General Howard, and many future writers (Bruce Hampton, Merrill Beal, Chester Fee, Thomas Sutherland, and David Lavender) to distort, minimize, or omit this event when writing about the war.

‡‡ Wood documents his appointment as officer of the day, responsible for "the guard, prison-

fate before them. Thoughts on the Indian as a human being, a man and brother. His strange history.* Inability to fuse with the white man. Difference in physical characteristics between these Indians and the Alaskans. Similarity of some of these men to the Roman type. Alaskans purely Asiatic.

July 18ᵗʰ { - *19ᵗʰ*} [Clearwater River at Kamiah to Camas Prairie]†

Breaking camp on return of Cavalry. Surrender of the young wounded "Eagle of the Light."‡ I am improvised a cudi and hear the woes and troubles of the innocent captives.§ I read them a lecture for general effect and say, "So go and sin no more."¶ Night march. No shoe. No nothin' now. Another "bivowk."[*sic*]**

---

ers, and police of the post or camp." (*Websters Revised Unabridged*, 1998). This night would be Wood's first extensive personal contact with individual non-treaty Nez Perces, a people he would admire, defend, memorialize, and write about for the rest of his life.

* Hamburger transcribes this as " His strange wisdom." Hamburger, *Two Rooms*, 48.

† A settler present the morning of the eighteenth described the river crossing: "The entire day was spent in recrossing. Ten men were taken over at a time in a boat (the one I had built six weeks before)." Francis M. Redfield, "Reminiscences of Francis M. Redfield, Chief Joseph's War," *Pacific Northwest Quarterly* 27 (1936): 66–77. Camas Prairie "was a favorite gathering spot for the Nez Perces,... one of the finest camas fields in the area." *Nez Perce Country* (Washington, D.C.: National Park Service, 1983), 196.

‡ The warrior Wood interviewed and probably sketched was not Eagle from the Light (Tipyahlanah Ka-ou-pu), a non-treaty Nez Perce chief "who even before the outbreak of the war had become disgusted with conditions in Idaho and had settled down with Flathead friends" in western Montana. Josephy, *Nez Perce Indians*, 573. More likely, Wood interviewed Temme Ilppilp, or Red Heart, Jr., one of Chief Red Heart's four sons. McWhorter, *Hear Me*, 333; Greene, *Nez Perce Summer*, 372.

§ *Cudi* is a legal loan word referring to a judge or juror. See *Oxford Latin Dictionary; Oxford English Dictionary*. Laura Mosher and Paul Nergelovic, United States Military Academy Library, email to author, April 1, 2004.

¶ Here, Wood ironically quotes John 8:11 (King James Bible), in which Jesus refuses to condemn an adulteress, then admonishes her—with these words—to change her life. After the "[military] commission could not make a finding in regard to the Indian prisoners," these innocent noncombatants—men, women, and children—were marched sixty miles on foot through heat and dust to Fort Lapwai, transported by steamer to Fort Vancouver, then imprisoned for nine months. Brown, *Flight of the Nez Perce*, 205; Greene, *Nez Perce Summer*, 100, 408–9n15; McWhorter, *Hear Me*, 331–2.

** "Infantry making night march encamped sixteen miles out." Adjutant Journal, July 19, 1877. Apparently, Wood's company elected to march partway to Cold Spring the night of July 18, then bivouac on Camas Prairie rather than bake all the next day in the heat, which can reach over a hundred degrees. "No shoes" may reflect the infantry's notoriously inadequate footwear. See Douglas C. McChristian, *The U.S. Army in the West 1870-1880* (Norman: University of Oklahoma Press,

July 19ᵗʰ { - *20ᵗʰ*} [Camas Prairie to Cold Spring]††

Horrible hot stifling march across a dry prairie.‡‡ No breakfast. No water. Men fainting and falling by the wayside.

July 20ᵗʰ [Cold Spring to Camas Prairie (Camp Wilkinson)]§§

In camp at Cold Spring. "Throck's" scare.¶¶ Waiting for the General. The afternoon march and camp on the prairie. Grass to our knees. Rolling hills. Sides speckled with herd and pack train. Men bustling about packs. Reminded of an Oriental camp in some desert, or steppe, and of De Quincey's *Flight of a Tartar Tribe*.***

July 21ˢᵗ [Camas Prairie to Lawyer Creek]

March to Camp Alexander in Lawyer's Canyon.††† Trout, ease, and comfort.

1995). In contrast, "Howard...marched his [mounted?] command 35 miles, to Cold Spring, in one day..." (Sutherland, *Howard's Campaign*, 13). Hamburger attributes this night march to Red Heart's band (*Two Rooms*, 48).

†† Intending to intercept the fleeing non-treaty bands in the Bitterroot Valley south of Missoula, General Howard had started his troops for Montana, but before he reached Cold Spring, he learned that the non-treaty warriors had attacked the treaty Indians who had betrayed them, stolen their horses and mules, and burned some property. Greene, *Nez Perce Summer*, 102-103. Wood's infantry company probably camped at a well-known Nez Perce site on Cold Springs Creek about halfway between the Kamiah area and the Lapwai Valley. Diana Mallickan, email to author, March 14, 2004.

‡‡ Refers to Camas Prairie west of Kamiah. Wood's Twenty-first Infantry company probably marched around nineteen miles in full sun to Cold Spring.

§§ Sutherland adds: "that night went into camp on the grassy table lands, where there was no wood for fires or for tent poles and the little water...was soon worked into such a mush of mud by the pack mules and cavalry horses that it was impossible to use it.... This camp I believe, was named in honor of Capt. M. C. Wilkinson, of Portland." *Portland Daily Standard*, August 1, 1877.

¶¶ Capt. Charles B. Throckmorton, Fourth Artillery; what the scare refers to is not known.

*** Allusion to the English Romantic writer Thomas De Quincey (1785–1859) and his famous historical essay, *Flight of a Tartar Tribe*. Wood may well have read the 1854 reprint of De Quincey's grandiloquent amalgam of history and fiction while a cadet at the United States Military Academy, where he "did an unusual amount of extracurricular reading...[in] works by Shakespeare, Spenser, Milton, and Sir Walter Scott." Bingham and Barnes, *Wood Works*, 5.

††† After praising the trout fishing in Lawyer Creek, Sutherland goes on to explain, "This beautiful camping ground was named after Dr. [C. T.] Alexander, chief of our medical corps, a gentleman of much intelligence and a rare fund of humor which he in vain tries to hide behind an effort to appear misanthropical." *Portland Daily Standard*, August 1, 1877.

July 22nd [Lawyer Creek]*

Sunday in the canyon. Arrival of Cushing and command.† I am promoted to Aide-de-Camp.‡

July 23rd [Lawyer Creek to Cottonwood Creek (Camp Alfred Sully)]§

Leave all about 6:45 a.m. for Croasdaile Ranch and camp at Chapman's ranch at about 10:45.¶ Nine miles.

---

* Lawyer Creek is named for Hallalhotsoot, or James Lawyer, a friend of the missionaries and head chief of the treaty Nez Perces. Misled by white officials, Lawyer arrogated to himself "the right and obligation to speak for all the bands and to sign away all the lands of Joseph, White Bird, and every other Nez Perce...who lived outside the [Idaho] reservation. Lawyer had neither objected to that act nor explained that he did not possess the right to do what he had done.... [To] those who were hurt by him or lost their lands as result of his action, he is still considered a man who betrayed the Nez Perces." Josephy, *Nez Perce Country*, 106–12.

† Capt. Harry C. Cushing, Fourth Artillery, stationed at San Francisco, was "the senior officer...whom Howard was to regard as a capable officer in the future and...Second Lieutenant Guy Howard, the general's oldest son who was soon made an aide-de-camp." Brown, *Flight of the Nez Perce*, 211.

‡ Captain Pollock notes, "Two of the members of his [General Howard's] staff are sick, Captain Wilkinson and Lieutenant Fletcher, so Lt. Wood is temporarily on the staff. The Lieutenant claims that the pure copper band he wears on the left wrist wards away sickness and bad humors." Pollock, *Grandfather*, 7.

§ The camp was named after Col. Alfred Sully, Wood's commanding officer, Twenty-first Infantry, at Fort Vancouver.

¶ "[Henry] Croasdaile is an ex-officer of the British navy, who owns two large sheep farms here, the houses on each of which were destroyed by the Indians. He is a very pleasant and well educated gentleman, clinging to all of his old English customs even to having a well stocked wine cellar." Sutherland, *Portland Daily Standard*, 8/11/77. The Nez Perces also may have taken "unusual rifles" and ".35 caliber exploding cartridges" when raiding Croasdaile's ranch, weapons and munitions that they used later in the conflict. Brown, *Flight of the Nez Perce,* 412–13.

Arthur Chapman was a controversial cross-cultural figure. By this date his house, barn, and outbuildings had been burned by non-treaty warriors and his horse herd, cattle, chickens, and pigs killed or driven off. He had settled on the Nez Perce Reservation at Cottonwood Creek in 1861. There, he married Mollie (1841–1896), a relative of Chief Eagle of the Light, and Yellow Wolf explains that "he and my uncle, Old Yellow Wolf, had lived in the same house, just as brothers." (McWhorter, *Yellow Wolf*, 55.) Father, husband, stockbreeder, trader, Chapman fought against the non-treaty bands, then became General Howard's scout and interpreter throughout the Army's pursuit. Wood published his sketch of Chapman—"A Scout"—in the *Daily Graphic* on August 3, 1877. At and after the Nez Perce surrender on October 5, 1877, Chapman translated for Joseph, including two interviews with Wood, then accompanied the surrendered Nez Perces to Fort Leavenworth. In 1879, he translated Joseph's famous speech in Washington, D.C., later published in the *North American Review* as "An Indian's View of Indian Affairs," a text that Chap-

"Mountain Passes in the Bitter Root Mountains." *This landscape and its original caption suggest Wood's respect for the daunting scale and beauty of the Nez Perces' homeland. Perhaps completed prior to the Army's crossing of Lolo Pass, this is one of five sketches in his second front-page spread in the Daily Graphic. Titled "Scenes of General Howard's Campaign Against the Nez Perce Indians," the montage was attributed as "Sketches by an Officer in the Field."* From the Daily Graphic, August 16, 1877. Chicago Research Library

man declared was "nothing more like his [Joseph's] statement than day is like dark" because the text had been extensively revised by A. B. Meacham and others (Chapman to Howard, February 18, 1880, Bowdoin College Archives, Brunswick, Maine). See also *Depredation Claim*, Arthur J. [*sic*] Chapman, Department of Interior, 12/17/86, Bk 2, No. 220; Arthur I. Chapman, *Report of the Secretary of War.* Vol. 1 (Washington, D.C. 1891), 191–94; *Pension Claim of Arthur I.* [*sic*] *Chapman, 1902*, Biographical Files, OHS Research Library; Katherine James, email messages to author, 2001–2002.

III.

General Howard needed help. While in Lewiston the weekend of July 21–22, Howard had read in national newspapers that "The [President's] Cabinet yesterday secretly but seriously considered the propriety of displacing Howard and putting [General] Crook in his place. Howard...has made such a sad mess of the campaign...," that it was "quite possible that he will be removed today."[33] Though the general believed he had just defeated the non-treaty Nez Perces on July 11 and 12, he seemed to be losing the fight for favorable opinion in the eastern newspapers—his home front. To defend himself, to execute his orders, and to create his record, the general needed literate, articulate, intelligent staff officers, but he had sent his chief aide-de-camp, Lt. Melville C. Wilkinson, to recover his health and recruit Indian scouts among the pacified peoples at Warm Springs.[34] Howard could not help himself. He had lost his right arm in the Civil War and could write only slowly and awkwardly with his left hand.[35] He needed someone who could write legibly, fluently, rapidly, intelligently. Riding from Lewiston to Lawyer Canyon, he realized the solution was obvious: promote his friend Lieutenant Wood to headquarters.

Lieutenant Wood's undifferentiated literary ability could now help the general in three prose-intensive personae. As the new aide-de-camp, he became a secretary who "sat up half the night to write orders and reports by the light of a candle stuck in half of a raw potato."[36] He composed and copied field orders, messages, and telegrams. As the new acting adjutant general, Lieutenant Wood became a chronicler responsible for General Howard's official daily log—a writing task he likely assumed from his predecessor, Lieutenant Wilkinson. Wood apparently delegated this second role. On two occasions after the war, he stated that he "turned over the duty of keeping a journal to a sergeant attached to headquarters who wrote an excellent hand."[37]

While both of those new roles extended Howard's efficacy, authority, and influence, they implicitly and tacitly generated Wood's third and most significant new persona, "Howard's Advocate," an imaginative press officer, writer, and artist, who—anonymously or publicly, with or without per-

mission, regardless of audience or occasion, capable of mixing fact and fiction—would speak, write, and draw to defend General Howard, rouse his troops, refute his critics, defend his record, and advance his cause. Lieutenant Wood leaked his first two anonymous press releases to the *Daily Graphic* in New York, where they appeared as front-page montages on August 3 and August 16. Both montages—attributed to "an officer of General Howard's staff"—were accompanied by text favorable to Howard, and the first included a Portland studio portrait. On August 27, the same illustrated paper published Wood's Camas Meadow article—signed with his initial—and on September 8, his anonymous Camas Meadow drawing.[38] In all this writing and drawing, Wood as Howard's Advocate omits or abstracts all evidence of army incompetence, human foibles, and humane details. On August 29, 1877, he composed his first signed military text, "General Field Order No. 6," an extended defense of Howard and his exhausted troops to which Howard ironically added only two words—"Under God."[39] This rhetorically skilled appeal to pathos would later be widely praised, circulated, and published by Army brass. Barraged by press accounts that erased or insulted General Howard after Chief Joseph's surrender on October 5, Howard's Advocate continued his counterattack: first, by anonymously leaking his poetic "Chief Joseph Surrender Speech"—which begins "Tell General Howard I know his heart"— to newspapers; then by publishing anonymous articles defending Howard in Chicago, New York, and Portland; then by acting as the general's secret envoy to President Hayes; and finally by co-authoring with Howard the heavily slanted post-war Army narrative of the campaign.[40] Promotion to aide-de-camp ended Erskine's personal, introspective diary on July 22, 1877, but Lieutenant Wood as Howard's Advocate would be created that day and continue until well after Howard's death in 1909. Eventually, Wood became explicitly critical of army conduct, published his disagreements with General Howard, and described his military service this way: "in my youth, I, stupid, fought / wearing the livery of that thing the State / Whose might is by the richest bought / a bully which protects the great." Once—late in his life and off the official record—he referred to Howard as "my ignorant superior officer."[41]

As suggested by his July 17 and 18 diary entries, however, Erskine simultaneously became a "Nez Perce Advocate." Admiring Nez Perce courage and skill and identifying with Nez Perce oppression, Erskine rejected military violence and defended the non-treaty bands. His first two montages for the *Daily Graphic* presented—for perhaps the first time in the national press—authentic images of Nez Perce clothing, villages, individuals, horses, and boats, and he accurately depicted some of the Nez Perce home landscape. In texts for the *Daily Graphic*, Erskine clearly praised the Nez Perces, "who are, mentally, as well as physically, by all odds the best developed and most advanced of all the aborigines in our Western country." After the surrender on October 5, he interviewed Chief Joseph, made drawings of Joseph and his infant daughter, sketched other surrendering Nez Perces, and published a third montage—all Nez Perce individuals—in New York on November 3.[42] As symbols of their developing friendship, he and Chief Joseph traded saddles.

Though he wrote the first sentence of his "Chief Joseph Surrender Speech" as Howard's Advocate, as Nez Perce Advocate he synthesized the remaining sixteen sentences for Joseph from Nez Perce facts (interviews with Joseph), translations (by Arthur Chapman), and his own observations and fictions (text, syntax, form, context). With this synthesis, he hoped to "redeem their [Nez Perce] suffering and the injustice of their situation through the grace and strength of impassioned language."[43] Although neither Joseph nor anyone else present on October 5 would ever confirm that they heard Erskine's "Chief Joseph Surrender Speech" on October 5, 1877, he would repeatedly publish, recite, and revise his subversive and poetic oration—disguised as artifact—until that disguised heroic sonnet became the most famous, controversial, and intercultural text in nineteenth-century western American literature. Masked as Howard's Advocate, drawing and writing without regard to race, Erskine as Nez Perce Advocate had, by the end of 1877, become the "one officer [who] rejected the fundamental assumption of American civilization's superiority."[44] That transformation begins in this diary.

In publishing his prose after 1877, Erskine probably considered this diary with great ambivalence. Burial of dead friends at White Bird, two "friendly fire" killings, failure to cross the Salmon, a week of absurd marching, jailing Red Heart's

"Camp of Nez Perce on the Clearwater River." *This original caption may identify a treaty band encampment Wood saw sometime after July 13, perhaps around Kamiah. Wood's attention to this peaceful domestic scene across the river suggests his diary entry on July 17: "thoughts on the Indian as a human being, a man and a brother," and his later poem identifying the Nez Perces as "my brown brothers / Of the wilderness /...[who] instructed my civilization."*   Reprinted from the Daily Graphic, *August 16, 1877. Chicago Research Library*

innocents, serving as judge on a kangaroo court—these may have been embarrassing weeks that Wood preferred to abstract, background, or delete. Except for narrating his Battle of the Clearwater experience in an 1884 article, "Chief Joseph, The Nez Perce," Wood did not publish any significant prose about his five weeks as an infantry soldier during the rest of his career. Instead, he focused repeatedly on the last two months of the conflict—especially the surrender on October 5 at Bear's Paw. If he told the whole truth implicit in this diary, those first five weeks at war might seem an absurd misadventure of the ridiculous, racist, incompetent, unjust, and ignorant.

In contrast to that evasive record in his published prose, Wood did use both events and language from this diary as a source for his published poetry. In composing and revising *The Poet in the Desert*, the hundred-page dramatic poem for which he "wanted to be remembered," he used the diary repeatedly.[45]

In the 1915 edition, for instance, he quoted his June 21 diary phrase "I was a soldier and have gone out to kill and be killed."[46] In that same edition, he re-called his June 27 entry: "I have stood with the soldiers, / Face to face with the great Mother, / And have wrapped the dead in their blankets,/ For the long repose."[47] Revising *The Poet in the Desert* in 1918, Wood again used that June 21 phrase but became more explicitly anti-military: "I was a soldier, and, at command, / Had gone out to kill and be killed. / This was not majestic."[48] In 1918, he also added sixty-three lines alluding to his July 17 entry, lines praising his Native American "brown brothers / of the wilderness /...[who] instructed my civilization..." and lamenting their tragedy. To protest all war, he also universalized his June 27 entry:

> I have seen War.
> I have heard it.
> I have smelled it.
> Even now I am waked from dreams
> By the stink of bodies
> Three days dead under the sun.
> Maggots filled their mouths.
> Flies crawled over their eyeballs,
> Buzzing up angrily as we threw
> Manhood into the pit of putrefaction.
> Weeds will grow upon the lips of lovers
> And grass flourish out of the hearts of fathers,
> But the father and lover
> Will return no more.[49]

In the 1929 revision, he added 178 new lines describing, praising, and idealizing Native American cultures in general and the Nez Perce implicitly.[50]

In Wood's unpublished work—drawings, poetry, and letters—the archival record suggests this diary's further significance. In his papers, Wood saved but never published or spoke about his drawing of the Salmon River crossing at White Bird—days that clearly suggested Army incompetence. Sometime after leaving the Army in 1884, Wood may have returned to this diary when composing a long narrative poem about the Wallowa band leaders and when drafting a Nez Perce War ballad sequence of six poems and one fragment. The latter, "Ballad of the Cottonwood Ranch," is grounded in his June 27 entry:

Ballad of the Cottonwood Ranch

Is it better to die all untarnished
Tho' life has but opened her gates
Or live and grow fat like a friar
With "coward" writ over your face?

We lay along the mountain side;
The Salmon River shot below
The sparks flew upward like men's souls
The rocks danced in the fiery glow.

"Swing low, sweet chariot," sang we all
The laughing youngsters stretched about —
And "Benny Havens,"—many a song
of love and war—and many a shout[51]

Wood probably abandoned this ballad sequence—as well as the Wallowa band poem—because the four longest ballads dramatizing Nez Perce individuals came from fantasy, reading, and hearsay. The unpublished poems grounded in his diary, such as "Ballad of the Burials," remain more significant. Confronted with mortality that he registered on June 27 as private horror and shock, this unpublished postwar elegy became an honorific memorial for the soldiers—and those who buried them—in Whitebird Canyon:

Ballad of the Burials

This was a man and a soldier —
But now so still it lies
With the buzzards winging o'er it
In its mouth the buzzing flies.

The sun shone hot, the infantry
Did sweat beneath their soldier packs
They sucked their canteens selfishly
They threw their blankets in their tracks.

The sun glared down as he would melt
The barren rocks. He burnt the grass.
The dusty column crawled its way
Toward the White Bird Canyon pass.

And all was still where devil din
Of shot and whoop and groan and cry

Had waked the cliffs. But now two days
The dead beneath the sun do lie.

Their faces stare into the sun
The polished flies buzz from their lips.
They lie so still, they shine so white
From boots and shirt and clothing stripped.

The spot is black where splashed their brains
Their bellies slashed with cruel art
And maggots all asquirm do crawl
Where once there lived a soldier's heart.

Hot glared the rocks. The flies swarmed up.
The buzzards marked the hidden spot
Where hopeless all, but fighting grim,
A man at bay had found his lot.

Jerome, the jester, knelt at ease
Behind a rock, still taking sight
But fell asleep till judgment day
When suddenly there fell the night.

And Blacksmith Joe, far up the cliff
Where he had climbed in desp'rate quest
Lay on the rocks, a lump of white
The buzzards hacked his splendid breast.

It was a field of dread and doom
Sown thick with what had once been men
Who spoke to us and were our friends
Now white like mushrooms through this glen.

Here stretched brave Theller on the rocks
Where to the last he stood at bay
And here a-sprawl with ghastly throats
Both Sergeant Jones and Piper lay.

And here the world came to an end
for drunken Fritz. 'Twas his last spree.
And here we swore the oath of blood
To send their souls much company.

The magpies hop and flutter near.
The little brook goes splashing on.
The sunflowers smile. The blessed air
Is sick with stench of carrion.

And sick the comrades' stomachs are
Who ply the pick and dig the holes
And down, with roar of angry flies
The dead fall in—God rest their souls!

And still, in midnight dreams, I see
The hundred corpses' blackened face.
I smell the smell, and wake for dread.
— It was a very charnel place![52]

In another unpublished poem from that postwar sequence, he continues as Nez Perce Advocate by expressing his admiration for the bands' skill in crossing rivers—a feat he witnessed and noted in his July 13 diary entry.

Ballad of the Flight across the Salmon River

The river runs foaming and restless
And hurrying down to the sea
Though never a drop returning
It flows eternally.

The saffron east pales into light
The dark squaws bind both bag and bale.
A noise like thunder nearer sweeps
And, tossing head and mane and tail,

Three thousand horses fill the place
A neighing, tossing, trampling throng.
Half naked boys on barebacked steeds
With shrilling screams do urge them on.

The packs are lashed, no pause is made
To drive that wild herd to the brim
of Salmon River. Then with shouts
Both men and boys forced them to swim.

The leaders plunge and, snorting, swim
And so, with many a cough and toss,
The river is flecked black with heads
Through eddies swift the herd doth cross.

The teepees and the parfleche bags
The bales and litter of the tribe
Are tied to manes and tails, or dry
Upon frail rafts of driftwood ride.

The babies on their mothers' backs,
The children clutch the horses' manes
And so they flit like passing birds;
Not any living thing remains.

Down stream and swiftly all are borne
All straining for the other bank;
The panting horses scramble out
And dripping stand with shining flanks.

As rides the last from out the flood
The first, far on the mountain, seem
Like flies; then buzzards from the blue
Drop down toward the silent stream.[53]

Among Wood's many unpublished letters, his 1918 response to an Idaho historian constitutes his only account of the Nez Perce conflict to include events from the first five weeks. Here, he defends the Army's river crossing recorded in his entries for June 29–July 1 and sketched but never published:

> You say we were halted three days at the Salmon River.... We had to cross a mountain torrent in a gorge not as the Indians did, by plunging in with their ponies and little light baggage, but with infantry-men and cavalrymen and a mountain-howitzer and ammunition and rations and pack mules. We got a rope across, by swimming with horses, and then rigged boats of willows, covered with canvas, and I think to cross an army under such conditions, very many of whose men could not even swim, was very creditable even if three days had been taken in the task.[54]

This 1877 diary, as a literary sourcebook to paradoxically use and avoid in his published and unpublished work, is perhaps as complex as Wood's later life. After approximately six years as General Howard's aide and advocate, Wood resigned in 1884 to become a Portland lawyer, writer, and civic leader—"probably the most influential cultural figure in turn-of-the century Portland."[55] In 1884, he also published "Chief Joseph, The Nez Perce," a highly-critical account of the federal government's dishonest negotiations with the non-treaty bands, and publicly declaring his role as Nez Perce Advocate, he argued that the non-treaty Nez Perces be returned from deadly exile in Oklahoma.[56] In 1888, three years after the non-treaty survivors returned to the northwest, Wood entertained Joseph at his home in Portland; in

"Chief Joseph." *Wood sketched this portrait between October 5 and October 15, 1877, and delivered it in person—along with perhaps as many as six others—to the New York Daily Graphic while en route to Washington, D.C., as General Howard's secret envoy to President Rutherford B. Hayes. Later, ghostwriting in Harpers (November 17, 1877), Wood explained: "Joseph has a gentle face, somewhat feminine in its beauty, but intensely strong and full of character. A photograph could not do him justice. A bullet scratch has left a slight scar on his forehead."* Daily Graphic, *November 3, 1877, Chicago Research Library*

1889, he arranged for the sculptor Olin Warner to cast a bronze medallion of Joseph. In 1892 and 1893, he sent his adolescent son, Erskine, to live summers with Joseph on the Colville Reservation. Basking in his history as Howard's Advocate, he received the Oregon militia title of colonel. For thirty-four years, he lived in Portland, loved his wife and children, practiced maritime law, and defended conservatives and radicals. He then fell in love with the young poet Sara Bard Field, sold a million-dollar land grant, resigned his law practice, set up trust accounts for his family, and, in 1918 at age sixty-six, moved with Field to California to make a new life together as writers and poets. They both became widely known. In 1927, Wood published *Heavenly Discourses*, a national bestseller that went through forty or more printings. In 1936, Wood privately confessed that his nationally published, admired, and accepted "Chief Joseph Surrender Speech" was "a literary item" rather than a verbatim transcript—as he had claimed since 1877.[57]

In March 1941, his June 27, 1877, diary entry—"The alarm shot at midnight. One of our own pickets shot by one of our men"—came back to haunt him. Lucullus McWhorter, an amateur historian researching the 1877 conflict, discovered a diary by Private Mayer in which "Lieutenant Wood, 21st Infantry, aide-de-camp" was erroneously named as shooting "Private Reed, Troop E, First Cavalry." McWhorter sent a copy of Mayer's accusatory diary entry to Wood and in *Hear Me, My Chiefs* (1952) published Wood's denial and explanation, in which Wood himself—sixty-four years after the fact—confused and conflated Reed's wounding with the July 7 killing of Private Michael Cassidy.[58] Assuming Wood's guilt and adding more guilt because of Wood's verbatim claim regarding the "Chief Joseph Surrender Speech," Mark Brown repeated in *Flight of the Nez Perce* (1967) McWhorter's false allegation that Wood had shot a fellow soldier. Brown also added more hearsay.[59] For reasons best known to them, many subsequent historians—until Jerome Greene—have repeated, let stand, or ignored this false allegation. In an unpublished appendix prepared for *Nez Perce Summer, 1877*, and in recent correspondence, Greene resolved this question:

> I don't think that Lieutenant Wood shot Reed. There would be something in Wood's ACP File in the National Archives if indeed that happened... It is possible that an enlisted man named Wood did the shooting. Mayer asserts that it was a picket who did it, and that would have been an enlisted man. Mayer's allusion to Lieutenant Wood, I think, simply confuses the two [June 30 and July 7] shootings.[60]

Neither that false charge nor any of Wood's writing nor the misstatements of historians ever affected Wood's lifetime of friendship and respect for the Nez Perce. In fact, Erskine's example—grounded in his diary entries of July 17 and 18—began a tradition of intercultural and interracial understanding that continues into the present as Wood family legacy. In October 1991, at the Congressional Medal of Honor Convention in Vancouver, Washington, the Wood family supported and participated in a "Celebrate Freedom" project exhibition titled "C. E. S. Wood and Chief Joseph: Brothers in the American West." Featuring displays of both traditional Nez Perce and U.S. Army clothing, ornaments, horse gear, weapons, ceremonial objects, daily equipment, and art, the exhibition also included a multimedia program of quotations from C. E. S. Wood's writings and Chief Joseph's 1879 speech.[61]

In July 1997, a more extraordinary event occurred in the Wallowa Valley when the C. E. S. Wood family—to fulfill an untransmitted request from Chief Joseph to C. E. S. Wood more than a hundred years earlier—presented an Appaloosa stallion worth twenty-five thousand dollars to Keith Soy Redthunder, the direct descendant of Chief Joseph still living in exile at Nespelem.[62] In a memorial statement, Mary Christina Wood, C. E. S. Wood's great-granddaughter and a professor of Indian law at the University of Oregon, spoke again of the Wood family's rejection of militarism:

> The 1877 campaign relentlessly pursued by the U.S. Government had pitted Indians and whites against each other in a conflict stained with injustice and coercion, but the relationship between C. E. S. Wood and Chief Joseph after the war was as families engaged in mutual and respectful bond of friendship.[63]

Most recently, the Wood family participated in another public event directly related to Wood's diary entries of July 17 and 18. On April 22, 2000, a "Reconciliation Ceremony" was held at Fort Vancouver to commemorate "the hardships endured at Fort Vancouver by Chief Red Heart's band" including the death of an infant boy. Sponsored by the Nez Perce Tribe, the U.S. Army, the City of Vancouver, and the National Park Service, the ceremony was led by tribal elders, soldiers, and Mary Wood. During the ceremony, which attracted more than three hundred people, Professor Wood promised "to always keep the story alive and teach the importance of what happened here."[64]

IV.

This 1877 diary is more than just the early personal writing of an interesting man with a complex personality. Many historians have found Wood's diary useful because his June 23 entry provides, as Jerome Greene states, "rare contemporary insight into the emotions of soldiers bound for the front during an Indian campaign...."[65] As a literary sourcebook for Wood, the diary proved more paradoxical: it cryptically recorded his awakening—as a Nez Perce Advocate—to racism, oppression, injustice, and militarism, the same forces he had resisted intuitively as a cadet at West Point. Simultaneously, his diary alludes to major personal transformations—his first face-to-face confrontations with war, death, and mortality and his promotion, as Howard's Advocate, to a position of military and linguistic power. As a survivor of the Nez Perce conflict, he could never forget what he had seen and done. The facts he learned and witnessed generated values, and those values generated rights, truths, insights, discoveries. How to transmit those discoveries without betraying both the Nez Perces and General Howard became a lifelong process, as Sherry Smith has explained: "Time and again throughout his life Wood returned to his Indian war experiences as he developed two themes—injustice and perfidy—that played important roles in his prose and poetry."[66]

In the end, Erskine chose friendship and respect for Joseph and the Wallowa band and rejected himself as Lieutenant Wood serving Howard's bellicose, intolerant ethnocentricity. He learned what Joseph Conrad wrote earlier in "Heart of Darkness:"

> The conquest of the earth, which mostly means the taking it away from those who have a different complexion or slightly flatter noses than ourselves, is not a pretty thing when you look into it too much. What redeems it is the idea only.[67]

Those choices and decisions and transformations begun in these scribbled thirty pages make both Wood's life and work essential and contemporary—with the Wallowa band still living in exile, the ownership of the Wallowa valley still an open question, and apology to and restitution for the non-treaty bands nowhere in sight.

Chapter 5 ▪ SOLDIER TO ADVOCATE

Preface to

RIDER IN THE WILDERNESS:
MINOR WHITE IN LA GRANDE 1940 – 1941

Searching for a historical cover image for *Oregon East (1950-1985),* I met Peter Bunnell, curator of the restricted Minor White Archive at Princeton University. He provided "Grande Ronde Valley from Mt. Emily," a rare 1940s print by Minor White, the young Works Progress Administration (WPA) Art Center photographer (at left) who later achieved international renown. Fast forward twenty nine years to early May 2004: *Calapooya Literary Review* editors Jodi Varon and David Axelrod asked me for a 750(+–) word essay on Minor White "setting up the La Grande WPA Arts Center during the 1940s." Deadline: June 15. So, I dropped all other manuscripts-in-progress to track down White and the WPA: reading sixteen months of local newspaper microfilm, finding and reading White's journals and letters, interviewing Bunnell and White's local student Fred Hill (lower right), and contacting archivists, curators, librarians, historians, biographers, photographers. By early June, I had a draft biographical sketch that I hoped fairly stated and accurately documented the young artist's historical context, character, behavior, and work—over 3,000 words. To avoid huge blocks of information—the bane of historical prose—I adapted the meditative essay collage which gave me brevity, white space, variation in voice and persona, and movement. The editors further enhanced the piece with White's newly-discovered 1940s images and some of Fred Hill's original images—ten in all. A few of those have been reprinted here, including a 1940 photo (left) of White and Hill by Fred's mother Etha.

Sources: *Calapooya Literary Review* 2 (2004): 21-26; Photos courtesy Fred Hill.

RIDER IN THE WILDERNESS:
MINOR WHITE IN LA GRANDE 1940–1941

"Need a car as badly as you do..."
—Minor White to Fred Hill, January 16, 1941.

June, 1940. When he descended from the eastbound train in La Grande that night, Minor White may have walked to his room in the Foley Hotel—battered suitcases heavy with cameras, film, photographs, clothes. Thirty-one, single, Minnesotan, impoverished, aspiring artist, White was a federal employee and amateur photographer without a vehicle. Around him lay Union County's 2,032 square miles of forest, mountain wilderness, rivers, pastures, fields, a county where 17,399 people—8.6 per square mile—were outnumbered by wildlife, a county seat of 7,747 souls situated in the most fertile valley east of the Cascades. In such country, being an outsider and a pedestrian would not lead White to discovery, much less to revelation. White needed someone to pick him up, drive him, drop him off, move him, carry him, transport him.

In rural, small, remote places, there is no serious art. That illusion generates others—sophistication is metropolitan; talent must be imported; important life is far away.

Six months before the Federal Arts Project carried White to La Grande, the people of Union County had been creating a vehicle for him and his work. In January, 1940, after the county court granted a year's free lease of the empty Mahaffey building, Mrs. Alan Christensen and thirty-seven local women—

"The Captains"—went door-to-door seeking $1 memberships for the new Art Center. They needed to raise $1,500 to renovate the building. To support their fund drive, Charles Bowes, editor of *The Observer*, published thirty-nine front page stories, ten news releases, two editorials, one letter to the editor, and one review—all before the center even opened. The paper reported that "The Captains" sold 700 memberships throughout Union County. Businesses, bankers, professors, doctors, farmers, priests, lawyers, teachers, PTA's, schools, clubs— everyone contributed and then some. The $1,500 was raised—and more. Art was in everyone. Except for materials, classes would be free. Teachers could volunteer. All students would be welcome. Local control was guaranteed. The WPA promised $10,000 for administration. By April, Jane Robinson of the Salem Art Center was hired as the first manager, and Bess Whitcomb, member of the Portland WPA Federal Theater Project, was appointed assistant manager. A local board of directors, officers, committees, constitution, and bylaws—all were chosen and set to work. On May 12, 1940, 1,200 people "from all parts of Northeast Oregon and from all walks of life" attended opening ceremonies at 10 Depot Street. A month before White arrived, The Grande Ronde Valley Art Center was up and rolling.

To defeat the Depression between April, 1935 and March, 1941, the WPA spent $600,556 on Union County make-work projects—parks, courthouse, reservoirs, roads, streets, sidewalks, airport, outhouses. On those same projects, Union County taxpayers spent $535,318 of their own funds.

The new Art Center would carry White, pay White, bog White down. His first act was installing an exhibition of his Portland cityscapes and explaining them. When Jane Robinson became ill and resigned in mid-July, White was appointed acting manager, then became permanent manager in early September. Like other artists cast or miscast as teachers and administrators, the young photographer would soon be overloaded: too many classes, no time to prepare them, inadequate darkroom, no studio, too much promotional and administrative work, no qualified assistants, no time for his own photography, no time to

SCHEDULE OF CLASSES
GRANDE RONDE VALLEY ART CENTER

MONDAY

	Time	Class	Instructor	Studio
Morn.	10:30--12	Children's Leather	Bell	B
		Children's Painting	Prudhomme	A
Aft.	2:00--3:30	Adult Crafts	Bell	B
		Speech & Diction (Adult)	Chambreau	A
Eve.	7:00--9:30	Adult Crafts	Be ll	B
		Pinocchio	Chambreau	A
	7:30--9:30	Beginning Camera	White	C

TUESDAY

	Time	Class	Instructor	Studio
Morn.	10:30--12	Children's Leather	Bell	B
		Children's Recitation & Music	Chambreau	A
Aft.	2:00--3:30	Adult Design	Prudhomme	C
		Pinocchio	Chambreau	A
	2: 00–4: 00	Weaving	Vanetti	B
Eve.	7:00--9:30	Adult Design	Prudhomme	C
		Weaving	Vanetti	B
		Wood Carving	Kirschner	na*
		Pinocchio	Chambreau	A
	7:00--9:00	Darkroom Technique	White	C

WEDNESDAY

	Time	Class	Instructor	Studio
Morn.	10:30--12	Children's Metal	Bell	B
		Children's Painting	Prudhomme	A
	11:00--11:15	Radio - KLBM		

* This entry was added in handwriting to the printed schedule.

"Class Schedule." *ca 1940 courtesy Fred Hill collection.*

write his "Memorable Fancies" journal. By December, 1940, White wrote to a former student:

> The old job has been keeping me busier than ever. About the only way I get to take any pictures at all is to have the Master Class do portraits, and get a few shots at the model myself, or run around the center shooting classes in action.*** I still like my job managing the A.C., but wish I had more time to take pix. Spent an awful lot of it trying to keep from teaching more than three classes a week.... J. Chandler is coming down with his camera club pretty soon for class work. That makes four, next term will have to have a new beginning class, that makes five. It has been suggested that I have a class Sat. night for the CCCs. That makes me mad. Maurice [Gekeler] The Mice is only around once a week now. I had hopes of making him into an assistant. He knows the stuff, but he talks so low, nobody can hear what he is saying.

As a WPA Arts Project administrator, White earned twice the WPA artist's $23.50 per week. "I am, at long last, getting a decent wage," White told Fred Hill.

That same December, Glen McKenzie, a young Summerville farmer and Federal Theater Project actor, picked up the new Art Center manager to show him the vast interior country—from the air. (Earlier that fall, someone had already driven White to Indian Rock on Mt. Emily where he'd taken a series of landscapes.) Sixty three years later, McKenzie remembered that day—December 8, 1940. He drove White to the airport and, since nobody had much money in those days, Glen rented the plane. Up in the freezing light, they cruised in great circles over the dun fields, snowy mountains, blue-green forests, meandering river. A little three-dimensionality would be good for the flatlander from Minnesota; a little apotheosis wouldn't hurt an abstracted mind. After the flight, White wrote to a student, "Went air planing today for the first time in La Grande, one of the cubs, had a wonderful time. Pictures were lousy, all of them blurred, had bumpy air."

Minor White, Wallowas, "The condition of my picture taking makes me unhappy. And as I consider the summer's work, I get no happier. Have about one good one. One of the Ice Lake shots. It really has some feeling to it, even I admit it. The only decent portrait has been of you."

—Minor White to Fred Hill, 12/8/40

Glen still had his WPA-built "Roosevelt House"—a spiffy outhouse with door, seat, vent, and he remembered Beth Whitcomb from the WPA Federal Theater Project: she came from Portland on the Friday night train, taught theater in the Art Center basement on weekends. For fifty years, Glen farmed and acted in plays, and in the 1990s, he and his wife Jean gave $10,000 to the new Eastern Oregon University theater that now bears his name. Glen loved being cast, becoming—for a while—other.

Another Art Center student transported White by land. "Minor did not have an automobile," Fred Hill wrote:

> When his schedule permitted, I would pick Minor up and we would
> go off on some photographic escapade around the area, usually end-
> ing up at our house [in Elgin] for the evening meal...High Valley was
> a frequent destination...small farms and old buildings about 15 miles
> away. Sometimes, after many pictures, we'd lie in the shade of some
> convenient tree and talk. One weekend we drove to Joseph, Oregon—
> about seventy five miles away... About dawn the next day, we drove to
> the trail-head, and with cameras in backpacks and carrying tripods, we
> hiked seven miles up to Ice Lake in the Eagle Cap wilderness...

Sixty three years later, a retired commercial photographer, Fred still treasured those 1940 images—White dabbling his toes in Ice Lake, White posing
by ponderosa on High Valley Road—and Fred also saved White's 1940 portraits
of him—as smiling innocent in High Valley stubble, as intimate with a wand of
gladiolus in the Art Center studio. The handsome twenty-year old kid from Elgin
who became White's only known and accomplished Art Center student—Fred
Hill moved White. He liked Fred's passion for pictures. He wanted Fred's companionship, attention, darkroom services, skills. Fred remembered his teacher's
pre-war encouragement.

Fred memorized and resented White's post-war sentence: "[E]ven if you are
not ever going to be an artist, you are going to be a pro, and you might as well
be a good one as not."

Fred's mother, Etha Hill, moved White too—in more private ways. She was
not like "the gossipy old women of this town [who]...seem...[to] try to escape a
reality more vicious than themselves in their own vicious way." In contrast, Etha
Hill on her Elgin farm gave White a persona and place to locate his secret self-described paradox—the "fear of women...yet desiring the intimacy—of mothering."
Writing her from Hawaii during the war, Private White praised "Maw" Hill's
friendly piety: "[Y]ou have become more dear to me since you have encouraged me in the way of the Lord." After R and R in Sydney, he praised Maw's
home-cooked meals and her welcome: "[Australian hospitality] was very much
like your own, just took me in, like a long lost cousin, got acquainted and fitted

me into their way of living in no time at all. Just like you did when I was beginning to think La Grande had nothing to offer in the way of friendliness." As her
sons boarded the train for the war, he empathized with her suffering, and told
her, "You are the laughing Ma Hill I like the best." Writing from New Guinea,
Sergeant White praised Etha Hill indirectly: "Among these [natives] are wom-
en who look as if they came from the farms of the Grande Ronde, the capable,
friendly serious characters." He told her he loved her and sent her a photo of a
naked, pendulous-breasted New Guinea mother suckling her baby.

*"When I looked at things for what they are (1940)," White wrote, "I was
fool enough to persist in my folly and found that each photograph was a mirror of my Self."*

After the Army called up Fred Hill in September, 1940, the passion of another student—Miss Isabel Kane—transported White. Graduate of universities in
California and Washington, resident and wanderer three years in Europe, traveler and teacher across America, lover of dancing, boating, cycling, hiking, swimming, Isabel Kane fell for her photography teacher while she herself was teaching Physical Education at Eastern Oregon University. Years later, Professor Kane
clearly recalled that infatuating winter of 1940 and the spring and summer of
1941: "My car and I were at his disposal...we were happy with each other and not
too aware of what was going on in the war.... We would take rides and he would
see a view and we would return as many as three or four times to get the right
light or the right angle." In winter, she drove him around the frozen dazzle of the
Grande Ronde, up to alpine snow-bound Anthony Lakes, and through spring
and summer, Izzy—White's nickname for her—was driving White to new views
of their fertile country: to Alicel where she watched him take the black-smoking
locomotive and boxcars between grain sheds and wheat elevators; to mid-val-
ley where she watched him take the saltbox barn, gabled tank house, coops, and
combine on their dryland furrows; to farms around Cove and Union where she
watched, waited, wanted him. A devout Catholic, White listened as she told him
about God and love and confession and revelation and ecstasy and theology.

With Izzy's passionate belief to accelerate his spiritual awakening, White shot the landscapes which would merit his first national award in New York, his first one-man show in Portland, his first national publication in *Fair is Our Land*.

In 1940 White wrote, "Straight photography, tight as sonnet-form, is all the scope I need. Experimental photography could also be sufficient scope, but I do not lean in that direction at this time."

In spite of gossip, the Art Center was cruising: two hundred individuals and eleven organizations donated to the 1941 fund drive; all kinds of national and Oregon and local art shows went up; classes for all ages in many media flourished; the daily paper published all White's articles and reviews; bureaucrats came from all the important places to congratulate. Writing to Fred Hill, White even imagined another typical WPA project he would apparently never complete: "to find persons who are representative of the valley and mug them with the valley as background. Have got my fill of sceenics[sic]."

My approach to photography at that time, first recognized during 1940 in La Grande, Oregon, was more or less as follows: "Surfaces reveal inner states—cameras record surfaces. Confronted with the world of surfaces in nature, man, and photographs, I must somehow be a kind of microscope by which the underlying forces of spirit are observed and extended to others."

—Minor White

In June, 1941, Isabel Kane resigned her professorship at the university. Free to spend vacation together, White and Izzy mounted a horseback trip into the Wallowas. Seeming innocents before the fall, they camped, swam, cooked, explored, played, photographed. "We were like brother and sister," she said later. One day, his "lust for pictures spent," White posed for Isabel above Ice Lake: bent to his tripod, overloaded with photo gear, covered by hat and clothes, alone in mountains of gray rock and dwarf trees. Later, in a wartime letter, White would ask Isabel about his epiphany that summer:

Do you remember the night we climbed out on a rock in Hurricane Creek?... In the uncertain light you remember that eerie spirit came eddying up the stream and caught up the white stuff of our souls in its whirlpool of air, and the three of us ascended the stream to the high valleys above where snow lay beneath the trees and lined the waterfalls, and where we ascended the air over the peaks like a thin white flame so in love with the world it danced and danced out of sight.

Isabel transcribed only the romantic and religious passages—like the one above—from White's letters, and, fearing discovery of his secret, she burned all his originals.

The fall of 1941, Isabel Kane organized the Art Center's annual fund drive, stayed with White as long as possible in La Grande, then drove north to her new professorship—teaching dance at Central Washington University. No more rides. On October 24, 1941, White made his last front page news: the manager of the Art Center had resigned "to the Portland WPA office last week...It was accepted Monday and will become effective November 1." After sixteen months in La Grande, White's sudden exit probably had multiple causes. The blitzkrieg in Europe was overshadowing every thing and every one. Fred Hill had gone to fight. No more rides. White was feeling insignificant. The local newspaper was sold to Californians. Charles Bowes, his supportive editor, had resigned. Art Center stories became merely La Grande news. No more front page. White's reviews no longer carried bylines. Before she left, Isabel Kane's management of the fall membership drive was in financial trouble. The superintendent of schools and an art professor resigned from his Board of Directors. Among La Grande public school art teachers, trouble was brewing over differences in arts pedagogy and principles, differences that White's reviews and lectures may have instigated but could not resolve. Though he posed as an arts administrator and teacher, White had no training or expertise in creating a coherent K-12 arts curriculum. He mailed a personal invitation to Etha Hill, but she was too busy to drive the twenty miles of dirt road to La Grande to hear White's August lecture—"The First Hundred Years of Photography." In Elgin, they were sweating out the harvest. Did gossip

Chapter 6 • RIDER IN THE WILDERNESS: MINOR WHITE IN LA GRANDE 1940–1941

and aesthetic differences and alienation accumulate? Perhaps. Perhaps not. The news reporter did state explicitly, "Minor White will not be present" at the Art Center Board of Directors meeting on November 3. When the westbound train carried him back to Portland in early November, 1941, the local WPA administrator took over.

"In 1939, Congress required that anyone who had been on WPA for eighteen months should be removed." —William O. Douglas.

In spring, 1942, after White received his draft notice, Isabel Kane drove from Ellensburg to Portland, picked up White for their last ride. She drove to a motel on the Oregon coast where, awake all night together, Isabel Kane would learn her love for White would always be unrequited. "He told me about his childhood and his feelings on marriage, an idea he didn't entirely rule out, though he never saw himself as a family man."

He confessed his fear of women, his love for her, but his sexual preference for men.

Four years after he left La Grande, White wrote to Etha Hill from the Philippines:

21 March 1945

Dear Maw

How you all today & why. So with a bang start I start. You can see what a pass this Army life brings a guy to when he can't think of anything better to say than some platitude like "I wish you were here," which grates upon the ear like nutmeg & as for sincerity—it ain't in it. I wouldn't wish you here, even for the trip. You would probably lose out, but are malaria, yams, ho-hums, dysentery, beri beri & *hari kari* worth it? I say no, no, no a thousand times no.

The above is known as "bucking for Section VIII" in GI circles, but a few years back in the lush literary circles it was known as the "stream of consciousness" style of writing. I am not sure but what the GI is righter.

The subject of this letter, that is, what it's all for, is to tell you I still love you—which outburst of emotion is brought on by the receipt of your Christmas package. Fred (you remember that camera-rabid son of yours?) swore it would have a brush in it, so I gather you must have changed your mind, because two cans of popcorn and one of nuts doesn't look like a scrub brush. I am not complaining you understand. I am just laying myself out like a rug trying to tell you how pleased I am that you should remember me. I thank you all over again, and if I were of a flowery turn of speech would go on at a terrific rate about how each seed of corn—as it popped—was like a prayer from you, or the sound of the corn popping in my mess kit sounded like your laughter as you watched me devour an egg.

But mostly I am very beholden to you because I have something from home to share with my tent-mates.

I am in an awful dither trying to decide how to spend my rotation period in the States. You are all so scattered and I would like to see you all and at the same time see as much of New York as possible. I am scared silly to go see the folks in Minneapolis. What will I talk about? I have not seen them for about six years. Cheerio sweetness, my many thanks and there's no help for it, and there are a few things left to say.

Had a letter from Maurice Geckler who is still at Lime, OR. Talk about shades out of a shady past and he tells me he got my address from Mrs. Hernshaw. I have been wondering why they remember when I had forgotten them about as if they had never existed. The one so slow, the other who never remembered anything I ever told her. That evidence of their remembering means quite a bit to me. I guess I still rankle a bit at having done so little that lasted in the town. I gained much, you, for one thing, experience, IZ, [Isabell Cain] but I fear I did not leave much behind.

Now do not get all het up and try to tell me I am all wrong, etc. I know I am, but I got to have my sentimental moments you know and get into profound contemplations to keep my metaphysics warm.

I see Fred now & then and am always amazed and amazed at his strictly dollars & cents sense that seems to have come out all over the place. Righto I say. And again my best thanks.

Love, Minor

In eight years (1935–1943), the Federal Arts Project employed more than 5,000 unemployed artists who created 2,566 murals, more than 100,000 easel paintings, 17,700 sculptures, and 350,000 fine prints.

Sixty years later, White's fear that he left no legacy in Union County seems mostly accurate. He stopped answering Fred Hill's letters. After the war, White continued to write Isabel Kane, but apparently stopped writing to Etha Hill. There's no record either Kane or White ever returned to visit "Maw" Hill or the Grande Ronde Valley. In 1954, while traveling through north Idaho to Portland, White—by then famous—did write that "seeing [the northwest landscape] again makes me realize that my early photos of Oregon are remarkably true to the experience." In his personal retrospective album, *Mirrors, Messages, Manifestations* (1969), White did reprint eight of his 150 images from riding in northeast Oregon. (In his 1942 Portland show, *Photographs of the Grande Ronde Valley*, there were sixty-one images in four groups: "Grande Ronde Valley," "Anthony Lakes," "Union and Baker Counties," and "Wallowa Mountains.") With one recent exception—the cover of *Oregon East 1950–1985*—White's entire northeast Oregon oeuvre can only be seen at the Princeton University Archive. Today, only biographers track down his eighteen amateurish reviews of national, WPA, Oregon, and student art shows published in the local paper. No one reads White's innumerable press releases, but his guest editorial on April 15, 1941, seems ironically contemporary: "La Grande has never had until this year something outstanding to offer the tourist while he is here in town. This year La Grande has an Art Center." The old Mahaffey building, where 1,200 people gathered May 12, 1940, to celebrate the opening of the Grande Ronde Valley Art Center is now a restaurant and White's basement studio and darkroom dry storage.

John Turner showed me his polished mahogany letter opener. In 1941, he took the "Wood Chipping" class at the Art Center. "It was a great place," he said. He was a seventh grader. His teacher was the Civil Conservation Corps director. For a few cents, Millers Cabinet Shop cut out the rough piece for him. He worked on that letter opener for weeks. Made it beautiful.

Let us now not praise famous men whose legacy is inaccessible and let us not dignify famous men who forget the community which welcomed them to the most fertile valley east of the Cascades. Perhaps it is enough just to illuminate their passage, to value their phoenix institution, to locate their remnants, and to recognize a few who bore gracefully such transients—these artists who seemed to be all tenor and no vehicle.

In rural, small, remote places, there is no serious art. That illusion generates others—sophistication is metropolitan; talent must be imported; important life is far away.

"Minor White Reconnoitering for a Photograph"
High Valley, Union County, Oregon 1940
Photo by Fred Hill

Down in my Heart

Peace Witness in War Time

William Stafford

introduction by Kim Stafford

NORTHWEST
Reprints

. . . .

Preface to

DOWN IN MY HEART: PEACE WITNESS IN WAR TIME

In a letter dated July 27, 1999, Marianne Keddington-Lang, the newly-appointed editor of the *Oregon Historical Quarterly* (*OHQ*) asked if I "would be willing to write a review of [*Down in My Heart*] for the *Quarterly*:" Eight weeks to write 500–700 words, minimal editing, two free copies, gratitude. Because she was a congenial and consummate professional and the first *OHQ* editor to contact me in 29 years of teaching and writing about Oregon literature, I accepted Marianne's invitation. Starting in 1971, I had read, met, traveled, worked with, and actually employed William Stafford. I knew his life and work in general but had not re-read this testament—his WW II pacifist autobiography—in several years. By October 11, I'd sent her my draft on which she performed minor corrective edits and sent me page proofs; I sent corrected proofs back to her on November 10. In my follow-up cover letter, I alerted Marianne to a critical omission I'd realized while editing the proofs: the book's seven introductions completely ignore the northwest Civilian Public Service (CPS) program, even the most obviously available texts in the *Oregon Literature Series*: David Johnson's interview/essay with William Everson on the Oregon CPS camp at Waldport, the literary contributions of Glen Coffield, the published diary of Adrian Wilson. As I explained, "an immense body of writing came out of those camps across the United States by many individuals. In this posthumous reprint, Stafford's place in that national body of writing goes unstated." (Note: A 2006 edition from OSU Press fills some of that void.)

Sources: *Oregon Historical Quarterly* 100.3 (1999): 339-342; Photo courtesy Lewis and Clark College, Watzek Library Archives and Special Collections.

DOWN IN MY HEART:
PEACE WITNESS IN WAR TIME

This reprint will be welcomed by readers who have not heard of William Stafford (1914–1993), by readers who know some of his writing, and by those who know enough to quote him. This memoir was both Stafford's first published book in 1947 and is now his most recent posthumous book. So anyone can easily read *Down in My Heart* and learn more about this Oregon writer and poet who—after forty years and thirty five books—achieved national and international stature. But the book is deceptively simple or, "Be ready,"—as Stafford would say. While you can read this in an evening, his stories of the World War II Civilian Public Service (CPS) camps for conscientious objectors may last a lifetime.

An exquisite classic miniature like this book needs front matter—frames and framers—to enhance the presentation: Robert Frank introduces the invaluable OSU Press Northwest Reprint Series; an anonymous biographer sketches Stafford's life; Kim Stafford gives his father's life and writing a thoughtful and intimate "Introduction;" an anonymous bibliographer lists some of Stafford's other books.

Then we come to the seventh frame—Stafford's original "Foreward" to his 1947 text. Typical of Stafford's other writing, his "Introduction" boldly claims high moral ground: conscription and war destroy human fellowship. He is a witness. He spent from 1942 to 1946 out in the cold in conscientious objector camps. That experience changed him. At one point, Stafford observes that "the forces of war incited frustrations and enmities that led to personal rebellion; but for us [CO's] a personal rebellion against other human beings became a capitulation to the forces we held to be at the root of war." (8-9).

Now, the eighth frame—the "Prologue"—can begin. Here, we're introduced to a hospital room. It's winter, dark, and snowing. The narrator, a hospital visitor, is talking to his friend George(no last name). George is not eating. The narrator has come to try to tell these stories to George: "I want to say these things because we are a lost people—you and I and some others—and we saw an event that few others could experience, a big event that made us silent and engulfed us quietly." (11) George does not answer. The narrator goes on, as does the reader—in hope that George may be listening, that he may awake. The art of reconciliation begins. Ironically, the man who most needs to hear these stories does not—we don't know why. This "Prologue" identifies Stafford's audience, purpose, occasion, and persona, while the message remains enigmatic, implicit, to be discovered. Stafford uses this prologue to make his spiritual autobiography cohere as implicit argument.

As we read the next ten chapters, we discover that George is the narrator's friend and fellow pacifist. Along with the other men, they've endured the CPS program—poverty, frugality, alienation, hard work, persecution, self-doubt. George appears in nearly every chapter. They have survived the underworld of aliens and outcasts, battled Forest Service ogres and fires, fought racism, ignorance, depravity, cherished natural beauty, companionship, music, tranquility, found apotheosis, seen evil as banality. While the narrator's patience, acceptance, imagination, and passivity have saved him, George has been destroyed by his intelligence, intolerance, conviction, aggression, passion to act. He becomes the narrator's foil—the pacifist turned rebel, criminal, anarchist. Unlike the narrator, George goes AWOL from the Civilian Public Service camp. The narrator and George become strangers. The narrator is an observer, a storyteller, a writer "learning everyone's language—more than ever before." (87) Unlike George, he won't "take a stand and do something without regard to the effect of my action on others." (90) George, he says, has been trapped by "the exhilarations of the outlaw, his personal freedom, and his constant living with rebellion." (92) The narrator has not. So, by telling George these stories, the narrator hopes to transform and illuminate their disastrous CPS years—an adventure if rightly considered. For ten chapters the reader learns how—among four years of other events—one man is saved and another lost—spiritual autobiography framed by implicit didactic intent in the tradition of Woolman and Ashbridge.

By the time we reach the "Epilogue," we realize that George lies comatose in a prison hospital on a hunger strike. He's become a martyr. Now, the narrator/ hero/survivor has told George the stories of their terrible road of trials. We realize the narrator intends to heal George, to awaken him, to reach him with the truth. We have overheard catharsis at its most profound. Will these stories awaken us—and rebellious George—to our common tragedy? Will their artistic language redeem the violence of our mutual lives? By writing and living, the narrator says he hopes "to change others, not alienate them." The storyteller in Stafford hopes to bring peace to George, to us all.

Finally, the narrator must leave. He reassures George—who has not responded—that he will "keep on saying those things we learned. It's dark and late now; the snow is white under the lamps, but the wind has stopped blowing." Still no response from George. He's ready for force-feeding now. While George dies abstracted, isolated, self-destroyed, the narrator goes out an agent of the living truth, a life-long subversive. The narrator is free to go because he has been faithful to the Sermon on the Mount. George is headlong toward activism, protest, martyrdom, Calvary, crucifixion, death.

Some night, when you're wondering why William Stafford eclipsed Robert Frost as the most widely-read poet in the United States, you might want to read this book. Beneath its accessible and simple surface, *Down in My Heart* shows how Stafford came to his vision that the freedom of art might reconcile us all, wake us up from all kinds of death, bring the peaceable kingdom down.

Chapter 7 • DOWN IN MY HEART: PEACE WITNESS IN WAR TIME

"Negotiating the Surrender." *In this sole eye witness sketch of the October 5, 1877 Bear's Paw site before Joseph arrives, six white men are waiting: General Howard (empty sleeve) and Colonel Miles are standing. Arthur Chapman (translator), Guy Howard, C. E. S. Wood, and Oscar Long are sprawling and difficult to identify. The two Nez Perce messengers, Old George and Captain John, are mounted but individually unidentifiable.*

(Original undated Guy Howard sketch from "Grace Howard Gray Scrapbook." Courtesy Oregon Historical Society.)

CHAPTER 8 | Critical/Textual Essay (1998)

Preface to

CHIEF JOSEPH'S "SURRENDER SPEECH" AS A LITERARY TEXT

Arguing that the "Chief Joseph Surrender Speech" seems to be a literary text, this essay has a complex, lengthy, and evolving history. Begun in 1994 and researched for two years; drafted and sent to Tim Barnes in 1996; revised and presented at the Pacific Northwest History Conference in 1997; published by *Oregon English* in 1998; revised, invited to the C. E. S. Wood Symposium, and rejected by *Western American Literature* in 1999 for being too informal; expanded and submitted for an NEH grant in 2002; revised and further researched 2006 to 2010; published June, 2012 on the Oregon Cultural Heritage Commission website and that 2012 electronic version is published here. These multiple drafts were generated (1) by hours and air miles to make discoveries in archives such as the C. E. S. Wood Papers at the Huntington Library and the Oliver Otis Howard Papers at Bowdoin College; (2) by new histories by distinguished historians Jerome Greene, Diane Pearson, and Elliott West all affirmatively citing the essay; (3) by a host of other sources too lengthy to list here. This essay's 20-year odyssey has attracted both disagreement and agreement and probably always will. For now, I rest my case. For further details, see the more elaborate treatment of Wood in my monograph *Soldier to Advocate*: *C. E. S. Wood's 1877 Legacy* (2006).

Sources: http://www.ochcom.org/pdf/Wood-Venn.pdf, *Journal* 20 (1998): 69-73

CHIEF JOSEPH'S "SURRENDER SPEECH" AS A LITERARY TEXT

October 5, 1877, Bear's Paw, Montana Territory

Cold wind, new snow, dying grass, northern plains, white mountains, bronze light. Below the open ridge, dead and wounded men lay in Nez Perce and U.S. Army camps. Wallowa Valley women, children, and men have fled 1,200 miles since June. That flight ended here. The five-day military conflict and negotiation finally resolved. Chief Joseph rode a black horse up the ridge, his hands crossed, his head bowed. Five Nez Perce men walked with him. Above him, the bulky silhouettes of waiting whitemen: Brigadier General Oliver O. Howard, Commander; Colonel Nelson A. Miles, Fifth Infantry, Yellowstone; Second Lieutenant C. E. S. Wood, Howard's aide-de-camp and adjutant; Second Lieutenant Oscar F. Long, Miles' aide-de-camp, Ad Chapman, and perhaps Nez Perce messengers Old George and Captain John. Joseph dismounted, offered his rifle to General Howard. Howard waved Joseph to Colonel Miles. Even though Howard and his troops had pursued the Nez Perce for 1,200 miles, the Nez Perce had—until Bear's Paw—successfully eluded or outrun Howard. Notified by telegraph, Miles had "caught" the Nez Perce by making a 200-mile forced march to Bear's Paw , surrounded the fleeing Indians, driven off their horse herd, and after failing to over run the Nez Perce, settled for siege until Howard arrived and negotiated with Joseph for a "surrender." To reward Colonel Miles, General Howard had agreed to give "The Official Surrender"—an honorific military ceremony foreign to Nez Perce tradition—to his junior.

Since that 1877 event, what Joseph said or didn't say after he handed his rifle to Colonel Miles has been disputed—possibly the longest dispute over a text in western American literature. C. E. S. Wood, the 25-year old aide-de-camp of General Howard, publicly claimed all his life that he wrote down verbatim a 155-word (+-) speech given by Chief Joseph after he handed over his rifle. No one at Bear's Paw that day—including General Howard—ever published anything corroborating Wood's text. While he had varying degrees of editorial control over the nineteen versions of the speech published between 1877 and 1939, Wood also revised the text, speaker, and contexts. After Wood's death in 1944, historians doubting Wood's veracity became more explicit, even though the "Surrender Speech" had become nationally-accepted as authentic Native American oratory. Since 1972, several historians have formally denounced Wood as "prostituting the truth," as being "unreliable," as "composing the famous speech himself," as not " being particular about the truth." As a result of their critique, Joseph is now represented in many anthologies and texts with "An Indian's View of Indian Affairs," his much longer 1879 speech in Washington, D.C. in which Joseph narrates the tragic Wallowa Valley Nez Perce story.

This attack by contemporary historians on a poet, soldier, attorney, anarchist—perhaps the most complex literary figure in the early Northwest—raises a cloud of fascinating questions. Neither Wood nor Joseph can clarify much now. Wood's ashes were scattered in 1944 in an oak grove above Los Gatos, California, and Joseph was buried on the Colville Reservation in 1904. During his lifetime, Wood never publicly retracted his "verbatim" claim: he was always the only person to record Joseph's reply to General Howard. Wood's 1877 journals end in Idaho—early in the Army's pursuit. Wood's original text—he always said—was lost by U.S. Army archivists. No other person at Bear's Paw ever directly quoted or repudiated Wood's text. So, consider for a moment that the controversy is still open: here stands C. E. S. Wood the soldier/poet/attorney now accused of lying his entire lifetime about the authenticity of the Chief Joseph "Surrender Speech;" there stand Wood's contemporary accusers. What follows here will be a few of many interrogatories for a grand jury of readers.

Did Wood ever say the "Surrender Speech" was not a verbatim transcript of Joseph?

Yes and no. In 1936, at the age of 84, the poet himself wrote the following unpublished letter to Lucullus McWhorter, his earliest chief examiner:

> My dear McWhorter—
>
> Don't expect me to correct all the misconceptions about Joseph—and at 84—I will not guarantee my own recollection—But as often happens I remember this surrender more clearly than the events of last year. Further General Miles nor anyone else knows Joseph's surrender speech accurately except myself. No one was interested to take it down—Oscar Long—Miles' regimental adjutant was there to take it down but did not—no one was told to take it down—I was not told—the speeches of Indians were not considered of importance—**I took it for my own benefit as a literary item** (GV emphasis)—and I have told you I at request gave it to the Adjutant General of the Army in Washington for the archives and it disappeared...." (1/31/36, WSU)

What might Wood have meant here—saying privately that the "Surrender Speech" was "taken as a literary item?"

He may well have intended the speech as a work of art and used commonplace literary conventions: selecting, arranging, and interpreting the facts to create an illusion that somehow made the facts more illuminating, truthful, comprehensive. Wood had many literary precedents here: he knew classical historians such as Tacitus were famous for inventing speeches to condense events and heighten drama; he knew the treaty speeches by Eastern chiefs such as Red Jacket who addressed whites with wise "King Solomon" oratory; he knew that Chapman's translation of Joseph would be literalistic, so he could create his own version of any translation he heard; Wood had read historical novelists, such as Walter Scott, who always pretended to be factual while writing fiction.

Calling the "Surrender Speech" a "literary item" also might have been Wood's way of alluding to his interest in poetic form. While the speech has always been printed as a prose paragraph, the three-part Shakespearean or heroic sonnet form seems to shape the piece. To be specific, consider a brief analysis of the version

Wood published as prose in *Century Magazine*, July, 1893, in his signed article, "Famous Indians: Portraits of Some Indian Chiefs."

To write a Shakespearean or heroic sonnet, the poet must first sustain a list of images that generates a consistent tension and emotion. Since Wood did not fight the Bear's Paw battle with Miles' troops, he learned this list of facts from Joseph, from interpreters, or from unknown sources. While Wood attributes these first fourteen lines to Joseph, no one but Wood has asserted that Joseph spoke them at the moment of his sunset surrender. As Wood writes the first 14 lines, the repeated short sentences (grammatical parallelism) accumulate great emotional force:

> Tell General Howard I know his heart.
> What he told me before-I have it in my heart.
> I am tired of fighting. Our chiefs are killed.
> Looking-glass is dead. Too-hul-hul-suit is dead.
> The old men are all dead. It is the young men, now,
> who say "Yes" or "No." He who led on the young men
> is dead. It is cold, and we have no blankets.
> The little children are freezing to death.
> My people—some of them—have run away to
> the hills, and have no blankets, no food.
> No one knows where they are—perhaps freezing
> to death. I want to have time to look for
> my children, and to see how many of them I can find;

This language, which also uses fractured five-accent meter and intense rhyme, displays great eloquence in defeat and shows Joseph is a noble adversary—not some stereotypical inarticulate savage. Joseph lists the Nez Perce dead in tight rhythmic parallels. He describes the Nez Perce suffering. By all historical accounts, this list is absolutely accurate—a fact never mentioned by Wood's critics.

After the sonnet's images of experience have been given, the Shakespearean or heroic sonnet requires the poet to prepare the reader for the ending statement with a transition or turn—a line, word, phrase, white space that signals the end of images and the beginning of statement about them. In this quasi sonnet, "Hear me, my chiefs" is the turn. With this invocation, Joseph is apparently pleading with his peers by revealing his own personal emotion. With this turn, Joseph also implicitly becomes the highest-ranking "surrendering general" in the Euro-American military tradition. This turn or transition may be Wood's most obvious sonneteer device, since no chiefs accompanied Joseph to the surrender, no uneducated translator would deliver such a perfectly-placed transition, and no Nez Perce would become so blatantly and personally emotional in a moment of such tribal military crisis. Who Joseph addressed with this phrase has baffled everyone, since only one Nez Perce chief—White Bird—had survived the Army siege.

To complete such a sonnet, an ending statement or couplet—prepared for by the turn—must somehow resolve the emotional tension created by all the previous lines. The specific images must add up, become assertion, statement, idea—something more than mere sensory impressions. Here, the speech's last lines make Joseph's desire for peace conclusive, clear, and absolute:

> From where the sun now stands
> I will fight no more forever!

Many others present at Bear's Paw agree that Joseph did, in fact, say something similar to this brief statement. Two years later, Joseph himself included similar language in "An Indian's View of Indian Affairs." These ending lines—which Wood may have actually heard from the interpreter Ad Chapman—may have inspired Wood to synthesize the earlier 14 lines of the poem. After all, great ending lines may be any poet's most difficult test. (From 1918 to 1939, Wood revised the last line to "Joseph will fight no more forever.")

No record shows that Wood criticized this July, 1893, version of his text. Over the next forty years, he would write, revise, and/or publish the speech seven times with the clear disclaimer that he was writing from memory. Confronted with multiple conflicting texts and revisions, in 1939, he sent his last version to Edward Lyman, publisher of Francis Haines' *Red Eagles of the Pacific Northwest* (1939).

Did Wood ever write a sonnet-length treatment of the speech?

Yes. Sometime after 1884, Wood drafted but never published a long narrative poem titled "Chief Joseph." Housed in the Huntington Library, that handwritten manuscript shows Wood wrote and revised the speech in 14 lines of sonnet length and style:

> Tell General Howard—what he said to me before,
> I have it in my heart—Maybe the Right is weak
> I do not know—Tell him that I am tired
> Of fighting—Too-hul-hul soot is dead—Looking Glass
> Is Dead—he who led the young men in battle—
> He is dead—Ah-laht-mah-Kaht—my brother.
> The old men are all dead—It is the young men
> Who say yes—or no—It is cold and we have
> No blankets—and no fire—Our children cry
> For food and we have none to give—
> My little daughter has run away upon the prairie—
> Perhaps I shall find her too among the dead—
> Here(sic) me, my chiefs—From where the sun now stands
> Joseph will fight no more forever—
>
> (WD Box 10 (20), 32-33)

So Wood publicly insisted throughout his life that the "Surrender Speech" was a "verbatim transcript," but privately admitted to McWhorter that the speech was a "literary item." What does this suggest?

From the beginning, he used formal English poetic strategies to select, arrange, and dramatize events he had heard about the battle prior to his arrival with Howard. From literary tradition, Wood-the-soldier knew he could adopt a double mask to conceal himself as Wood-the-poet: when writing the speech, he masked himself as Chief Joseph. To conceal his identity in 1877, he first gave his text to Thomas Sutherland, the correspondent who accompanied Howard throughout the campaign, and Sutherland leaked the speech to the press for him in Bismark and Portland.

Calling the speech a "literary item" also acknowledged that Wood had—over his lifetime—clearly edited, revised, recited, and published as many as nineteen versions of the speech. For example, after 1877, he always deleted "I am tired." In 1895 and after, he moved the lines about Joseph's little daughter from the prose frame into the speech itself. In 1895, he changed "Our chiefs are killed" to "Our chiefs are dead," but in 1939, he still wasn't sure which was correct. From 1918 to 1939, he revised the last line to read "Joseph will fight no more forever." Between 1877 and 1939, he revised his spelling and his treatment of Ollicut—Joseph's brother—three times: first he objectively "led" the young men, then he ironically "led on" the young men, then he pseudonymously "led-the-young-men-in-battle." In 1877, he added the word "wet" to a version published in Oregon, and deleted Chief Too-hool-hool-zote from a version published in New York. In the prose frame of the speech, he also revised speaker and context.

So what might Wood's motives have been? What was driving this text into print?

Regardless of how much he invented or how much he recorded at Bear's Paw, Wood-the-poet wanted to speak for justice, intelligence, compassion, mercy, peace. Through this speech, he could show the Nez Perce as human beings, as people with voices, emotions, souls. Surrendering in intensely poetic Shakespearean English and form, Joseph would not be silenced. He would be heard. Since the failure of the Lapwaii Council which basically started the Nez Perce War, being silenced was a critical problem. Even General Howard had arrested Too-hool-hool-suit just for speaking against all Howard's presumptions. Also, while Nez Perce did not use any such poetic form or style in such moments, the formal Euro-American eloquence and compassion created and projected by Wood showed Joseph's greatness and humanity. Thus, Joseph's suffering—translated by Wood-the-poet—became explicit, personal, eloquent, public and Wood-the-soldier has successfully "humanized the enemy" and subverted military values.

The rest of Wood's career also supports the view that Wood-the-soldier was at war with Wood-the-poet. While he was supposed to be killing Native Americans, Wood, in fact, empathized with them and embraced their culture and literature. Wood's first published poem, "Song of the Salmon Fishing," adopted the point of view of an Alaskan Chilkaht girl, and his later work included poems and folk tales in Native American personae and style. He revised his famous book-length poem, *The Poet in the Desert* (1929), to include in Part XLIX

another quasi-Nez Perce speech synthesized from several sources. Throughout his life, he remained friends with Chief Joseph, sent his son to live with Joseph on the Colville Reservation. In 1997, the Wood family presented an Appaloosa horse to the Nez Perce at Chief Joseph Days in the Wallowa Valley—the Nez Perce homeland in northeast Oregon.

This self divided between conscience and power—one of many oxymorons in the heart of any "Christian soldier"—was not Wood's problem alone. Dr. Fitzgerald, a surgeon with Howard's army, reported that many of Howard's soldiers regretted shooting at the Nez Perce because they felt the Nez Perce were innocent. So, the psychological crises haunting Howard's troops may have been serious and unresolved, but admitting them would have been taboo. How could there be any dignity in killing the very people who rescued Lewis and Clark? Kept a seventy-year peace treaty? Peacefully welcomed and traded salmon, horses, and cattle with Oregon Trail immigrants? Owned herds of beautiful horses and cattle? Dressed and acted in honorable ways? Militarism alone could not resolve these conflicting emotions. Among soldiers in Howard's command, outward aggression may have ceased but—as delayed stress syndrome shows—inward aggression, doubt, fear, guilt go on and on.

Writing this speech, Wood might have been trying to resolve this dilemma. With poetic language creating the Euro-American illusion of a "formal military surrender," Wood appealed to and evoked an acceptable, formal, and familiar emotion—the human cry for an end to war. Writing this speech may have allowed Wood to identify with Joseph's pain, guilt, and suffering and thus offer catharsis on all sides. In the speech, Joseph shows his humane conscience in absolute terms, but Joseph might also be speaking for many of Howard's soldiers—perhaps even for Wood himself—who wanted no more racist war caused by greed, betrayal, and ignorance. As Dr. Fitzgerald reported, many soldiers already knew there was nothing heroic about such conflict.

So how and why could Joseph's speech become a national text that has been published, read, anthologized, and taught across the United States for more than 100 years?

The power to create the illusion of dignified closure where no dignity or closure actually existed may be one reason the speech became and remains even now a national text attractive to historians, teachers, writers, students. As a poetic text appearing near the end of continental expansion, after the Civil War, at the end of this penultimate Indian conflict, the "Surrender Speech" exposes the racist violence of empire, cries out for an end to that violence, and asserts that the overt "Indian Wars" are finally over—forever. Departing from many other texts that glorify "westward expansion," the speech invokes universal humanitarian values, appeals to pity, mercy, peace, and love—the emotions denied by militarism. This synthesis of Wood and Joseph seems to speak without racist myth or patriot veneer. Like Picasso's "Guernica" or Shylock's "Does not a Jew bleed?", the "Surrender Speech" becomes mythic, essential, timeless, authentic—a human cry for peace. (Even the popular defense attorney Gerry Spence has published it in his latest book on winning arguments.)

Due to this complexity—white soldier calling out for peace through an Indian persona—Wood may be the first northwest modernist poet. As described by Milosz, modernism has a complex heritage: "Art is used to triumph over others, to dominate, to command obedience and surrender, while the artist's other half, through distance, militates against his selfish instincts." Applied to Wood, this paradox may help to define Wood's persona here: he clearly used Joseph's tragic experience to subvert racism and militarism while simultaneously denying any personal, financial, or career benefits—which were numerous. From 1877 on, Wood sold articles, poems, sketches, and stories about the Nez Perce and Native Americans, and gained both renown and notoriety for them. Another good reason to consider the speech as a literary text may be that Wood intended to elevate Joseph and salvage humane feeling from annihilation, but Wood's national success with the speech may have ironically contributed to the perpetuation of the "Vanishing Red" stereotype—that painting reproduced all over the United States of the naked mounted brave at sunset—head bowed in defeat. For instance, Native American editors Elizabeth Woody and Gloria Bird have criticized the perpetual teaching of such "surrender speeches" because they are too frequently published, read, and taught without any larger account of what happened to the Wallowa Valley Nez Perce either before or after 1877.

While this controversy may never be over, readers might value the literary complexities in the "Surrender Speech" which Wood's more superficial critics have overlooked. It seems possible that Wood learned—after the fact—the tragic facts from Bear's Paw, then, for complex aesthetic, political, ethical, and personal reasons, transformed those facts with quasi sonnet form that, sounding like authentic Native American oratory, became part of the American national canon for more than 100 years. This 1877 work—which Wood never copyrighted or published in his books—may have exceeded all of Wood's intentions or expectations.

Some evidence suggests that Wood was haunted by his claim to a "verbatim transcript" throughout his life. He was always asked to explain the origin of the speech—which he may never have been able to fully disclose. In 1923, at the age of seventy, Wood wrote a one-act play *Odysseus*, which was performed in San Francisco. In this play, Wood may have again used literary strategies to identify, address, and interpret the crisis of credibility he had created for himself and to dignify and resolve that crisis. In Wood's brief play, the main character is the old and dying Odysseus. At one point, Odysseus and Dictys, a young Theban boy, have the following dialogue:

> **Odysseus:** Zeus!—I seem like to be, and turn to a grasshopper. Here is a jewel for you—Let your tongue speak truth. It will be profitable to you—I did not do it. Men are such fools. O I could make a lie seem very truth. I am an old man now. You have a courtly tongue. Stick to the truth, young boy. It is more profitable.
> **Dictys:** Great King; was not your Trojan wood horse a lie?
> **Odysseus:** No. No. Horses do not lie. I was the liar—I was the master liar of them all. And I, the master liar, say train your young tongue to truth. There is a jewel for you from an old man who has seen some things. Yes. Has seen some things; and done some things. Yes, done some things. Ha...." (Wood, *Collected Poems...* 149.)

In Wood's play, there is no final revelation or confession by Odysseus. The hero walks into the sea with his secrets. He dies. The play ends. How could Wood explain—after seventy years—that, as Picasso said, "Art is a lie that tells the truth?" How could he confess that he had feigned a verbatim transcript of Joseph in order to create credibility for a quasi sonnet that would become more well-known than anything he ever wrote?

I suggest that the "Surrender Speech" should not be dismissed for its failures to meet some arbitrary factual test. Instead, the speech should be understood as a literary text designed to transform the oppression that outrageous and intolerable racist facts created. Did Wood write what military history still attempts to annihilate by abstraction? Did Wood write what he and other soldiers needed to hear? Did Wood write what should have been said by any individual of conscience? Did Wood write to support General Howard? Did Wood write so Joseph and the Nez Perce would not be silenced? Did Wood write what all humane tradition required? Did Wood write to create catharsis for everyone?: Any or all of these may be true. Whatever the case, the "Surrender Speech" shows that, for more than 100 years, Wood's poetic language—parallels, image, rhyme, quasi sonnet form, statement, paradox, persona, voice-transformed ignoble violence into humane statement. As William Stafford once said, "Poetry is finally subversive."

Chapter 8 • CHIEF JOSEPH'S "SURRENDER SPEECH" AS A LITERARY TEXT

ABOVE: Leslie Fiedler (1973). UM Mansfield Library photo. CENTER: Theodore Roethke (1952). UW Libraries photo. LEFT: William Stafford (ca. 1960). L & C Watzek Library photo. RIGHT: Bernard Malamud (1958). OSU Libraries photo. (Please see PERMISSIONS AND CREDITS for full citations).

Preface to

WILLIAM STAFFORD IN NORTHWEST LITERATURE

After William Stafford's death in 1993, I was invited to join "The Original Stafford Group" to discuss how best to honor and perpetuate his legacy. At the group's first meeting on July 2, 1996 in Portland, I read and distributed a single-spaced two-page draft of this essay. The response by those present—including the Stafford family—was highly affirmative. In March, 1997, I participated in a Northwest Regional NCTE Conference evening symposium hosted by John Daniel and featuring fourteen presenters: composer Todd Barton, translator Lars Nordstrom, West Linn High School students, poets Paulann Petersen and Marvin Bell, videographer Mike Markee, and Stafford family members—Kim, Kit, Dorothy, and Barbara. For that occasion, I read a revision of this essay to a large and friendly audience, then sang *a capella* two stanzas of the old camp song "Down by the Riverside"—a lyrical coda approved by Dorothy Stafford for an audience of some 1500 English teachers who joined me in the chorus. Submitted to and accepted for publication in the *Oregon English Journal,* the following text has been revised. A printed copy has been deposited in the William Stafford Archive at Lewis and Clark College, and a videotape of that 1997 symposium is also housed there.

Sources: *Oregon English Journal* 19.1 (1997): 16-17.

WILLIAM STAFFORD IN NORTHWEST LITERATURE

Shortly after World War II ended, four writers immigrated to the Pacific Northwest to take up teaching, writing, and literary life: Leslie Fiedler returned to the University of Montana in 1947; Theodore Roethke arrived at the University of Washington the same year; William Stafford came to Lewis and Clark College in 1948; Bernard Malamud arrived at Oregon State University in 1949.

These four writers came to the most recently-settled and most invisible literary region in the United States, a region represented in all American high school literary anthologies published between 1917-1957 by only one poet and poem— Edwin Markham's "Man With the Hoe"—and by one prose writer of literary folktales, James Stevens' *The Saginaw Paul Bunyan* (1932). Even though a vigorous northwest literary community had developed between the wars, most national literary maps—like national anthologies—perpetuated northwest invisibility by showing Lewis and Clark, Chief Joseph, *Free Air* (1919) by Sinclair Lewis, and on only one map, the poet Mary Carolyn Davies. Instead of naming northwest writers who had achieved some national significance—Davis, McNickle, Reed, Wood, Whiteley, Holbrook, Fisher, McDonald—national literary maps tended to fill the blank far corner with those neat little icons—conestoga wagon, fir tree, salmon, mountain, river, desert. If we couldn't yet have culture, at least we had nature.

Three of these four immigrant writers responded to that resource colony status in much the same way—as ambivalent sojourners.

In Missoula, Leslie Fiedler—Eastern, leftist, liberal, ex-Communist, Jewish, articulate, combative—brought with him a fortress of abstractions that caused him to judge Montana faces as having "no adequate physical expressions even for

friendliness and the muscles around the mouth and eyes were obviously unprepared to cope with the demands of any more complicated emotion...the poverty of experience had left the possibilities of the human face in them incompletely realized" (Fiedler 77). Disregarding the sophisticated Montana writers of the period—A. B. Guthrie, Gwendolyn Haste, D'Arcy McNickle, Dan Cushman, Fiedler's critique of the northwest attracted wild kinds of attention: he was adopted as Heavy Runner into the Blackfeet tribe; he was attacked for his Montana-baiting in newspaper editorials across the state; he caused political investigations of the English Department. After twenty three years, his "long loving battle with Montana," the "mountain madhouse," ended and Fiedler chose to leave Missoula in 1964 for Buffalo, New York, where he became national news for alleged drug use in 1967.

From Seattle, Theodore Roethke competed with eastern poets for an eastern audience he had left behind. Allegedly declaring himself to be "the only poet within 500 miles of Seattle," Theodore Roethke imported literary modernism—emotional volatility, outward aggression and inward division, self-dramatization, confession, metrical lyricism—and slowly gained a national reputation. Before and after his death from a heart attack in 1965, Roethke's writing and teaching also shaped many poets—a major modernist phalanx: Kizer, Wagoner, Haislip, Wright, Huff, McPherson, Carlile, Hugo, and others who later taught or are still teaching in the region and elsewhere. Roethke's poems became the first by a poet residing in the northwest to be consistently anthologized in national collections—though the "North American Sequence"—his most northwestern work—was usually not among those canonized. Roethke's national reputation, his successful students, and his body of work created the false impression that Roethke was—in fact—the *only* poet of stature and talent in the region—a delusion that still endures today in Seattle—among other places.

Bernard Malamud endured Corvallis from 1949–1961. While there, he wrote four books and established his national reputation, though his most important northwest book is still a solitary one—the academic satire about teaching among the English faculty at Cascadia College, *A New Life* (1961). Malamud's other fiction, frequently included in the national canon, is usually not associated with the

Pacific Northwest—though a posthumous work did incorporate the Nez Perce retreat. Malamud's most influential student, who actually rejected much of what Malamud taught, has become—in the west, at least—the essayist and fiction writer William Kittredge.

For all three of these writers, the Pacific Northwest seems to have been—first of all—a place to write and reflect on the life of elsewhere. The best example of this tendency may be Ernest Hemingway, who first came to Idaho to write in 1939, and who regularly worked in the West "not only on drafts of *A Farewell to Arms*, but [also] *Death in the Afternoon*, *For Whom the Bell Tolls* and *A Moveable Feast* (Putnam, 17). In his twenty two years of visiting Idaho, where he died a suicide in 1961, Hemingway wrote only one short story set in the West—"Wine of Wyoming." Unlike the northwest emigre writers who were fleeing to Mexico (H. L. Davis), New York (Mary Barnard), Russia (John Reed), or Asia (Opal Whiteley), these three immigrant writers all seem—like Hemingway—to be ambivalent sojourners. As visitors, they could mostly ignore—with a few exceptions—the northwest complexity around them: a vigorous emerging literary community, a maturing Native American literature and culture, increasing industrialization and declining radical labor, developing nuclear energy, growing Asian-American traditions, the felling of the last old growth forests in the lower United States, the damming of the greatest coldwater river in the United States. All those neat little icons on the literary map were changing and those changes seem to have had little or no significance for these three men.

In contrast to Fiedler, Roethke, and Malamud, consider the life and writing of William Stafford. For forty-five years, Stafford's poetry engaged the culture, history, literary community, and cosmos around him, but not—as in Roethke—in a directly egoistic, fame-seeking, self-dramatizing, self-conscious way. For example, at the beginning of a Pacific Northwest poetry symposium in the 1975, Stafford shocked Roethke students by calling Roethke "a great big exotic...[who] slowed the Northwest school by being so significant and salient and un-Northwest"(Broughton 6). In the middle of another panel on Roethke in the northwest, Stafford explained that he felt no literary influence from Roethke whatsoever. At a meeting of Roethke students, this was not quite the right thing to say. After Stafford's statement, Richard Hugo made sure Stafford understood the great Seattle shadow everyone was supposed to be standing in by shouting out to Stafford and the audience—"Thank you, Martin Boorman"—thus suggesting that Stafford's denial was equal to the denials by Hitler's secretary about Hitler (Kizer).

Roethke, modernism, and Roethke's students met their counterpoint in William Stafford. Let me name just a few ways those differences were played out. Stafford rejected Roethke's Freudian stereotype of poets as sick people trying to heal themselves. For Stafford, art "was a healthy process" (Stafford/Hugo 46). Great art did not draw attention to itself or necessarily aggrandize the poet. Poetry was closer to witness or testimony than to dramatic performance. Great art might well efface the poet and reveal the mysterious world beyond both poet and language. Stafford's pedagogy respected the silence at the center of all things, did not intend to dominate, or try to impose a whole universe. Stafford welcomed any thought. He did not advocate, as did Hugo, that writers should only write about their obsessions.

Stafford's poetry also became contrapuntal to the intellectual tendencies in Fiedler and Malamud. Stafford criticized local life, but not in a simplistic, reductive, abstract, or condescending fashion—as was Fiedler's tendency. The faces around him were human beings and everyone—after all—was not necessarily a descendent of Huck Finn, an orphan who lit out for territory. Stafford reminded readers over and over again that life is larger than anyone's ideas about it, that too much intention endangers creation, that writers refuse to abstract what they love, that writers extend tradition by violating it, that writers should not let modernism—or any literary precedent—determine what anyone else might want to say. While Stafford understood satire as Malamud wrote it (e.g., "At the Klamath Berry Festival") and literary criticism as Fiedler practiced it (e.g., "Whose Tradition?"), he also knew the dangers in satire and judgment by outsiders: local complexity, the subtle lives beyond obvious surfaces and imperial icons, may never be recognized or discovered.

So, unlike Malamud, Roethke, and Fiedler, Stafford lived the Pacific Northwest for forty five years—long enough to achieve a profound and abiding understanding of the way things are, what the mountains mean, what many people, animals, rivers, plants, wind all might know, what immigrants feel beyond colonial icons, surfaces, stereotypes. Because of this sense of enduring habitation and imaginative vision, William Stafford's body of writing is the most extensive—and so most inclusive and authentic—poetry we have after World War II, a poetry created, as Stafford himself would say, "from immediate relation to felt life," a poetry that turned every old icon upside down. Unlike our three more ambivalent sojourners who came to the Pacific Northwest after World War II, Stafford's legacy is that of a settler, an insider, a local, an immigrant become native. Stafford had lived here long enough to work his way through all the psychological phases of immigrant life: initial euphoria, subsequent depression, slow and difficult accommodation, and ultimate acceptance.

William Stafford's legacy is also inclusive and authentic because he never wavered from his vision that the "means to art is the life of all people" (Stafford 92). Even though he came to the most icon-ridden, edenic, and invisible literary region in the United States, William Stafford welcomed any thought. He taught that authentic life requires the oldest spiritual virtues—self-discipline, modesty, acceptance, forgiveness, good will, good sense, ethical commitments, restraint, humility, resistance to authority, and grace. He taught the necessity to recognize and love "the world beyond all violence and pose." He engaged, challenged, and enriched the literary community, schools, readings, conferences, homes, and was the last Oregon poet to even attempt to educate the Oregon legislature.

This Stafford legacy—the pacifist as heroic settler of conscience arrayed against *any* form of empire—may be too complex to be received, held, or understood by any single person alone or any particular region. Understanding Stafford's life and work invites many contexts. That he was—like Roethke, Malamud, and Fiedler—a post-war immigrant to the Pacific Northwest is one of those. "It's like living on an island," he once told me. Yes, I thought: home at once remote, immediate, universal.

Chapter 9 ▪ *WILLIAM STAFFORD IN NORTHWEST LITERATURE*

Beginning in Fall 1997
in the Northwest
and the Southwest

StoryLines America:
A Radio/Library
Partnership Exploring Our
Regional Literature

StoryLines America

Northwest
StoryLines America
program list

1. *The Way West*
A.B. Guthrie, Jr.

2. *Coyote Stories*
Mourning Dove

3. *Honey in the Horn*
H.L. Davis

4. *The Surrounded*
D'Arcy McNickle

5. *A River Runs
Through It*
Norman Maclean

6. *No-No Boy*
John Okada

7. *This House of Sky*
Ivan Doig

8. *Runaway*
Mary Clearman Blew

9. *Owning It All*
William Kittredge

10. *One Flew Over the
Cuckoo's Nest*
Ken Kesey

11. *Housekeeping*
Marilynne Robinson

12. *Of Wolves and Men*
Barry Lopez

13. *The Business of
Fancydancing*
Sherman Alexie

Southwest
StoryLines America
program list

1. *Ramona*
Helen Hunt Jackson

2. *With His Pistol in
His Hand*
Americo Paredes

3. *Death Comes for
the Archbishop*
Willa Cather

4. *People of the Valley*
Frank Waters

5. *House Made of Dawn*
N. Scott Momaday

6. *Ceremony*
Leslie Marmon Silko

7. *Pocho*
José Antonio Villarreal

8. *Bless Me, Ultima*
Rudolfo Anaya

9. *All the Pretty Horses*
Cormac McCarthy

10. *The Milagro
Beanfield War*
John Nichols

11. *Face of an Angel*
Denise Chávez

12. *In Mad Love and War*
Joy Harjo

13. *The Brave Cowboy*
Edward Abbey

HUMANITIES

Preface to

STORYLINES AMERICA:
A 20th CENTURY NORTHWEST READING LIST

From January 1995 to December 1997, I served as a Scholar/Consultant to one of the largest—if not *the largest*—regional literature projects in the United States. Titled "StoryLines America: A Radio/Library Partnership Exploring Our Regional Literature," the project was sponsored by The American Library Association(ALA), and was funded by a $390,000 grant from the National Endowment for the Humanities (NEH)—one of the largest awards the agency made during the 1990s. According to Susan Brandehoff, ALA Project Director, that funding "reflects the excellent scholarship and project organization contained in the proposal as well as NEH's belief that this project is an important one and of national significance."

As proposed and executed, the generous grant was used to produce thirteen call-in radio programs presenting and discussing thirteen outstanding works of literature in two regions: the Southwest (Arizona, New Mexico, southern Utah, southern Colorado, and West Texas) and the Northwest (western Montana, Idaho, Oregon, and Washington). For two hours on Sunday nights, between October 5 and December 28, 1997, a live, large, diverse, and attentive audience—estimated at 104,000 per program for both regions—heard experts and authors discuss and read those thirteen books on the air, and—if so moved, listeners could dial an 800 number, call in, and offer their comments.

Before broadcasts, of course, a lot of organization, planning, scripts, study guides, and details had to be completed, specifically annotated book lists for the Southwest and the Northwest had to be developed. Who would select those books for *StoryLines America* programs? By what criteria? December 20, 1994, just before Christmas vacation—the short notice emergency arrived from Montana: the ALA grant required a list of northwest books to be in Chicago in early 1995. In about a week, I alone was supposed to create even more text:

Source: Photo: Montana KUFM organizers Lowell Jaeger (left) and
Paul Zalis (right) October 1997; Photo courtesy Paul Zalis.

a narrative overview of Northwest literature, highlighting some of the following: What makes the Northwest unique? What questions about place and people's lives will the literature develop? How does the identity of the Northwest contribute to national identity? What books would be used (your suggested reading list) with a brief description of books and authors and how they relate to overall themes? (Paul Zalis to GV 12/20/95)

Declining the requested historical narrative and extensive research, I sat in my office for most of that snowbound vacation and wrote annotations for the thirteen-book list below, then faxed that list to Paul Zalis on January 7, 1995. In Chicago, ALA incorporated that list in the initial grant submitted to NEH in July. Afterward, Susan Brandehoff, national ALA Project Manager, described my list:

> George Venn... contributed to the original NEH proposal an annotated list of readings to be used in radio programs in the Northwest. His selections and annotations reflected the diversity and breadth of literature of the Northwest region and were an important factor in the proposal's success.... As project manager for the ALA, I value Mr. Venn's work highly and look forward to working with him on what will be an important and continuing national radio project." (Brandehoff 12/31/96)

In December, 1996, NEH rejected the proposal, but encouraged ALA and Montana organizers to revise and resubmit their regional literature program grant with a new emphasis on serving rural rather than just regional audiences. Another booklist revision was required. By summer, 1996, Montana organizers had sent me book lists from two other Scholar/Consultants: Garrett Hongo, University of Oregon, and William Kittredge, University of Montana. So I synthesized my initial list with theirs, made some revisions, then sent the revision to Lowell Jaeger, the lead Montana editor on June 26.

In September, 1996, NEH funded the grand project, so Montana staff began forming the final booklist by fax and conference call. Based on low interest in a previous Richard Hugo program, poetry was ruled out—even the poetry of William Stafford. By January 22, 1997, Lowell Jaeger and William Kittredge had finalized the northwest booklist for radio broadcasts, the same list to be given brief coverage in Lowell Jaeger's booklet, *Northwest Series Discussion Guide*

(1997). On that final list of thirteen, eight of my original booklist—authors and/or titles—remained. Five writers and/or books had been replaced with five other writers—three from Montana. (For revisions by Montana staff, see bolded text below my following annotations.)

According to the June 5, 1998 "Final Report" by ALA project director Deb Robertson, *StoryLines America* was widely and successfully promoted, publicized, heard, appreciated. The combined audience for both regions was estimated at 104,000 per program. Across the northwest, ninety eight libraries made specific efforts to spread the news, feature the books, promote the shows. When the *StoryLines America: Northwest Series Discussion Guide* by Lowell Jaeger was published, each library received twenty five copies, as well as bookmarks, posters, and publicity kits. Media—regional and national—were contacted with press releases.

Nineteen regional radio stations broadcast the two-hour programs. Call-in comments numbered from six to sixteen per program—five to six being the average. In the northwest, seven living authors took part in the live discussions of their books. (On October 19, 1997, I completed a very brief live interview on H. L. Davis' classic novel *Honey in the Horn*.) In June, 1998, ALA published cassette tapes of all twenty six (northwest and southwest) programs, and they were sent—gratis—to thirty participating libraries. Copies of those tapes were made available to anyone anywhere.

Source: *StoryLines Northwest: Cassettes 1-13.* National Endowment for the Humanities & American Library Association, June, 1997.

STORYLINES AMERICA: A 20ᵗʰ CENTURY NORTHWEST READING LIST

Mourning Dove *Coyote Stories* (1933)

Born in 1888 into the Okanogan tribe in northeast Washington, Mourning Dove's first novel, *Cogewea* (1927) was "perhaps the first novel written by an American Indian woman." Assistance from Lucullus McWhorter probably adulterated that first book, but her second book, *Coyote Stories*, is generally agreed to be much more authentic. It is also the first published collection of Native American oral stories told by a Native American woman. As this book introduces the imaginative complexity of Plateau cultures, it raises questions about the simplistic stereotypes of Native Americans, and offers the challenge of understanding the major literary figure for Plateau tribes—the trickster Coyote. For a contrasting personal account of the devastating meeting of Indian and White cultures, see the first autobiography by a northwest Native American woman, Sarah Winnemucca, as recorded in her *Life Among the Piutes*.

H. L. Davis *Honey in the Horn* (1935)

Born at Rone's Mill, Oregon, in 1894, Davis first won national recognition as a poet when he received the Levinson Prize in 1919. With encouragement from Menken at the *American Mercury*, Davis began publishing short fiction in 1929. Written in Mexico, his first novel, *Honey in the Horn*, won two national prizes—the Harper Prize (1935) and the Pulitzer Prize (1936.) When Davis satirized the settling of Oregon, he attracted serious public criticism, and eventually returned to Mexico—where he wrote and published in all genres until his death in 1960. Through realistic portraits of colonial characters—golden pioneer, helpless girl, innocent community, noble savage, lost orphan boy, Davis raises questions about the mythology of American innocence, and through his main character's quest, he rejects and revises Twain's version of the frontier myth of escape.

D'Arcy McNickle *The Surrounded* (1936)

Born in 1904 at St. Ignatius, Montana, McNickle has been called "the earliest Native American prose stylist, the earliest craftsman of the novel...." His first novel, *The Surrounded*, is also "the first novel by a Native American to make a sharp break with traditional chronological narrative." Widely respected as an academic, scholar, and activist, McNickle was the first director of the Newberry Library's Center for the History of the American Indian, and a founding member of the Congress of American Indians. He was also a "vocal proponent of the Native American right of self-determination." By dramatizing the cultural and personal conflicts created by forced assimilation, McNickle raises important questions about white supremacy, cultural imperialism, and the integrity of indigenous cultures.

James Stevens *Big Jim Turner* (1945)

Warren Clare has argued that James Stevens was "the finest novelist produced by the Pacific Northwest in the first half of this century." His earliest national appearances came in the *American Mercury*, where he published a folkloristic narrative Stevens had learned in northwest lumber camps. In 1925, Alfred Knopf published a collection of these Paul Bunyan stories, and Stevens became instantly and nationally famous. As a result, that earliest work—folkloristic, journalistic, stereotypical—has always obscured his more important role—a writer who demanded authentic life be portrayed in fiction—and his most mature means to depict that aesthetic demand—a *kunstbildungsroman* about a boy from Idaho. The picaresque narrative raises important questions about how innocence is lost in an industrializing northwest, and whether it is possible to achieve maturity and art—beyond stereotypes—through hard work, girls, public libraries, labor wars, and religious quarrels.

(Deleted and replaced by Ivan Doig's *This House of Sky*)

A. B. Guthrie *The Way West* (1949)

Oregon Trail fiction, an unstudied American canon, includes more than ninety works of fiction written since 1859. Among those writers who have dramatized the crises of an expanding empire, "none has so humanized and personalized the experience as Guthrie's" *The Way West*—for which he won the Pulitzer Prize in 1949. This book is one in a series of six novels in which Guthrie, Montana's most prolific major novelist, evaluates and explores the historical west from the 1830s to the 1960s. In this novel, Guthrie seems to test the frontier hypothesis of Fredrick Jackson Turner—that as Americans moved west and encountered the wilderness, they were purified by their ordeal and became a new and better people. The novel further examines the American heroic code—self-respect, stoicism, courage, endurance, heroism, forgiveness. For a more ironic vision, see Archie Binns' *The Land Is Bright*. Also, see Honore Willsie Morrow's classic, *On To Oregon*.

John Okada *No-No Boy* (1957)

Asian-American writing begins in the Pacific Northwest in the 1890s as Japanese immigrants—on both the coast and in the interior—formed literary societies for writing and sharing haiku, senryu, tanka, and other traditional arts. John Okada's novel is the first, best, and most important literary work of that northwest community, or, as Frank Chin wrote, "John Okada is the only great one [Asian American writer]." The book dramatizes the quest for identity of a young Pacific Northwest Nisei man who rejects both military service in World War II and relocation camps. After spending the war in prison, Ichiro returns to Seattle, parents, friends, veterans, institutions—all of which generate conflicts which Ichiro must resolve. *No-No Boy* raises significant questions about being an American, an Asian immigrant, and a northwest artist.

Ken Kesey *One Flew Over the Cuckoo's Nest* (1962)

Ken Kesey has lived on a farm at Pleasant Hill, Oregon, since 1967. Counter-culture guru in the 1960s and subject of Tom Wolfe's *The Electric Kool-Aid Acid Test*, Kesey's 1962 novel features the heroic, tragic defiance of a logger named

R. P. McMurphy. His conflict with "civilization" is told by another inmate, a Native American chief, from inside their asylum—where Nurse Ratched rules with lobotomizing power. Also adapted for the stage and made into a major film, this novel raises one of the enduring questions of northwest literature, and shows that literature's connection to romanticism: "What can be done about the life-denying force of institutionalized civilization?"

Ursula Le Guin *The Lathe of Heaven* (1971)

Ursula Le Guin's novels have been recognized with more national literary awards than any other northwest writer, including Hugo Awards, Nebula Awards, and the National Book Award in 1972 for *The Farthest Shore*. In *The Lathe of Heaven*, her only work explicitly set in the Pacific Northwest and a work also adapted for national television, she uses her rich prose to explore the mad futuristic world of utopian dream researcher Dr. Haber, who is supposed to be healing the dystopian dreamer George Orr by releasing him from his dreams—which he fears. As in her other works, Le Guin here presents what she calls a "thought experiment" for readers—a study of the dangers of utopian expectations. Whose dream will we inhabit in a future northwest? Whose do we live now?

(deleted and replaced by Norman Maclean's *A River Runs Through It*)

Barry Lopez *Desert Notes* (1976)

When *Of Wolves and Men* (1978) became a national bestseller and was awarded the John Burroughs Medal, when his *Arctic Dreams* (1986) became a Book-of-the-Month Club selection and earned a National Book Award, some in the Pacific Northwest looked back to *Desert Notes: Reflections in the Eye of a Raven*—Barry Lopez' first, smallest, most comical, most evocative, most reflective, most magical northwestern book. While Lopez has lived for years near Finn Rock, Oregon, on the dense, populous, heavily-vegetated, wet side of the Cascades, he explores here—in the most subtle ways—the dry, sparse, empty, other—the desert. In *Desert Notes*, he raises the same questions his longer and later work addresses: "Is it possible to know the cosmos as it is—without human projections? Is it possible to re-imagine our place and ourselves as participants in the biosphere instead of the stereotypical conquerors?"

(deleted *Desert Notes* and replaced with Lopez' *Of Wolves and Men*)

James Welch *Fools Crow* (1986)

In his first two shorter novels, Jim Welch dramatized the anguish of contemporary northwest Native American experience in powerful, spare, surrealistic prose. For these works, he received national recognition, e.g., front page of the *New York Times Book Review*. After *Winter in the Blood* (1974) and *The Death of Jim Loney* (1979), his perspective shifted, and *Fool's Crow* became the first and only northwest novel to successfully reconstruct Native American tribal life prior to white contact. In this epic, Welch dramatizes daily life among the Blackfeet in a "culture where people felt whole with themselves, whole with their past, whole with power." The novel raises the same question Welch faced as a writer: Is it possible to enter a time before empire—disease, racism, arrogance—had begun to destroy what it did not understand? Dee Brown says, yes: "This book may be the closest we will ever come in literature to an understanding of what life was like before the cataclysms of the last century."

(deleted and replaced with Sherman Alexie's *The Business of Fancy Dancing*)

Lex Runciman and Steve Sher *Northwest Variety: Personal Essays by 14 Regional Authors* (1987)

The fourteen writers collected here have addressed what it means to live and write in the Pacific Northwest. To be included, a writer or poet had to currently reside in the Northwest, to have published three or more books, and to represent a larger group of novelists, poets, dramatists, journalists—from Oregon, Washington, Idaho, and Western Montana. *Northwest Variety* is the first and only such collection. Essayists include Halperin, Rutsala, Gallegher, Pintarich, Gale, Hoyt, Wren, Kittredge, Jensen, Deemer, Inada, DeFrees, Hamill, and Wrigley. The essays raise several regional paradoxes worth discussing. For instance, why do northwest writers believe they must invent a context for themselves and their work, while simultaneously resisting any northwest regional context?

(deleted and replaced by William Kittredge's *Owning It All*)

Mary Clearman Blew *Runaway* (1990)

Literary short fiction by northwest women may begin with Mary Hallock Foote's *The Cup of Trembling and Other Stories* (1896), four stories about the Idaho frontier. In the 20th century, that tradition expanded to include more than 100 "settlement novels," ranch novels, and autobiographies. In his *American Scholar* article, "Unknown Novels," Roger Sale identifies *They Came to a River* (1941) by Allis McKay as among the best of these. In these short stories, Blew focuses on rural, northwestern women who have departed—somehow—from the stereotypical norms of western frontier myth, and she asks again and again—"What happens to women seeking validation for their new life?" Juley, a recurring character who escapes into university life, provides one kind of answer. Like *The Women's West* and *Women Poets of the West*, this book continues to show that western experience—without women's fiction—cannot be understood.

Primus St. John/Ingrid Wendt *From Here We Speak* (1993)

This book is Volume 4 in *The Oregon Literature Series*, a six-volume historical anthology of Oregon writing, and a collection distinguished by the National Council of Teachers of English Multicultural Publishing Award in 1994 and further distinguished by a National Endowment for the Arts "Exemplary Programs Grant" in 1992. While there have been more than 100 anthologies of northwest writing published in the last 100 years, 99% of them have not been "historical." This collection contains the only comprehensive survey of poetry completed in the region—from Native American lyrics to Issei haiku, from Stewart Holbrook awards to National Book Awards, from cowboy poets to a founder of Associated Writing Programs, from originals to translations in six languages, from pre-contact to 1991. Thus, this collection best represents—in one volume—the range, diversity, and complexity of Pacific Northwest poetry. The volume was edited by one of the region's most accomplished Black-American poets, Primus St. John, and one of the region's most articulate feminist poets, Ingrid Wendt.

(deleted and replaced by Marilynne Robinson's *Housekeeping*)

OREGON LITERATURE SERIES
(OCTE/OSU PRESS, 1993 – 1994)

THE WORLD BEGINS HERE
An Anthology of Oregon Short Fiction
edited by Glen A. Love

FROM CIE GOULET © OCTE

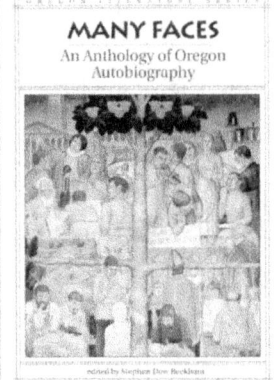

MANY FACES
An Anthology of Oregon Autobiography
edited by Stephen Dow Beckham

FROM A. & A. RUNQUIST © OCTE

VARIETIES OF HOPE
An Anthology of Oregon Prose
edited by Gordon B. Dodds

FROM CAROL RILEY © OCTE

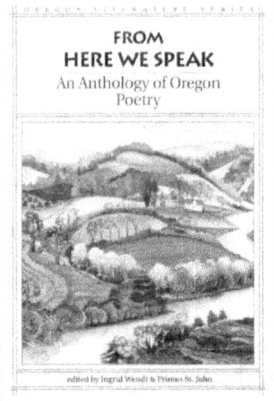

FROM HERE WE SPEAK
An Anthology of Oregon Poetry
edited by Ingrid Wendt & Primus St. John

FROM JENNIFER JOYCE © OCTE

THE STORIES WE TELL
An Anthology of Oregon Folk Literature
edited by Suzi Jones & Jarold Ramsey

FROM PLATEAU, UMATILLA, 1915 © OCTE

TALKING ON PAPER
An Anthology of Oregon Letters and Diaries
edited by Shannon Applegate & Terence O'Donnell

FROM SARAH HAWLEY QUILT (sic), 1876 © OCTE

DECLARED A NATIONAL MODEL BY NEA.

"MOST REMARKABLE ENDEAVOR
IN [OREGON] LITERARY HISTORY."
—THE OREGONIAN.

SOLD OVER 20,000. SIX VOLUMES. STILL IN PRINT.

CHAPTER 11 | Keynote Address (1995)

Preface to

EDITING AN INVISIBLE LITERATURE: FRAMES AROUND
THE OREGON LITERATURE SERIES : An Address

In 1988, I proposed creating six anthologies of the best Oregon writing to the Oregon Council of Teachers of English (OCTE). From 1989 to 1995, I served as General Editor for what became *The Oregon Literature Series*: innovative genre-based historical anthologies for general readers and schools to be edited by Glen Love, Stephen Dow Beckham, Gordon Dodds, co-edited by Ingrid Wendt and Primus St. John, Suzi Jones and Jarold Ramsey, Shannon Applegate and Terence O'Donnell. After the series' successful publication by Oregon State University Press, unanimous positive reviews, an Exemplary Programs Grant from National Endowment for the Arts, the 1994 Stewart Holbrook Award from Oregon Institute of Literary Arts, a 1995 Multicultural Publishing Award from the National Council of Teachers of English, I was invited by Kay Stephens (OCTE president), Peter Sears (Oregon Arts Commission), and Anita Helle (Oregon State University English Department) to present a keynote address to an all-day professional workshop titled "Teaching *The Oregon Literature Series*." Delivered at Oregon State University on January 28, 1995, circulated as a video, rejected by the *Oregon English Journal,* the following text—published here for the first time—is a slightly revised version of that keynote. (For further details, please see the six volumes.)

Source: "Keynote Address: Editing an Invisible Literature: Frames Around *The Oregon Literature Series*." Videotape. Oregon State University, Corvallis. 28 January 1995.

EDITING AN INVISIBLE LITERATURE: FRAMES AROUND **THE OREGON LITERATURE SERIES**: An Address

> *It is utterly part of our nature to want roots, to need roots, to struggle for roots, for a sense of belonging, for some place that is recognized as mine, as yours, as ours.... Learning about one's roots, one's place, one's territory is perhaps the central fact of existence.*
>
> —Robert Coles

Oregon

One morning in September, 1993, a grade school teacher on the Oregon coast took *The World Begins Here*—the short fiction volume and first to be published in *The Oregon Literature Series (OLS)*—to her classroom. Without telling her students what the book contained, she simply asked them to pass the book around the room, and to look at the book for a few minutes. As the first student was leafing through this collection, she looked up at the teacher and said, "There's someone from Oregon in here." "Oh?" said the teacher—straight-faced. The girl was surprised. She passed the book on, and the next student looked through the collection and said, "Here's another person from Oregon." And the book went around the room in this way until finally one student asked in disbelief, "Are *all* these people in this book from Oregon?" The teacher nodded. The students were amazed. One of them asked, "Are *you* in this book? Mrs. Gaffney?" The teacher said, "Yes." "What page, what page?" they asked her. The students were dumbfounded, pleased, surprised, delighted, and slightly incredulous. That Oregon, that Oregon writers, that their teacher enjoyed the validation of print—this was unknown to her students.

Oregon teachers had frequently noted this same disassociation: the culture around them was not included in their nationally-published school texts. An Oregon social studies teacher wanted students to study Oregon Native American life, but the official textbook published information only on the Navajo and Chippewa. Oregon's native peoples were not mentioned—anywhere. An Oregon English teacher wanted students to study and appreciate the traditional Oregon sense of humor, but school text examples of the tall tale were all taken from the Mid-west exploits of Mike Fink and the southwest yarns of Pecos Bill. There were no references to Hathaway Jones on the Rogue River, or Reub Long in the Oregon desert. An Oregon history teacher wanted students to read diary entries by women and children on the Oregon Trail, but school textbooks passed over the great migration in one or two paragraphs—if they mentioned it. An English teacher wanted to introduce the Oregon logging and lumbering in poetry and fiction by Oregonians, but this industry is represented in school texts—if at all—only by James Steven's Paul Bunyan pseudo-folk tales—which barely present the authentic experience of the men and women who have done the work. Where in the school texts could the social studies teacher find the Oregon experience of Greek, Japanese, Basque, or Chinese immigrants and their traditions? They simply weren't included. Instead, teachers were expected to present some other region's writing and/or literature. For example, a 1991 study by Michael Snider showed that in four supposedly "national" English textbooks with an average of 89 authors each, only *one* of those textbooks contained *one* Oregon author. On the average, over four fifths of the selections in these "national" textbooks were written by authors from the New England and Mid-Atlantic regions.

If this first paradox defines part of the Oregon context for *The Oregon Literature Series*, the first historical anthologies of Oregon literature, then consider a few others.

These six books appear in a state with no written literary history; a state where 17th century British theater is now a multi-million dollar Ashland industry; a state in which literature has the least patronage of all the major arts; a state

"*Oregon Literature Series* Editors and Publisher." *L to R (seated): Terence O'Donnell (letters and diaries co-editor), Ulrich Hardt (managing editor), Jo Alexander (OSU Press publisher), George Venn (general editor), Shannon Applegate (letters and diaries co-editor). L to R (standing): Primus St. John (poetry co-editor), Stephen Dow Beckham (autobiography editor), Ingrid Wendt (poetry co-editor), Gordon Dodds (prose editor), Suzi Jones (folk literature co-editor), Glen Love (short fiction editor), Jarold Ramsey (folk literature co-editor).*

in which librarians are regularly asked, "Who are Oregon's writers anyway?"; a state in which few teachers have formally studied the body of writing done in Oregon; a state in which the 19th century heritage tends to be both honored and dismissed; a state in which major reference works omit poetry and fiction; a state with immense archives not known to many citizens; a state in which ethnic literary traditions are generally unknown; a state with no current poet laureate; a state with a literary lecture series which excludes Oregon writers from the podium.

Paradoxically, individuals from Oregon have received nearly all types of national and international recognition—Nebula Awards, National Book Awards, Nobel Prizes. In the last ten years, William Stafford was identified—in a national poll—as the most widely-read poet in the United States. In the state and region, new cultural and literary organizations have been multiplying. Between 1980-

1990 these organizations and others like them were created to seek out, evaluate, recognize, display, share, and otherwise discuss Oregon's heritage. To name a few: Oregon Trail Museum, High Desert Museum, Warm Springs Museum, Tamastslikt Cultural Institute, Oregon Institute of Literary Arts, Oregon Literary Map, Guide to Oregon Publishers, Oregon Authors Annual, *NW Writers Handbook* and *Writer's Northwest Newsletter*, Fishtrap Gathering, Northwest Writing Institute, *Left Bank* Magazine, Northwest Reprint Series, *Calyx* Magazine, Northwest Native American Writers Association, Oregon Cultural Heritage Commission, Northwest Writers, Inc, Oregon Book Awards, *Glimmer Train,* Andres Berger Awards, and others.

From federal agencies such as the Bureau of Land Management and the Forest Service, to Native American tribes, librarians, readers, and writers, thoughtful people across the state seem to be part of this paradox, as I noted during the development of the Oregon Trail Museum in Baker City. When the museum was first proposed, Bureau of Land Management officials (BLM) said that they had no interest in a museum. They were in the resource management business— grass, water, forage, cattle, sheep. Within five years, the BLM reversed their position and provided land, money, and expertise to the multi-million dollar museum construction project—the first and only federally-supported cultural institution east of the Oregon Cascades. This case may show another aspect of the Oregon paradox: Out of the dying 19th century illusion of endless natural resources we give birth to the wealth of cultural resources for the 21st century.

Individuals who supported the series during its planning stages also recognized another aspect of this paradoxical condition: The wealth of Oregon literature was known, but no one had created ready access to Oregon texts. Richard Lewis, then Executive Director of the Oregon Council for the Humanities said it this way: "I think the proposed series of volumes is well-conceived and would offer the state what it does not now have: a compact, readable record of outstanding Oregon writing suitable for use by students and the general public." John Erickson, then State Superintendent of Public Instruction, agreed: "Oregon school children and teachers have never had access to a comprehensive collection of the fine writing which has emerged from this state.... I applaud the efforts of OCTE and encourage others to support this valuable project." Brian G. Booth, then President of the Oregon Institute of Literary Arts, identified the same problem: "Oregon has produced a rich and varied body of literature. Unfortunately, this body of work is not readily available except to those few who comb through used and rare bookstores.... Oregon is perhaps the only state in the West which has not had a press actively involved in publishing its writers of the past."

Several other paradoxical details may give even greater definition to the Oregon context.

Who actually gave the money for this project? Who did not support it? These were the *OLS* patrons and the cash amounts they contributed:

> Oregon Council of Teachers of English (OCTE), $42,000
> Oregon State University Press (OSU), $54,000
> Oregon Council for the Humanities, $40,000
> Portland State University, $33,000
> National Endowment for the Arts, $39,000,
> Oregon Arts Commission, $ 4,000
> Oregon Center for the Book, $ 3,000
> Jackson Foundation, $ 2,500
> Eastern Oregon University, $2,000

Most of this generosity paid expenses and honoraria to the individuals who edited and produced the six volumes. Editors were chosen for their expertise from a field of 130 applicants who answered a national call. A value equal to twice the cash donations was contributed—as staff, time, and resources—by editors, institutions, OSU Press, Advisory Boards, OCTE, and others—too numerous to list here—who assisted them.

Who was invited to financially support this project but did not respond?: The Oregon Historical Society, nearly all of the private, corporate trusts in Oregon and the northwest. Presented with the opportunity to support the first historical anthologies of Oregon writing, they balked. It's never been done before. Who's heard of this? Since none of them were explicit in their rejection, even now it is impossible to tell why they did not support these books and the eleven editors who made major sacrifices to complete them. So, we did them anyway.

And the paradoxes continue.

Who recognized the series at the beginning, who recognized it after the fact? At the beginning, only one Portland television station and one newspaper reporter answered the invitation to the August 27, 1990 news conference at which the eleven editorial appointments were announced. The *Oregonian* did not answer the invitation. Though *The Oregon Literature Series* set a national precedent, Oregon media published little or nothing from the news release announcing the beginning of the project. Since the volumes have been released, more than 100 reviews, articles, notices, announcements have appeared statewide in many Oregon newspapers and magazines. After the fact, all of the journalistic coverage—with one egg-faced exception—has been general praise. Even radio stations have reported on the series.

Some after-the-fact coverage shows that many journalists, reviewers, and scholars seem to have difficulty grasping the work before them, while others clearly recognized what had been done. Some newspapers gave full-page coverage and major reviews, but others just didn't recognize a historical anthology when they saw one. After a luke-warm review, one Portland journalist finally requested a complete set of the books for use as reference volumes. They had already become indispensable. Some reviewers clearly understood the significance of what they read while other reviewers showed they hardly knew how to describe, much less evaluate this historical anthology series. Reviewing the entire set of six anthologies remains more than any reviewer has been willing to attempt—so far. Generally, reviewers seem to not be able to grasp the context, size, scope, and significance of what they've been given—all of which suggests that we've done something right: *The Oregon Literature Series* eludes preconceived ideas. Even one volume editor, a sophisticated, highly-informed, lifelong scholar of Oregon and author of several books, said to me, "Until I read *The Stories We Tell, An Anthology of Oregon Folk Literature*, I would never have believed there was any real cultural diversity in Oregon." This kind of reversal of expert opinion has not been confined to oral literature Other volumes also created similar changes—especially *From Here We Speak, An Anthology of Oregon Poetry*. All in all, these books showed that there was more significant Oregon literature than anyone—including me—had previously contemplated.

Among all these paradoxes, Oregon teachers and librarians turned out to be more savvy, supportive, and consistent than the popular press, reviewers, foundations, historical societies, and the scholarly community.

Before publication, a statewide survey of 549 individuals in public education established that nearly 100% of Oregon teachers supported the project. During the project, the OCTE board president Tim Gillespie, a public school writing consultant and teacher, reminded the editors, "Trust the teachers," and they did. Teachers were integral to completing the work at all stages. Teachers served on the editor selection panel. Teachers' regional conference fees generated the OCTE financial support. Teachers served on all panels which reviewed the draft manuscripts.

Since publication, teachers seem to be adopting the *OLS* in many different ways. One high school reports buying a complete class set, that it would offer an Oregon literature elective course for juniors. Another high school reports that the volumes have been added to the reference collection for each classroom. One high school teacher told me that one of her Advanced Placement English students came up to her at the end of their class and said, "*Varieties of Hope* is the best book in our school." Social studies teachers are interested in some volumes for their Oregon history courses. Grade schools seem to be exploring how to use the books. One school district was going to consider adopting the prose volume for all eighth grade social studies. Several junior colleges and four year colleges and universities report that they have already used a variety of the books as class texts in literature and composition. One university professor told me, "I was just shocked at the diversity in *From Here We Speak*," the poetry volume. Teachers at all levels are inquiring about them, about how to use them, about what they present.

From the beginning, librarians across Oregon never wavered in their support. Former state librarian Wes Doak, former president of the Oregon Library Association Michael Gaston—these keepers of Oregon literacy knew the problem intimately. The State library supported the project from beginning to ending. Since publication, the librarians I've talked to are delighted. To celebrate the end of the series, the Oregon State Library and new state librarian Jim Scheppke sponsored

a gathering at the state capitol. In January, 1995, the complete *OLS* was present-ed to Norma Paulus, Superintendent of Public Instruction, as Governor Barbara Roberts had been presented with a set in 1994. Across Oregon, librarians now have a comprehensive reference source to which they can refer anyone who wants to know "Who are Oregon's authors anyway?"

So, I'm suggesting that *The Oregon Literature Series* was completed during what may be a transition period defined by conflicting tendencies: most Orego-nians seem to ride along blindly-encapsulated by the old 19th century corporate, federal, triumphal mythology of subjugation while simultaneously creating 21st century institutions to foster a mythology of enduring habitation.

"OCTE and OSU Present *Oregon Literature Series* at the Capital." *L to R: Debbie LaCroix (OCTE Board), Jeff Grass (OSU Press), Kay Stephens (OCTE Board), Alan Howard (OCTE President), Barbara Roberts (Oregon Governor), John Byrne (OSU Presi-dent), Tim Gillespie (OCTE Board), Joe Fitzgibbon (OCTE Board).*

Northwest Region

Spiraling outward now, consider some regional contexts.

After a presentation about the *OLS* in Kennewick, Washington, last September, a high school teacher said to me, "I wish we had something like this." "I don't think there's any equivalent text for Washington state except *Washington: A Literary Chronicle* (1969) by W. Storrs Lee," I responded. Another Washington teacher joined the conversation and said, "There's just nothing in Washington like this."

"The northwest needs to collect its folk literature," wrote a Vancouver, B.C. reviewer. We have started that in *The Stories We Tell: Oregon Folk Literature* (1994). However, the majority of oral literature is still generally unknown—in archives, memories, shoeboxes, family records, attics, old newspapers.

Boise State University had published *The Literature of Idaho* (1986) by the dedicated scholar, James Maguire. Working with the help of librarians and consulting with other scholars, Maguire produced a one-volume anthology jammed with excerpts and bibliographies that clearly merited its place on scholarly and library shelves, but seemed unlikely as a public school text. I recently learned that the Idaho Council of Teachers of English has now begun a similar project to the *OLS*. They have some precedents to look to. Over the past ten years, Idaho publishers have released *Idaho Poetry* (1988), a historical anthology; *Way Out In Idaho* (1991), a volume of Idaho folksong; *Idaho Folklife: Homesteads to Headstones* (1985), a collection of essays; *Where the Morning Light's Still Blue* (1995), an anthology of personal essays. All of these useful, important, and thoughtful books serve a more limited and specific audience than the *OLS*, and some—one in particular—was completed without the broad collaboration that created *The Oregon Literature Series*. The differences in results can be significant. For instance, more than 50% of the works in the 1995 essay collection are taken from just *one* Boise magazine, and more that 90% of the writing is by living writers. Several writers have two essays in the collection. There's no critical or historical perspective.

Montana, of course, generated *The Last Best Place* (1988)—a monumental one-volume anthology we studied carefully while designing *The Oregon Literature Series*. We guessed that the 1,100 pages of the Montana book would probably not be held in the hands of students, carried in backpacks, used in classes. Yes, it was formidable, but bulk was not necessarily congenial. For all of its numerous virtues, the Montana volume also had some limitations: no texts from oral traditions among groups other than Native Americans; uneven range and representation of genres—belletrist, popular, and folk; no translations from immigrant languages; more cultural dualism than pluralism. In talking recently with one Montana anthology editor, I learned that the book was intended as a kind of bomb aimed at the "mythic Montana" past that needed to be repudiated.

In the larger context of northwest literature, the *OLS* volumes also make several contributions. The northwest still has no competent or complete literary history. Significant biographies of northwest writers can be counted on one hand, collections of letters by writers on the other hand. Only one book-length study of regional literature has been published recently, William Bevis' exemplary *Ten Tough Trips* (1990). While more than one hundred anthologies of northwest writing have been published, most anthologists don't seem to approach their work historically. With a few notable exceptions, regional literary scholarship tends to be mostly occasional essays and pamphlets which are more or less visible and of very uneven quality. The last significant collections of critical essays, *Northwest Perspectives* (1979), and *Regionalism and the Pacific Northwest* (1983), the only collection of autobiographical essays, *Northwest Variety* (1987), the second collection of interviews, *At the Field's End* (1988)—these show the small number of secondary sources. While there are a few university courses in northwest literature, no full professorships in northwest literature are ever advertised—even at the major universities. Much of northwest writing still awaits discovery, analysis, evaluation, and interpretation. After nearly 150 years of writing, this complex body of literature seems to have been marginalized by the critical and scholarly community.

In a regional context then, the *OLS* books—with introductory essays, author photographs, art, texts, head notes, and bibliographies—were designed to serve teachers, students, and general readers in ways that no collections in the region have done previously—comprehensive overviews in a single collection of nearly two hundred years of writing. They also begin to fill that void created by the absence of a northwest literary history, and the absence of endowed professorships, regularly taught courses, literary criticism, and scholarship. For example, Glen Love's essay in *The World Begins Here* traces the process by which *space* becomes *place*—and he shows how Oregon fiction evolved in those terms. In that role, these books and their apparatus also challenge the cheapest stereotyped image of a regional/colonial literature not worthy of anyone's time. While the *OLS* books challenge that easy stereotype, northwest literature may still be several generations away from being respected in the northwest with the same status as, say, southern literature and culture are studied, taught, and discussed at The Center for the Study of Southern Culture.

United States

Spiraling outward further, more paradoxes and models appear.

Because they document major shifts in literary and social norms and values, new American anthologies are also significant for anyone attempting to understand the history, present, and future: *The New Poetry* (1917) ushered in literary Modernism; *The Book of American Negro Poetry* (1922) announced the Harlem Renaissance; *I'll Take My Stand* (1930) announced the Southern Agrarian consensus; *Understanding Poetry* (1938) introduced the New Criticism; *Five Poets of the Pacific Northwest* (1965) introduced Northwest modernists; *The Big Aieeeee* (1976) introduced Asian-American poetry; *Dancing on the Rim of the World* (1990) introduced Northwest Native American poetry; *The Heath Anthology of American Literature* (1990) introduced the issues of the expanded canon, canon formation, and postmodernism in American literature. These Oregon collections may also be signaling a major transition in American literary history: the "national" is being redefined by the "regional."

"Six books? I don't believe it. There's not that much out there." This response from a New York editor was coupled with a request for copies of all six *OLS* volumes. Since that statement, he's been planning a similar project in New York state, said he already had a potential sponsor.

"Can you send us all of the information on how you did this project?" An arts administrator from Wyoming wanted to know everything about *The Oregon Literature Series*.

The National Council of Teachers of English presented the *OLS* with a Multicultural Publishing Award in 1994—one of six awards given across the nation. A paradox also haunted that award. The feature article about the series in the nationally-circulated *Council Chronicle* made no specific reference to the multicultural content of the Oregon volumes which, in fact, contain more multicultural writing than any of the other six award recipients. In all six volumes together, there are more than 90 translations from more than 20 languages: Spanish, Nez Perce, Nehalem Tillamook, Northern Paiute, Sahaptin, Coos, Alsea, Clackamas, Talkema, Kalapuya, Modoc, Japanese, Chinese, Greek, Chinook Jargon, Basque. Eleven of these translations appear side by side with the original language, and four translations appear in more than one version.

In that *Council Chronicle* article, some other state literary anthology projects were also described. All of these we had evaluated very closely.

In Maine, eighth grade teachers were required by their legislature to begin teaching a Maine Studies course. Recognizing that there was no textbook, a group of Maine teachers created a single-volume anthology of Maine writers. We were told by reputable sources that the book, *Maine Speaks* (1989), was criticized on the floor of a National Endowment for the Arts meeting because the volume did not include Native American texts. Looking at the volume, we were uneasy with the quality and variety of selections. The eighth-grade audience required the Maine editors to limit the length, diversity, and complexity of the writing. The legislatively-mandated model seemed too narrow.

Minnesota teachers had created *Braided Lives* (1991), an award-winning reader for high school students by anthologizing Native American, Latino/a American, African American, and Asian American writers from across the United States. In contrast, our intent was to locate and integrate the best writing from all ethnic writers and communities in every volume. In our view, isolating the ethnic writing from all other writing became a liability. It suggested a divisive model.

Mississippi presented us with still another model: *Mississippi Writers: Recollections of Childhood and Youth* (1985). This four-volume series was prepared by a single editor employed by the Center for the Study of Southern Culture. The manuscript was reviewed by the editorial board of the University of Mississippi Press. Once the books were finished, they were presented to public school teachers for use. In contrast, the *OLS* volumes all had one or more separate editors, were reviewed by all editors, and presented many subjects. Oregon teachers told us they wanted range, depth, complexity, variety. We did not believe that one editor—however knowledgeable—would be able to meet the demands of Oregon classrooms and general readers.

Nationally, then, Oregon and other states were apparently doing something similar. However, as the National Endowment for the Arts chair, John Frohnmayer told an Oregon Arts Commission meeting in December, 1991, just before the NEA awarded us the $39,000 Special Projects Grant in 1992, "*The Oregon Literature Series* is considered a national model, and will be duplicated in at least three other states. Another wonderful Oregon project." As of today, that distinction remains. No other state enjoys such a historical anthology.

To complete the national frame around these books, I want to point out that the northwest— as a literary region—has almost always been omitted from national literature anthologies. One place this negligence can be documented is James Olson's *The Nature of Literature Anthologies Used in the Teaching of High School English 1917–1957.* In Olson's final table, "Authors Consistently Among the Fifty Most Frequently Represented In Anthologies", no northwest authors appear. In another table, "Fifty Selections Ranked According to Frequency of Occurrence," the only poet listed who has been associated with Oregon is Edwin Markham and his famous "The Man With the Hoe." James Stevens of *The Saginaw Paul Bunyan* (1932) fame appears only during the period 1946–57. On national literary maps, the northwest begins with Lewis and Clark, progresses from Chief Joseph to the poet Mary Carolyn Davies, then to James Stevens and Paul Bunyan, then the poet Theodore Roethke. To fill the vacant blocks of space created by the absence of writers in Montana and Idaho, mapmakers may throw in Sinclair Lewis' *Free Air* (1919). Even after the nationally-published best sellers, such as *Opal, The Journal of an Understanding Heart* (1920) by Opal Whiteley, *Swift Flows the River* (1940) by Nard Jones, *The Egg and I* (1945) by Betty Mc-Donald, even after the national literary prizes awarded to H. L. Davis, William Stafford, Ursula Le Guin, and Ken Kesey, school textbook editors elsewhere still tend to believe that Paul Bunyan, Theodore Roethke, or Gary Snyder can somehow represent the entire region. There was no northwest Native American literature except speeches by Chiefs Seattle and Joseph. There was no northwest Asian-American literature. While *The Oregon Literature Series* cannot immediately reverse that national ignorance, these books may—I hope—become known to national editors reshaping the national canon.

American School Curriculum History
Now, I'll attempt to extend this contextual description to the classroom.

In his book *Tradition and Reform in the Teaching of English: A History* (1974), Arthur Applebee describes how literature worthy of study in American schools has evolved over 300 years. To summarize, 17th century students initially studied famous classical Roman and Greek authors; eventually, famous British authors were mixed in; still later, that Classical/British mix was combined with contemporary New England authors—Hawthorne, Bryant, Longfellow, Lowell. Eventually, the Roman and Greek authors were dropped and British authors were reduced—except for Shakespeare. After the Civil War, southern writers were added to the canon of school authors. A few western authors were added—very few.

As Applebee points out, this process partly reflects changing priorities in American society, in definitions of literacy, in university entrance test requirements. But the process is significant. It shows that schools have always needed anthologies that are connected to the culture, history, traditions of their students, anthologies that represent the issues, values, insights of the community of writers, readers, teachers, citizens.

To bring this process into better focus, consider several Applebee examples in detail.

The British school anthology, *A Protestant Tutor for Youth* (1679) was first published in London by Benjamin Harris and widely used in British schools. When Harris emigrated to Boston, he brought *A Protestant Tutor...* with him, but revised, adapted, and shortened it, then changed its title to become regionally appropriate: *The New England Primer* (1686–1690). This anthology became the basic school text for the next one hundred years in New England. Eventually, Noah Webster's three books, *Grammatical Institute*, *Blue Backed Speller*, and *An American Selection of Lessons in Reading and Speaking* (1759) show that new more diverse school texts were being incorporated into the curriculum and *American* has now appeared in the title—though none of the reading selections were by American authors—not yet. According to Applebee, Webster's anthology was widely used in American schools for more than 50 years.

However, and this is significant, regional variations on Webster's textbooks were also published, adopted, and taught: anthologies by Lindley Murray (1799–1801) and John Pierpont (1820–30). Murray's anthology was the first to include contemporary poetry—which made up half the volume. (*From Here We Speak* repeats that model—half of the volume is contemporary Oregon poetry.) Pierpont's anthology included the first writing by American authors to be used in American school anthologies.

Applebee further explains that American literature did not enter the American curriculum as a separate course until 1900. After approximately 200 years, New England regional literature finally became a subject worthy of serious study in American schools. When this happened, New England writing was also the only American literature thought appropriate for schools. Until other regions matured as New England had matured, "New England literature" would be synonymous with "American literature." This process created a major historical force still at work in curriculum—among other places. For example, not very long ago, every American student was still expected to know the work of Robert Frost. The first regional literature to mature became "the national literature" in American classrooms.

What's the connection between that process and Oregon teachers, curriculum, and *The Oregon Literature Series*?

The American question that haunts these Oregon books is also the same question that haunted Pierpont's anthology in the 1820s: is the school curriculum door closed to new writing and writers from here, from the new place? Will Oregon teachers accept Oregon authors in these new school anthologies? Will William Stafford be given the same school audience opportunity as Robert Frost? In Oregon, will Oregon writers be considered worthy? Are they good enough to be studied? Taught? As we know now, Pierpont discovered an open door—since we know that his anthologies were accepted, and we know that by 1900 American literature had actually become an independent course. For 300 years, adding new American regional literature to the school curriculum has been the norm. In fact, adding new regional literature to the American national canon and curriculum may be the best and oldest means to create a dynamic national literature. National textbook publishers shouldn't be able to arrogate to themselves the right to say that such an important process is now—somehow—over.

Cultural History

The creation and use of literary anthologies in schools is also an ancient and universal act. The 305 poems of the *Shih Ching* (7th to 12th centuries BC) and the *Book of Odes* did this work for the Chinese empire; the *Greek Anthology* (13 volumes in the 4th century BC) did this work for Hellenic culture. These Oregon collections are part of that ancient cultural tradition.

Another universal act implicit in these collections is called *regionalization*—a process which occurs when literature or other arts move to new places, engage those places, begin to interpret those places, invent those places as worthy of attention, as sources of illumination. Such movement creates discontinuity among language, person, and place; text does not include self or community in the new context. White settlers had no stories or songs uniting them with Mt. Rainier, Columbia River, Crater Lake, Hellgate Canyon, the Big Blackfoot River, Lake Pend Oreille, San Juan Islands. Because this problem pervades literary history in every culture and in many literary forms—from myth to poem to novel, discontinuity has to be addressed if people are to be at home in the cosmos, in themselves, in their communities.

Suzi Jones explains this process in "Regionalization: a Rhetorical Strategy:"

> details from the local environment are picked up, replacing names of more distant people, places, objects, and concerns.... Environments are loaded with meaning for their inhabitants, from the very primal notion of 'home' which a simple place name can evoke to the elaborate cosmo-logical schemata which have been imposed on landscapes.... Signs of the local environment...can be thought of as a rhetorical strategy...one of the strategies of persuasion available... (Jones 111).

The *OLS* attempts to give readers a wide selection of oral texts that show this process of regionalization, since both sides of the Cascades in Oregon have generated their own traditional literature. We have also included texts that, as Jones explains, have not been regionalized and may not be. Their forms seem to be too traditional to be influenced by the new place.

In cultural and literary history, we recognize how regionalization works in even more complex ways: the novel emerges from the 16ᵗʰ century Spanish picaresque tradition, moves to England and is changed by Fielding and Smollett; the sonnet starts as an Italian song form that is adopted by poets and exported to England where it is regionalized by Spenser and Shakespeare into something of their own; the sacred Judaic poetry of the desert that became the "Psalms" of *The King James Bible* became the poetic cadence of Whitman and Ginsburg. This process of literary forms moving, adapting, changing, also intrigued William Stafford, as can be seen in his poem, "That Time of Year"—a sonnet in which the traditional quatrains have been replaced by haiku tercets, in which the couplet has been replaced by a one-line ending, "There is still time." In these Oregon anthologies, readers can finally study how major literary forms, themes, illusions, and expectations arrived on the Pacific Coast, and evaluate how Oregon writers have responded.

Under the influence of regionalization, a colony such as Oregon also begins to show other universal processes. The new place becomes a cultural matrix different from the place left behind. In a colony, there is a dynamic relationship created between the conservative forces arguing against any change from the original place, and equally powerful forces arguing for adaptation and innovation. Other forces also work to keep a colonial matrix roiling—exploitation, racism, and environmental degradation which may not have been tolerated or considered civilized "back there" are practiced daily in the colony. Places like Oregon become moral, ethical, philosophical crucibles where every value associated with civilization is tested, broken, ignored, revised, and every edenic utopian fantasy may be acted out. In colonies, the inherited definitions of civilization undergo regular testing and revision. Also, the immigrant colonies have the potential for the widest racial, ethnic, and religious mixtures, so social and linguistic life in the colonies may be much more complex and fluid than in "established" societies. Colonies may raise radical questions of class and status, wealth, questions of individual superiority and self-worth, questions of self-inflation, degradation, theft, and escape, questions about the integrity, value, or significance of the original place. In colonies, there is continuous dynamic tension between the indigenous and the imported, the wild and domestic, the old and the new, known and unknown, legal and illegal, power and conscience.

Over time, those dynamic relationships—which neither government nor elites nor corporations can dictate—may generate a demand for synthesis—as every relationship between new and old is explored, evaluated, revised, rejected, reinvented, improvised upon. As a result, mature literature extending all traditions becomes possible. As this demand for synthesis, for resolution, for unity increases, colonial literatures come of age. Colonial writers recognize the conflicts inherent in their condition and their writing becomes the means to understand, order, resolve, and share them. These *OLS* anthologies show that process at work in many areas. I list four that occur to me: settler anxiety vs. settler peace; Native American stereotype vs. Native American reality; emigrant expectation and immigrant reality; the conflict between nature and culture.

When this universal process of seeking synthesis is suspended, when our world is not discussed or presented in our books or schooling, when there is no continuity between our world and our stories, it is easy to conclude that our world, and our lives must not be very significant. While students in the sciences explore the world beyond the classroom and discover its meanings, students in history, social studies, and reading must generally assume that nothing important has happened in their region. They live in a place which appears to be without culture, without history, without the stories that generate humane knowledge and values. Without such collections as *The Oregon Literature Series*, we lose one of the most ancient sources of orientation and humane connection to the world—our language. We become placeless, disconnected, alienated, ignorant, and abstracted. Like the Greek giant Antaeus, we can now be easily defeated because we have been disconnected from knowledge, from place, lifted off the ground, made rootless, powerless.

That literacy generates values is implicit here. Up to a certain point, writing validates what we value most. What does not appear in writing must be less significant. Translated into these terms, texts without Oregon references suggest that our place must not be valued among Oregon adults. Important life must be going on in other communities someplace else. Thus, the possibilities of taking literacy seriously are reduced, and the possibilities of developing a literacy inferiority complex are increased. Texts that include Oregon writers can develop in anyone a sense of themselves as members of a literate community where readers value writers and writing and writers value readers and reading.

A final cultural universal is also implicit here—that literature is our best source of accurate knowledge of our community, its history, principles, and values. Without reading these books, Oregonians can carry into adulthood the completely false view that Oregon holds no cultural diversity, linguistic complexity, or historical vitality. An adult who has grown up in Baker City, The Dalles, Lakeview, or Astoria might unfortunately conclude that everyone in Oregon is a white, Anglo-Saxon Protestant, that everyone has always spoken English, and that life presents few choices beyond those which television provides. If, as a student in such communities, that adult had read Oregon literature, he/she would have quickly discovered that these communities have complex ethnic mosaics, that several languages—from Chinese to Chinook jargon—were spoken in their towns during the 19th century, that their communities have tragicomic histories of surviving change, and that all of those communities have generated significant writing. Without access to and study of Oregon literature, it is easy for anyone—fed enough television—to swallow many simplistic generalizations about

the nature of their lives—Is everyone really racist, sexist and capitalist?—generalizations which billions of tax dollars for prisons and police may never be able to contain or reverse.

To conclude, the order of this essay implies a message: these concentric frames expanding outward from local to universal attempt to recognize that any particular regional literature has universal, national, regional, and local implications—but without the local, none of the rest will matter. Since mass culture continues to homogenize our lives, this assertion of the local is important work. Leonard Lutwack makes this clear in *The Role of Place in Literature* (1984), when he says that placelessness has become one of the most pervasive sources of American malaise. As Simone Weil states in *The Need for Roots* (1952), rootedness "is automatically brought about by the place, conditions of birth, professional and social community," from which the individual draws "the whole of his moral, intellectual, and spiritual life." "Rootlessness is an American illness," writes William Cass in a review of Gertrude Stein. And the list goes on and on. Malcolm Cowley chronicles what may be the fate of the generation that grew up between the world wars: "Looking backward, I feel that our whole training was involuntarily directed toward destroying whatever roots we had in the soil, toward eradicating our local and regional peculiarities, toward making us homeless citizens of the world."

Here, then, are these six volumes: 2,100 pages containing 580 authors selected by 11 editors and reviewed and adopted by all 11 and by 40 advisory board readers; they cost around half a million dollars; they took six years (1989–1994) of work. They constitute the clearest labor of love I know. They intend to show that Oregon is a complex, beautiful, and authentic place where anyone can leave the trivial surface of stereotype and cliche, achieve depth and complexity, embrace contraries, discover universality in the particular. As readers, as teachers, as citizens, as writers, I hope you find their challenge entertaining and enlightening. I, for one, have been inspired and humbled by the immense collaboration required to bring them to you, by the boon of complexity they contain.

Preface to

REMEMBERING WALLACE STEGNER

After the renowned western novelist and historian Wallace Stegner died in April, 1993, the northwest literary community did not forget his achievements: founding the Stanford creative writing program, publishing over thirty books of award-winning fiction and non-fiction, and advocating environmental ethics and regional awareness: specifically, he "proclaimed that Northwest literature had finally realized a strong regional tradition." To celebrate and honor Stegner's life and work, John Daniel organized and hosted "A Tribute to Wallace Stegner"—an October 10, 1993 program at the University of Portland. On that evening, an audience of 425 gathered in the Buckley Center Auditorium to hear John Daniel, James Hepworth, William Kittredge, Terry Tempest Williams, Barry Lopez, and myself offer our fifteen minute tributes. The following text was my invited contribution to that occasion and at the end of my statement I sang "Big Rock Candy Mountain" which generated a standing ovation. Supported directly by the University of Portland, by Rev. Art Schoenfeldt, C. S. C., by Suzanne and Fred Fields, and by John and Marilyn Daniel, the entire evening was videotaped (105 min) as an event in the Schoenfeldt Distinguished Writers Series.

Sources: *A Tribute to Wallace Stegner.* Videotape. Univ. of Portland, 10 October 1993. 105 min; Photo: Wallace Stegner, USU Western Writers' Conference Barbecue, Logan Canyon, 1972 courtesy Merrill-Cazier Library, Utah State University Special Collections and Archives.

REMEMBERING WALLACE STEGNER

On January 17, 1971, Wallace Stegner wrote me a letter. I'd sent him my first Western American Literature syllabus and a reading list and asked for his advice and critique. I didn't expect him to answer me, and I concealed from him that I hadn't yet read any of his books. Even though his writing had not been included in any of my formal education—graduate or undergraduate—he was still a respected name on my horizon. He had founded and directed the creative writing program at Stanford. He had published many books and was about to win the Pulitzer Prize for *Angle of Repose* (1971). So when I received his letter, I was amazed and delighted. This was generous and kind. One of the elders had taken time out from writing the DeVoto biography to answer my query—a full typed page from South Fork Lane in Los Altos to 4th Street in La Grande:

> Your western literature list looks to me very sound. It includes a few has-beens and a couple of never-will-be's, but on the whole it's pretty close to the list I would make up myself for such a course. You omit Eugene Manlove Rhodes, whom I think I would put in there well ahead of Charlie Siringo, and you also omit Edward Abbey, who though I once had a quarrel with him is a hell of a good writer. For young ones you might throw in Tom Mayer or Larry McMurtry, especially McMurtry. Kesey is less a writer than a cult leader, the poor man's Charley Manson. Allison McKay and Anne Shannon Monroe I don't know. There are some Mormon writers, especially Virginia Sorenson, who might go in, and I don't see how you can leave out Bernard DeVoto, who despite the fact that his histories are more significant than his novels, did write an awful lot, awful well, about the West.

Where to get dope on these people is nothing that I can help you with—or, perhaps, should. I honest to God have enough to do without working up other people's bibliographies. The DeVoto papers are here at Stanford—I'm working on a biography of him now. The Mari Sandoz papers are at a state college in Chadron, Nebraska. H. L. Davis is dead, but God knows where his papers are. Try the Oregon Historical Society. Or look up the Book of the Month Club news for the date of *Honey in the Horn*. That should have some biographical dope.

I'm glad to see you've put Scott Momaday in. He's a good Indian, and not according to the old proverb. He, McMurtry, Abbey, and Mayer were all writing fellows here. So was Tom Horn, another young one you might look up. So, for that matter, was Kesey. I wish you luck in your course. And before I leave you with it, maybe I should suggest that you throw into your large and bubbling pot the name of Alfred Henry Lewis (Dan Quin) whose Wolfville stories certainly belong in any extended course in western fiction.

Sincerely,

Wallace Stegner

As I read, I recognized a welcoming tone—personable, forthright, honest. Later, I realized that he was recommending his students to me, but he was also treating me as though my course mattered, as though the western canon mattered, as though I existed. Teaching at the smallest, the most isolated, most remote four-year college in Oregon, you can begin to have doubts. For me, this letter became a kind of trail head, an entrance, an invitation. One year out of graduate school, I simultaneously began to read his work, teach Western American literature, and write.

In June, 1972, I hitch-hiked to Logan, Utah, to attend the Western Writers' Conference at Utah State University. Stegner would be there, along with William Eastlake, Frank Waters—the elders I had read and not read. I needed to see them. My good-luck ride—non-stop La Grande to Logan—came from a mining engineer who'd been inspecting the disaster in the Coeur d'Alene Mining District that spring. While the engineer snored in the back seat, I herded his big Oldsmobile all night across the moonlit Idaho/Utah desert. On the Logan campus the next morning, I pitched my tent in a landscape planting of pine and juniper right across from the meeting site—Oregon higher education didn't believe in paying lodging or travel for writers' conferences. (Maybe poverty was supposed to keep us honest?) Tucked away in the thicket, I was perfectly concealed in my free canvas room, and took it easy there—until the automatic sprinklers came on at midnight.

Because of my all-night ride, I was two days early for the conference. Browsing through the campus paper, I discovered that Wallace Stegner was to be the graduation speaker on Sunday, June 3. I decided to go. Sitting in the massive Utah State pavilion, I turned on my tape recorder and listened to Stegner's address. His silver hair and rich baritone gave him an aura of great dignity as he explained to the graduates the dynamics of being an American. As you might remember, this was a time of violent dissent, radicalism on campus, protest against the Vietnam War. He had been caught up in this conflict at Stanford. His three pieces of advice to the graduates came straight to me:

> (1) Question the impulse to repudiate the past.... A man may think experimentally within very narrow limits—his profession or his job—but outside it he is very likely to be guided by the uniformities of action and habit that he doesn't even inquire into.... Most experiments, like most biological mutations, are monsters and cannot live.... You can only question from a [historical] base. You can't high jump from a pan of jello.

> (2) Question the questioner. A lot of things wrong in the world may be wrong in ourselves. The aim of our lives is conduct, which is a very different thing [than behavior]. [Conduct] involves a code of personal ethics and an obligation to personal integrity. There are things which are too cheap, too dishonest, too self-indulgent for a good man to do—or a good woman. Know what they are. Knowing them is more important than affiliation with any cause...."

> (3) Question the impulse to perfection, to demand perfection. Idealism is almost invariably self-righteous. That's a hard thing to tell the young. Sooner or later, militant idealism always seems to wind up with a gun in its hand, a machine gun, a Molotov cocktail, a rock; it winds up encouraging violence and repression. Or else, if the militant idealist balks in his impulse to coerce others into

right thinking, he often drops out, withdraws in disgust and tries to create one of those enclaves of perfection where the "handouts grow on bushes and hens lay soft-boiled eggs and little streams of alcohol come trickling down the rocks" and children grow up as part of the wildlife.

He concluded with an analogy that clarified the dynamic process of democracy and democratic identity better than any I had ever heard:

> [Americans] are built like an atom: as a matter of fact, we bombard ourselves with a constant electron stream of questioning and dissent. An elder can suggest to you what the nucleus contains. He can tell you somewhat reluctantly that even the nucleus is open to bombardment—if you chose to bombard. Go ahead. Bombard it. See what particles you can knock off. But understand that you bomb the nucleus at your own risk, because that is where, if anywhere, lies our unity as a people and our hope as a people and it's not to be attacked lightly. But it is also true that that nucleus, by itself, alone and inert, is not enough. What really holds us together is the electrical charge, the tension that exists between the positive core and the negatively charged electrons called "challenge" and "choice" and "change." Neither inertia nor chaos but the two together is what those of you who graduate today are graduating into.

This was the most eloquent speech I had ever heard about being an American. Stegner made both dissent and tradition acceptable and warned all sides about the limits of both. My own mountain of paradoxes began to make sense: vigorous challenges to tradition were traditional; criticism of the powerful and elite was traditional; orthodoxy was traditional but so was doubting it; both convention and departure from it were traditional. Cultivating and understanding these paradoxes were all part of being a citizen, a faithful minority, of being an artist, of being human. Because of Stegner, I could also translate them into the process of being a writer. Mostly, I could give up the mindless demand for "one right answer" which had dominated my upbringing. Stegner actually described the Protestants well. "They always wanted to be more dominant than they actually were."

Later, during the writer's conference, Stegner made statements that for the first time, described the literary wilderness I was headed into—as though he had the whole territory mapped and memorized: on risk, he said that the greatest risk of all was being traditional, not experimental; on character, he said that the archetypal characters in the western novel were a man looking for paradise and a woman who wanted to settle down; on conservation, he said the west was both beautiful and full of crimes against the land; on writing, it meant going out there every day to the little shack and putting black on white; on Joe Hill, he was fascinated by songs people had died to and for; on integrity in writing, there is no choice: you have to know the country and the people; on biography, writers have to take the lives of other writers seriously or no one else will.

He went on and on like this, giving the multiplicity of roles a writer needs to understand: citizen, witness, realist, regionalist, democrat(in the historical sense), conservationist, scholar—all with important responsibilities to land, self, and community. The solipsistic egotistical whiners, the isolated self-loathing self-pitying nihilists that I had studied in graduate school—they were all suddenly exposed and I knew why I had not been able to subscribe to their offers of membership.

Why, exactly, I felt—at the age of 29—as though I were a kid listening to a wise old man I couldn't say then, but I finally learned more about that feeling in 1974 when I read *The Sound of Mountain Water* (1969) and Stegner's essay, "Born a Square." As I began to read this essay, I realized that—for the first time in my life—I was reading a writer who knew and understood more about my background than I did, and he was writing about my life in more vivid and accurate prose than I had ever read before: "Let us imagine some native white Protestant second-or-third generation immigrant kind of boy who grows up in Corvallis or Ogden or Great Falls, eating well and getting plenty of air and exercise and being a reasonably healthy animal in an essentially pre-industrial, pre-urban society: in short, born lucky."

After nearly ten years of serious reading in Biblical, Greek, Roman, Spanish, Latin American, Chinese, English, and American literatures in two languages, Stegner's was the first prose that included my personal experience and referred to my landscape. In a burned-out Idaho milltown of 600 people, I'd been a four-year letterman, a student body president, a National Honor Society member. In my grandparents' logging community in western Washington, I'd learned to fish, hike, hunt, drive truck, keep bees, set chokers, buck bales,

haul wood, build houses, fix anything, cook, butcher lambs. As a preacher's stepson in Washington cities and towns, I was required to memorize whole books of the *Bible*. In college, I'd learned to sing solos in the major European languages for any size audience, to play leading roles in plays and musicals. I'd learn to value silence, wilderness, wild animals, free-flowing water, quiet places, places where there weren't any people. I'd learned the heroic virtues Stegner described—fortitude, resolution, magnanimity.

I continued listening.

> And our Westerner—does he then sing his smiling sunny song and tell his Pollyanna stories about noble pioneers and win book awards with them? Hardly. I have already said that he needs a present to come home to, even if his present is only his identity as an orphan with an inadequate tradition. But he must discover that the full range of doubt, magnanimity, pettiness, the abrasive grind of class and caste struggle, the generation of all sorts of power needed to run the future, even the full measure of alienation and a fuller-than-average measure of hope, are as native to Salt Lake City or Idaho Falls or Minot as to Saul Bellow's Chicago or Baldwin's Harlem or Camus's Oran or Faulkner's Oxford. The western writer should go away and get his eyes opened, and then look back. But not back into history... All [the West] has to do is be itself at the most responsible pitch, to take a hard look at itself and acknowledge some of the things that the myths have consistently obscured—been used to obscure.

In these few sentences, Stegner had unwittingly described my life. As an undergraduate, I'd been away two years—one in Latin America, one in Europe. I've been looking back ever since. I've been trying to be myself, and trying to see what western myth has hidden. This has turned out to be the work of a lifetime. How could Stegner know this? Outline who I had been, where I had come from, my experience in higher education, a group of elders I had claimed, a lifetime of work to do, a code of aesthetic values, a sense of hope, the trail I was on? "Born a Square" became for me a declaration of identity. The library card shows that I have checked out and read *The Sound of Mountain Water* six times since then. Even now, I rank it with Conrad's "Preface" to *The Nigger of the Narcissus*, Faulkner's "Nobel Prize Acceptance Speech," Cervantes' *Quixote*, Jimenez'

Platero, Euripides' *Iphigenia,* the stories of Chekhov. Unlike James Stevens and H. L. Davis' attack on northwest regional writing in *Status Rerum* (1927), beautiful as a diatribe against the commercialistic teaching of hack writing, Stegner's statement was a kind of credo—an affirmation I could accept, understand, and identify with—one I had lived.

Through John Daniel, whom we should all thank for putting this evening together, I was finally able to thank Wallace Stegner and personally acknowledge my debt to him—though this evening is my only formal declaration. In October, 1986, he agreed to read the manuscript of *Marking the Magic Circle* (1987), my third book—a collage of photography, poetry, translation, autobiography, fiction, and history—and a book emulating the multiple genre mix of Stegner's own *Wolf Willow* (1962), where I had learned that Stegner himself came from a place even more remote than rural Idaho and Washington. In a two-page review of the manuscript he wrote for Oregon State University Press, he alerted me to the need to be explicit about my intention in the book's organization. "My guess is that readers won't see your schema without ...an explanation," he warned. He was right.

I wrote a letter thanking him, telling him about hearing him speak in the 1970s in Utah, then set about rewriting my introduction. Eventually, I sent him two different drafts, and he responded immediately with a card: "I greatly prefer the second and shorter one. It's both explanatory and provocative, and that's exactly what you want. Good luck yourself." (Nov. 28, 1986).

So, I celebrate tonight with you Wallace Stegner—an exemplary life which embraced the complexity of the western writer's roles: novelist, scholar, teacher, critic, biographer, editor, conservationist. I celebrate a life with the fullest range of responsibility a writer can accept: for his own work, for the work of others, for the culture as a whole, for the language, for the biosphere itself. His example inspired me, and I have some vague hope that my work moved him. He called my title essay to *Marking The Magic Circle* "first rate." No one ever said that to me— no one except my publisher. Stegner did. *The Oregonian* dismissed the entire 200-page book in three or four sentences.

"Stegner Tribute Writers/Sponsors." *L to R: Barry Lopez, Terry Tempest Williams, Bill Kittredge, Bro. Donald Stabrowski, CSC, Rev. Art Schoenfeldt, CSC, John Daniel, George Venn, James Hepworth.* Photo courtesy University of Portland.

I want to conclude with a verse and chorus from what I have come to recognize as a Stegner theme song—lyrics I first heard him quote in Utah, and was amazed that any writer knew folksongs that I knew, lyrics he used for the title of his novel published the year I was born, lyrics he used as a title for his last book of prose: that song is "Big Rock Candy Mountain." It hovers among us all tonight as the evocation of idealism, paradise, promised land, and ease—the illusion we dance with still, the myth Stegner taught us to see through and look out the other side to possibilities more authentic, less dangerous to the biosphere, to ourselves, to others.

The Big Rock Candy Mountain

INTRO: *One evening as the sun went down*
and the jungle fires were burning
down the track came a hobo hiking.
He said "Boys I'm not turning.
I'm headed for a land that's far away
beside the crystal fountain–
I'll see you all this coming fall
in the Big Rock Candy Mountain.

VERSE: *In the Big Rock Candy Mountain*
it's a land that's fair and bright
the handouts grow on bushes
and you sleep out every night.
The boxcars are all empty
and the sun shines every day–
I'm bound to go
where there ain't no snow
where the sleet don't fall
and the wind don't blow
in the Big Rock Candy Mountain.

CHORUS: *Oh the buzzing of the bees*
in the cigarette trees
by the soda water fountain
by the lemonade springs
where the blue bird sings
in the Big Rock Candy Mountain

VERSE: *In the Big Rock Candy Mountain*
you never change your socks
and little streams of alcohol
come trickling down the rocks.
The shacks all have to tip their hats
the railroad bulls are blind.
There's a lake of stew
and ginger ale too
you can paddle all around it
in a big canoe
in the Big Rock Candy Mountain

Chapter 12 ▪ REMEMBERING WALLACE STEGNER

"1988 Panel." *L to R: William Kittredge, Ursula Le Guin, Marc Jaffe, George Venn (moderator), Julian Bach, Rich Wandschneider (director/non-panelist).* Photo courtesy Fishtrap and OPB

Preface to

A DIALOGUE ON MYTH AT WALLOWA LAKE

At the first Fishtrap Gathering in 1988, I was invited to serve as moderator for one of four panel discussions. At the Methodist Church campground that Saturday morning, the first panel addressed the topic "East/West Perspectives on Western Writing." To prepare, I formulated some questions: (1) " How do Eastern critics view writers and writing in the Northwest today? What are their aesthetic or thematic expectations? How have these originated? (2) Do Northwest writers attempt to fulfill the historical genre expectations of Eastern publishers? How have those expectations affected their writing and their lives?" Readings and discussions by Craig Lesley, Jim and Lois Welch, Ursula Le Guin, William Kittredge, Kim Stafford, and me were offered to a welcoming audience that also included small press publishers Jim Hepworth (Confluence Press), Jim Anderson (Breitenbush Books), and Charles Ackley and Rich Wandschneider (Pika Press).

In July 1990, Fishtrap invited me to engage once more in the rich conversations between writers and readers. That year, the schedule promised readings and panels with Terry Tempest Williams, Molly Gloss, Jonathan Nicholas, Kim Stafford, Lawson Inada, Simon Ortiz, John Rember, Sue Armitage, William Kittredge, Pat Mulcahy, Ursula Le Guin, Joy Johannessen, and Annick Smith. The Native American poet Liz Woody and I were invited to lead off the Saturday morning program with a poetry reading addressing the theme "Patterns." Afterward, we both fielded numerous questions from the audience—some dialogues continuing for days. The "Questioner" below is a composite of some of those literary conference conversations.

Source: "Fishtrap Gathering Reels in Eastern Publishers." *Arts East* 5.4, 1988:1.

A DIALOGUE ON MYTH AT WALLOWA LAKE

Note to readers: As we talk, mule deer wander around us on ground that was first owned by an Ice Age glacier, then by creek water and granite boulders, then by the Nez Perce, then by an Oregon State Game Refuge, and then by the Methodist Church and then by—

Questioner: I don't understand what you're really saying in these poems.

Geo: I said northwest writers are attempting to create a mythology of enduring habitation in a society that has always dreamed its believers will escape into space—the next paradise.

Questioner: Why should that be necessary? I mean, mythology isn't true, is it?

Geo: Myth embodies the authentic values of a people. In particular, myths discriminate between acts that preserve and perpetuate life and acts that degrade and destroy life. All serious writing continues this mythological process.

Questioner: So what does this have to do with the Northwest?

Geo: Writers here inherited a mythology of subjugation which once made "settlement" heroic, but that mythology is destroying us.

Questioner: But there must be some goodness in our traditions. Look at us. We're the most powerful nation on earth. I just can't reject everything I believe.

Geo: I'm not asking you to reject what you believe. Just try to recognize the liabilities of its accompanying myths.

Questioner: I don't know what you mean.

Geo: Western literature best portrays the assumptions of subjugation myth. Let me list a few : (1) violence against anyone or anything who opposes advancing civilization is acceptable; (2) escape from the restraints of civilization is

possible, desirable; (3) natural resources are unlimited, free, and exploitable by any agricultural or industrial means; (4) only male heroic emotions are approved: stoicism, simplicity, naivete, power; (5) anxiety over and fear of females is constant; (6) plundering a community—human or ecological—is acceptable. Sound familiar? Most of them are derived from the enslavement analogy, the dictatorship analogy, the Roman Army mentality.

Questioner: Like a John Wayne western. Sounds dangerous.

Geo: But they didn't always sound that way. Civilization has used such assumptions to justify expansion for centuries.

Questioner: But violence is happening all over now. Pollution, endangered species, toxic waste, soil erosion, battered women, abandoned children, drugs, gang violence, racism, energy shortages—you name it.

Geo: Does that sound like a world without end, a world of continuous habitation?

Questioner: Not really. Maybe the end of the world is coming—like Revelation says. (A mule deer doe approaches.)

Geo: I'd say that subjugation mythology is destroying living communities everywhere. The present generation of Northwest writers has witnessed this undeniable destruction.

Questioner: That sounds too easy, too black and white for me. Besides, there are lots of good Christian and non-Christian people.

Geo: Can you deny that Christendom devours more natural resources than any civilization in history? Can you deny that Christendom has the most violent attitude toward nature of any religion?

Questioner: Maybe this is changing. The Pope named St. Francis the patron saint of the environment this year. Is that part of this new mythology of habitation—as you call it? (The deer stands still. Her deep shining eyes stare at the Questioner—as though in a trance.)

Geo: Token symbolism is better than nothing?

Questioner: Well, how *is* this mythology of habitation formed?

Geo: Let me list a set of assumptions which seem to be shaping habitation my-thology: (1) the native and indigenous—in all their forms—must be defend-ed from degradation and violence; (2) the human must be restrained, must relearn cultivation, must practice cyclic processes that do not degrade ecosys-tems; (3) limited natural resources can only be used if that use preserves the long-term (200 year) integrity, stability, and diversity of ecosystems; (4) full emotional range of awareness is necessary—the childlike, the feminine, the masculine, the plant, the animal, the river, the rock, the sky, the star—and complete emotional expression is essential—the tragic, the comic, the satir-ic, the farcical; (5) the female sense of home, compassion, cultivation, and nurture must be understood, taught, and practiced; (6) community integrity and individual genius must be asserted in all microcosms in order to generate continuing wisdom and art. Most of these new assumptions are based on the marriage analogy, the regenerative dance of opposites analogy, the imagery of wholistic and organic interdependence.

Questioner: But I just heard two academic historians say, "No more mythology. Let's just have the facts." (The doe takes a step toward the Questioner, who seems to recoil from her approach.)

Geo: It's too late. The transition from subjugation myth to habitation myth is already happening everywhere in the Northwest.

Questioner: This deer is looking at me. How do you know?

Geo: One primary habitation myth figure, the archetypal wise old woman in her many masks, is already demanding cleanup, restoration, repair, rehabilitation, justice, respect for children, plants, animals, fish. She becomes a corrective to the excesses of subjugation myth. In a younger version, she is the outraged Antigone determined to see justice done.

Questioner: Is the subjugation myth changing? Look at this thing. (The Ques-tioner points to the staring doe. Her great, soft, silken purse ears slowly and continuously listen on all sides.)

Geo: I think so. The penitent, self-pitying male, guilty of all the extremes of sub-jugation myth, has become both a predictable literary pose and a fictional character. While film westerns and their silent strong stereotypes lose their audience, real cowboys have suddenly become poetic and loquacious. Writers of all ethnic backgrounds are now taking indigenous and prehistoric life se-riously. Writers and poets everywhere are practicing the disciplined spiritual observation it takes to become intimate with a place.

Questioner: So you think there's any hope for us?

Geo: Writers have always asked the same question: what generates and per-petuates abundance, and what degrades and destroys it? To make and keep a habitable world, everything is subjected to that test. Elsewhere, writers have been making that imaginative test for centuries, and northwest writers will have to make that test here now. Wallowa County was the last county "settled" in the lower forty eight states, so this is almost the last place where subjugation myth worked its destruction. Isn't it fitting that we talk here now about this new mythology? Salmon, forests, rivers, owls, soil, children, women, men, air, grass—everything is saying we have to invent a new story for our lives or we will perish. What we do to the cosmos, what we do to others, we do to ourselves.

Questioner: (The doe comes closer to the Questioner and shining black nose sniffs the air around the conversation.) What is this deer doing to me? (The Questioner moves away from the doe.) What does she want?

Geo: Wilderness sends wide rainbows upward out of stone.

Questioner: What's that supposed to mean?

Geo: Ask the deer, the native, the indigenous systems. They have lived here 10,000 years. They will show you the dream of enduring habitation, a world without end.

Writer's Northwest Handbook

a h e w s o i b

3,000 Market & Resource Listings
Articles ◆ Essays ◆ Tips

4th Edition

This dialogue also illustrates how writers' conferences—where editors, agents, and journalists hunt for talent—can generate publications. At the 1990 conference lunch, freelance editor Bill Woodall asked me if the *Writer's Northwest Handbook* (*WNH*) edited by Dennis and Linny Stovall (pictured at right) might publish an article based on my subjects: "writers' mythologies about the West that didn't work and don't work now...and that we need new visions." After accepting the dialogue for publication, Linny Stovall wrote: "Thanks for an original format and most of all for putting this theme in the positive form you did." Building awareness of the regional literary community with their tabloid *Writers Northwest* (75,000 circulation), the Media Weavers 230-page *WNH* became, for over ten years "the best possible reference guide to the literary life of the Northwest. A book for writers, students, publishers, teachers, librarians, and of course, readers."

Sources: "Wilderness Sends Rainbows Upward Out of Stone." *Writer's Northwest Handbook* (4th). Eds. Dennis/Linny Stovall. Hillsboro, OR: Media Weavers (1991): 12-13; Photo courtesy Stovalls.

Chapter 13 ▪ A DIALOGUE ON MYTH AT WALLOWA LAKE

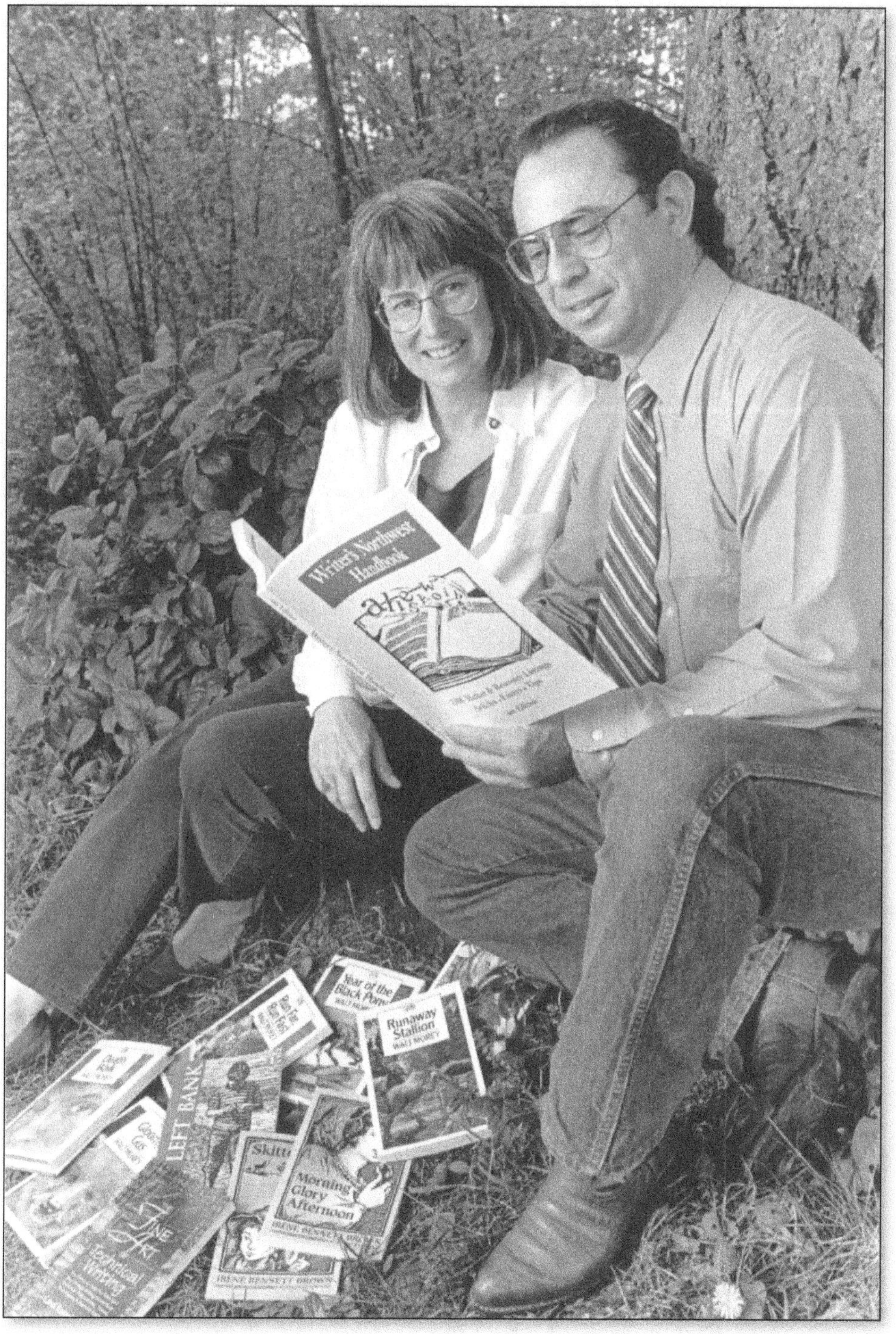

ALL THAT COMES TO LIGHT

Poems by
Lisa Malinowski Steinman

YELLOW

Poems by Anne Pitkin

Preface to

ALL THAT COMES TO LIGHT by LISA STEINMAN
& YELLOW by ANNE PITKIN

In 1978, I reviewed *Railroadin', Etc* by J. J. Greenbriar for the prestigious quarterly *Western American Literature* (*WAL*). Over the next decade, I wrote and/or published—somewhere—at least one review each year, so when Dana Brunvand, Assistant Editor at *WAL*, asked if I would "write a double review of two collections of poetry by northwestern poets," I accepted. It was mid July, 1989. By mid-September, 500 words total for both books. No mere plot summaries, identify major themes. Compare to other books, works. No long quotes. In short, editor Thomas J. Lyon wanted a concise canon review. I struggled. On September 17, I sent Brunvand the 1,000 word review below, with this note:

> This was a difficult assignment. I've never had to review two books at the same time before, and the word limit worked against my instincts—all the way.... However, I did quote a full poem from each book, make some evaluative and interpretative comments, and give the books a frame that might wake up a few people in the back row. In the future, please let me review *one book* at a time. Please? It may be that poets aren't as important as they should be now, but *WAL* doesn't have to subscribe to that cliche. After all, we do live in the age of instantly obsolete prose, don't we?

When the review appeared, it was featured as an "Editor's Essay Review." Never heard a word from the poets, but Brunvand thanked me for "tackling such a difficult task" and "In the future your wishes will be honored—no more requests for a double review."

Sources: *Western American Literature* 25.1 (1990): 53-56; Photos courtesy Lex Runciman and authors. Steinman cover by Chi Meredith; Pitkin cover anon.

REVIEWS OF
YELLOW by ANNE PITKIN
ALL THAT COMES TO LIGHT
by LISA STEINMAN

For a frame around this review, consider that the colonial northwest is crashing down around our ears. Oregon votes to ban log exports, old growth forests and spotted owls are recognized as ecosystems, Idaho bans nuclear waste shipments, Washington signs a historic pact with native American tribes. When the dangerous clearcut simplicities of a colonial civilization are challenged, all forms of diversity and complexity will assert themselves—these two fine books of poems: both by college professors, both widely published in literary magazines, both in mid-career, both from the great raincoast of North America.

Lisa Steinman's *All That Comes To Light* is a hard-edged, intellectual, witty book that defies stereotypes about women poets. Implicitly or explicitly, her poems pose problems and arrive at abstract solutions. She does not wear her professorial learning lightly; the majority of poems begin with epigraphs, many are salted with allusions, some are about language as language. She is a thinking reed and a judgmental one: words like *good, bad, right, wrong* appear frequently in the poems. She likes nothing so much as a poem which begins with an abstract statement in the title or first line:

The Often Regrettable Ease With Which Things, Through Death or Dissolution, Enter the Category of Stuff

I have been hanging onto the title of this poem
by my fingertips for days.
From such a perch, one studies pacts of closeness:
the bushtits suspended in their soft nest, odd angles protruding
—a beak, the trace of a wing.

The crackle of opening pine cones spreads seed like wildfire.
They violate the rule of the jungle:
never let go of one vine until the next is firmly in hand.
On the other hand,
we turn things over and over in our minds like dogs settling into sleep:
tedious, vestigial moves.

Yet Spring astonishes, this year.
Wisteria drips from a neighbor's porch; morning glories, Oregon
Grape, Bewick's wren.

Fledglings leapfrog like popcorn in the underbrush.
From now on, a rule of thumb:
pure motion, scattered sound, catching things on the wing.

By the sea, we notice a sandpiper running before the tide,
like a small skiff teasing the waves.   (p. 34)

While no poem can represent an entire collection, the tendencies in this poem appear throughout Steinman's book. She likes this mix of image and statement, concrete and abstract language. She seems to be free-associating here, but her leaping is carefully controlled antithetical, synonymous, and climatic parallelism. As the first two lines show, Steinman is a self-conscious artist determined to be seen, and she wants to control her medium so that it does not become mundane. She is uneasy with the mundane, with disruptive noise, with an inhospitable world, but neither the refuge of abstract intelligence nor cultural sophistication leave her at peace. At their best, the poems in *All That Comes To Light* become wise, become themselves. When imagination fails to transform the facts into a possible world, which is the critical colonial dilemma, her grievances begin to sound pedantic, pretentious, cute.

The voice in Anne Pitkin's *Yellow* is more musical, philosophical, pictorial. The book is structured by an autobiographical sequence that begins with the death of her first husband and ends with her listening to the singing of her second husband. Her implicit journey through death, grief, memory, escape, travel, realization, regeneration, and finally, love again—that journey gives Pitkin's forty-two poems an intimate and epic quality, and much greater formal variety.

Pitkin's voice can be exemplified by a poem from the last section of her book, "What Remains Is The Traveler:"

March

What was tentative
is losing patience. Yellow,
for example, splatters the side of the house
as forsythia races into bloom. Yellow
bulges thinly through splitting seams of dandelion buds.

The children in the day-care yard
were never tentative. This afternoon, they are yelling
in unison, all mouth and violent sunflower
on their stalks. Be trees,

the teacher says, and they are,
branching and leaving like mad through this sudden concerto
for wind and robins, and jays racketing over the rooftops.

Something here is traditional.
Maybe a wedding, an occasion when summer and winter
         reconcile briefly

like divorced parents. Or think of a door annually opened

and a flowershop's whole supply of corsages and boutonnieres
torn up and flung in every direction. Think

of a dog galloping through the mess.   (p. 67)

While Steinman appeals directly to readers with her learning and intelligence, Pitkin's appeal is more indirect, emotional, musical. Her passion for a new life is absolute, and she makes her journey with poise and insight—no fanfare. Sometimes, that insight becomes mere report, other times, revelation. While Steinman grows through acts of will, Pitkin evolves through acts of perception of the world around and within her. While Steinman tends to abstract what she feels and knows, Pitkin stays close to and trusts the sensuous world and achieves regeneration: a colonial hope is also implicit here—it is possible to live through grief and go on, to end the moaning over a destroyed frontier.

So the linear, masculine, extractive forces that subjugated the frontier have exhausted their passion just as those same forces have nearly exhausted regional resources. Now, feminine energy—cyclic, regenerative, insistent—comes forward with force, insight, and reform. Ursula Le Guin is writing far better novels than her peers, Molly Gloss has written the first frontier novel to feature a woman protagonist, Shannon Applegate has written a best seller—her family's Oregon history. Like their contemporaries, these two poets know that men—alone— cannot create a civilized humane lasting world. They can only make a Hemingway colony. These new books by Steinman and Pitkin show the means for reinventing the colonial northwest: honesty, humor, intelligence, compassion. Listen: regeneration can begin. Like Kurtz before him, McMurphy is also dead.

Photo by Lisa Kroeber

Hear

Ursula Le Guin

"One of the greatest science fiction writers of the century"

May 24 - 8 pm - Inlow Theatre

EOSC Campus — La Grande

Free public reading sponsored by Arts Poetica & Student Activities Board

EASTERN

Eastern Oregon State College   La Grande, OR 97850

CHAPTER 15 | Group Interview Transcript (1988)

Preface to

URSULA LE GUIN AT EASTERN OREGON UNIVERSITY

From 1961 to the present, Ars Poetica at Eastern Oregon University (EOU) has officially hosted live literary readings. During those fifty four years, authors of all types—regional, national, international—have been invited by EOU to present their original work to an audience of students, faculty, townspeople, and visitors. In addition to their evening readings, visiting authors frequently give guest lectures, offer writing workshops, hold press conferences, attend public receptions, complete book signings. On May 24, 1985, the afternoon before her Ars Poetica reading from her new novel *Always Coming Home*, Ursula Le Guin agreed to a taped interview with Eastern students and faculty—David Memmott, Misha Chocholak, Katherine Harmon, Suzanne Madden, Frankie Osborne, other students, and myself—impresario for Ars Poetica from 1970-1988. Listening to the distinguished winner of Hugo Awards, Nebula Awards, Locus Awards, and World Fantasy Awards, I found her comments memorable, historical, and informative, so I transcribed and edited that audio text, sent it to Le Guin for review and permission, and in 1988 she agreed to publication in *Oregon East,* the campus literary magazine. In September, 1998, I again sought her permission to reprint for a larger audience—a northwest anthology. Le Guin reviewed, edited, and approved the version below, and wrote me, "I'm very glad this worked out...one of these days I would love to come back to La Grande—it's such a pretty town—and see the heronry again." In 2014, she was awarded the National Book Foundation Medal for Distinguished Contribution to American Letters.

Sources: "Ursula Le Guin Interview." Ed. George Venn. *Oregon East* 19. (1988): 37-50; Photo by Lisa Kroeber; Poster courtesy Ars Poetica Collection, Pierce Library, Eastern Oregon University.

URSULA LE GUIN AT EASTERN OREGON UNIVERSITY: A 1985 INTERVIEW WITH LOCAL WRITERS

Question: What should you do to get started?

Le Guin: Be sure you want to write. Also, you have to find out what kind of writing you want to do.

Question: How did you thread that maze yourself?

Le Guin: I started as soon as I learned how to write, and when I was 12, I sent a story to a pulp magazine called *Astounding* which became *Analog*.

Question: And they rejected you?

Le Guin: But I'm very proud of that rejection slip; I kept that rejection slip for a long time. I had a real rejection slip like grown-ups did. It satisfied me completely. But when you get a little older the rejection slips don't satisfy the way they used to. Of course, the first thing you do is write. After you've got it as good as you think you can get it, you submit your work. That seems to be a very hard step for some people; they can write, but find it very hard to submit it to an editor. So, you have to write endlessly, you have to submit endlessly, and you have to get used to your writing coming back endlessly—with printed notes from editors.

Question: Do you encourage an apprenticeship period before you start to send your writing out?

Le Guin: Well, writers need to read the kind of published work that they want to write. Also, you need to find out who the competition is, as the musicians put it—what other people are doing, and what their level of skill is. I don't know any artist that isn't really interested in what other artists are doing. That interest doesn't have to be competitive or ugly, but there is definitely a comparison of self with others going on all the time. This is hard for writers. It is easier for musicians because they work together, and even painters tend to get into one another's studios. However, a lot of writers work completely alone. They have no group whatsoever to show work to.

Question: What about criticism by a friend?

Le Guin: What seems to be more important is to have a writing group. It is hard to criticize one to one. There is no way to keep it from becoming personal. If you have a group, it becomes diffused. Of course, you keep personalities out of it. Everybody starts talking about the story, and the critics start bouncing off each other too, saying "Noooo." The person whose story it is has to just sit there quietly until it's all over. Ah, it's very strengthening to the character. (I didn't mean that.)

Question: Was a writing group important in your development as a writer?

Le Guin: No, they hadn't invented writing groups yet.

Question: So, who responded to your early work?

Le Guin: A professor. You turned your story in to the professor on your knees, and the professor took it home, marked it up, brought it back, and said "Veddy good job." (laughter) I was so depressed.

Question: Who were your teachers?

Le Guin: There was one. I had a spare cranny in my sophomore year and I took one creative writing course and that was it. (chuckle) I knew I was a writer then. I didn't know if I was a good writer, but I knew I was a writer. And I knew I didn't need this nonsense. But then, long after, when I had become a writer and had some reputation, I was invited to do a workshop—the first Clarion West Workshop in Seattle. That's where I learned the workshop technique, which by then was getting highly refined, and which has by now taken over most creative writing courses in colleges—because it works. You can't teach writing, but you can share and develop skills that work.

Question: Why does this group criticism work?

Le Guin: I don't think that anybody knows exactly why it works. There is something about attaining self-criticism through the group situation. Criticizing other people's manuscripts, you then can come back and read your own stuff with the detachment that you must have as an artist. I don't really know what it is, but I know it works.

Question: What suggestions do you have for writers who are trying to publish science fiction and fantasy stories?

Le Guin: Well, congratulations in the first place because you are in one of the few paying markets. So, read the markets, read *Locus Magazine,* always read *Locus Magazine,* send work out until you get something accepted, and as soon as you have something accepted, join the Science Fiction Writers Association and get their marvelous packet of information. Once you've had a couple of acceptances, people begin to know your name. If you keep at it, they will remember you. This is true both in the magazines and in the novels. You may not get paid very well, but they don't either. (laughter) You will get printed and read, which is the big thing when you're starting.

Question: And after that initial success?

Le Guin: If you're serious, if you are writing a novel every couple of years and some short stories in between, then you should think of an agent because an agent will take all the load off you. But there's no use thinking of an agent unless you are really a serious and prolific writer. Otherwise, an agent won't want you. You would be wasting each other's time.

Question: Do you read the magazines where you want to publish?

Le Guin: I think it's important, if you're writing for a market, to read that market.

Question: Do you also read the collections of short stories?

Le Guin: Yes, that's sensible. Some years ago, I OD'd on reading science fiction, so I find it hard to read very much of it now.

Question: Is there a lot of good new science fiction coming out now? I've seen a lot of reprints lately.

Le Guin: There are about five major paperback publishers releasing new paperbacks, but most of them are deliberate schlock. It's junk food. They take paperbacks off the stands within six weeks, if not three weeks, and they pulp the book and start over. They literally pulp the book. It is an attitude that assumes no difference between books and magazines—all are disposable, like Kleenex. I don't think quality stuff is any more rare than it used to be, but there's more schlock around.

Question: The problem I found was that in fantasy writing, everyone was imitating everyone.

Le Guin: Unicorns, unicorns. (laughter) Unicorns used to be rare, remember? Now there's a dragon every time you turn a page. Trilogies. Boy, is anybody else sick of trilogies? It's a great deal for the publishers. They figure, "If readers liked volume one, then they'll buy volume two and volume three." Apparently readers do.

Question: Did you ever try to interpret *Dune?* (laughter)

Le Guin: Frank Herbert was so insistent that *Dune* was a trilogy, that I always doubted him. I think he wrote *Dune,* saw he had a winner, then wrote the other two books.

Question: Recently there seems to be a tendency for mature, big name novelists to do novels together. Jerry Pournelle has done novels with several people. Can collaboration be helpful?

Le Guin: Maybe Jerry Pournelle needs it. (laughter) Don't ask me to be polite about Jerry Pournelle, please. Our politics are a little different, to put it mildly. Collaboration is probably a game to play when you get a little along, but there's no way I could collaborate on a book. I get my fun with other people working on a screen play, or making a film, or working with some art form other than writing. My books are my books and I don't want anybody else's little fingerprints in them. It's a matter of temperament. But if you get sick of working alone, as many writers do, it must be kind of nice.

Question: What books or writers influenced you other than science fiction writers?

Le Guin: I read a little science fiction when I was a kid, then I didn't read it at all 'til I was about 30. But I was reading more or less everything else that was ever written: all the kids' books, all the fairy tales, all the novelists—English novelists, and Russian novelists—and the poets. When I went into French in college, I read the French writers. I kind of avoided American literature for a long, long time. I'm coming back around to it now through the back door—mostly womens' writing. I didn't find much that was down my alley in American literature except Mark Twain. From childhood on, I've read Mark Twain. The great writers from the east coast—most of them didn't have much to say to me. So, I can't say who's influenced me because it was everybody.

Question: Do you see any danger in imitating other writers?

Le Guin: Well, I imitated like crazy when I was a teenager and young. I'd write a whole short story and realize, when I let it cool off and re-read it, that I'd been imitating Dickens or somebody I had no business imitating. But it didn't do any harm. Painters and composers imitate each other. I don't think there's any harm, as long as you've realized what you've done. It is a form of practice—of playing scales...

Question: So how important is wide reading for a writer?

Le Guin: Reading is a major part of being a writer. I have met young writers who didn't read, or who read very narrowly-maybe just science fiction. That's all they ever read. They got on to it when they were 10 or 11, and have never branched out, except whatever they were forced to read in high school. They didn't learn what you could do with the language. They had no idea what an instrument they had to play, because they just hadn't read anything very good. To know your instrument you really have to read the best writers. Again, this is true of the other arts. All the musicians I know are always listening to music. They're soaked in music. Most artists enjoy their medium. They do kind of live it. So it's hard on your eyes.

Question: In his recent book, Russell Baker especially remembers listening a lot as a child. He was listening to conversations, to endless verbal play. Did that occur in your household as well, and would you think that atmosphere important for a writer?

Le Guin: Ours was an immensely articulate household, and rather large. I had three brothers and parents, and an aunty. My mother said she didn't realize I could talk until my last brother was drafted, but (laughter) then I opened my mouth and it never closed. Yes. There was real conversation, not argument. Both my parents loved to get an idea roaring around the table, and they had interesting friends who were also articulate people. That was a Berkeley, California, professor's household, so it was high-level stuff. A kid sits there and soaks it all in. It was great. It is also a little unreal, since most people don't live that way. You come out being articulate and that can terrify people. I know. I do it. But I do think it helps the writer's ear, because you hear the language spoken with intelligence and passion.

Question: Do you read your own work out loud, Ursula?

Le Guin: Poetry, and sometimes dialogue, yes. Sometimes I'm appalled when I read something and realize that I have done a sound echo or something like that, but I don't make a lot of mistakes of a certain kind because I do seem to hear the voices as I write them.

Question: How do you feel about fantasy and science fiction writers borrowing ideas from other writers? For instance, in one of your books, you have characters go into another world. I like that concept, yet a lot of readers relate it to *Alice in Wonderland*.

Le Guin: That one was conscious and deliberate. I was trying to find a different way into "the other place," and I found there was no other way. You don't move those gateways. Those gateways are there, believe me. You have two things working here. One is this: in good fantasy you're working with what Jung called the archetypes—ways of perceiving and thinking that seem to be deep in all of us. Whatever language we speak, whatever culture we're from, there are certain commonplaces that seem to come out. Within one culture, and one language, those get developed in a certain way, so in English we say "the world of fairies' or "the other world" or "the place where it's light when it's dark here. " That's one of our stock places. In fantasy, if you don't use those places, what are you going to use? Those places are where fantasy comes from. The other thing is this: within science fiction, there is a very healthy tradition of stealing ideas. Because science fiction is intellectual, it's like science. Everybody uses every idea in science. Right? The same is true in science fiction. Of course, there is plagiarism, but a healthy, nonplagiaristic re-use of someone else's idea is just taken for granted.

Question: Are you saying these two things make science fiction distinctive?

Le Guin: Yes, in a way. This borrowing is one reason I like science fiction a lot. It's much healthier than a lot of mainstream fiction where everybody is carefully making sure that they don't sound like anybody else. They get a little paranoid. A healthy art form is one in which ideas and things are passing around freely, and people don't worry so much about "Am I being myself? Am I expressing myself, and nobody but myself?" Well, what's that matter? Other people are going to read you, so you have to be expressing them too. The person you're always collaborating with is your reader.

Question: Should a writer be thinking about the reader?

Le Guin: Your story doesn't exist, except for you, until that other person picks it up and reads it, and their reading of it is just as important as your writing of it, in a sense. This is something which, as young writers, you cannot be too conscious of. It's important to remember that writing is to be read. The writing is not an end in itself, except for you. A story has an intense life apart from the writer. You can't control what a reader puts into your story. That's out of your hands. Readers will do all sorts of weird stuff, but a story still goes on its own little tour.

Question: When you write, do you think of an ideal reader?

Le Guin: Lots! Lots of them! (chuckle) No. (Laughter) Not an ideal reader, no. Anybody, anybody who wants to read. It's lovely to know that people are reading your book. This is the basic validation for a writer. I don't mean that you have to be a best seller, but just to know that a lot of strangers are going to read your book—that is something amazing.

Question: When you first started writing science fiction, how did you overcome the fear that your science fiction might be thought of as silly?

Le Guin: Well, science fiction doesn't have total universal appeal. You will find people who, not through snobbishness, not elitism, but just through taste, don't like the stuff. You do meet kids who don't like fantasy, although not very many. Most of them will go for Dr. Seuss, and the legends, and the fairy tales, if allowed to. But as they grow up, some people, for whatever reason, lose that taste and, if they want fiction at all, they want something realistic. But also, there is a lot of snobbishness and ignorance and fear about science fiction. People think it's written for men, people think it's highly intellectual, and people think you have to know physics. These are all errors—or prejudices. Some of the best fiction being written in the United States now is science fiction. For instance, Gene Wolfe is published as science fiction. Phil Dick is one of the great novelists of the 1960s and 1970s.

Question: Do you think it's harder for a woman to break into science fiction?

Le Guin: Not any more. The generation before me were using initials or pen names, but there was a little phalanx of us who arrived with our heads down, and the doors opened. We just marched in and editors were happy. There were some women editors who made a big difference, too. As beginning writers, I don't think women have the cards stacked against them now. But, as things go on, womens' books do seem to go out of print faster, and more often. It's complicated. Poetry has been a man's game, but now they just gave Carolyn Kizer the Pulitzer. A wonderfully surprising winner. So things have been changing for the better, but this is still a male-supremacist society.

Question: Are there any particular qualifications for good science fiction writers or good science fiction writing?

Le Guin: Well, good prose. Learn how to use your instrument; learn how to play the piano before you play the sonata. You have to say that in fantasy, because there are so many klutzes writing. In science fiction, the writer must additionally have a certain respect for scientific fact. If you don't know what's going on in the science that you're using in the story, you're going to make great big ugly bloopers. Chip Delaney said that "Science fiction does not deny what is known to be known in science." In other words, you take the state of the art in science now, and work on from that. You can make up things, but you don't go back and falsify science. Now this is not entirely true; in science fiction, for example, spaceships often deny Einstein by going faster than light; but that's a common exception, agreed upon for practical purposes. People have to get about the galaxy, after all.

Question: Do you read articles that are written about your writing and how do you react to them?

Le Guin: Usually with something between depression and rage. (laughter) Some critics have enlightened me as to what I was doing. Some critics have enlightened me as to the way critics' minds work, which is not very useful to me. If you can find a critic who is on your wave length, that person may be a wonderful sounding board or guide. But in general, I don't think artists do listen very much to the critics. For one thing, critics are talking about work that's done, and any artist who's alive probably has something entirely new in mind now and doesn't want to be bothered by all that old stuff. However, I sometimes do get value from critics. For instance, I recently discovered the feminist criticism that's been going on in the United States and England during the last ten years, which I was deeply ignorant of, and I discovered that these critics are talking about literature in a way that finally makes sense to me. This criticism has influenced my whole approach to my writing. I'm discovering I have ancestors that I didn't know about.

Question: How do you respond when critics pick out images that you didn't know you put in, or find underlying meanings that you hadn't intended?

Le Guin: Well, you've got one of two things there. You've got either this imaginative, inventive reader who is putting their own symbols and deep meanings in, or, you've got a real sharp critic who's seeing something you didn't know you were doing. If you've done something that's worth doing, you've done something you didn't know you did. You'll see it yourself sometimes. Maybe much later. I know much more about the *Earthsea* books now than I did when I was writing them. I was just following—like a trace through a labyrinth—when I was writing those books. I couldn't have told you what they were about. Now I could give you some idea what I think they're about. But my opinion now is because I'm not a trained critic. Never believe an artist talking about her own work.

Question: Do you have any work that's your favorite?

Le Guin: Always the one I'm working on.

Question: What about those past?

Le Guin: Well, the first *Earthsea* book, *The Wizard of Earthsea,* was the best-shaped book I have ever made. Also, writers tend to be fond of books that didn't get very much attention paid to them, so I have a kind of weakness for

Lathe of Heaven and *The Eye of the Heron,* both of which have been left out when people get serious about my books.

Question: You said you started when you were 12...
Le Guin: That was the first story I sent out.

Question: How did you survive that first eight to ten years—the hard time when writers write but don't earn anything?
Le Guin: It's hard. You have to have absolute unreasonable self-confidence, and you have to have some other way of making a living. I married it. (laughter) That is one means. Well. Don't laugh. People have been doing this for a long time... If I hadn't married a Ph.D., I would have gone ahead and taught French at the college level. That was a deliberate choice which my mother and father and I talked over. My father was particularly insistent. He said, "Look, if you try to make a living out of your writing, you're going to have to write it the way the editor says. You're not going to take that. You're too rebellious." And I said, "Oh, no, I'm not rebellious." (laughter) But he was right. I had to have a part-time skill. It doesn't have to be anything as fancy as teaching French. It can be any skill that you can use, but there's got to be some way to keep the bread coming.

Question: Has publishing changed much since you began writing?
Le Guin: The worst thing that has been happening in publishing is that most of the publishers have been bought up by big corporations. People are now publishing books who don't know anything about publishing books and don't give a hoot. They think it's a quick money business, and, of course, it's not. Publishing has always been run by ladies and gentlemen. It's an incredibly old-fashioned business. It's very slow, and the money is slow. Writers got real money, but it came from royalties, not from advances. Now, all the real money is "up front," as they call it. It's all the great huge advance—50,000 to half a million—and forget royalties. Now, they're not really doing books; they're doing a product. Believe me, this is destructive. I'm really frightened. Dalton

and Walden Books and now Crown are beginning to run the publishing trade. They're saying, "We want 42 nursing novels and a couple of pseudo-serious, New England, upper-class-family novels." They're telling the publishers what they want, and the publishers tell the writers, and the writers provide. Well, that isn't writing. That is the word industry. I could call it "word processing," but that's been taken over. (laughter) It is done on processors because it has to be done very fast. Here, I get very gloomy.

Question: Is there any way out of this crass commercialism?

Le Guin: I don't know, except to patronize those publishers who still publish serious books seriously. Also, keep your eye on the small and local presses, where hope has always been for off-beat writers and poets. Sometimes, for science fiction and fantasy writers, the small press is a little freedom department. The trouble with them is that they don't have much circulation, but don't forget them.

Question: So how does a novelist make a living?

Le Guin: It depends on what you call making a living. If you can write one $30,000 novel a year, that's a living. Then there's Uncle Sam, who hits artists like an absolute ton of bricks. There is no way to defend your income as an artist. They take the maximum. So, there are easier ways of making a living. If possible, go into plumbing, for God's sake. (laughter)

Question: I had a teacher who once said that if you like to write, give it up for six months. If you can't stand it, then go back and write again.

Le Guin: This is Gene Wolfe's cure for writer's block. Writers say, "I can't write, I can't write." So, for three days you don't write or read anything. You can't even write a laundry list, and you don't even read the labels on aspirin bottles. You don't watch television and you don't listen to radio. Gene Wolfe says that if you are a writer, you'll be back at your desk by eight o' clock on the fourth morning whimpering, "Please, just let me do a word or two..." I've known people who've tried it, and they say it works.

Question: Suppose you're writing a novel which you intended to be a futuristic psychological novel and some agent or publisher comes along and says it's science fiction and rejects it.

Le Guin: So, the person who wants to put it down says it was sci fi and pays no more attention to it—the ultimate put down. Forget it. If it's psychological science fiction set in the future, it must have the internal coherence and consistency of science fiction. The psychology of your people has to relate to the rest of their world, and their psychology is probably going to be different from ours. This consistency works for both fantasy and science fiction. If you make up a world of any kind, if you do what Tolkien calls a "secondary creation," it must be internally consistent. This is the failing in so much of what's being written now, particularly these fantasy trilogies. They are not thought out. They say, "Well gee, we'll have this band of Amazons here, and then there are these real mean guys over here that ride rhinoceroses," but there's never any food for the rhinoceroses, and you don't understand the Amazon economy, and so the book is just a heap of little cute ideas. Schlock! This is where science fiction and fantasy are harder in some ways than writing realistic fiction. Everything is up to you.

Question: So you say just write the book and let the publisher put the label on it?

Le Guin: That's what happened to me. I get labeled all sorts of funny ways. Publishers are going to put the label on a book that they think will sell it. That's their business, after all. The book seller needs that label, too. They have to know where to shelve it. I kept finding Saul Bellow's *Mr. Sammler's Planet* in the science fiction section. I bet it made him mad. (laughter)

Question: What about writing a fantasy now like *The Earthsea Trilogy?*

Le Guin: When I wrote *Earthsea* in the mid-1960s, there wasn't much of a tradition of that kind of book. There were some writers, Tolkien above all, who just dumped you in the middle of a fantasy world and developed it completely from there. Since then, that kind of book has become a commonplace.

Question: What about the writer's role as a story teller vs. role of the prophet?

Le Guin: Same thing. Same difference. By "prophet" you would include ethical commentary, and so on. Isn't that what story tellers have always done? No story is innocent; no story doesn't have a moral. Every story, whether the author means it or not, is telling you something about life. And it just depends on how much of a soap box you build before you start telling your story. I am conscious of having preached sometimes, and preaching definitely damages art. Preaching is not story telling. In fact, they may be almost incompatible except in something like a parable.

Question: Can I get you a cup of tea or something?

Le Guin: You know what I'd like? A root beer.

La Grande, Oregon
May 24, 1985

NARD JONES

Author of "This Mad Heritage," a five-part story
which begins in the July number of the
Up-to-the-Times Magazine.

CHAPTER 16 | Novel Reprint Introduction (1987)

Preface to

NARD JONES, WESTON, AND *OREGON DETOUR*

In spring, 1978, one of the students in my Western Literature course introduced me to Nard Jones and *Oregon Detour* (1930)—his first novel that local residents allegedly kept stealing from Weston Public Library. In spring, 1981, supported by an Oregon Council for the Humanities (OCH) research grant, I set out—Weston, Pendleton, Walla Walla, Seattle—to find answers via family and friends' interviews, newspapers, magazines, archives, libraries. In August, 1981—my final report for OCH completed—I left for a year to teach at a Chinese university. Back in Oregon, I presented public lectures in Portland, Pendleton, and Athena. Subsequent publication in *Marking the Magic Circle* (1987) generated less than grateful responses from various Weston residents, but later this essay drew a positive response from Oregon State University Press editor Jo Alexander:

> There is a passage in Venn's essay about *Oregon Detour* that sums up one of the reasons why it is important to reprint our regional literature. It expresses his powerful belief that literature matters in kids' lives, in all our lives, and that is particularly important for those of us who live in places like Oregon. It's too easy to believe that literature is something that happens in New York City, that writers live on the East Coast or in California, that nothing important happens in Oregon. Let me read this passage to you: *** I was fascinated by Venn's story; I went to the library, found a copy of *Oregon Detour*, read it and enjoyed it. And suggested to the Director of the Press that we should reprint it. He said yes, but not in isolation, and suggested a reprint series (*Burnside Reader* 1992).

So, when the novel became the first volume in the Northwest Reprint Series edited by Robert Frank, I was able to incorporate my Weston critics' comments in that 1990 "Introduction."

Sources: *Marking the Magic Circle.* Corvallis: OSU, 1987. 156-172. Rpt. in *Oregon Detour* by Nard Jones. Corvallis: OSU Press, Northwest Reprint Series (1990): vii-xxxi;
Photos: Author's Weston home (1993) Jan Boles photo; Nard Jones ca 1936 courtesy Penrose Library Archives, Whitman College.

NARD JONES, WESTON, AND OREGON DETOUR

I.

One January day in 1978, as students were bundling up to leave my Western Literature class at Eastern Oregon University, a young woman who always sat in the back row approached me at the lectern. She asked me if I'd heard of a writer called Nard Jones and could she read one of his books for a paper due in three weeks. I didn't know this student well. She was a freshman. She'd done C work in the course so far. She'd been absent a time or two. I asked her which book she was interested in.

"Well, there's this one that people keep stealing from the library at home," she said. I thought I saw a kind of gleam in her eye. I must have looked doubtful. "Really, it's true," she said.

"Where's home?" I asked.

"Weston. Over by Walla Walla," she said and pointed fifty miles northwest.

"Which book is it that people steal?" I asked.

"I don't know. My mother's got a copy, I think. She's friends with the librarian."

"You grew up there?" I asked.

"Twelve years," she said.

"Well, it should make an interesting paper. Find out as much as you can. Talk to the librarian. Let me know if I can help."

"Oh, good," she said, and I'm still sure she went out with a great smile on her face, as though something about her life was suddenly worthy after all.

That was my introduction to *Oregon Detour* (1930). The student did read the book and wrote her paper, but her project raised more questions than it answered. For instance, she said that the author had been run out of town, that he'd been sued, that he'd written an awful book about the town's good people, and that everyone stole the novel. As I read this, something in me began to doubt. Was something being left out?

I started to wonder: is any of this true?

To begin, I looked through my own research files for a survey of libraries in Eastern Oregon I'd done in 1973, to find what the librarian of Weston had, indeed, said in response to my question: "In your judgment, who are the most important authors who've written about Eastern Oregon?" The Weston librarian had replied: "DeVoto. Probably best known. Parkman. I think Nard Jones progressed into a good writer.... I can't think of any more really important ones."

Given the Weston student's paper, this answer seemed mysterious. I looked through the librarian's responses for more information about the controversy or the novel itself. She had listed all of Jones's regional works except *Oregon Detour*. Something seemed to be left out? That began to bother me. In the five-page questionnaire, I'd clearly invited any librarian to mention any fiction about the region. (See Chapter 24 below)

Since there was no Jones biography, I began—with a modest research grant—to search for Nard Jones's literary past in libraries, among Weston residents, in newspapers, among the Jones family. From those sources, I discovered that Nard Jones (1904–1972) had cast himself a complex career. He'd edited Miller-Freeman trade publications in Seattle and New York for nearly 24 years, but when his struggle with alcoholism reached crisis in New York in 1952, his family left him and returned to Seattle. Eventually, Jones rejoined his family and went to work for the *Seattle Post-Intelligencer* in 1953, where he held various editorial posts, including chief editorial writer, until his retirement in 1970. During his career, he'd also written and published more than 300 stories in popular magazines, and done numerous radio broadcasts. He had also published twelve novels, including his national bestseller, *Swift Flows the River* (1941), *Evergreen Land* (1947)—a history of Washington, and *The Pacific Northwest* (1963), a regional history co-authored with Stewart Holbrook and Roderick Haig-Brown. Whitman National Monument was still selling Jones's popular history of the Whitman Mission, *The Great Command* (1959). *Seattle* (1972), a history and memoir, appeared posthumously from Doubleday.

After about six months of research, I finally uncovered the story of *Oregon Detour*, the first novel by a Northwest writer to use the aesthetics of the "New Realism" established by Sherwood Anderson, Sinclair Lewis, and Scott Fitzgerald, and a novel which has apparently been the object of fifty years of censorship in Weston, Oregon. This seems to be what happened.

II.

In 1926, Maynard Benedict Jones graduated from Whitman College with highest honors in English and returned to Weston, Oregon, to live with his family and to work in the family general store. During that year at home, he continued the literary career he had started at Whitman. Jones was not afraid of controversy. At Whitman College, he had scandalized the campus his senior year by writing and publishing an underground sheet called *Spasm*. His editorship of *Blue Moon*, the campus literary magazine he founded, had been constantly challenged for publishing "blue" literature rather than writing of the "sunny side." He wrote fifteen stories for the popular pulp magazines, a New York market he had been quick to understand. He also wrote weekly editorials for the *Weston Leader* publisher, Clark Wood, who was also Jones's literary mentor. Jones's weekly columns showed the major literary influences of his Whitman education: the polemic style of H. L. Mencken, the New Realism of Sinclair Lewis, and the small town interests of Sherwood Anderson. His *Weston Leader* columns were often pure provocation. He'd probably started *Oregon Detour* at Whitman when he learned from Professor Russell Blankenship that a realistic novel in the manner of *Main Street* (1920) had not been written about any Northwest community.

In September 1927, Jones moved to Seattle to work on two Miller-Freeman trade publications, *Pacific Motorboat* and *Western Woodworker*. In a sense, re-

turning to Seattle was going home. He'd been born in that city in 1904 and had lived there for the first thirteen years of his life, a time when he had enjoyed great personal freedom because his family had owned a hotel there. Now, after eleven years away—California, Eastern Washington, Eastern Oregon—he returned as a fast-rising magazine writer, recent college graduate, new editor, and budding novelist. He moved into a hotel, edited for Miller-Freeman during the day and, bolstered by shots of whiskey which could make him dangerous, wrote fiction and worked on *Oregon Detour* in the evenings. Apparently, Jones's shots of whiskey could increase to fifths during an evening's writing. When drunk, Jones could become violent, poetic, or both. When he was sober, his sense of humor and compassion returned. In June 1928, he married Elizabeth Dunphy, the daughter of Walla Walla's leading lawyer and member of a wheat-ranching pioneer family. In March 1929, he hired Brandt and Brandt, literary agents in New York, and sent off the *Oregon Detour* manuscript. Within fifteen days, his new agent had sold the book to Payson and Clarke for $500 plus 10 percent royalties to $5,000, 15 percent thereafter.

Here, then, was a Northwest literary boomer. At 25, he was a veteran of print, a quick learner, a skilled amateur actor with a fatal taste for whiskey, jokes, and self-dramatization. Short, dark-haired, fluent, quick, handsome, slender, ambitious, Jones was a compelling presence. To complete this picture of sudden success—comparable to none in the region—all Nard Jones needed to hear was the comment of William Rose Benet, Assistant Editor of *Saturday Review* and Payson and Clarke's chief editor: "Your book seems to be one of the most promising first novels that I have read in some time." After some correspondence between Benet and Jones about revisions, Jones's novel went to press and was released in early 1930. From coast to coast, *Oregon Detour* quickly attracted critical approval.

In Weston, Oregon, a conservative rural farming town of 600, events had progressed toward publication somewhat differently. Clark Wood, the *Weston Leader* publisher, had been trying for nine months to prepare the Weston audience for his protege's novel. Wood had published a letter from Jones, April 19, 1929, in which Jones wrote: "The hero of this book is the harvest. And any of my friends who circulate the rumor that any of its people are such-and-such persons will be shot in cold blood—even though I have to do it myself. This will take months of time, as I am the most damnable shot in the eleven Western states."

In October 1929, Wood had reprinted a complimentary national review of the novel containing the statement that "There is no bitterness in the book. No sarcasm. In writing of his people, the author has not forsaken them." Just before the novel was released, Wood further not-ed that "Weston is [the] locale but charac-ters are fictitious." This evidence suggests that both Wood and Jones knew contro-versy was rising like thunder heads over Weston Mountain.

On January 17, 1930, *Oregon Detour* went on sale in the local drugstore, just a few yards from Jones's home on Water Street. (His father was mayor of Weston, a leading businessman, and an avid com-munity booster.) All copies of the first shipment sold immediately for $2.50 each. Those who couldn't afford to buy the novel rented a copy from friends at 25 cents and read it. The Weston librarian,

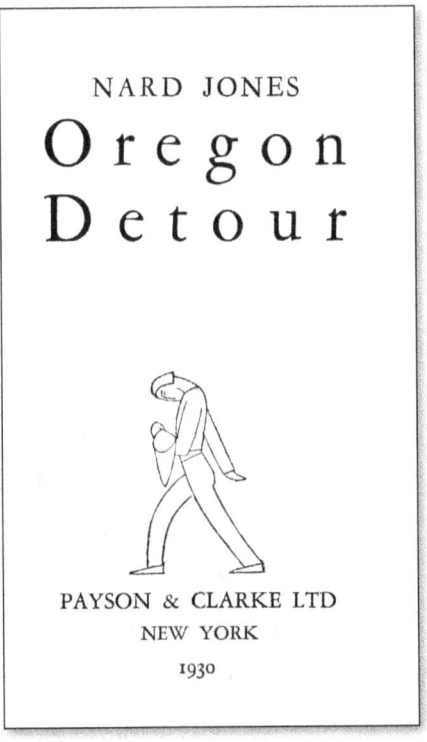

NARD JONES

Oregon Detour

PAYSON & CLARKE LTD
NEW YORK
1930

Josephine Godwin, another of Jones's literary mentors, added the book to the public library. It was immediately checked out by a family friend, then by the doctor's wife who read the novel aloud to her husband at bedtime. They laughed over each page and considered the novel a "boy's look at his hometown." Many of the surrounding wheat farmers who did business with the Jones and Jones Mer-cantile also bought copies of the novel. They felt it was a good-humored use of risque local events. Some snickered that the pious now appeared only sanctimo-nious. Young married couples in the community—Jones's peers—were especially anxious to read the novel because the word quickly spread that *Oregon Detour* contained "real people."

Nevertheless, a segment of Weston's six hundred people were furious. They were reading *Oregon Detour* as reporting. They called the novel "vulgar." They objected to its "hard-talking sloppy lingo," and to Jones's use of salacious names like "Fanny Breast" and "Rev. Alfred Horliss." They objected to his explicit use of sexuality. Those who protested were generally members of two socially powerful groups in Weston, the Methodist Church and the Saturday Afternoon Club, both dominated by socially-prominent women who held formidable powers over cultural life in the community. For instance, the Saturday Afternoon Club gave monthly literary programs, reviewed proper books, encouraged musical events, controlled the library board prior to 1955, and at one time owned the city park—which they later gave to the city of Weston. Their membership was by invitation only.

According to Nard Jones's sister, who was still living with her family in Weston when the novel appeared, a Saturday Afternoon Club member approached her on the street. As she recalled the encounter,

> This woman said, I'm not sure what her words were, but it was something like she thought it was terrible that Nard might have put people in Weston into his book. I remember I was so shocked. I was fifteen, I guess, and I turned around to her and I said, "Mrs.___, I really think that people must feel terribly important to think that they're in somebody's novel." I turned around and walked away.

Many women in this group refused to read the novel after they heard about its characters and language. It was publicly stated to this writer that there was also a mass book burning to rid Weston of *Oregon Detour*. It was also suggested that somewhere in a Weston attic lies a trunkful of copies waiting to be discovered.

Even though he lived in Seattle several hundred miles away, Nard Jones immediately felt the tremors of outrage created by his novel in Weston. His response, published by Clark Wood in the January 24 edition of the *Weston Leader*, is worth reprinting here in its entirety as the only document of its kind in Northwest literature—a New Realist asking his subject community to read their lives as literature rather than as reporting:

It's Only Fiction

To whom it may concern: It has been brought to my attention that individuals are looking upon certain passages in *Oregon Detour* as reflective of truth. This is regrettable and far from the real purpose of the author.

Only three actual names appear in this volume: they are merely mentioned in one or two sentences and this mention is intended as a compliment. All other characters are fictional, though necessitating common names which would naturally be duplicated in this and thousands of other books and communities.

It is perhaps needless to say that what happens in "Creston" may happen in a hundred other wheat towns. It is also needless to say that the writer would not intentionally speak in a derogatory manner of those toward whom he has the highest regard.

Authors are frequently confronted with this situation, and it is no new thing. I am sure that the great majority of my hometown people will read the book purely as a story, not attempting to weave into it any information which happens to be in their own minds—but which was not in the mind of the author as he wrote.

Very truly yours,

Nard Jones

Apparently, Jones's effort to encourage his Weston audience to accept his fictional mask did not succeed. In Weston, the novel was read in 1930 and was still read in 1981 as "about Weston" by the majority of residents. Trying to figure out or trying to remember who the "real people" were in the novel is still a local pastime. There is no evidence that the novel was ever understood as literature, as a statement by Jones that Northwest small town life is—at best—a dangerous idyll.

Biographical evidence also suggests that "It's Only Fiction" was as much a feigned professional pose as it was an effort to claim his innocent intentions. Thus, the professional innocence projected here only conceals a part of Jones that was iconoclastic—as his Whitman career had already dramatized.

However, other evidence suggests that Jones was not invulnerable to the snarl of the Weston status quo. Most significant in this respect must have been his now

lost letter to Clark Wood in April 1930, to which Wood responded on April 16, 1930, as follows:

> Dear Nard:
>
> Have no regrets about your novel. It was a good yarn—the proof being that I was absorbed in it myself when usually I don't care a damn about anything except a detective story with a mysterious murder in the first chapter—preferably a double murder.
>
> The sex stuff naturally caused some comment around here, but they ate it up. Those who didn't buy the book borrowed it. I realized that you had to put in this sort of stuff in order to sell the yarn and I thought you handled it with extreme skill.
>
> Some of the descriptive work—notably the flood and the wheat harvest—was strongly done, and was almost as good as yours truly could have evolved.
>
> Forget it, boy. You haven't lost any real friends around this burg.
>
> Woodsy

The tone of Wood's letter suggests that Jones needed to be reassured about his potential loss of popularity at home. Evidently, behind the young New Realist's mask lived a writer both sentimental and nostalgic about Weston—a town where he'd actually been given the impetus to become a writer, a town he would visit annually for most of his life, a town where he gave copies of his books to the library, a town he wrote about in both fiction and journalism for the rest of his career. Private sources also confirm that Jones himself was "very, very shy... he was not a daring person. He hated flying and avoided autograph parties as much as possible." Even though he could call on national reviews, Clark Wood, and New Realism to shield him, a part of Jones was still vulnerable to the possibility of local dishonor.

Of course, Jones tried to convert this furor into a joke for Northwest writers who read *The Frontier*, the region's leading literary magazine. In the November 1930 issue, Jones reported his recent news in this fashion:

> Nard Jones, Seattle, is finishing a second novel, *Sin of Angels*, for spring publication. He has two long stories and a short to *College Life*:

"Hollywood," "Expatriates,"and "Please May I Have Another?"' For the past three years Mr. Jones engaged in trade journal work. Recently he took the Oregon Detour by auto—"without being shot at, or hanged."

While levity here worked to preserve some professional dignity, more important adjustments were going on at the typewriter, where Jones had just finished his second novel, *The Petlands*, and was at work on his third, *Wheat Women*. In advance notices for *Wheat Women* published in the *Weston Leader* in November, Jones continued to respond:

> I am doing another wheat novel in order to show the other side of the picture depicted in Oregon Detour. That book showed many of the faults of the wheat land; this new wheat story will show many of its virtues. It will probably, therefore, be longer.

Is Jones attempting here to recover from what he's decided were his excesses in *Oregon Detour*? Is he playing to an offended audience with tongue in cheek? Is this the final evidence that he himself was unprepared for the implications of his first book? All seem likely. He was also careful to add a disclaimer to the front matter of *The Petlands* (1931), in which he reminded his readers that the "story of this book is fiction."

Subsequent events in Weston allegedly took several turns against Jones and *Oregon Detour*, turns which seem to have been dominated by the Saturday Afternoon Club. Most conspicuous were those hostile moves alleged in the local narrative about *Oregon Detour* recorded by the student writer, namely that Jones was sued and run out of town. There seems to be no base in fact for either of those charges. No evidence of a lawsuit exists in Umatilla County courts or in the memories of more than thirty informants. Also, Jones was clearly not run out of town, since he had lived in Seattle for three years prior to the novel's publication. Further, Jones returned to Weston in June 1930, for a two-week summer vacation with his parents. According to family sources, Jones's father, Nelson Hawk Jones, would never have allowed the young novelist to return for the Pioneer Reunion if there had been any threat of violence against him. Jones also returned to Weston for Christmas that same year, and usually made an annual trip to Weston the rest of his life.

Thus it appears that those who faulted *Oregon Detour* attempted to honor their own opinions by literalizing the novel and defining the novelist as criminal and outcast. In fact, there was never unanimous Weston disapproval of *Oregon Detour*. Jones did not lose his rapport with the majority. There was no suit. There was no expulsion. In 1981, Jones's novels could be found in many Weston homes and many Westonites remembered him fondly—jokes, boozing, pranks, stories, and favors. For the rest of his life, he wrote about Umatilla County people and, especially the Pioneer Reunion, a work which he revised and included in *Evergreen Land*.

However, the allegation that Nard Jones's first novel could not be regularly kept on the shelves of Weston libraries between 1931 and 1981 has an apparently factual basis. Shortly after the novel was published, a student at Weston High School gave a book report to his English teacher on *Oregon Detour*. She immediately removed the book from the sophomore reading list and the high school library. Weston Public Library records show that the book was added to the Weston branch in 1930, but soon had to be re-ordered from the main Umatilla County Library in Pendleton. The librarian confirmed that this could only mean the book was no longer in the Weston collection. In 1935, the novel seems to have been restored to the Weston branch collection, but by 1936 *Oregon Detour* again had to be ordered for Weston readers from Pendleton. Evidently the novel was being stolen, a conclusion supported by a retired Umatilla County librarian, who stated that she was told "not to send *Oregon Detour* to Weston because it would never come back." In a recent newspaper report the current librarian "concedes the novel was not on the shelves when she took over in 1955..." For a multitude of possible reasons—lost, missing, burned, stolen, misplaced, banned, worn out—*Oregon Detour* could not regularly be found in the Weston collection until 1981, when the current librarian's 20-year search for a copy of the novel ended successfully: three copies of the novel were suddenly given to the Weston Public Library subsequent to my 1981 research.

This apparent popularity of *Oregon Detour*—as a book with a doubtful reputation—was matched by an equally durable outrage about the novel that appeared in various guises during my 1981 interviews in Weston. The angry were generally old "native" members of the Saturday Afternoon Club or directly related to them in some way. One interview, for example, contained these comments:

Why you going around trying to get the skeletons out of the closet? Looking for a nigger in the woodpile? I can't see any good in it. I'm not going to tell you anything even if you want me to. I heard you was going around doing this. Why stir people up again over something that happened fifty years ago? You should let well enough alone.

Other members of that group refused to be interviewed. Still others feigned ignorance of the entire event and its consequences, even though they were recommended as highly informed sources. Evidently, the small segment of the community that initially felt it had been slandered by *Oregon Detour* still feels that their reputations have something to lose some 51 years later.

Whatever the causes of their silence, the Saturday Afternoon Club and the women of the Methodist Church have made their judgment about the novel and its controversial status a fact of community life. Only one opinion about *Oregon Detour*—the Saturday Afternoon Club opinion—seems to circulate in the community. Research at Weston-McEwen High School in 1982 revealed that no current students had heard of the novel or read it, and only a few of their parents had heard of the novel at all. Even though the high school librarian had heard of the book herself, the book was not housed in the high school collection.

Yet banned book status for *Oregon Detour* by the offended minority is qualified. In 1980, a farmer on Weston Mountain called Nard Jones's son in Walla Walla and asked if he could still buy a copy of the novel. Also, a woman who'd spent her summers in Weston for forty years finally sought out a copy of the novel in 1982 and read it herself. Her conclusion: the book was tame. Finally, the novel is in demand. Umatilla County Library records show that, between 1937 and 1959, one of two main library copies circulated 22 times for 3 weeks each. Another Umatilla County Library copy circulated 29 times between 1966 and 1973, including three successful circulations to the Weston branch. Most of the individuals interviewed during 1981 wanted to know where they could find a copy of the novel, or if there was one in the Weston library. There wasn't at that time: only two noncirculating copies of *Oregon Detour* remained in the central Umatilla County Library in Pendleton, and both were in moderate demand even though they had to be read in the library. There seems to be a continuing if not increasing readership for *Oregon Detour*—the local classic, which competes with

that other unknown northeast Oregon classic, *Beyond The Black Stump* (1956) by the Australian novelist Nevil Shute.

III.

Why all this fear of a book? There are three factors at work here—all very concrete and powerful—which might serve to explain what happened in 1930. First, the events and characters in *Oregon Detour* were neither genteel nor romantic, and didn't fit with the formula romances and westerns that dominated popular reading tastes in Weston at that time. Realistic treatment of local sexual adventures and authentic descriptions of wild, small town characters were unprecedented in Northwest fiction, which even caused the novel to be a best seller in Portland for more than two months.

Also, whatever he claimed, Nard Jones had actually changed these events and characters very little, and where he did alter events those alterations were not understood by his Weston audience. Adopting New Realism, Jones had written a contemporary pageant without the benefit of historical distance. For Weston readers, fact and fiction were difficult—if not impossible—to separate. The only place name Jones changed was Weston, which became "Creston." All other place names—Walla Walla, Pendleton, Portland—remained the same. No common landmarks in the community were renamed, local character names were only slightly altered, e.g., Clark Wood became Clark Tipp, and some local character names were not altered at all—as Jones acknowledged in "It's Only Fiction." Local events—a flash flood, the Pioneer Reunion, and high school graduation—had been altered for fictional purposes but those alterations were not understood as acts of literary naturalism. For example, a major flash flood swept through Weston on Sunday afternoon, July 1, 1927. Carefully reported by Clark Wood in the *Weston Leader's* next issue, Jones included the same flood in *Oregon Detour* (74–88), but made major changes. In the 1927 event, Newt O'Harras's home was completely washed away, but no one was killed. In the novel, the flood kills an innocent woman, Lura Dyer, which causes one of the main characters, Etta Dant, to blaspheme. Where Jones needed plot material, he took it directly from community rumor, public event, or his own experience among his peers—including all sexual antics. Numerous interviews with Jones's peers confirmed this literalism. Many informants either knew or recalled without assistance the individuals in the community who had served Jones as models for Etta Dant, Florence Larson, Peg Nettleship, Swede Mongsen, and Charlie Fraser. However, many interviews also confirmed that Jones made composite characters, concentrating separate historical events into one character's experience in the novel. Thus, suspension of disbelief was impossible for the Weston audience. For many reasons, Jones's mixture of fact and fiction could not be separated, partly because Jones had so completely bound together taboo subjects with literal events, places, and individuals.

This fracturing of genteel literary expectations by *Oregon Detour* extended itself to become a second cause of uproar—and popularity. The community's illusions about itself had been threatened by a New Realist novel—a common event in the decade. As Donald Meinig has noted in his historical geography, *The Great Columbia Plain,* the Weston-Walla Walla area "during the first decades of this [20th] century seemed to be overshadowed by the massive influences of a crass materialism, strident boosterism, and a frantic concern to be in the forefront of 'progress.' " Like other New Realists, Jones had stripped away Weston's white enamel of piety, progress, and propriety to show local individuals becoming the natural victims of their own ignorance, fear, violence, customs, and self-deceptions. The sons and daughters of the golden pioneers were not only masters of a beautiful landscape; they were also slaves to their inner landscape, especially their sexuality, loneliness, and insecurity.

Third, *Oregon Detour* also reversed community power structure and social privilege, a potent change which Jones himself might not have recognized would occur when he wrote the novel. Suddenly, an "outsider" had exposed the "natives" to the possibility of public censure. In many Northwestern towns, these two social classes are defined by the Oregon Trail experience. The ancestors of the "natives" came overland, homesteaded, founded the community, created its institutions, and commanded its wealth. According to Weston sources, the "natives" did not hold their members up to public censure. In contrast, the "newcomers" were those individuals whose families had settled in the community after 1900. More than likely, the "newcomers" bought land from one of the "natives," or carried on business, services, or other forms of labor. They would not be invited to join the Saturday Afternoon Club, but would form the Fun and Fiction Club. At the Pioneer Reunion, they would not be eligible to nominate the Pioneer Queen. When *Oregon Detour* appeared, the "newcomers" were not threatened, since Jones had taken his major characters largely from "native" wheat families whose lands surrounded "Creston." However, the life beyond reproach that the "natives" enjoyed had been redrawn by some newcomer who'd kept his eyes and ears open. Ironically, it is the outrage of the "natives" that has kept the novel alive in the community.

IV.

This microcosmic conflict and its causes are not unique. Such conflicts are universal in literature—Flaubert, Steinbeck, Wolfe, Hergersheimer, Lewis—to name a few. However, in the Northwest this is the first and oldest case of local censorship and of public furor between a novelist and members of his community—perhaps a sign that literary culture had begun to rise from those authentic sources called for by H. L. Davis and James Stevens in their 1927 Mencken-style polemic, *Status Rerum*. With the single exception of Vardis Fisher's agrarian novel, *Toilers of the Hills* (1928), the modern Northwest novel did not begin to appear before *Oregon Detour* was published. In fact, Northwest novelists whose works are still reprinted and studied today all began to publish their major books after 1930: H. L. Davis, James Stevens, D'arcy McNickle, Vardis Fisher, to name a few. Thus, it may be fair to conclude that *Oregon Detour* was the region's first modern novel, certainly the Northwest's first exercise in "New Realism."

V.

I thought this *Oregon Detour* inquiry had culminated when, one April after-noon in 1983, I stood before the assembled student body of Weston-McEwen High School in Athena, the school Jones himself would have attended if he were growing up in Weston today. Waiting in that shining gymnasium for silence, I reviewed my notes and watched the energy and excitement in the bleachers turn to attention. I hoped I was ready. For about half an hour, I told them the *Oregon Detour* story as I'd been able to find it. At the end of my talk, I read them part of a chapter about high school seniors from Weston going to Pendleton after graduation for a night on the town. The bleachers began to whistle and cheer. I stopped reading, looked up, waited, then read a few more sentences. They laughed. I read on, stopping while they responded, then reading on again. They loved it. Only when the bell jangled at the end of the day did they let me stop. Busses were coming, cars waiting.

On my way out, the principal stopped me in the front hall. He was a big man who'd gone to school locally and returned to teach. "Nothing's changed," he said. "That part you read? I did that too. These kids will do it too. It's all still the same. Even graduation." As he spoke, students were streaming by with coats and books and packs—voices rich, magnificent, and opening to the spring outside. I hoped there was another novelist among them. At least, I thought, they now have heard that writing fiction was a possibility—even here. At best, if I'd done my work well enough, *Oregon Detour* might again be included as a worthy interpretation of its generative community.

However, the *Oregon Detour* story was not over.

After the initial publication of this essay in *Marking The Magic Circle* (1987), I received less than grateful responses from various Weston residents. Thankfully, their accusations provided me with new information which was partially incor-porated in my 1990 "Introduction" when the novel was republished by Oregon State University Press—the first volume in the Northwest Reprint Series edited by Robert Frank. According to recent Oregon State University Press reports, the novel has sold 133 hardbacks and 1,450 paperbacks since being reprinted in 1990 and is still in print as of 2016.

Chapter 16 ▪ NARD JONES, WESTON, AND OREGON DETOUR

SEAL ROCK

John Haislip

Preface to

SEAL ROCK BY JOHN HAISLIP

In 1979 *Northwest Review* editor Michael Strelow asked me to review *Flying over Greenland*, Stanley Radhuber's new book of poems. I worked hard to be fair, honest, clear. After reporting that my review was better than the one he requested from another writer, the editor resigned. A year went by, then his successor John Witte rejected my Radhuber review. Surprised and disappointed, I moved on. In 1985, Frank Walsh, the editor of *Publishing Northwest*, asked me to write reviews for his new regional newsletter. Three reviews and a year later, irony came calling: John Witte, the *Northwest Review* editor who'd rejected my Radhuber review, asked me to review John Haislip's book *Seal Rock* (1986). He called *Seal Rock* "a flawed, but perhaps not mortally flawed book?" I suddenly felt strangely respected. Once again I'd been asked to write for perhaps the most reputable literary journal in the northwest, to write about a book by a student of Theodore Roethke, to evaluate a poet teaching at Oregon's major liberal arts university. To fairly review such a book would be to assert an attitude and aesthetic out of the main stream, a poetic practice contrary to, for example, William Stafford. So, the review would be contrapuntal. When I sent in the text below, John Witte replied in three words: "Accepted, with gratitude." In 1987, I was one of three judges who awarded *Seal Rock* the first Oregon Institute of Literary Arts Hazel Hall Award for Poetry. Haislip passed away in 2011.

Sources: *Northwest Review* 25.2 (1987): 157-160; Photos: "John Haislip, Editor, *Northwest Review*, 1969." by William Stafford courtesy Lewis and Clark College Watek Library. Cover painting by John Rock: "Oregon Coast—Fog Lifting."

REVIEW OF **SEAL ROCK** BY JOHN HAISLIP

Seal Rock shows that John Haislip has chosen poetry over poetic ambition. Throughout his career as a poet teaching at the University of Oregon, he's exercised a restraint that many of his contemporaries have not. Instead of forcing himself to observe the cliche—"get another book out right away"—after *Not Every Year* (U. of Washington, 1971), Haislip has taken his time and written what he had to write, or as William Heyen says on the jacket: "contemporary American poets do not very often earn their books, as Haislip as earned *Seal Rock*." "Earn" here has nothing to do with money, and everything to do with the cumulative effects of real experience that allow a poet to reject mass production, self-imitation, and intentionality—those forces that operate the poetic marketplace—and embrace patience, necessity, and craft—those forces that generate lasting poetry. This book feels more like a "selected poems" than a "latest book," which shows the merits of Haislip's way of writing and his attitude toward publication.

Time and patience have generated a delightful variety here. In the twenty-two poems and the eight prose pieces in *Seal Rock*, there are many personae: father, son, husband, lover, friend, warrior, fisherman, sailor, beachcomber, naturalist, folk historian, biographer. None of them are easy masks adopted temporarily to get a poem written. None of them come to quite the same conclusions, though they are all conscious of the cliff, the wind, the sea, the human. There's that multiplicity of a real human being attempting to always be himself, to not sacrifice his own growth to some more dangerous necessity—like self-imitation. Instead of a "latest book" of poems, which are usually all quite similar and reveal the poet's latest "idea" about "how to do something different," this book contains long poems, short poems, mid-length poems, parodies, sonnets, elegies, love poems, catalogs,

prose poems, didactic poems, narrative poems—as well as eight prose pieces(or fewer, depending on how liberally you define prose poem.) Such diversity in a single book is simply unmatched by most of Haislip's contemporaries.

The prosodical variety which time, necessity, and craft have produced here is equally diverse. Both metrical and non-metrical work is present. Long lines, short lines, stanzas, no stanzas—the variety is lively and interesting. Haislip does, however, have his characteristic moves: the 3-stress line, the double parallelism, Latinate mixed with Anglo-Saxon diction. His characteristic poetic acts are at once simple, rhythmic, and regenerative—naming, counting, coloring what he loves. The poet is orienting himself at the edge of the continent. However, his orientation is terribly complex because it is carried out within the context of a community, a family, a tradition, a nation—all of which may bring home into doubt, as the Russian fishing fleet succeeds in doing here:

Seal Rock: Dec. 1967

I knew. Who didn't know?
I remembered. Who could forget?
Butcher boys of every nation
scribbling the same report,
we're winding down on food.

Then why take my fish
out of a bay that's been
winding down for years?
No salmon to speak of,
bluebacks are getting scarce,
steelhead may be gone.
And all that bottom fishing
inside the jaws is dead.

Listen, you sons of bitches,
decode this message fast:
everyone's moored on somebody's truth,
but this Coney Island crap game has got to go.

Another amazing fact about this book is that John Haislip hasn't been flooding the mails with his poems. Instead, he's elected to observe what Horace recommended—keeping poems at home for ten years. He's let them work on him as he's worked on them. Looking at Haislip's essay called "Seal Rock", which prefigured this collection when it was published in *American Poets In 1976*, and which was the first essay by a contemporary northwest poet to identify the human and literary significance of living and writing in the northwest, it is easy to see that Haislip has been revising. For instance, he's left out the explicitly interpretative portions of the initial essay, included three sections of the prose, but given each prose piece a new position and title, and included them in *Seal Rock* with three poems from the initial essay: "Missing The Old Boy," "For Robert Blanchard," and "Hunting for 'Blues' In The Rain." To the best of my knowledge, these constitute more published revisions than those of all of his peers put together.

Also, Haislip has experimented throughout the new book, in a way he had not experimented in the essay, with the effects of juxtaposing prose pieces and lyric poems. While that effect might look simple, it is not. For example, the opening page is a prose piece titled "M.P. 150" and in it Haislip states explicitly what seem to be the geographical and personal facts about the place called "Seal Rock" on the Oregon coast. However, what seems to be literalistic here is actually figurative, since "M.P. 150" establishes the mythological substructure of the entire book—that quest for and discovery of a real home and abiding friends. (Note that it starts with "my village" and ends with "our village.") That same first prose poem also invokes the mythical symbolism of orientation when Haislip identifies for himself and his readers what north, south, east, and west have come to mean. Such gestures create a world with a center that holds. The book, in fact, persistently pursues the meanings of those directions and that center. Late in the book, Haislip challenges—by parody or directly—the eastern establishment and its facile condescension to his poetics:

Hunting for 'Blues' in the Rain

So it's **not** all piss ants in the rain after all
when the great agates roll up out of the surf
in and around the flat round stones and up our
long beach coming down hard on me is a fat old
woman in her rain gear black comes right through
sheet after bruising sheet of water like a Crone
through tough Fifth Avenue plate except this is
has got to be that other end of the continent you
better believe we are shattering more than glass
out here busting up more than silence plowing
into finding more than little "blues" in the rain.

The prose pieces here are so artistically diverse that they elude any generalization. Some scan. Some roar. Some talk. The mixture of prose and poetry, which none of his peers have attempted, symbolizes the dialogue at work in *Seal Rock* between the lyrical and the historical, the brief charged moment of insight and the long years of residence at a moral address.

A final dimension of this book to notice and admire is Haislip's refusal to participate in the "tourist poetry" binge that hit the northwest in the late 1970s— that effort to stop in damn near every town long enough to write some instant view of nowhere with a place name in the title. Instead, the poet of *Seal Rock* has given his careful and perceptive attention to a single place and his discoveries there. That stance, above all, shows that he's rejected the mass-produced, snapshotting of the present and kept his poise: see, understand, but reject—finally— what the tides bring in this day:

Kelp

Its holdfast gone; its every last
Rawhide tentacle torn by the high tides
And the winter storms' demented beatings,
The kelp, loosened, will slowly surface
Inside the coves—tumbling ton by ton,
Out of the great waves, across the sand.

What a welter, what a ferment of coils
And knotted mounds of excrementitious
Horror: look, look there, and there!
Such dotage, in brilliant moonlight too.

Seal Rock is a book that has fundamentally rejected most of what passes for poetic ambition—self-imitation, mass production, tourist poems. Instead of conforming to the present, Haislip has been patient, careful, and thereby original. This book gives us a compelling and complex microcosm—a place where real is still possible. Haislip has held to his art by finding and holding his ground.

Chapter 17 ▪ REVIEW OF SEAL ROCK BY JOHN HAISLIP

Marking the Magic Circle

an intimate geography

poetry, fiction, and essays
by George Venn

Preface to

MARKING THE MAGIC CIRCLE

In August 1983, Louie Attebery, The College of Idaho Vice President, invited me to give a guest lecture and poetry reading for the course titled "Regionalism in American Literature." By this time, I'd learned the some of the stereotypical connotations of "regional" and "regionalist"—19th century local color, 20th century Southern Agrarians, quaint customs, geographical differences, provincialism, etc. I'd also received generous affirmation from publishing two books of poems and winning a national Pushcart Prize. Over four months of drafting and revising the lecture, I discovered the meditative essay collage, a form I could enrich with memories of people, place, ideas, trees, winter, harvest. In that process, I also discovered that region—beyond stereotypes—is a universal organizing metaphor and principle with specific values. After presenting on January 5, 1984, I was told that this essay inspired a College of Idaho sociologist to rewrite his entire lecture, and the essay later became the title work for my third book—a collage of poetry, essays, fiction, Jan Boles photographs, and translations—*Marking The Magic Circle* (1987). Because that book defied any single genre, Oregon Literary Arts judges granted a "Special Award for Oregon Literature" (1988), and in 2005 the book was further honored by the Oregon Cultural Heritage Commission and Oregon State Library by listing on "Literary Oregon: 100 Books, 1800–2000." The book's success was due in large part to the talent, good faith, and commitment of Jo Alexander, Editor, OSU Press. Between June 1986 and February 1987, she dedicated herself to collaboratively shaping and enhancing the eclectic mass of manuscripts and photographs.

Sources: *Marking the Magic Circle.* Corvallis: OSU Press, 1987: 2-20;
Photos: Cover by Bernard Thomas; "In Waldo Hall 1980s" courtesy Jo Alexander.

MARKING THE MAGIC CIRCLE

December night, end of the year. Late. A blizzard roars through the bare trees outside and drives freezing rain against the windows. Ice storm. On the ridge, not even the deer move from their beds in thick timber, their nostrils venting steam to the night. All public power is gone. All lines down. I go to the window to look out, but the glass is wrinkled and frozen into a sacred blur, so I return to this page by an old kerosene lamp, its three flames receding into the storm beyond the windows. Behind me, lodgepole logs shift and settle in the stove; the fire's heat surrounds my shoulders but leaves my knees and shins chilled. I listen. Blizzard subsides, then gusts, subsides, then blasts a white whirlwind past my window. The glass trembles. I am at home. The dog barks at some sound in that storm I cannot hear. "What?" I say to her. Getting up to see what she heard, I feel the old farmhouse sway like a ship.

• • •

This is why writing begins for me—an immediate place and moment demanding attention, inviting names, suggesting reflections, encouraging exploration. If I'm lucky, something will appear. That doesn't always happen. Maybe it won't happen here, but language does have this power to create an immediate sensible cosmos out of the blizzard—whatever it might be—and the inaudible sounds inside it.

On another night like this one, caught between personal loss and inexpressible anger, I wrote this poem and found through it some order where none seemed possible before:

Chapter 18 ▪ MARKING THE MAGIC CIRCLE

Winter Sailor

Even the trees reef now.
The blizzard screams.
I sway and moan inside
ready to jump into the maw
of any whale.

Cut loose, I'm blasted
leaves wrenched north.
There on the bald ridge
light rides over snow—
something dies.

A horseman comes.
His silver bridle gleams
to me for miles.
I reach out to this
plain dream
of slight new rein.

▪ ▪ ▪

Space is organized around a sacral center ... let us remember that not only so-called primitives but literate and sophisticated peoples are disposed to structure their worlds this way.

—YI-FU TUAN

Back inside, I check the fire, add a round of lodgepole, then come back to this desk by the window. The lamp still gives its three receding flames to the storm. Salvaged from my grandparents' basement, the lamp's round glass base is etched with a nine-pointed star. Above the base, the round belly of lamp oil rises—incarnadine—nearly half gone. Inside that reservoir, the old wick coils like a snakeskin. I have never changed wicks—this must be my grandmother's work. The brass round chimney base sits like a dusty hat on top of the glass reservoir. From the groove in the narrowing crown, a tongue of soft yellow flame—blue centered, almost invisible—sways in the drafts of storm leaking in around the old wood casing. The glass chimney is broken and gone. On a clear cold night, you could see this lamp inviting you in from the dark fields. Tonight, it would be useless. The whiteout has come. I scrawl on.

. . .

As an old family lamp might create a center that could transform a better night, so in my own life there are centering places that give arrangement to my experience. The houses I was born into or learned to live—replete with attics, basements, hideaways, kitchens, barns, stumps, creeks, lakes, rivers, animals, plants, friends—all became centers of protection where holy facts were shown to me: love's hands and milk, strong wood walls and fires, singing and death, water and the answered cry, silence and the voices of trees, animals and light—the true edges of all things. Those sanctuaries I carry with me, always returning to them, considering them, writing about them. They are fires where cedar burns uncon-sumed. They are mountains where wrestling angels wait. But they were separated by miles and years, and the greatest demand of my growing up seemed to be to hold them together, to call them all one name, to see them as one. From Louie Attebery, then Harold Merriam, I learned that a river—south fork murky, north fork clear—might unify those places, those lives. I called them Northwest. All secrets, truths, mysteries resided there. Northwest became my dream house, my Mt. Analogue, a place to stand, a landscape of possibilities. I was at home in that space marked by the Columbia River. I had a world with many centers and a real edge—a region.

Later, I learned that people universally scribe a similar sacred circle with their lives and homes at the center, a circle with a meaningful series of concentric rings spiraling outward from that center toward an edge—an opening, a passageway to the infinite, the unknown. Though often hidden from us, that magic circle and its positions have given centuries of arrangement and expression to human lives. Saying *well-rounded, rounded out, coming full circle, come around, on the edge, on edge, edgy, far out, outcast, exorbitant, extremities, heart, core, outback, out west, eccentric,* I touched the top of the circle's linguistic mountain. In the cosmogra-phies of 6th century B.C. China, ancient Greece, and medieval Europe, I found recurrent images of the sacred circle. In *Mental Maps* (Penguin, 1974), 1 learned from Gould and White that human information, understanding, and emotional involvement decrease with the distance from home. From my students, I also have good evidence that everyone—no matter where they moved—created a magic circle as I had with home at the center and meaningful concentric rings moving outward to the edge. "Being is round," says Bachelard. While the boundaries and centers on that internal symbolic map may change, its topography and contours are apparently archetypal.

Probably never found in the geography texts, that circle I traced around the Columbia drainage gave definition to the region where I felt I belonged. Frequently, that map becomes more concrete—the work of poems.

Early Morning: Washington 12 Toward Ohanapecosh

Along the dammed Cowlitz River
stump ranch fields are thickening
with swampgrass and buttercups.
Blackberries are always overgrowing
cedar stumps jutting like monuments
in the pasture. Alders jump the fence
ferns move in, moss takes the shake roof
and swallows fly out the kitchen window
over mole hills and rank thistles.

I could be farming that homestead
long enough to see my own posts rot
my fences rust and disappear in floods.
I was born to this land; land is my name.
Here means my first father died, my uncles
aunts and cousins live, my brother and I played
summers away in grandfather's timothy and clover.
I know the faller's ax, polaski, froe,
peavy, scythe, the crosscut saw.

Davis Creek, Tilton River,
Rainy Valley, Packwood, Mossyrock—
the small loggerheaded towns asleep
in the century of their own sawdust

the logging trucks aiming their reaches
like howitzers at the silent Cascades.
Sawlogs wait prisoner at the mill;
teepee burner glows like rusted hell.
Bare bulb of the yard light burns over
the yellow crummy streaked with dew.

I could be a gyppo sleeping in that shack
where the junked-out cars are full of dust.
I could be swinging out of bed on hoot owl
caulks and hard hat my only human hope.
I could be pulling green chain at the mill
packing a black lunchbucket, driving home
half drunk from the Ashford Tavern payday.
I've chased chokers, borne off cants,
slung tongs, stickered and stacked on bunks
until I didn't know who my own hands were.

As sun burns around the corner
I give this valley all the names I have
drive myself for higher country on Rainier—
Indian Bar, Summerland, Mystic Lake—
the alpine park no man will ever cut
where I'll camp tonight and sleep
a glacial sleep for lives I'll always be.

When I come down, no one in these towns
will know my name or consider the avalanche
of lupine melting in my hands like laws.
I'll see the second growth and death of work
then fly like a shining crow for the river.

. . .

The symbolic circle can also become an imperfect shape, might appear as fragmented or fracturing, as this poem suggests:

My Mother Is This White Wind Cleaning

out. Everything. From Grandma's house.
Laos is a refugee. Laos needs a place.
Laos is sponsored by her church—
those singing fundamentalists.

Out old clothes. Out thirty years of dirt.
Nothing's to be left.
Salvation's Army marches here—
converting love to modest rent.

Oh she has reasons heaped holy
on a silver platter, theological as
the head of John the Baptist.
Order, too. There's a box to Dump

there's a box for Goodwill, a box to Burn.
I'm reeling from them all.
I stay away and help. Late at night,
she asks me what I'll want to take.

"Save me Grandma's diaries, the morning
in June she called me outside to see
the salamander slide under the door,
odor of geraniums in the air.

Save me that place I slept and dreamed
for thirty years," I say.
She writhes. Gold rings twist themselves
around her fingers. She's down to blurt:

"All this must be done. Your aunt
and I are just sick of these decisions."
I nod. I know it is too late to teach
her to leave the soul of just one

earthly home alone or call it love's
unvendible estate. She knows not where
she comes from or where she goes.
She is borne again by her far God—

the cleansing homeless storm. I'm still
her son, the troublemaker. Here, growing,
a tree bent again by all her prevailing.
Where next, oh righteous tornado?

. . .

The illusion of superiority and centrality is probably necessary to the sustenance of culture. When rude encounters with reality shatter that illusion the culture itself is liable to decline.
　　　　　　　　　　　—Yi-Fu Tuan

The phone jangles. I leave the desk again. It is Elizabeth working late at the hospital in town. She tells me all the mountain passes—Cabbage Hill and Ladd Canyon—are closed. All the valley roads are a frozen impasse. No one can get in or out of the Grande Ronde tonight. Two hundred trucks have pulled off and parked She wants to know if she should stay there and sleep at the hospital to-night. "Give me half an hour," I say, wondering how deep the drifts might be across our road by now, but not doubting my ability to get there and get her back here—somehow. That confidence is not built by chains and front-wheel drive alone. There is more to it. I hang up the phone and look around again: there is the larder on the porch full of peaches, applesauce, beans, mushrooms, pickles, chard, honey, peas, potatoes, Walla Walla sweets, lamb, trout, carrots—maybe five hundred pounds of food from the garden, pasture, mountains, rivers. Thinking of that abundance, I am stronger. The wood—split, stacked, dry lodgepole—four cords at least left: thinking of such work done, I am reassured. Putting on my wool hat, windbreaker, and boots, I remember Idaho winters under Mt. Spokane and how deep snow was a kind of joy for me. I check the fire, turn on the water, feel it cross my fingers cold, and go outside. The wind has died some. Looking back inside, I see the grandmother lamp burning—that single tongue of energy—but from outside, there are fewer reflections inward. The light seems more shallow—some-how. Above me, a white swirling mass breaks up as I head down the road to check the depth of the drifts, the shimmering white crust breaking like china plates under my boots. Behind me, I think of the beds, tools, diaries, children, cats, sheep, horses, sleds, stoves. Beside me, the dog—all mongrel confidence—trots along on top of the crust, the Puck of this mid-winter dream. Starving on Lolo summit, would I eat her?

. . .

If there's any discovery here, it may be that confidence is generated by marking the magic circle—the region—and asserting its centers. Even from biologists like Ardrey, we have learned that the animal who fights or defends home ground is doubly strong and likely to win. If not from biology, then from the mythic Antaeus we can see that defeat will come in battle only if he is abstracted into space. If not from myth, then from medicine we might be persuaded that the patient who heals at home heals faster and more surely than the patient who heals in hospital. If not from medicine, then from war, our war, Vietnam, we might learn that those who fought for home were impossible to kill, outnumber, even find. If not from war, then from the continuous assertions of small colleges and small town chambers of commerce who publicize that they are "the cultural, educational, and religious center of the intermountain west," or that they are "the regional center." This power of the magic circle to generate confidence also generates spiritual allies—strength, health, belief, optimism. Mere existence may go on elsewhere, but within the circle we thrive. The freight of weakness, helplessness, alienation, anguish—all that grinds without the bearings of the magic circle—is well known.

El Greco overcame those feelings by carrying clods of Cretan soil in his pockets all the time he lived in Spain. A northwest writer who moved to New York took a wall-sized photograph of Mt. Rainier with him for his office. If this confidence becomes excessive, it becomes dangerous; literally, chauvinism, less literally, nationalism. At its best, it is the result of love for home—that passion of Native Americans, 17th century Dutch, and others. This is never the same as love for a nation. Your region is not your nation. Thus, as the magic circle creates confidence, so the whole force of a region generates, nurtures, and sustains vitality, creativity, energy, delight.

Sometimes, that confidence comes from just one tree.

Larch in Fall

All my life I've seen you slowly going gold
slowly letting go your shade another year
felt your needles ticking down your limbs
to soothe the summer duff to sleep again—
your soft voice falling in October light.

Your gold tongue is spotfire on the ridge
saying silently that change must come where all
those changeless conifers believe that any turn
from official hue can mean the end, and still
you flare and freeze on steep north slopes.

In Idaho, you asked what color I would be.
I stared at you, said subtle green, said gold,
brown, black wet, and living in Montana
you gave me fence and roof and beams, and here
your form still gives me shape in cavities of snag.

You stand now as ghost women on the mountain whose
blood is sinking in my veins at night
whose double names I take to like confounding hope
whose heartwood is the tough straight muscle that
gives me light, whose fire is fire that speaks as

it burns up. I chose you, Larch, to all those
splattering loud leaves in hard and famous forests
in some country far from this interior, this west.
Hold to that ridge for me another year, hold to
that brilliance mottling the falling light

so still and clear—my changer who remains.

Chapter 18 ▪ MARKING THE MAGIC CIRCLE

* * *

The circle and its four directions may be regarded as symbolic of the need for psychic orientation.... In terms of psychological symbolism, the circle expresses the union of opposites—the union of the personal temporal world of the ego with the non-personal, timeless world of the non-ego.
> —ANIELA JAFFE

The Toyota engine purrs steady on gas and oil from the Paleozoic swamps, the cylinders cast from Chinese ore. I wait, thinking of my wife at the hospital, wondering if when I met her hitchhiking in Spain she would ever have imagined herself, a sun-seeking Aussie, stranded on a December night in Oregon. (From nowhere comes the feeling that I'm suddenly writing this in a cave and looking out at Scotland.) The vehicle is warm now. Is the tenor? I shift to reverse. The frozen wheels break away from the red fir planks suddenly and I roll backward into the white road. As the lights swing over the fields, I recall the biggest drift at the highway and the night of the Pattersons' Christmas party thirteen years ago—before we moved out here from town. This same old blizzard suddenly began to blow while we were all inside drinking hot spiced wine. For us, the blizzard was new. No one had come prepared for 60 mph winds and freezing rain and snow. How could we have known? The ground was nearly bare. A few began to talk about leaving, but most stayed on. The wine was good, the Pattersons good hosts. I remember my friend Glen Davis—all confidence that his front-wheel drive could go through anything—plowed his Saab into that drift, high-centered, and he and his wife had to walk back up the hill to the party to save themselves. When they straggled in about midnight—Glen's beard frozen white and filled with ice, and Alice's whole body nearly frozen—some chose to leave their cars and ride in our old VW van which had better clearance, traction, and chains. We roared down the road past the high-centered Saab and luck got us to the highway where the Haufles, our future neighbors, were just being dropped off from a party. They began to attempt the 50 yard walk home through the drift against the driven snow and rain, the wife falling in the knee deep freezing mass, the husband, bent by the wind, lifting her out. We waited in the van watching them, and when she fell the second time and when we saw them hesitate and start back, two of us got out, went after them and brought them to the already-loaded van. There must have been fourteen of us packed like wet dogs in that old VW bus. (Later, as Jean Haufle lay dying, she told me her red weasel dream, and asked me to give the eulogy at her funeral.) I roll forward downhill, hitting drifts, blinded by snow, accelerating too high, slogging from side to side, the Toyota's front-wheel drive taking hold, the crust scraping the undercarriage as the bed of snow jostles me like a whale. I keep up the rpms like Joe Sander taught me and the big drift is there and I hit it and break through the berm of new-plowed snow onto the plowed highway feeling like I've suddenly been born. Fighting to slow down, sliding, turning into the slide, straightening out, on my way—I laugh.

. . .

Another value created by the magic circle is wholeness; appearing here in a brief winter road, so also found in the spiraling lines that reach out from the center of a region to the edges of time, place, memory, nature, sexuality. That growing from the center can go on forever, each experience laying on another growth ring over that first home—that place to stand. "Our life is an apprenticeship to the truth that around every circle another can be drawn; that there is no end in nature," says Emerson. That continuously enlarging circle, drawn and redrawn, but with its magic center sure, becomes a region's metaphor for the possibilities of wholeness. Turning inward, that circle can generate a life of continuous revelation—heartwood. Turned to nature, that circle can become ecological, asserting the unity of all life and requiring that we must come into harmonious relation with what we cannot create. In a region, in one watershed, in one household, that wholeness with nature is an individual possibility. I can oppose a dam on a local creek, a clearcut on a municipal watershed, a loss of local wilderness, and be effective. I cannot—fundamentally—generate the same demands for ecological wholeness elsewhere. Turned to human life, the circle invites a vision of human stability through resident generations, of human strength from families—their cycles, their picnics, their quarrels, their wisdom. From the long effects of time in place comes a kind of spiritual ecology, an intimate genealogy, a novel. Turned to individuals, the circle spirals away from mere acquaintances toward abiding friends.

Reports of those who only pass through the magic circle are likely to be tourist snapshots of a place still seeking mature portraiture. Yes, someone must be the wind, and the wind has its mystery, motion, depth, detail, and demands, but I'm willing to let someone else be the wind. I am studying how to know its local names—Chinook, Wallowa, Northwester—and how that wind feels when the barn door blows off on Columbus Day, how that wind shapes the trees, the people, the ridges, the prayers, and all of their relationships. Such a whole view creates a usable past, binds conscious to unconscious, dead to living, living to unborn, natural to human. Such unity is possible in a region, if it is possible at all. It takes years—sometimes—to just see something, as I was recently reminded:

From Half-Dead Grass

These infinite rise
all under town—purple, white—
quietly resurrecting dead lawns

with doubtless weeds.
Even before the cold trumpets
of hothouse Easter lilies

begin to preach gaudy white
in the crisscrossed churches
these small bright explosions

live and bloom through snow.
Why has it taken me
twelve years to see them

well enough to write this down:
Dwarf violets. Again.
In the cemetery. March 15.

Grande Ronde Valley and River from Mt. Harris.   *Dave Jensen Photo*

Through every human being, unique space, intimate space, opens up to the world.
—RILKE

At the hospital, the parking lot is pure ice. I sit out waiting for her, thinking of how far she is from the gum trees, kookaburras, wallabies, kangaroos, koala bears, platypi, uncles, Merino sheep, aunts, brothers, horses, cousins, Murray Greys, drought, sunlight, beer, fruitcake—a whole other magic carried inside her. Eventually, she appears, tired, coming home, coming down, my Scheherazade who saves our lives in stories: the 18-car wreck in the canyon, the scalp of Mrs. Awe from Spirit Lake, Idaho, sewn on and did I know her; three basins of blood and water to rinse out the glass fragments, the doctor changing his clothes three times; a baby born without pain; an old man setting himself on fire; a young man injured, drunk, and swearing; a nurse driving in through the storm who hasn't missed a night shift in twenty years; her son, dying of cancer stranded in Baker; who knows how long he has to live. We ride beyond the city's midnight, scrabble our way up the road home. Inside and warming by the fire, she tells me how hundreds of people are eating and sleeping overnight. Temporary shelters everywhere in town. We make tea and talk, her stories slowly letting us down from the blizzard's crisis. Undressing by the old lamp, her naked body softening in the light, her voice coming down to whisper as she pulls the quilts up over her ears, her hands on me freezing cold. We argue briefly about tomorrow's weather, I voting for the returning sun, the solstice so near, and she voting for more cold—sure the world is against her. I find ways to warm her—old, familiar as lovers—and afterward she wants to trade sides of the bed. Mine must be warmer. I hear the stove cooling down ping by ping. Deer will come down again tonight to find the old Jonathans fallen under snow.

How does a region generate intimacy? In the magic circle, any experience can become a lover's dialogue—a shared story because confidence allows anything to be said—right down to criticism that becomes encouragement, not simple correction. As I hear my wife's stories, so any dweller in the magic circle can be listening for that momentary revelation brought along by storm, calm, animal, plant, person, place. The exportable surface imagery of a region—the quaint postcard world of mountains, rivers, cowboys, loggers—tends to lose that intimacy imbedded in the fabric of daily lives. True intimacy can't travel outside the circle. Poets are always listening for those feelings and exploring them. All literature seeks—at its best—to further that intimate dialogue which nurtures and sustains the sacramental relationships on which our lives depend. Fed on public speeches from far away, we may all starve. Mass media can create mass malaise. Knowing the news doesn't mean anyone gives a damn.

Intimacy in a region also becomes the opening to universality. After I first learned the name of the rufous-sided towhee at Malheur Refuge, I gave myself to learning the names and lives of all those birds and now see more clearly when the tundra swans return from Argentina, when the robins return from Mexico.

Once I was introduced by Ward Tonsfeldt to shaggy manes along the Clark Fork, I set out to find the real differences between toadstools and mushrooms, and followed those differences to the black woodear in the soups of China. Because I knew the story of the Chinese miners murdered on the Snake River, I lived cautiously in Hunan Province for a year, though I did see the *guo gi* (wild chicken) in the marketplace—the bird whose cry surrounds the edges of northwest grainfields, whose flashing neck and feathered rainbow explodes out of dry grass by the river. Going to Albertson College of Idaho with Tom Jaramillo, Raul Welder, Jose Nasser, it was easier to live undergraduate years in Ecuador and Spain and understand that Spanish is not just a foreign language—it marks another magic circle which can be revealed to anyone who refuses to become a tourist. Thus, the intimate within the region becomes the opening to the universal—the needle's eye holds the binding thread of everywhere. The ancient fight for that intimacy goes on and on:

Voice from Another Wilderness

A long time
we were living old
in the north before the Romans.

We watched them march.
They wanted slaves.
Our fists tightened on our spears.

We strung our bows
with fierce belief
and waited for the dark. Romans are easy

to kill at night.
They cannot see us
painted as we are with clay and ash.

We fight them now
for everything we love—
our deer, our wives, our trees.

They say Romans will never
go home. We can't leave these hills.
Tonight, we attack the garrison and retreat.

Be with us, gods
of the river. Caves
in the mountains, wait for us.

Caractacus, we come.

○ ○ ○

*From the shapes of men's lives imparted by the places where they have experience,
good writing comes.*
—WILLIAM CARLOS WILLIAMS

Here, it is morning now. Long dreaming drifts have laid their curves high
and deep across the roads. Public power is still off. Not even the mailman or the
paper carrier will make it through today. White shifting skiffs of snow still move
over the fields flowing like currents over riverbed. I build up the fire again and the
stovepipe begins to ping, the drafts wheeze, the fly ash circles softly upward, then
disappears. Water for coffee heats on the stove. But for the skittish wind, there
is no movement outside. I wait at the desk. Suddenly, a red-shafted flicker lights
among the ice-glazed branches of the apple tree and begins to peck its way into a
frozen core. I watch that black half-moon on its breast as it pecks, stops, a black
shining eye cast upward, then pecks again. In the frozen field, the horses wait for
their oats and alfalfa and I see the shapes of two pheasants by their feeders—*guo
gi* picking up the smallest kernels of grain. Everyone still sleeps. I close the draft
and damper on the stove. The dog has finished her morning dance and whine and
is ready to go out.

At the open door, I see the Blue Mountains darkened with pine, the lower
slopes open, white, smooth. I remember my earliest crayon-scribbled pictures on
that heavy paper from grade school: huge white mountains in the background,
a foreground of trees on green hills, blue creek coming down, and in the center

always a gabled house, smoke scrawling gray out the chimney, a few stick figures with hats. I think of my grandfathers and grandmothers in their coastal graves in the shadows of Mt. Rainier, of my wife and children in their inland beds asleep, of the Columbia waiting for all our lives to melt as this snow will soon. I go inside to the silence, surrounded by the old wood walls with openings to the light, openings leaking wind. It is warm. I will make Elizabeth some coffee now.

∘ ∘ ∘

A region is a microcosm—a magic circle centered on home. The values generated by that circle are many, but I have limited myself here to three—confidence, wholeness, and intimacy. For me, the authentic map of the universe is composed of these microcosms—a mosaic of specific human constructs crossing all abstract political, geographic, economic, and racial boundaries. This view of region as *microcosm* stands in contrast to the more dangerous metrocentric fantasy of region as *province*. When defined as *province*, region becomes an edge in a far remote place, a fragment of some empire with a far-away center. When the magic circle is defined as *province*, local life can be drained of significance, since only those who live at The Center are real. Thus, local intimacy, confidence, and wholeness are threatened. In contrast, region as *microcosm* enables an artist living anywhere—including the Northwest—to get work done, to achieve character, belief, aesthetic, purpose, and style. Region as *province* imposes a centralizing political and demographic metaphor which can artificially elevate the significance of artists who live in political or population centers, and artificially dismiss significant artistic achievements that are not centralized by nonartistic forces. An artist who chooses not to live in political or population centers, who chooses not to become an alien to the oldest and most immediate sources of human nurture, who chooses not to become a victim of nationalism—such an artist must assert the region as *microcosm*—this locust flowering, that hive by the Columbia—and where do you live?

Chapter 18 ▪ MARKING THE MAGIC CIRCLE

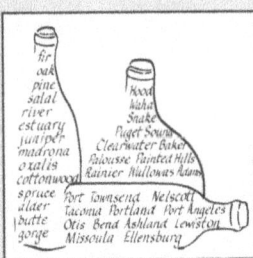

NORTHWEST VARIETY:
Personal Essays
By 14 Regional Authors

Edited By
Lex Runciman
and Steven Sher

Preface to

NORTHWEST VARIETY

In August, 1983, Frank Walsh of Coos Bay, Oregon founded *Publishing Northwest*, a bi-monthly newsletter focused on adult non-fiction from small presses in the Northwest, Alaska, and British Columbia. In August 1985, Walsh invited me to contribute reviews of literary books by regional publishers, a service also begun that same year by Seattle-based *The Northwest Review of Books*. I knew nothing about Walsh, but Vi Gale, Portland poet and my publisher, recommended him, so I accepted. Over the next five years, I contributed reviews: poetry by John Woods, Jeanne Walker, and Corrine Hales; short fiction by James Thomas; two regional prose collections: *Northwest Variety: Personal Essays by 14 Regional Authors* (1987) and *At The Field's End: Interviews with 20 Pacific Northwest Writers* (1987). While both those collections were preceded by *Dialogues With Northwest Writers* (1982), all three serve as worthy sources of Northwest literary history. However, *Northwest Variety* editors Lex Runciman (below) and Steve Sher (above) created an invaluable symposium by asking thirty of the region's foremost living writers and poets to discuss the central question of regional identity: "What does it mean to be a Northwest writer?" In my review, I offered some specific values seemingly held in common by those Northwest literati.

Source: "A Very Important Exercise in Literary Self-Examination."
Review of *Northwest Variety: Personal Essays by 14 Regional Authors*.
Eds. Lex Runciman and Steve Sher. *Publishing Northwest* 5.5 (Sept/Oct 1987): 1-2

REVIEW OF **NORTHWEST VARIETY:** PERSONAL ESSAYS BY 14 REGIONAL AUTHORS

This is an extremely important 151 pages. Fourteen northwest writers and poets have addressed in essays (supplemented by a recent photo and a bibliography) what it means to live and work in this region. The invited writers and poets were selected according to the following criteria: be a current Northwest resident, be the author of three (or more) books, and be representative of a broad mix of writers—both popular and literary—from Oregon, Washington, Idaho, and Western Montana. The editors have pledged 12% of the purchase price of each volume to the Richard Hugo Scholarship Fund to benefit student writers enrolled in the University of Montana's graduate writing program.

All of those are important signals for readers who have been watching the northwest literary community—the last to mature in the U.S. and currently the most significant in the country. While scholars have produced two useful recent volumes *Northwest Perspectives* (1979) and *Regionalism and the Pacific Northwest* (1983), there has been no such book of essays by writers and poets. While there have been a few scattered individual essays on being a writer in the northwest, John Haislip's "Seal Rock" in *American Poets in 1976*, and Tom Robbins' "Why I Live Where I Live" in *Esquire*, Oct. 1980, this book is literally the first and only volume of its kind in the region. There is only one remotely related volume, *Dialogues With Northwest Writers* (Northwest Review Books, Eugene), and that volume includes only one poet who is also included in *Northwest Variety*, Lawson Inada. (He deserves the coverage.) The search for a diversity of opinions in this volume is also distinct, since most such collections tend to only include "literary" writers from within academic

walls, or "established writers"—both of which categories become reductive and exclusionary. Thus, the northwest canon is being expanded and revised in this book, with essays by Mark Halperin, Vern Rutsala, Tess Gallagher, Paul Pintarich, Vi Gale, Richard Hoyt, M. K. Wren, William Kittredge, Laura Jensen, Charles Deemer, Lawson Inada, Madeline DeFrees, Sam Hamill, and Robert Wrigley.

The effort to support the Hugo Memorial Scholarship Fund is a final signal that these editors have seen the need to make public and traditional a means of formal support for northwest writing students. While the northwest has a massive investment in financially supporting the literature of Great Britain and Europe, it has practically no formal investment in supporting northwest writers and writing.

Thus, Runciman and Sher have seen the tenuous literary situation in the northwest and seen it clearly. They recognized that autobiographies by northwest writers can be counted on one hand, and that collections of letters by northwest writers on one finger. (Rumor has it that the University of Idaho is about to publish H. L. Davis' letters—a first.) There are few serious literary biographies of northwest writers and poets. There has been no comprehensive literary history written in the northwest since 1930. Northwest classics, such as *The Surrounded* (D'arcy McNickle), *Big Jim Turner* (James Stevens), and *Honey In The Horn* (H. L. Davis), have all gone out of print and then been reprinted outside the northwest. Literature is the least-supported of any of the state arts programs in the territory. *Northwest Variety* attempts to fill some of those voids.

At first glance, their reflections show a collection of writers and poets who seem to have no sense of a shared region. However, the volume shows that there are shared assumptions in *Northwest Variety*, assumptions worth listing here since readers may themselves be searching for that elusive northwest core, that unarticulated sense of literary community that the editors were perhaps hoping to discover. Thus, a brief *Status Rerum* for the northwest in 1987, some 50 years after the first, published by Davis and Stevens in 1927. Northwest writers and poets are more or less aware of one or more of the following:

- All seem to believe they are faced with the task of inventing a context for themselves and their work. Simultaneously, there are also a lot of efforts to avoid any context that is northwestern. Thus, the real paradox of the volume.

- At this edge of the continent, the domesticating and endangering of an Edenic landscape generates a sense both of territoriality and paradoxically a sense of loss of that pristine world we inherited. While the last great forests fall, we lament their falling on paper made from them.

- We face four ways: the Far East of Asia, its culture, images, and immigrants, and the Far East of New York, its publishing industries, critics, and agents; to the south, we are aware of a moral border; to the north, an international border that we should know more about. None of those directions can be ignored.

- We are also intensely conscious of a 3-dimensional spectacular cosmos: sea, mountains, plains. West-running rivers make the connections among these. We are dry sage in wind, we are cedars in fog. Salmon hold us together; dams also generate doubt.

- There is an uncompromising sense of cultural pluralism that derives from Native American influences, early and recent immigration, cultural sophistication, and the mixing of these. This sense of pluralism is also international in scope, influence, and interest. Paradoxically, that cultural pluralism does not extend itself to support for cultural pluralism as it translates into regionalism. There is only an unsteady and suspicious embrace of, say, the well-documented U.S. cultural differences among the northeast, south, southwest, midwest, California, and the Rocky Mountain west. Still becoming aware of ourselves, we are only comfortable with ethnic diversity.

- There is a profound sense of isolation from the literary centers—also the population and publishing centers in the east—and being "out here" on a cultural frontier makes the siren song of success sound loudly from **Anywhere**, and makes the need to be connected with or pretending to **Sophistication Else-where** essential. Paradoxically, there is the belief that good writing can occur anywhere and always transcends its context.

- There is the need to construct, discover, or import a usable past which means inventing for ourselves a history (family, literary, or personal) that allows us to take ourselves seriously as writers, and which also means inventing for ourselves some relationship to place, which, paradoxically, may mean rejecting—through critique—much that is northwestern.

Northwest Variety is a very important exercise in literary self-examination. While the essays are somewhat uneven in both writing and thinking, this is an essential collection for anyone anywhere. Runciman and Sher will be thanked for this volume by serious readers for years to come. What we need most—criticism, history, biography, and autobiography—they have gathered.

Northwest Variety shows the present in northwest writing: a highly-diversified and talented literary community which has won all national awards available to writers (see *Contemporary Northwest Writing* (Roy Carlson, OSU Press) but a literary community which has not effectively asserted itself as a community since about 1939; it has granted to scholars the primary act of definition, which they have not yet done: the last history of Oregon literature was published in 1930; and the northwest literary community has not made any specific efforts to perpetuate itself. In fact, the opposite seems to be true. Outside of a few symposia whose proceedings have been published, this book attempts to address many of the most important issues in northwest literature for the first time. An ambitious and worthy task.

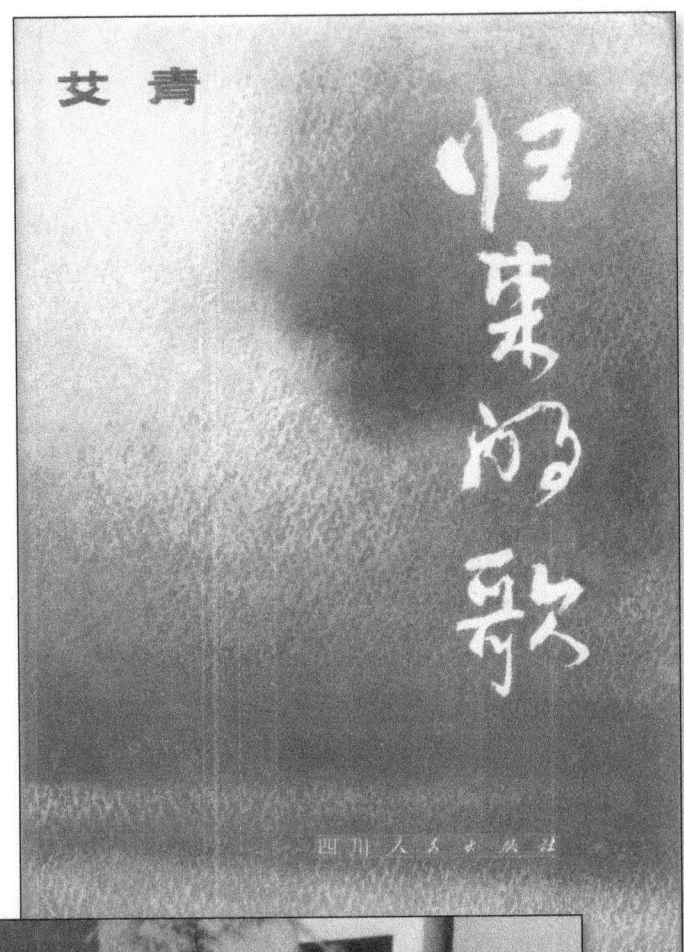

CHAPTER 20 | Chinese Poet's Biography (1984)

Preface to

THE PARADOX OF AI QING

On January 29, 1979, President Carter and Chinese President Deng Xiaoping established full diplomatic relations. About a year later, after being twice rejected for tenure by the Eastern Oregon University president, I answered a Chinese Foreign Experts Bureau ad for English instructors. Falling out with Russia and opening to The West, English had replaced Russian as China's official second language. Everyone, even old Russian teachers, wanted to learn English now. I was hired. In August, 1981, my wife and children and I flew to China to teach at what is now Central South University in Changsha. By December, to escape difficult living conditions, my wife and children flew to Australia. After the new year, Liu Pei Wu, Dean of Foreign Languages, and I agreed to translate a sheaf of poems from *Songs for Coming Home* (1980) by the modern Chinese poet Ai Qing. When we wrote to Ai Qing about a proposed bilingual edition of his work, he approved, and sent us a signed copy of his book (left). With only superficial biography, we translated sixteen poems. Returning to the states via Beijing, I interviewed the poet at his apartment (left). Back in Oregon, I realized my collaborator had effaced the poet's experience. Seeking justice for both poet and translations, I researched the essay below, submitted the entire manuscript to University of Washington editor Don Ellegood and to *Northwest Review* editor John Witte. On May 22, 1984, Witte replied: "We would like to use part of this marvelous submission of Ai Qing's work for the forthcoming issue." (Most recently, Ai Qing's son, Ai Weiwei, continues his father's rebellion. See "At Large: Ai Weiwei on Alcatraz." September 27, 2014–April 26, 2015 at Alcatraz Island.)

Source: *Northwest Review* (Fall,1984):100-105 (poems translated from *Songs for Coming Home* with Lu Pei Wu) and 107-115 (essay).

THE PARADOX OF AI QING

In 1912, two years after the poet Ai Qing was born, the last Chinese emperor abdicated and the people of China began half a century of political, military, and artistic conflict. This turmoil defined Ai Qing later, but did not affect his early years. A landlord's son, he studied painting, then abandoned art school as a freshman and sailed to Paris where he studied for three years. Returning home in 1932 as Japan's policy toward China was growing more hostile, Ai Qing joined radical organizations in Shanghai and was eventually arrested. During his two years in jail, he wrote his first memorable poem, "Dayanhe." By the time the Anti-Japanese War began in 1937, Ai Qing had become a leftist poet sympathetic—as were many writers—to the cause of China's liberation from the invading Japanese army. His humane sympathies, his interest in artistic freedom, his interest in social reform all came to temporary resolution in 1941 when the young idealistic poet escaped the Kuomintang and joined the Communist movement in Yenan.[1]

To this isolated Communist camp in Shensi Province, many Chinese writers and artists—full of hope and confidence—retreated, partly because of effective Communist war leadership, partly because the mountains were a refuge from chaos, and partly because writers there could safely continue to attack the Japanese. In Yenan, Ai Qing and his most accomplished contemporaries talked with Mao Zedong and continued to write and publish freely. However, in March and April, 1942, the scene began to change.

Ting Ling, Ai Qing, Lo Feng, Wang Shih-wei, and Hsiao Chun all published writing during these two months which contained literary attitudes dangerous to Communist ideology. One of the main literary offenders in Yenan was Ai Qing.

In his article, "Understand Authors, Respect Authors," published on March 11, 1942, Ai Qing stated that

> The writer is the recorder of emotions, the nerve or the eye of wisdom of a nation, i.e., in the sphere of emotions, impressions, thoughts, and mental action, the loyal soldier who protects the nation or class to which he belongs. In his work, the writer crystallizes his own and other people's impressions, emotions, and thoughts in imaginative language, and through this language he sums up the whole life of his people or class and introduces order into it.

Thus, the writer was seen by Ai Qing as an independent spiritual force. A leading critic further summarized that Ai Qing

> considers self-examination or self-respect as the aim of literature. He is also of the opinion that a poem, a novel, or a drama may have the political effect of an increase of inner determination to overcome the enemy, but he denies any tangible utility to literature... Ai Qing thinks that the writer should attend spiritual health as a physician attends to physical health . . . Ai Qing demands that the writer's only privilege be freedom to write and the opportunity to work independently...[2]

Two months after this essay appeared, Mao Zedong called the Yenan Forum to "exchange views" with more than two hundred Chinese artists and writers. This apparent dialogue finally became a Stalinist monologue by Mao Zedong, who issued his now famous *Talks At the Yenan Forum on Literature and Art* the day the forum ended. In part, Mao's statements repudiated Ai Qing's independent view. Instead of separating art from politics, Mao Zedong declared the Communist Party's prescription for the political control of literature, a position which, generally, still governs Chinese writers today. The following brief quotes and precis summarize Mao's utilitarian views:[3]

- *social position*: literature and art should "fit properly into the whole revolutionary machine as one of its component parts."

- *social function:* "literature and art should awaken and arouse the masses and impel them to unite and struggle to change their environment."

- *audience:* "literature and art must serve the broad masses of workers, peasants, soldiers, and urban petty bourgeoisie" and elevate their cultural level.

- *point of* view: to serve the masses, we "must take the stand of the proletariat," use "socialist realism," and adopt Party spirit.

- *correct style*: literature and art must use simple language, as in posters, folksongs, folk tales and must use national forms and national styles.

- *artists' lives*: "all revolutionary writers and artists must for long periods of time, unreservedly and wholeheartedly, go into the midst of the masses . . . of workers, peasants, and soldiers."

- *correct subject and tone:* "all dark forces which endanger the masses must be exposed while revolutionary struggles of the masses must be praised."

- *taboo subject:* "these works which depict the so-called 'dark side' of the proletariat are certainly poor."

- *evaluation:* "every class in every society places the political criterion first and the artistic criterion second"; thus a work of art is judged for its correct political thinking before its aesthetic qualities.

- *final purpose:* "But will Marxism not destroy any creative impulse? It will; it will certainly destroy the creative impulse that is feudal, bourgeois, petty-bourgeois, liberal, individualistic, nihilistic, art-for-art's sake, aristocratic, decadent, or pessimistic and any creative impulse that is not of the people and of the proletariat. As far as the writers and artists of the proletariat are concerned, ought not these kinds of impulses to be done away with? I think they ought; they should be utterly destroyed, and while they are being destroyed, new things can be built up."

Thus, Ai Qing had suddenly become a military-artistic recruit in an army whose leaders' views on literature directly violated his own. Autobiographical evidence suggests that he may have been converted to Mao's vision of literature, yet as early as 1939 he'd written that "the sound of poetry is the sound of freedom. Suppression of the people's speech is the most cruel oppression." Just before the Yenan Forum, he published a collection of essays, *On Poetry,* which was "distinguished by its independent thinking and its awareness that language is the only material of poetry." Nevertheless, he seems to have accepted the Party's literary policy and by that drumbeat he began to march. He taught at the Party's literary academy in Yenan until 1945, edited the Party's poetry magazine, published new books, and became a serious student of Marxism. In 1945, he became a full-fledged member of the Communist Party.

After the Communist armies triumphed in 1949, Ai Qing was appointed to important positions in the new government—editor, organizer, administrator. His visibility increased. He explained Party arts policies in essays, published new books of propagandistic verse, traveled to Japan, Chile, and the Soviet Union. He saw his work translated into ten languages. His *Selected Poems* appeared in 1951. He savoured popular acclaim because his work was simple, compassionate, and clear. He enjoyed Party patronage, partly because he'd been able to follow the prescriptions of Yenan, and partly because he'd been able to write convincing war poetry—*Face The Sun* and *Torch*. Unlike other writers who had made their opposition to the Yenan prescription obvious—Hu Feng is the best example—Ai Qing seemed to have made his transformation complete. However, he had failed—by his own admission—to write any successful new poems by socialist rules between 1942 and 1945:

> In this period, my creative style underwent immense change. I became acquainted with a few heroes from the working class and wrote some journalistic essays. I learned to write poetry using the folk-song forms. Since most of these are mere exercises produced during the process of learning, I decided not to include them in my collection.[4]

A paradoxical image of a major Communist Chinese poet begins to unfold here—a man serving simultaneously the Communist prescription for literature and his own aesthetic. This commitment to two masters—perhaps three if, 'the people' is added—would eventually combine to bring him down, then cast him out for twenty years of exile and silence.

In March, 1956, the attack on Ai Qing quietly began. Along with other writers accused by the Party of resisting political control over literature, Ai Qing was singled out at the Second Session of the Council of Chinese Writers Union for his failure to bring back from the Korean War front at Chusan a poem praising the heroes of naval defense squadrons. Instead, Ai Qing had written *Black Eel,* an epic poem with a "folkloristic love story as its theme." "How we long for good poems written by him and by other older poets," a high Party leader despaired.[5] There followed shortly the Hundred Flowers Policy, a campaign which brought about great literary activity and permitted the view to develop that literature might be comprised of more than the prescriptions of Yenan. Ai Qing was considered to be a leader in a group which advocated revising the Party's literary policies. In July, 1956, *On Poetry,* his book which had appeared just before the Yenan Forum and was repudiated by Mao in 1942, was reprinted in Beijing. While Ai Qing acted as a go-between for writers such as Ting Ling, who were also coming under attack during this period for their outspoken opposition to the Party's prescription, he himself kept silent, apparently working behind the scenes for revision of the Party's absolute control.

However, in September, 1957, he was finally attacked himself for his "unhealthy emotions," "bourgeois individualism," and for an absence of "political enthusiasm." He was further accused of promiscuous relations with women, put under surveillance by the Party, then sentenced to half a year of menial work. Early in 1958, he was critically attacked by a more orthodox Party poet, Feng Chih, whose rebuttal of Ai Qing's "Understand Authors, Respect Authors," served as the public hatchet to Ai Qing's literary position. Later in that same year, Feng Chih reviewed Ai Qing's poetry, labeling it "reactionary formalism" which violated the prescriptions of Yenan, especially in its "cosmopolitan" dimension. He also charged that Ai Qing's poems lacked a "plain message" for the people, failed to create a convincing "positive" hero, and demeaned the workers, peasants, and soldiers. He was quickly excommunicated from the Party, and along with thousands of other Chinese intellectuals, he was sentenced to manual labor in the countryside.[6]

Twenty years later, the poet described this sudden reversal in a brief auto-biography:

> In April, 1958, with the help of a general and the consent of Premier Zhou Enlai, I went to a state farm in the northeast to "observe and learn from real life." I was deputy head of a tree farm and spent a year and a half there living together with lumberjacks. During my stay I wrote two long poems. Unfortunately, both works were lost.
>
> In the winter of 1959, 1 went to Xinjiang where I spent sixteen years in a reclamation area with production and construction corps.[7]

These five sentences written in 1978 gleam with monumental and symbolic silence, with paradox become bitter irony. What happened? Obviously, he'd become a prisoner of the revolution that he thought would free him and free China, a prisoner also of the Yenan prescriptions he'd apparently subscribed to in the chaos of 1942. While the poet has intentionally obscured these twenty years, the "Lost Years" as they are called in the text,[8] it is possible to piece together some of what lies behind this grim face-saving prose.

As a convicted "rightist"[9] sent down to the countryside for "re-education from the masses," Ai Qing was first removed from all of his official responsibilities, including the editorial board of *Shih Kan* (Poetry) from which he disappeared in 1957. Of course, he would also be required to dismember his household: abandon his personal library, give away his life-long collection of cactus, leave behind family, friends, and relatives. Also, in reducing himself to a "cultural worker" in the Big Leap Forward, he would be cut off from an active literary career which had made him one of China's most popular poets—loved even among the illiterate—and exile would also cut him off from his growing international audience. Like other poets in Chinese history, he was sent to the most remote, primitive, and isolated frontier region available—the Bei Da Huang area in Xinjiang along the Soviet-Chinese border. In exile, he was "assigned to the latrine detail and slept in a cellar."[10] With two minor exceptions—a children's story and lyrics for one song—he was for twenty years totally silenced as a poet publishing in China. Access to libraries, foreign press, or periodicals were largely denied him.

All his manuscripts from exile—with a few exceptions—he describes as "lost." How many poems? He himself would not say. While he was allowed to continue to write in exile, apparently all or most of his manuscripts were confiscated or otherwise destroyed. In 1978, he returned from Xinjiang blind in his right eye, partly because he wasn't allowed to come to Beijing for treatment for three years after his cataract condition had been diagnosed in 1972.

When the Gang of Four fell in 1977, Ai Qing and his wife were finally allowed to permanently return to Beijing. In April, 1978, his first poem in twenty years, "Red Flag," appeared in a Shanghai newspaper. Little by little, the moderate government of Deng Xiao Ping made the poet's reinstatement a symbolic act of redress. Again, Ai Qing was granted a passport and traveled to Europe and the United Sates. His *Selected Poems* appeared in China in 1979, and the bilingual version edited by Eugene Chen-Eoyang has recently appeared in the United States and China. Ai Qing was also restored to positions in the federal arts establishment, including the editorial board of China's leading poetry magazine, *Shih Kan*. Again, he enjoys access to friends, relatives, libraries. Now, at 72, he lives with his wife, Gao Ying, in a hotel suite in Beijing while waiting for his home quarters to be completed.[11]

His first book of new poems written after his return was *Songs for Coming Home* (Sichuan People's Press, 1980). Even the book's introduction, "A Poet Must Tell the Truth," reasserts the old paradox in Ai Qing's vision—the conflict between concrete individual feelings and the prescriptions of political life. While he can write a common Marxist view that a poet "must identify with the people, share their feelings and draw his wisdom and courage from them ... and must have 'political sensitivity' which should agree with the desire of the people," Ai Qing can also state the more dangerous individualistic view that

> a poet should be loyal to what he feels. What is called 'feeling' is but the reflection of the objective world. Of course, telling truth may cause you some trouble, even some danger. But to write poems, if you really want to, means never telling lies against your conscience.

Chapter 20 • THE PARADOX OF AI QING

For Ai Qing, such paradoxical statements are not new and should not be surprising. They began early in his life when, as a student returned from Paris, he had
separated art from life. He carried that dualism to Yenan where, when confronted
by Mao Zedong's prescription, he seemed to become a good literary soldier for
the revolution. However, he apparently could never quite abandon his view of life
as separate from art, or his view of life as laden with necessary opposites—one of
which is art. Those complexities finally caused his exile for twenty years in Xinjiang. Now returned, paradox still seems to rise naturally from most of his new poems. His artistic terms—like the terms of experience—always modify each other.
He seems to remind us that there is no single absolute.

Five Poems By Ai Qing Translated By Lu Pei Wu And George Venn

Fish Fossil

The way you darted
The way you leaped, shimmering
From swell to swell
Free to dive deep or swim

Then, bad luck. The volcano? Ground swell?
Some upheaval boomed.
Your play and flash all smothered
In evolutionary ash—your tomb.

Billions of years later
A new federal assayer hammered
Found you, life-like as ever
In some remote dark stratum

But you're hushed now
Not even a breath
Scales and fins all perfect
Petrified, petrified.

You're all inert
Your give and taking gone
No vision for sky or wave.
An ear for surf left? None.

Staring at just one piece of you
Any numbskull can see that
Arrested movement means
Slow obscure hardening to death.

The living need to strive
To act, to move, go on
Then die
Like candlefish who burn, burn...

"Fish Fossil." *Lithograph from* Songs for Coming Home *(Sichuan People's Publishing Co., Chengdu, 1980): page 13. The image by an unknown artist symbolizes the poet's initial freedom and the effects of twenty-year exile.*

Hail

Hides inside a storm
Hangs out with thunderheads

Like gangs of grasshoppers
Yells wrack and blood

Gets with the blitz
Gets with heavy rumbling

Hits fast
Pulls out quick
What's left
A real nightmare

Beat limbs
Busted glass all over

Shot-out streetlights
Everyone cussing, moaning

Persian Chrysanthemums

Red, fuchsia, white
These flowers numerous, exquisite
Like night-scattered stars
Hovering above Daqing

In the oil drillers' yard
By the guesthouse door
Beside the refinery road
These flowers sing for autumn now

Those years in Yenan
Before the caves at Yangjialing
Qaorgou, Wangjiaping, Zhaoyuan
These flowers grew—fair as girls

Who knows who brought them
These seeds from Yenan to Daqing?
Wherever these flowers bloom
They remind us still—Yenan

Burning the Wasteland Grass

Small, small—just one match
Strikes open this frontier

Empty steppes—ocean of flames
Ah, god, what a fire

Red blazing pillars writhe
and, flare—gone for glory

More fleet than any wind
Flames leap like gold driven deer

Smoke billows at the sun
A rush of crimson cloud takes form

Wildfire laughs amuck
Through underbrush goes great

Fire marches right, left
And trembling lives retreat

This feral grass must fall
Before spring grain can rise

Now, sharpen our bright plows
And open these new fields to time

The Lost Years

Not like losing a bundle
Waiting at the lost and found
Lost years
Can't find where they went—
Disappeared bit by bit
Lost twenty years ago
Lost in hubbub cities
Lost on far empty steppes
In rush hour stations
By lone kerosene lanterns
Lost years
Aren't scattered pages you may gather
More like water poured on loess
Dried—not even a stain left
Time's stream
Can't be dredged or seined
Time's never solidified
If fossilized, it could
Centuries later, be a shape in rock
Time's all evanescence
Like smoke from a driven train
Lost years
Are like a friend
Who suffered. You lost touch
Suddenly, news from somewhere comes
He's long long gone.

Preface to

CAROLYN KIZER AT CANNON BEACH:
A 1981 INTERVIEW WITH TIM BARNES

During graduate school, I read Carolyn Kizer for the first time in *Five Poets of the Pacific Northwest* (1964). Later, I found her July 1956 article, "Poetry: the School of the Pacific Northwest" in *The New Republic*—a declaration that she and other Theodore Roethke students had become prime movers in the teaching and practice and publication of regional poetry. In 1959, she—along with Errol Pritchard, Nelson Bentley, Richard Hugo, and Edith Shiffert—founded *Poetry Northwest*; in 1960 she published her first poetry collection *The Ungrateful Garden*. A year later, she became the first director of the Literature Program for the National Endowment for the Arts, and became a major figure in American poetry—books, prizes, honorary degrees.

Tim Barnes and I met and became friends during the Portland Poetry Festival. A professor and poet teaching undergraduate composition, literature, and creative writing at Portland Community College, Barnes and I shared similar positions and interests in original writing, Arts-in-Education, literary publications, and western American literature. On one occasion sometime between 1982 and 1983, Barnes showed me his rough transcript of his 1981 taped interview with Carolyn Kizer. By coincidence, I had booked Kizer for an April 4, 1984 Ars Poetica reading at Eastern Oregon University. Seeing the possibility of enriching and publishing helpful background details about Kizer, I offered to edit Barnes' rough transcript, then show the edited draft to Kizer when she read in La Grande. Barnes approved. I set about formatting, editing, retyping, then sent the edited text to Barnes. He approved my polishing.

On April 4, 1984, the afternoon before her second Ars Poetica reading—she first read at EOU in 1966—I gave that edited draft to Kizer. Sitting at my desk in Inlow Hall, she read every page and approved the text—critical in one passage of poetic bureaucrats—for publication in *Oregon East* (1950–1985). In September, 1988, when I asked her permission to reprint this interview in a northwest anthology, Kizer agreed with one qualification: "if you omit the comments about the Iowa Writers Workshop. Things change in time, sometimes even for the better. Fifteen years have passed. Gerry Stern is not Marvin Bell!" The version below observes her requested omission. While this manuscript was being prepared for publication, Carolyn Kizer passed away in October 2014.

Source: *Oregon East* 15. (1985): 133-142; Tim Barnes photo courtesy Ilka Kuznick; Carolyn Kizer photo courtesy Thomas Victor and Carolyn Kizer.

CAROLYN KIZER AT CANNON BEACH: A 1981 INTERVIEW WITH TIM BARNES

Barnes: What do you think about doing poetry workshops?

Kizer: Workshops have a value. Their most important function is to give people a little distance on their own work. You can achieve much the same effect by throwing a poem in a bureau drawer and not looking at it for six months. But if somebody is able to give you a detached view of it, a kind of critical objectivity, show you certain techniques of revision, you can make a lot of improvements. The two classes I've had already (both in Newport) were very different, but also had some curious similarities: the first day consisted of people who had some talent, but weren't very experienced, so all I did was talk about language and sentence structure. The second day I had people who had been published a bit and could manage the basic structure of language. Then I talked about getting the poem to move across the page, to have either a dramatic or dialectical form. So, I was busy ripping things apart and putting them back together again in various curious ways. It was a totally different process from one day to the next and that is one of the things that keeps the teacher interested. Also, occasionally, you find somebody who has really got it. I was lucky enough yesterday to have a woman who is by God going to become a good poet.

I started teaching in 1970, when I was middle-aged, and I am lucky I didn't teach when I was younger. It's obvious that today we have people graduating from poetry workshops and going into teaching with no intermediate stops. They don't have any life experience, nothing interesting happens to them. They go from being students to teachers and, by and large, their poetry is dead and boring. Unlike the poets of my generation, you can't tell these younger players without a program. You can recognize the difference among the voices of Denise Levertov, James Wright, Galway Kinnell, Gary Snyder, and Adrienne Rich. You don't even need to look at the bottom of the page. But with your pure workshop product, for the most part, there is a deadly sameness. They write about the same things in the same way. It's mostly this sort of unstructured free verse delivered in a grey, matter-of-fact voice.

I think my generation is lucky because we're not the products of poetry workshops. I took a course from Theodore Roethke—this was in the middle 1950s—but Roethke's emphasis was on *reading* poetry which I think is sound. His class was called "How To Read a Poem." It was not like the contemporary workshop, where the primary emphasis is not on how to write, but how to get published and how to learn how to suck up to influential people. It's the politics of literature that is being taught *nowadays* for the most part. I disapprove violently of this. People shouldn't start trying to publish, shouldn't start trying to make a name for themselves before they know how to put a decent poem together. Of course, there are exceptions to this, but I think this is the general thrust of many of the famous workshops.

Barnes: Your work has dealt with loss—I see it in "Chinese Imitations" and "A Month in Summer." How do you manage to capture that bittersweetness so well?

Kizer: It's very difficult to express suffering and/or loss in poetry without sounding self-pitying, without uttering inarticulate shrieks. What I really did then was find a vehicle, through the forms of another culture, through which to express pain and loss. That gave me a way to mute, control, and discipline the work which—on my own—would probably have disintegrated into something less attractive than I would like to have appear in public. Now that I am really into joy, I don't have those preoccupations, but I find I still like to write a formal poem.

There is always this confusion in the public mind between the life and the work. One has to be careful not to forget that distinction. We must honor the convention of the persona in even the most overtly confessional poet. But it is true that we discharge pain into the work and relieve our life of it. Sometimes I'm shocked when people say, "Oh you must have been suffering terribly at that period." And I say, "Who? Me?" I don't ever want to be caught advocating poetry as catharsis or as therapy, but certainly experience and pain are somehow defused by writing about them. It never hurts quite that badly again, and sometimes you really don't want to give up the pain if it is a precious relic or a valued experience. If you're in mourning for someone you've lost, you realize you are going to diminish some of the charge of that emotional experience by writing about it—to quote myself (in "Not Writing Poems About Children"), the deliberate "sacrifice to a cold stanza." You just decide the poem is more important than the suffering.

Of course, we're all so multifaceted that part of us could be hurting while part of us is jumping up and down having a good time and sending up balloons. It depends on which segment of yourself you happen to be dealing with at the time. One of the things about writers that drives non-writers nuts is that in some situations, such as a passionate love scene or a passionate renunciation scene, the other person realizes that part of the writer is watching and taking notes. That makes them think that there is a certain lack of commitment there, but this is not necessarily true. The two acts can go on at the same time. This is one of the things that makes a writer: these trains leaving on two tracks simultaneously—the watching track and the operating track.

Barnes: I haven't seen your work in many places these days. Are you publishing much right now?

Kizer: I don't send out a lot. I get lazy about that, and also I get more interested in writing poetry than I do seeing it in print, but I have a new book which is nearly finished. I have to retype it and God knows how long that'll take because I'm probably the world's leading compulsive reviser. I couldn't agree more with Valery who said "a poem is never finished, just abandoned." It is very hard for me to let go. I had the same difficulty when I was pregnant.

Barnes: Where was "Pro Femina" published in full?

Kizer: It has never been published in full.

Barnes: Will there be more sections?

Kizer: Who knows? Quite possibly. When I published it, I said, "From Pro Femina" because I thought, well, this could go on and on. It did not go on, but let's not slam the door, eh? I agree not only with that statement of Valery's but I agree with the general notion that one writes *one* poem in one's life. What you do is drop in the pieces at various times. It's like doing a jigsaw puzzle. You say "'Well, there's a large hole here in the shape of North Dakota. Now can I write North Dakota and drop it in there?" Sometimes, you can and sometimes you can't. I'm not a bit infected with the need to have a book every other year. A number of my dear contemporaries who happen to be friends of mine are writing books that they really shouldn't have published. They weren't ready. The poems weren't good enough, but they feel that pressure to stay in the public eye. I've never been very ambitious in the worldly sense. I think I'm terribly ambitious about the work. I'm not one to see something in print that is going to cover me with blushes. And, I've always spent a lot of time being happy and having love affairs and a good time generally.

Barnes: How do you feel about the relationship between living and the writing?

Kizer: Well, by God, you'd better do some living, you know. One of the poets I most admire among my contemporaries is the poet C. K. Williams. Do you know a book called *With Ignorance?*

Barnes: He has another one, too.

Kizer: Oh God, I know. I went out and paid a king's ransom to buy his early books when I read *With Ignorance* because I just went bananas over it. Now, there's a man who is living. He's hanging out with people in taverns who have been to Vietnam and are beating their wives and are in trouble with the police. It's real urban grit. It's what life is like for most people and I really dig it. I think Levine gets into quite a bit of real grit, although Phil does it by diving into his own past a lot. I admire Williams because he's not just sitting in his study chewing his pencil thinking about how to revise the fourth stanza. He's out there talking and listening. I don't know why he is not a household word.

A couple of years ago I was reading to lifers in the Oregon State prison's maximum security section. I said, "Don't tell me what anybody did. I don't want to know." I knew they were all multiple rapists and murderers. A finer bunch of guys you could never hope to meet. I somehow felt my poetry wasn't quite the thing for them, so I read them C. K. Williams. They just went apeshit, they loved it. I always meant to write Williams and tell him about them and I regret to say that I haven't gotten around to doing that yet.

Gary Snyder and I both feel there has to be a way of extending the audience without compromising the poetry. I think there are all sorts of ways of doing it. A lot of it has to do with subject matter. You don't have to write like Rod McKuen or Erica Jong, whom I'm carefully mentioning in the same breath, but I think a lot of their appeal is in the ability of the audience to identify with them.

Barnes: How did you like being Director of the Literature Program of the National Endowment for the Arts?

Kizer: I loved it. For two reasons. I've told this story already, but not here. When I applied for the job and got it, I was sitting in a restaurant on University Way in Seattle with a bunch of my friends. Somebody said, "Carolyn, why did you apply for that job?" And another friend said "Well, you know how idealistic she is. She wanted to go and help people." Somebody else said, "Is that why you did it?" I said, "No, I want power! I want to know what it feels like. I've never had any!" That was the honest answer. I did enjoy it very much.

Barnes: How long were you there?

Kizer: Well, Nixon fired my boss, Roger Stevens, who ran the Endowment and I quit the next day. Some little Watergate creep sent for Roger and said "You can clear out your desk on Monday." I think it was Gordon Strachan. Stevens had been working for nothing. I saw him at a party that night at his house, and he was just gray. So I marched in Monday morning and said, "Get me a Form 57." That's the form you quit on. And I thought "Shit, if I know the number, I better get out of here. Been a bureaucrat long enough."

The Endowment was a new agency. There were no rules, no regulations. You made up programs; you flew by the seat of your pants. You tried it, and if it didn't work, you tried something else. Must have been very much like the early days of the New Deal when you went by what Roosevelt called "trial and error." Nobody ever had had a federal arts program in this country before, so we had no precedents. Poetry-in-the-Schools? Yah. That would be good. How about prisons? What about subsidies to fine presses? And then we'd go storming in to Roger Stevens and say "Why don't we do this?" He'd say, "Oh God, if I let you do this, the next thing you'll be doing is poetry for paraplegics," and I'd say "Dynamite. Let's try it." No matter how outrageous the plan, he would always let me have a shot at it. He was fussy about who he picked though, and then when he chose people he had faith in them and let them run. So, he was great to work for. You know that old saying that "No man is a hero to his valet." Supposedly, if you ever work for someone, you see the soft underbelly and you don't believe in them anymore. In the case of Roger Stevens, who is now running the Kennedy Center, this was absolutely not true. I idolized that man. If he called up tomorrow and said, "Uhh, I have good reasons for asking you to go to Ouagadougou and establish a ballet company," I'd say "OK, send me the ticket." I have blind faith in him. He's a marvelous man.

Barnes: In Washington, the politics of art was not so hard on you?

Kizer: Well, you see it got bad later, but when I was there it was fun. Stevens also said, "Let's not have a lot of complicated forms and stuff. If people are going to apply for grants, let them fill out one page," and I certainly agree with that. Then, it turned into octuplicate, you know... nine sheets of this and blah, blah, blah. The way things happen in bureaucracies. The little men in the back room, the people whose jobs depend on shuffling paper, the lawyers and the standard bureaucrats take over. So I was there in the halcyon period when there was a lot of excitement generated. We had a wonderful time. We were very understaffed and overworked, and we didn't have any money. We really had to improvise a lot. The literary budget was $80,000 for the whole country including every state. What can you do with $80,000? You can do a lot, and we did it. Now they've got millions, and they haven't had a new idea in ten years.

Barnes: How would you see the Endowment and the Literature Program now?
Kizer: Well, I don't really think it would be tactful of me to talk about that. It might sound like sour grapes, and also I don't want to knock them while Reagan is after them. Reagan may allow a few shards and fragments. What I suspect Reagan will do is continue institutional support to opera houses and symphonies and art museums—the big stuff—so that the big Republican contributors to these things won't feel the necessity to give to the arts. Then they can concentrate on the really important work of life which is raising money for Reagan, right? This government is subsidizing art for the rich, which I think is ridiculous. At any rate, our arts program is still just a drop in the bucket compared even to a country that is tottering on the brink of bankruptcy like Great Britain. I read some statistic the other day: our entire theatre program for the NEA is less than the British contribute for the National Theatre alone.

One thing the NEA has done is to stimulate grants from the private sector by these challenge grants, and corporate giving has increased by leaps and bounds. But the trouble with corporations and foundations is that they're terrible cowards, and they have no taste, and they want their judgment validated by the federal government saying "It's OK to give money to them because they're OK," and then they'll do it. But if you go in to them cold and say, "We've got this great innovative program here, Judy Garland and Mickey Rooney are going to start a theatre in the barn," the Ford Foundation says, "Get lost." If the government comes in and says, "Well, we'll put up forty thou, if you put up forty thou," then that's OK. It makes it respectable and there's no question of the corporate and foundation creeps having to make value judgments which they're terrified of doing anyway. You know that's the good part of the Federal arts program. But to criticize it in any detail, I think, would not be the thing to do at this particular moment.

Barnes: What are you working on now?

Kizer: Well, I don't know. I never know what is going to come next. Of the poems I've written recently, one is addressed to God, one is about the children of the sixties, one is a love poem to my husband to whom I've been married for six years. I'm sure they form a pattern but I haven't seen it yet. I'm interested in the whole genre of writing about women's lives, particularly women who were attached to famous men as servants, lovers, mothers, sisters, whatever. This is a feminist concern, a subject I find very interesting. One great thing about being a woman writer: there is so much that hasn't been written. You really feel like an adventurer going out to discover new lands or territo-

Carolyn Kizer and W. S. Merwin, NCTE Conference, New Orleans, 1966.
(William Stafford photo)

ries. We were talking about that this morning in the car, about how a lot of people are made uncomfortable by the personal, intimate quality of a lot of women's writing. Well, they better get used to it because women are trying to say things that have never been said before and I think it's very exciting. Of course, there's a lot of bad writing, a lot of self-pity, a lot of anger. On the whole, I'm most interested in character, the impact of one person or situation on another. That subject hasn't been dealt with much in poetry since Browning. I like to deal with it.

Barnes: Did you find that character is a subject women seem to explore well?

Kizer: I wish they did. No, I don't think so, not at present. They're still trying to explore feelings or attitudes which have been considered taboo or just unexpressed. Also, because I'm writing autobiographical essays and reading a number of books on male autobiography, it struck me that distinguished men tend to write a cleaned up, edited version of themselves as they wish to appear to posterity. Now, I don't feel any interest in that kind of character exploration at all. The whole point of autobiography is to find out what happened, and to find out by being as truthful and honest about yourself as you possibly can, to explore the whole mystery of human relations. My mode is not to present to the future the way I want people to think of me, but to find out the truth about my parents, about my society, about the particular segment of history that I live in. In both prose and poetry it seems to me that you simply start at a given point and find out as you go along what you want to say, or what you need to say in a shapely way.

Barnes: What contemporary poets are writing like that?

Kizer: I don't pretend to keep up. I've never quite recovered from the fact that when I was at the Endowment, I read every issue of every literary magazine being published in the United States. I always staggered home with stacks of magazines, which were all over my bedroom, and read them all the time night and day. I really O.D.'d on literary magazines and for a while I couldn't look at one. I've sort of sneaked back in now. I read *Kayak, Antaeus, Shenando-*

ah, and just recently I've subscribed to *The Northwest Review,* which is good and lively these days. Also, some of the university quarterlies are interesting: *Georgia, Iowa, Ohio.* As to poets, I love Margaret Atwood; I think she's wonderful. She's dealing with the life experience of women and the history of male/female relationships in a way that interests me extremely. I think she is as gifted as anybody living.

Barnes: Prose and poetry both?

Kizer: The novels interest me a lot, but I'm talking about the poetry.

Barnes: Did you like Adrienne Rich's *A Dream of a Common Language?*

Kizer: I'm crazy about it. I find with her late poetry that the more you read it the more you like it. Even if I have an initial resistance to some of her ideas, and disagree with her, I think her poetry is magnificent. You succumb to its glory, and anyone who doesn't is simply not seriously reading poetry. They're prejudiced by her opinions and attitudes and they're letting that get in the way. Levertov is writing magnificently too. She's right at the top of her form. I heard her in San Francisco not long ago. It was overwhelming. I like Maxine Kumin's work. I like Louise Gluck. I like Olga Broumas a lot. I love Naomi Lazard. She's got two books. One is called *Ordinances,* a 1984ish book of poems written largely in the voice of someone very like Big Brother. It's a protest against the increased mechanization and bureaucratization of our lives. It's a dazzling book. The other book is called *The Moonlit Upper Deckerina,* poems about animals and about her mother and her sister . . . and her lovers. It's wonderful.

Barnes: How have the relationships between your work, marriage, love, children, worked out in your life?

Kizer: Between marriages, I had twenty years off for good behavior. I don't know if that's a world record, but I was divorced in 1955 and I remarried in 1975. At any rate, I was unmarried for a long time and I had little children whom I raised.

There used to be a feminist magazine called *Aphra*. They once wrote and asked me to do an essay on marriage, and the little conceit of my essay was that I kept trying to stay awake long enough to write an essay on marriage. It was filled with nice little aphorisms like, "Marriage is a nice place to visit, but I wouldn't want to live there," and various cracks like that. The piece ends, of course, with my falling asleep. In 1974 I was giving a reading in Baltimore, and I read this piece aloud. At the end of it I said, "I would like to take this opportunity to announce my engagement."

I still think marriage is boring. I still think it is an institution and I don't approve of institutions on the whole but ... these second marriages are great stuff, I'll tell you! or these late marriages. You've grown up; you're no longer trying to make the other person fulfill your dreams for you. You don't have those fantasies about what they are going to do for you. You're able to approach it from the point of view of companionship and sharing and fun and richness and adventure, but you're not putting that intolerable burden on the other person of fulfilling your fantasies. You're perfectly willing to take the responsibility for your own life. Until people do that, they shouldn't get married at all which I think is why this whole trend toward getting married and having babies in your thirties is terrific. The first marriage in our society has generally been a sort of graduate education: your practice time in learning how to be a civilized human being. That is an extraordinarily painful way of doing things. It would be a lot better if people could get themselves in shape before embarking on marriage rather than afterwards. I think things have gotten a lot more civilized in this country in the last few years. I told my husband I could not enter into a conventional marriage again. No way. It has to be a full partnership. I'm not about to go back and be a housewife at my age. Forget it, Jack. That's fine with him.

Barnes: How might you characterize a good partnership?

Kizer: Recently, I finished a poem on that subject—or perhaps, more accurately, it expresses the mood of a sublime relationship between equals. It was in-

spired by something Dick Hugo said to me on the telephone in 1975. We had both recently remarried, after a long drought. He said—and this is verbatim—"You spend your whole life developing a tragic vocabulary, and then look what happens!" My poem is called "Afternoon Happiness" and, like all poems which express emotion, particularly the emotion of joy, it was rejected by *The New Yorker*! My favorite bit, because of the nice rhymes, is:

> My former husband, that old disaster, is now just funny,
> So laugh we do, in what Cyril Connolly
> Has called 'the endless, nocturnal conversation
> Of marriage,' which may be the best part.
> Darling, must I love you in light verse
> Without the tribute of profoundest art?

I speak of light verse there, because I set myself, as a kind of exercise, to write a poem which begins lightly and humorously, and gradually becomes more serious and I hope profound. It ends this way:

> No, love, the heavy poems will have to come
> From *temps perdu,* fertile with pain, or perhaps,
> Detonated by terrors far beyond this place,
> Where the world rends itself, and its tainted waters
> Rise in the east, to erode our safety here.
> Much as I want to gather a lifetime thrift
> And craft, my cunning skills tied in a knot for you,
> There is only this useless happiness as gift.

Barnes: What gets you sitting down to write a poem?

Kizer: I think there are two things. One is a sense of outrage, passion that really drives you to the typewriter to do a poem. But then there's that other moment when a phrase, a vision, a memory, something physical, something visible, simply sets off a whole constellation of things. In other words, there is a kind of moment around which all sort of things from your past simply spring like nails to a magnet—what the old English critic Maude Bodkin called an "image cluster." The poem happens when you get that last piece that makes everything come together. To me, this is the true creative moment out of which the best poems come.

Don't you sometimes wonder how people cope with life who don't write poetry? They don't have any way of putting the pieces together, and no way to make sense out of life. But the sense that poetry makes out of life is only for the life of the poem. It's not a permanent acquisition by any means, but for that moment it works. All writing of poetry is an act of translation, because the poem is there inside you, and you're trying to get it out, but your vocabulary is inadequate. You do the best you can, but you almost never finish a poem with the sense that you've adequately translated that thing that was inside of you onto the page. On occasions when you come close, that's when you feel good. But most of the time, you realize that the poem is garbled and imperfect and you're not getting the whole thing out because you lack the language for it. In the same way, the vocabulary of dreams is quite different from the vocabulary of waking life, yet one feels in dream a profound truth about one's situation. One knows that our dreams are trying to educate us, trying to tell us what's happening to us, and we, with our inadequate, imperfect command of dream language, try to extract the sense from dreams that will help guide our lives. I think that relates very closely to what our poetry is trying to say.

Chapter 21 ▪ CAROLYN KIZER AT CANNON BEACH

CHAPTER 22 | Symposium Transcript (1980)

· ·

Preface to

NORTHWEST POETRY AND THE LAND
By Dr. Brian Attebery

A conference entitled "Northwest Poetry and the Land" was held on January 15 and 16, 1980 at the College of Idaho, sponsored by the College of Idaho English Department and the Snake River Valley Regional Studies Center with funding from the Association for the Humanities in Idaho. Hosted by the widely-published critic and scholar Dr. Brian Attebery (left) and his wife the distinguished folklorist Dr. Jennifer Eastman (left), the Conference brought nine writers to read from and discuss their works before an audience of teachers, students, writers, and interested community members. The nine writers included poets from Washington, Oregon, Idaho, and Montana: William Stafford, Richard Hugo, Madeline DeFrees, George Venn, Kim Stafford, Steve Wallin, and Tom Trusky. The others were Ann Copeland, a fiction writer from New Brunswick, Canada, who was then Writer-in-Residence at The College of Idaho, and Peter Balakian, an Armenian poet and scholar from Brown University, who was then completing a dissertation on Theodore Roethke. The major event of the conference was a panel discussion the last night. Balakian served as moderator. After that final panel, letters to George Venn suggested some posing. One participant wrote, "I don't think everyone there was entirely honest (not lying, but evasive) about the relationship of their work to the environment." Another wrote more bluntly: " 'Survive my lies.' So many busy words." (With the permission of Dr. Attebery, the introduction and transcript reprinted here were edited, condensed, and first published in *Oregon East* (1986).

Sources: *Oregon East*. La Grande: Eastern Oregon University (1986): 33-42;
William Stafford photos courtesy Lewis and Clark College,
Watzek Library Archives and Special Collections.

NORTHWEST POETRY AND THE LAND

Introduced and Edited By Dr. Brian Attebery

Moderator Balakian began with a prepared statement on regional poetry and the special importance of the physical environment for writers in the Northwest. He described the sense of space which struck him, as an outsider, in the work of Northwest poets. The Northwest poet, he said, is still a voyager, still faced with a landscape grand and inhuman. As opposed to the disengaged and cosmopolitan work of many Eastern poets, Northwest writers seem to be rooted in their region. They have the sense of place that Isaac Singer says is indispensable for literature.

The poets' responses to this introduction seemed to be, in many cases, resistance. When asked about landscape, they said, in effect, "My poems are not about landscape, not exterior landscape at any rate." William Stafford was particularly insistent on the freedom of the imagination to create or alter landscapes and the continuity of human experience, the traditions that cross regional boundaries. However, when

Peter Balakian (*Stafford photo*)

Richard Hugo *(Stafford photo)*

the conversation turned to the sources of inner landscape which all the poets insisted on, some very profound acknowledgments of the importance of natural surroundings emerged.

The younger poets, like Kim Stafford and George Venn, seemed to find it easier than their elders to credit environment for aspects of their poetry. The younger writers, who have not established a national audience, are looking for a tradition to build on, and they are likely to consider the common link in the art of the Northwest to be the use of landscape as a complex store of metaphor and a vantage point from which to view the human condition. The panel soon moved to a recognition of the complex and fertile interrelationship of land, culture, and the individual.

HUGO: The thing about a lot of writers—Faulkner and Singer are two, and certainly a lot of poets—is when you talk about writing out of a particular area, say for Faulkner this one little county in Mississippi or for Singer this small town in southern Poland, is that it's really a psychological matter, that is to say, it's a way of stabilizing the base of operations from which you work as a writer. It's what I often tell beginning poetry students: if you're in Missoula, you can go to Peking, but if you ain't nowhere, you can't go no place. You've got to start in some area; the imagination, I think, wants to have a kind of stability, a stable base from which to operate, and if you localize it, make it rather finite and limited, I think it makes it that much easier to write. And I think that's one reason writers do it. It's very hard just to write on air. If you're not any particular place when you start a poem, that is one more problem to solve, and it seems to me you should solve as many problems as you can before the poem begins.

DEFREES: I think it's important to distinguish that you need not be physically in that space at that time. I was just thinking about something that came up today: people were discussing how they might write when they're in transit some place, that seemed like a good time to write. And maybe part of that is that once you know a place and your imagination takes possession of it, when you have some dis-

Madeline DeFrees (U Montana)

tance from it, then the imagination...then it's idealized in some way.

HUGO: Yes, that's a good point. I didn't mean that you actually had to be in the place when you were writing. In fact a lot of my early poems take place in a certain point on the Duwamish River that I never would go to, except when I wanted to write a poem, I always imagined myself there and that's where I took off from. So it's a place in the mind, really, though it helps if it has a particular name. Even that is a source of stability. But Madeline's quite right; it's not a matter of physically being there. You might be writing anywhere. But it's where your mind says to you, "This is where things start. This is where things begin. I am here, therefore I'm able to speak." You can actually fantasize places that are ideals as a basis for your writing. You don't have to be there. But usually you would have been there if it's that obsessive that you can use it.

DEFREES: I remember when I had a friend who worked in Poetry in the Schools for a long time, and she was going to a different school about every week

or two. That particular year I was using a book in class, Bachelard's *The Poetics of Space*, and she decided that she was going to read that book and use it for Poetry in the Schools. So the first thing that she did in every school that she went into was to ask each of the students to be quiet for a while, you know, put your head down on the desk or whatever, and imagine the place that you're going to go to write in. For some it was a tree-house; for some it was some place outdoors that they really liked. But each one had that place, and she encouraged them to see it in great detail, and from then on, whenever it was time to write a poem they would first go to that place. So they were creating a stable base. And she got some really fantastic poems out of that.

HUGO: In my book *The Triggering Town*, one thing I do is...there's a student who turned in a very bad poem about deer mating, and he tried to use the drama of the event to carry the poem. Of course it was a mistake, and I pointed out as an exercise that had he had the deer mating in a particular spot, let's say an abandoned mining camp, that he then had these words available to him like "slag" and "ore" and "silver" and "flume," and there was a whole vocabulary, beautiful language that he could then work into his poem, instead of some words he had which were rather abstract and not particularly engaging. I mean there's your vocabulary, in that abandoned mining camp, and here are the deer mating, and so you don't have to just concern yourself with the mating act itself, but you've got all this other background to draw on. I happen to be a sort of person who believes—and this is absolutely silly, but I believe it anyway—I believe that where something happened is just as important as what happened there.

W. STAFFORD: It sounds as if, when we come to a meeting like this, as if there is a location that forms us, and then we interact with it, and that environment is something that we are sort of giving back to people around us. If you can see better, you tell them more about it; if you can hear better, and so on. But I have another kind of feeling about this that I want to enunciate just to see how it works. First we create the environment, then we let it influence us. I want to quote Madeline from this afternoon in class. She said, "Since perception

William Stafford (uncredited photo)

itself is selective, and memory selects even from that..." You see, she's backing away from something objective out there. And I would like to embrace that tendency that she's saying, and say that it makes me a little bit restive to speak about being from an area and thereby formed by it. Sounds as if the trees, or some kind of tradition is in the air, and so on. Perception is selective. We create a background for ourselves: legends, stories, a way of seeing things. One way I thought of to bring this down to earth is to say that once Hugo moved to Montana, Montana changed. I mean for me it changed. It's over the mountains somewhere: I can read all sort of statistics about it; but the feeling of Montana comes from some kind of interaction between the people and the place.

VENN: It seems to me that the pattern in our experience as a people has been toward uniformity and standardization. And it seems to me that the base for this kind of conversation is to make us more aware that some of the institutions which we might be justifiably proud of can tend to jeopardize the very things we want to hold on to. I'm thinking in particular of mass communication, mass production, and mass transportation. What we are trying to do is counteract that sense of uniformity, of standardization, of people as interchangeable parts that I think works against how we want to be. The best illustration I can think of was offered by Bess Lomax Hawes, director of the national folk arts program. She told the story of visiting villages in Alaska and hearing from people there that for as long as they could remember they had held public dances, ceremonials, feasts, and various kinds of celebrations. Within six months after the Telstar satellite went over, those festivities that had defined that people for hundreds of years were all stopped. They were over. And that's not an isolated fact. It seems to me that's part

George Venn (*Stafford photo*)

of the way we live, to work toward homogeneity. In schools we have the same kind of activity. The English teacher is taught that regional slang is not a language we're supposed to write, even though Twain made it into art. So, for instance, in the Northwest, if somebody says, "I drug the log under the fence and snuck on home," we recognize that as spoken language, yet we sense that we're not supposed to talk that way. The word is "dragged," and the word is "sneaked." For me the whole act of talking about this question is an act of seeking somehow to counteract what I think is a very dangerous and even very subtle leveling.

W. STAFFORD: In a way we're here inventing ourselves tonight. We're inventing our background, to justify ourselves. I want to be leery of self-conscious identification with a chosen background, because every act of thought should put at hazard all other thoughts. Every work of literature must be ready to violate its own tradition, as a means of extending it. I just think it's that complex. So in a way we're struggling to keep from having simple identification with a background someone's chosen for us.

COPELAND: I'd like to say something as one who's not from Idaho, not from the West, but who's walking around these days trying to see the region. I've only been here a week, and the first set of scales is dropping from my eyes. But I do know that there is something very mysterious about how you see a place the first time. You think you're seeing and then a few days later you realize you weren't. I look at the mountains and try to see them. What I know while I'm doing this,

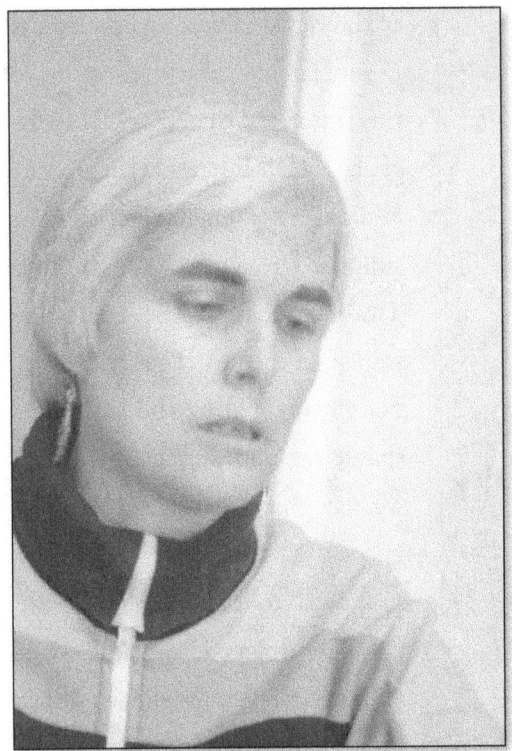

Ann Copeland (Stafford photo)

having been writing long enough to have tested this and experienced it, is that whatever I'm seeing now will in some mysterious way later come out as some kind of Idaho, some kind of region, transformed imaginatively, I hope, in a way I can't imagine now. And it may take ten years.

HUGO: That's very interesting. I do the same thing, except when I write a poem I do it very rapidly. That is to say, I see a place for the first time—it takes me almost no time at all to convert that place to the place a poem needs, then appropriate the place I've created out of the place I've seen to the poem. I do exactly what she's talking about except I do it very fast. Then I quite often have the name of the original place that I first saw in the title of the poem. A lot of people think the poem's about that place, but it isn't at all.

W. STAFFORD: Dick, I get a vision of you going across Montana like these big milling machines. You've got to go back: you've got to go put Montana back. (Laughter)

VENN: I want to offer a challenge here. What I hear is that the place that the imagination conceives of holds a greater integrity than the actual generative place. We don't want to be fixed into a particular locale. Now I want to offer just a comment about that. When I think about two of the most profound images that we have, at least in traditional literature, for absolute suffering, in the Christian

tradition that image, as it's been described, comes out of a very specific conscious-ness of death in the desert, so that the vision of hell in Christianity is derived from that lack of water, isolation, wandering. The celestial image there, of course, is ur-ban. There is the City of Gold: it is a city. The contrary is true in Nordic culture, where the image of absolute suffering is objectified by freezing, by going through what it's like to die in winter in the snow. What I begin to wonder is if we're not having a kind of traditional American fantasy whenever we say that imagination isn't tied to any particular place? Or does the imagination derive its strength and its authority and its power from a particular territory? Are we having this feeling that we are supreme to the world and that we can go any place and have any vision of ourselves, in the manner that Williams describes the Puritans: as though they carry the universe they want inside of them and don't have to find with that ex-ternal universe some more immediate relation than one just desired by the mind?

W. STAFFORD: Well now, George, I don't have to feel supreme in order to identify with that idea, which I do. All I have to do is realize that I can easi-ly be subjugated by the superior imagination of Dante or somebody else in the great Northlands. I would side with this position without claiming any kind of supremacy, just saying that I am subject to many kinds of influences including human influences, which are very powerful.

BALAKIAN: I find that notwithstanding the very large differences among poets who have written in the Northwest, there is some quality that emanates from a sense of vista, space, of other phenomenological reality, of living not only in the imaginative world, but in a world that engages one. I do find a dif-ference between the poetry of James Merrill, John Ashbery, et cetera. I think that difference has something to do with place, and maybe you could tell me how you feel about that.

DEFREES: I know that any of these generalizations are going to be too easy, but I've been thinking about that a little before I came, and one thing that oc-curred to me is that if you are dwarfed by landscape, that can be a kind of restorative dwarfing or a kind of fruitful contrast. I've always had these sort of symbolic postures that I work from. That sounds really crazy, but...it would be helpful to me, for example to think of myself as riding on a bicycle just against a backdrop of sky, something that big, against all that. I don't know why. Something in the juxtaposition of the minute and the huge.

BALAKIAN: Culture obviously dictates needs, and needs dictate how we respond in our poems.

DEFREES: I think very often when you have too many people for a given amount of space that it doesn't have the same kind of effect, and that the way of dealing with it is to retreat into an inner world that has little apparent connection with anything that we know out there,

HUGO: We think of poetry not so much as adding to literature or even as literature at all, but as an artful way of validating one's own life and one's own relations with the world. I think that's a much stronger Western tradition than it is an Eastern tradition. To me a book like *Mirabel*, by Merrill, whatever its values, always strikes me as a little contrived. Not the poem itself but the basis for it. One wonders, was all this necessary? Did he have to do this? Well, probably he did have to write. I think that's not quite the way Western poets work. I think that the impulse to write and the impulse to live are probably less separable out here. I think what we're doing out West with our poems is validating our own humanity, keeping something alive, keeping alive our right to love our responses to things.

DEFREES: I think in order to write—maybe to do certain other things too—you need some kind of anonymity or apartness, but also some kind of community or feeling of being with. And it may be somewhat different for each person who writes, but when the balance of those two things is disturbed to a degree that makes it wrong for you, then I think it's difficult to go on doing it. When I first went from Montana back to Massachusetts, one way to keep on writing was to try to get back there [to Montana], or to...just to talk about the distance I felt from it.

HUGO: Try to get back to the West.

DEFREES: Yes, even though the subject of the poem might not have been that.

BALAKIAN: I'd like to throw out another question, about the formal matter of making poetry: form, technique, the way you handle lines and rhythms, and if you feel that writing where you do affects them.

HUGO: I have something to say to that. When I lived almost forty years in the Pacific Northwest, out around Seattle, and when I studied under Roethke, as helpful as he was as a teacher, one thing that didn't help me much was his own writing. This is an odd thing to say, but I never cared much for Roethke's poems, and I didn't like them especially when I was a student. I like them better now, but I didn't like the way he heard the language. I thought he had an ear for what I called a soft language, that is to say the unaccented syllables were clearly unaccented, and it just wasn't the language my ear somehow obsessively wanted to hear. Now, since I was a native of the region and Roethke was not—I don't know if there's any actual connection, but certainly there's a similarity between the kind of language I wanted to hear and the kind of topography I was in. Now around Seattle and Portland, you know, things grow very fast. Grass grows...if you don't mow your lawn three times a week in the spring, you've had it. It just overtakes you. Everything is thick; the brush is thick; you go fishing and you have to beat yourself through swamps and weeds and vines and trees, and everything is clogged, jammed. There's always something in front of your face. A country of surprise: you round a corner on a road and there's a big mountain right in front of your eyes. And I wanted a kind of jammed language, an intense language, a language without much air between the words. I wanted it as thick as the undergrowth of the Pacific Northwest, the salal and the greasewood and so forth. Now, when I first read Bill's poems, I admired this language that was slow, seemingly unambitious and doing so very very much. And I wrote a poem one time called "In Stafford Country." It was written on a train—I was going through North Dakota, and that open area just seemed the kind of country that Bill's early poems about Kansas had come out of. But then when I got to Montana and found things more panoramic... When you go fishing in Montana—I thought it was paradise when I first got there—when you go fishing on a stream in Montana you just walk along the bank of the stream! I couldn't believe it. You don't have to climb over logs, you don't have to beat your way through brush, you just walk along. And furthermore there's lots of fish. But the main thing was that there you could see things coming from far off. There's very little surprise. You can mostly anticipate what it is you're going to see, and it was there that my line started to loosen up, my rhythms, that more space got in between the words. The language began to soften, and I hope for the good. Anyway I think so. I don't know if the landscape ever had a direct effect on my style, but there was that curious parallel. There was that landscape and there was that style.

VENN: It might be a corollary, Dick, if you look at something that some people have suggested about indigenous art: that the art that came out of that plateau flat country is almost exclusively two-dimensional.

HUGO: That's right. More sculpturing among the Indian tribes on the West Coast.

VENN: It may have something to do with the life that grew there. The question about space and style that Dick answered reminded me of some work I did once, an essay talking about how people who came here in the nineteenth century seemed to be bringing with them from another territory, in this case the landscape of England and Scotland, a kind of language and a sense of space and style, so that the poems, for instance, in early Northwest writing are populated by terms like "glen" and "dale" and "brae" and "down" and various other Scottish or English topographical terms, as well as a lot of other kinds of things that came along with that tradition. These terms suggest that their sense of space was something they carried with them to the Northwest, the same way you can see fenestration in buildings coming across the country: barn styles coming across the country; a lot of that tradition carries with us. Yet if you look at the evolution of poetry in the Northwest, you see a gradual falling away of all of those terms from about 1900 to about 1930. People who grew up here didn't tend to use that vocabulary that came out here, and then there's that other vocabulary that begins to be generated by where we are. One of my favorite instances of regional inheritance is to ask students in class what "chinook" means. Students from the Northwest have a very definite sense of what "chinook" means, although they don't always agree what direction it comes from. And the students from California know what "Santa Ana" means. "Chinook" is a name—at least that's one of its meanings—in Washington for a wind from Eastern Washington down the Cascades that melts everything, floods everybody, and maybe that's something—some way of using vocabulary there that's derived from space or from a sense of what happens there.

B. ATTEBERY: You obviously can't build poems around here out of banks and braes and bonny doons and so forth. But even if you have the right terms, where do you go from there?

Kim Stafford (anon photo)

HUGO: I think you're asking a fundamental question. That's really throwing us back to basics.

B. ATTEBERY: Does that go back to something that's the same everywhere, or are there other things that the region gives you?

K. STAFFORD: I have an answer to that. One thing I did on the Poet in the Schools program is write a whole bunch of local words up on the board, names for things in the landscape, names for things in a barn, whatever, and it's like a Rorschach test for the students: try to use all those words in your poem. Well, the poems are incredibly different, because that's not it as you say, it's not those names. One thing I keep thinking about rises from a number of things people have said. Borges has this story about this encyclopedia that appeared, and it described the world not as it is but as it should be. And it was such a convincing description and vision that pretty soon the world was like that. Now the world was changed because it was enchanting the way this encyclopedia described it. And I thought, in a way that's what any kind of art, and certainly in the Northwest...we're trying to write the encyclopedia which purports to be descriptive but is a vision. We're trying to bring them together....

Chapter 22 • NORTHWEST POETRY AND THE LAND

PORTLAND REVIEW

Vol. 22   1976

Poetry/Prose/Drawings

$3.00

CHAPTER 23 | Critical Essay (1976)

Preface to

THE SEARCH FOR SACRED SPACE
IN WESTERN AMERICAN LITERATURE

During my first five years in Eastern Oregon, I'd become an outspoken conservationist, an advocate for free-flowing streams and for the preservation of national forests as wilderness. As a reader of William O. Douglas and Aldo Leopold, it seemed disingenuous to pose silent and neutral while old growth forests were being clear cut, the Snake River dammed, salmon and top soil and clean water sacrificed to industrial corporate greed. So, in December, 1975, after *Portland Review* editor Victor Trelawny invited me to "do an article about western writers...a rather learned look at western writing historically. Primus [St. John] suggested yourself...," I was ready. In one essay, I could synthesize my testimony defending uncut forests and undammed rivers with the northwest literary situation—a synthesis of environmental ethics and literary practice. Without edits or comments, Trelawny published this essay in *Portland Review*— the deleted bibliography now added in Part V. In his June 16 follow up letter, Trelawny wrote: the piece was both "historical and critical...[and dealt] with mythos, that undercurrent we all live with here whether we recognize it or not.... Primus St. John (left) read it as soon as the book came out and he was quite happy we had managed to get such a thoughtful article on this subject." Later, the piece earned the praise of critic Lars Nordstrom for seeking "that correspondence between inner and outer reality which leads poems into a poetry where place exists as a metaphor." Also, it is the precursor to the more widely published essay "Continuity in Northwest Literature."

Source: *Portland Review* 22. (1976): 6-19; Photo: Primus St. John (1974) courtesy Ars Poetica Archive, Special Collections, Pierce Library, Eastern Oregon University; cover calligraphy by Manuel Izquierdo reprinted courtesy of archives, Portland State University.

THE SEARCH FOR SACRED SPACE IN WESTERN AMERICAN LITERATURE

The complex body of indigenous mythology that survived the period of conquest and settlement in the American West demonstrates that the indigenous imagination had transformed an amorphous mass of neutral, homogeneous places into a space where substantial qualitative differences and the spirit of place had been perceived. Undoubtedly, such a transformation of space took thousands of years of continuous habitation, thousands of priests and poets with a gift for mystery. Generally, primordial myths of the Indian, which are the sources of true history (the history of the human condition), indicate that there was a profound animistic belief that trees, plants, animals, mountains, lakes, and rivers had guardian spirits—spirits of place—which had to be addressed and appeased before any destructive act in space was possible. Also, the numerous etiological myths indicate that Beaver, Raven, Spider Woman, and Coyote all created fixed points in space from which tribal experience took its meaning. Hells Canyon was a trench Coyote dug. Cedar trees were prayed to before their bark was stripped. Salmon were not simply fish and camas or kouse were not simply roots; they were both the embodiment of gods. The relationships that were established in this large body of mythic literature make at least one conclusion clear: the encounter between space and the human imagination sacralized the territory and declared ethical positions and attitudes for human conduct in sacred space.

Used in this context, *sacred space* implies home, a heterogeneous landscape in which humans have both privileges and responsibilities. It contains enduring qualitative differences. It has fixed points, centers from which all human activity takes its meaning. It endures beyond any particular individual as a source of objective reality. In sacred space, there is continuity between internal and external space; humans seek that continuity and bind themselves to it. We claim space as part of ourselves. We identify with it. Hence, humans become part of the landscape and know their place in it. We know what the mountains mean, and we know their names. Sacred space is constructed through a prolonged period of orientation, as I noted above. In sacred space, humans tend to be at rest, more concerned with *being* than *doing*.

Historically, it is clear that the sense of sacred space and the spirit of place which had been achieved by the indigenous imagination was not transmitted to Americans during the conquest and settlement of the American West. With few notable exceptions, the invading conquerors tended to isolate themselves within their own traditions and, as William Carlos Williams says of the Puritans, "The jargon of God, which they used, was their dialect by which they kept themselves surrounded as with a palisade." The belief in American cultural and technological supremacy and the conviction that Christianity was unique probably contributed to this ethnocentric walling out of local traditions, assuring the transplanting of Judeo-Christian mythology into the territory. Thus, the West became a New Eden, a New Jerusalem. Pioneers became new Children of Israel wandering in the wilderness. The Mississippi became the River Jordan. The Indians became Devils. Settlers thought of themselves as Christ's Army. As William Gilpin declared, frontiersmen never forgot that

> one of their chief aims was the expansion of pure Christianity; they viewed with satisfaction the replacement of the savage yell with the songs of Zion. Settlement and religion went together.

Burning with such absolutes and pure ethnocentricity, it is easy to see how the accomplishments of an indigenous imagination, the sense of sacred space and spirit of place, could be ignored, misunderstood, or passed over as pagan mumbo jumbo. Even today, most Westerners know very little about indigenous myth, except what they might find on a Roadside History they were going too fast to read.

That a transplanted Christianity should be pushing the missionary and mold-board plow across the Great American Desert to Oregon is no accident. As Mircea Eliade states:

> Whether it is a case of clearing uncultivated ground or of conquering and occupying a territory already inhabited by "other" human beings, the ritual taking possession must always repeat the cosmogony. *For in the view of archaic societies everything that is not "our world" is not yet a world.* A territory can be made ours only by creating it anew, that is, by consecrating it. (Italics mine.)

In the conquest and settlement of the West, I am going to argue that the Judeo-Christian cosmogony was, in fact, repeated. Our entrance in the West was made under the terms established by the Genesis mythos in which humans are commanded to increase, conquer, and subdue the earth, and have dominion over all living things. Animals and plants and people exist to be used, and although people are made of clay, we are made in God's image, and like God, enjoy (or perhaps suffer from) a separation from nature. Further, people are aliens cast out of an ideal universe, we are aliens doomed to wander, sin, and labor. If this mythos is coupled with the historic antipathy of European civilization for arid, uninhabited territory, and uncultivated ground, and an even more intense antipathy for pagan (from *paganus*, villager, from *pagus*, village; corrupted to mean *pagan* by Roman Christians who considered civilian villagers in Northern Europe as lost souls) animistic religions, it is perhaps easier to comprehend the destruction of wilderness, wildlife, American Indians, as well as the current ecological crisis. Undoubtedly there were other settlers who did not see their mission in the West as clearly founded in myth, but who perhaps accepted Manifest Destiny—the political version of a "promised land"—or the Homestead Act. But generally, western conquest and settlement, the ritual taking possession of a new territory, required that Americans think of the West as a *profane space*, inhabited by "howling savages" which had to be sacralized through the introduction of Christian gods and heroes of the Genesis mythos who enjoyed divine sanction for human dominion over all life.

Used in this context, profane space implies a territory in which people believe they have all privileges and no responsibilities. Space is homogeneous and neutral, hence without any enduring experiences of qualitative differences. Profane space appears and disappears as a result of expediency and necessity. It is space to pass through more than space to call home. In profane space, people feel a profound discontinuity between internal and external reality, and confronted with that discontinuity over a period of time, people are emptied of themselves and confront absolute "other." In profane space, things have no names, or only the most general names. In it, people are aliens, orphans, wanderers, strangers; we belong no where and must keep moving to get somewhere, but when asked, we do not know where that where is. People do not know what the mountains mean or their names. It is a spiritless world and all is relative in it. In part, it produces what has been described as *The Homeless Mind* by Peter Berger and others.

The imaginative ethnocentric act of transforming the American West from a sacred space held by indigenous peoples into a profane space which would have to be sacralized by the Genesis mythos has had profound and dramatic consequences for everything alive in Western space during the conquest and settlement. For buffalo and other wildlife, it meant near extinction, then the establishment of refuges and sanctuaries. For Indian peoples, genocide, then reservations. For wilderness, exploitation, then finally protection through law. For rivers, damming, then some protection by the Wild Rivers Bill. And if the pattern continues, all natural objects may someday enjoy protection from the Genesis mythos as has been admirably prepared for by Christopher D. Stone in *Should Trees Have Standing*? However, for poets and writers, the creation of profane space in the American West generated a difficult imaginative task—confronting profane space and responding to it, establishing relationships with it, and a constant search for means outside the Genesis mythos to sacralization.

In the remainder of this essay, I hope to explore how some of the three or four generations of western writers of the conquest and settlement and modern periods have responded to the profane space declared to be open for consecration by the Genesis mythos. In that process, I believe that the dualism of sacred and profane space may be helpful in understanding our own place, traditions, and writers. Although this dualism employs what appears to be theological terms, it is my intention not to use them in that limited sense; instead, I hope the terms will be useful as a means of showing how the writer or poet invariably stares into both worlds in a search for unity.

I.

The evidence shows that the early periods of American encounter with the West did not create a sense of sacred space. In general, the frontier was declared profane territory and the plants, animals, and people on it were thought of as objects to be subjugated, exploited, and capitalized upon—the Genesis mythos at work. Mountain men, fur traders, and early explorers treated the space around them as though all of the abundant natural resources had been created exclusively for their convenience, profit, and temporary gratification. People and objects in space took and held meaning in relation to an economic system in Europe or the East, not for their own sakes. License, lawlessness, and violence—the projected traits of the "primitives" without their accompanying and sacralizing animism— were generally the specific human traits attributed to these early American wanderers in profane space. In addition, many of the "free" trappers who appear in the novels of the second generation West are also orphans, wanderers, and prodigals. For instance, consider A. B. Guthrie's *The Big Sky*. That Boone Caudill killed Jim Deakins, fathered a blind baby, and abandoned his Indian wife Teal Eye, all argue that Guthrie saw the mountain man's failure to sacralize the wilderness and the life he lived in it. Like Adam and Esau, Boone Caudill is doomed to destroy his space and his heritage through his own blind ignorance and lack of identification with his past, his friends, and his space. Boone is an archetypal orphan, a violent wanderer in profane space. In Vardis Fisher's novel, *Mountain Man*, Sam Minard becomes Fisher's means to praise the mountain man's way of life in a natural land-scape without Guthrie's sense of tragedy. Revenge against the Crow who have killed his bride dominates Sam and the novel, and the slaughter and destruction of other life in profane space is seen as cause for celebration. In both Fisher and Guthrie, we see characters who take all privileges and no responsibilities for the space around them, yet in both novelists there is a profound nostalgia for that lost Eden in the wilderness where their characters wander like new Adams.

That this paradoxical view of the mountain man is characteristic of second generation novelists suggests that once profane space is gone, it then becomes sacred space to those children of settlers who grew up identifying with it after it was conquered. Fisher writes about that transformation; as a result of growing up in Idaho, he has become

> incurably a mountain man, a man of the American West.... When he went East he had thought that he would never want to see the West again. He had not known that he was and always would be a mountain man.

Wallace Stegner makes the immediate experience of the second generation child more clear in his opening "overture" to *The Sound of Mountain Water*:

> All I knew was that it was pure delight to be where the land lifted in peaks and plunged in canyons, and to sniff air thin, spray-cooled, full of pine and spruce smells, and to be so close-seeming to the improbable indigo sky. I gave my heart to the mountains the minute I stood beside this river with its spray in my face and watched it thunder into foam, smooth to green glass over sunken roots, shatter to foam again.

I submit that these are the claims of the territory which begin the creation of sacred space. Such realizations were not available to the mountain man who, like his later edition—the miner—suggest an exploitative response in the traditional Genesis mythos to profane space. Second generation novelists like Stegner, Fisher, and Guthrie looked back on the mountain men and saw their heroic tragedy that was certainly the beginning of our current ecological crisis. Nevertheless, that early profane space that allowed wilderness to be ransacked would become sacred space as a result of poets, writers, and magicians who grew up with it inside them.

II.

Another distinguishable response to profane space by Western writers and poets has been rejection. In short, leave this country. Find another country in which space is already sacralized. In the larger context of American literature. this seems to be the nature of T. S. Eliot's retreat to England, and perhaps even Mark

Twain's final flight to Medieval Europe in *The Mysterious Stranger*. More effective evidence for Western writers might be found in the innumerable characters in settlement novels like *My Antonia* who come to the prairie from Europe, but who cannot adapt. They do not like this "kawntree." They go insane from the discontinuity between internal and external space, retreat to Europe, or create isolated European enclaves to wall out the surrounding profane territory.

I know of only one definitive statement of this rejection/retreat response to profane space in western writing—Kenneth Hanson's poem "First of All" in *The Uncorrected World*.

First of all it is necessary
to find yourself a country
which is not easy.
It takes much looking
after which you must be lucky.
There must be rocks and water
and a sky that is willing
to take itself for granted
without being overbearing.

There should be
great gods in the background
and on the mountain tops.
There should be lesser gods
in the fields, and nymphs
about all the cool fountains.
The past should be always
somewhere in the distance,
not taken too seriously
but there always giving perspective.

The olive trees
and the orange trees and the cypress
will change your life, the rocks
and the lies and the gods
and the strict music. If you go there
you should be prepared to leave
at a moment's notice, knowing
after all you have been somewhere.

Although these excerpts from the poem do not represent all of Hanson's vision, they document the rejection of profane space on a cultural frontier and the adoption of the sacred space of Greece. Contrary to Robin Skelton's "Preface" in *Five Poets of the Pacific Northwest*—"the departure of a poet for Italy...or for Greece (whence Kenneth Hanson has just returned), is...much less an escape from the Northwest than a further exploration of it"—this rejection of profane space may also be seen as a retreat into a space sacralized by all of those factors mentioned in the definition of sacred space—a world where myth and reality meet in landscape, objects, and the imagination.

Most of the popular literature of the West demonstrates that this meeting of myth and reality has not occurred here with the resultant sacralization. Instead, the mythic West—wild, shoot-'em-up, black-hat-white-hat-West—has been so successfully interposed between ourselves and profane space that the choice to read or write the "horse operas" itself constitutes another form of rejection/retreat. Early popular fiction that stocked the Eastern pulp markets is still hatching today in the thud and blunder romances of television and the formula western film or novel. From Buffalo Bill to Paul Bunyan to Pecos Bill to Roaring Ralph Rockwood the Reckless Ranger, the Genesis mythos has again spawned a wild series of romantic conquerors whose human exploits and ethnocentric excesses obscure the fact of profane space. Instead of coming eye to eye with the environment around them, Americans come eye to eye with the latter day saints—Roy Rogers, Dale Evans, and Trigger. Such writing did not bring the 19th century to a sense of its own space in the West, and has not brought the contemporary West any closer to its space either. Instead of sacralization, such fiction and film constitute a rejection of profane space, and thus we are still not at home in our own territory. (In most westerns, the territory is a kind of dead stage that film makers can also find in Spain or Mexico or Italy.) Before the West can be sacralized, it must be discovered instead of destroyed or used as a stage for the exploits of dunderheads. Popular fiction and film cannot bring us to even a truce with the territory of profane space through which its characters move us.

III.

The imaginative ethnocentric act of transforming the American West from a sacred space held by indigenous people and their gods into a profane space which would have to be sacralized by the Genesis mythos has given us a body of literature which, by and large, has been written in response to that sense of profane space. To this point, I have indicated several possible responses: act out the conquest and despoliation of the very space we came to, reject profane space and retreat to another country, or bury our collective heads in the homocentric pulpish nonsense of the "horse operas." That the response to profane space has been destruction, rejection, or retreat suggests that Western writers have responded in detail to what has only been recently articulated in public print—that the Genesis mythos is inadequate for the sacralization of space. Such a statement finds substantial elaboration in several writers which I believe deserve to be present here. First, Mircea Eliade himself:

> The cosmic liturgy, the mystery of nature's participation in the Christological drama, have become inaccessible to Christians living in a modern city. Their religious experience is no longer open to the cosmos. In the last analysis, it is a strictly private experience; salvation is a problem that concerns man and his god; at most, man recognizes that he is responsible not only to God but also to history. But in these man-God-history relationships there is no place for the cosmos. From this it would appear that, even for a genuine Christian, the world is no longer felt as the work of God.

Another writer who has seen this inadequacy of the Judeo-Christian mythos to implicate the cosmos, thus creating sacred space beyond the church buildings, is the American historian Lynn White Jr. In his article "The Historical Roots of Our Ecologic Crisis," White states that

> Especially in its Western form, Christianity is the most anthropocentric religion the world has seen.... Christianity, in absolute contrast to ancient paganism and Asia's religions...not only established a dualism of man and nature but also insisted that it is God's will that man exploit nature for his proper ends.

This historical perspective provided by White and Eliade was also contained in one of the most cogent statements of Aldo Leopold in his essay "The Land Ethic:"

> The first ethics dealt with relation between individuals; the Mosaic Decalogue is an example. Later accretions dealt with relation between the individual and society.... There is yet no ethic dealing with man's relation to land and to the animals and plants which grow upon it.

From all three of these writers, it is clear that the Genesis mythos is simply inadequate to the construction of sacred space. The god of the conquerors is not implicated in the cosmos, that God has enjoined his people to dominate and subdue the earth and its creatures, and the conquerors had only an exploitative ethic. It is not surprising to consider that Western writers must respond to profane space, and that the response to that space dominates much of Western literature. Assuming that writers and poets are sensitive to this inadequacy in their traditional inheritance, I would now like to look at those writers who have sought out a means to create sacred space.

IV.

One of the prominent areas where this search for a tradition capable of creating sacred space has concentrated is the indigenous mythology. Such a search has taken a multitude of postures among various writers in the West who have sought to discover some unity between themselves and the space around them. If the Indians of Cooper's novels are preliminary explorations of this possibility, it has lately become very obvious in the work of many Western writers—Frank Waters, Walter Van Tilburg Clark, Frederic Manfred. William Eastlake, D. H. Lawrence (while in Taos), Margaret Craven. Jack Leahy, and others.

It is inevitable that Frank Waters and his avowal that people's "conflicting relationships to the earth has provided something of a thematic continuity in all my books" be submitted here as exemplary of this search by Western writers. In a television interview series published in 1971, Waters declared that

> ...after all, we are interested in our relationship to our land, to our own
> earth, and the Indians are indigenous to this continent. The Indian is
> much different from our European white, so I think we have a great
> deal to learn from their expression of it in their own idiom.

I believe it is accurate to say that most, if not all, of Waters' books and articles explore indigenous sources of the sense of sacred space, their conflicts with the American mythology of profane space, and some means of resolution of those conflicts. Of course. Waters' exploration is more often dedicated to consciousness in a more elaborate fashion than can be indicated here. Nevertheless, he writes continually that Americans, unlike the Indians, have not yet achieved the sense of sacred space in the West,

> the deep rhythms of its wide and bitter earth, its immense and lonely
> skies, the thunder of its mountains, the tide-suck of its pelagic plains.
> Not yet rooted in a living homeland—not yet at peace with its breath-
> ing spirit of place—strangers all, alone and lonely! And so forever rest-
> less, hurtling back and forth from horizon to horizon, moving at every
> and any excuse.

This same searching in the indigenous sources of sacrality is also found in the work of Gary Snyder. Consider, for instance, Snyder's statement in a 1965 film:

> We won't be white men a thousand years from now. We won't be white
> men fifty years from now. Our whole culture is going someplace else.
> The work of poetry is to capture those areas of the consciousness which
> belong to the American continent, the nonwhite world...ultimately
> getting in contact with the natural world, which we've been out of con-
> tact with so long we've almost destroyed the planet.

Of course, Snyder has made many other statements which elaborate on this declared search as the poet's responsibility; in *Earth House Hold* he wrote a section titled "White Indians" and another statement which serves further to confirm and illustrate that the indigenous sources of sacrality are another possible means of transforming profane space. In discussing the possible ways of approaching local soil, of contacting local powers, Snyder says that

> For many, the invisible presence of the Indian and the heartbreaking
> beauty of America work without fasting or herbs. We make these con-
> tacts simply by walking the Sierra or Mojave, learning the old edibles,
> singing and watching.

The specific language here is a direct move beyond rejection of profane space and beyond domination or conquest. Such attention to the indigenous and to our immediate responses can transform profane space by putting us in touch with the sense of the sacred which was originally achieved by the peoples of what they called *Turtle Island*. A final modern instance of this search for a sacralizing tradition appears in a recent novel by the British Columbia writer Margaret Craven; in her book, *I Heard The Owl Call My Name*, an Episcopal priest walks into the invisible aura of sacred space that implicates the entire cosmos of the Vancouver Island tribe that he has been sent to minister to:

> The Indian knows his village and feels for his village as no white man for his country, his town, or even for his own bit of land. His village is not the strip of land four miles long and three miles wide that is his as long as the sun rises and the moon sets. The myths are the village and the winds and the rains. The river is the village, and the black and white killer whales that herd the fish to the end of the inlet the better to gobble them. The village is the salmon who come up the river to spawn, the seal who follows the salmon and bites off his head, the blue-jay whose name is like the sound he makes, "Kwiss-Kwiss." The village is the talking bird, the owl, who calls the name of the man who is going to die, and the silver-tipped grizzly who ambles into the village, and the little white speck that is the mountain goat on Whoop-Szo.

Unlike certain of his missionary predecessors who found themselves dead, the Episcopal priest responds positively to this indigenous sense of sacrality. Instead of forcing Newtonian space and white supremacy down the throats of local totems, the priest finds himself intentionally participating in the indigenous sense of sacrality out of respect for its images of life, death, and community. In all three of these writers, it seems clear that they are searching indigenous tradition with long, careful stares. Whether this will end in a synthesis of cultures, as Snyder has predicted, is not agreed upon; they do agree, however, on the place to search.

The search for a means of transforming space is also present in the work of many poets and writers who have not found indigenous tradition amenable to their vision. Such writers are then forced into a sacralizing posture which they must achieve alone. For instance, the poetry of Robinson Jeffers suggests this mode of searching in a poem like "The Beauty of Things."

To feel and speak the astonishing beauty of
things—earth, stone and water,
Beast, man and woman, sun moon and stars—
The blood-shot beauty of human nature, its thoughts,
frenzies and passions,
And unhuman nature, its towering reality—
For man's half dream; man, you might say, is nature
dreaming, but rock
And water and sky are constant—to feel
Greatly, and understand greatly, and express greatly,
the natural
Beauty, is the sole business of poetry.
The rest's diversion: those holy or noble sentiments,
the intricate ideas,
The love, lust longing: reasons, but not the reason.

Here, I believe that Jeffers charges poets with the most elemental act required
for the achievement of sacred space. That this was a major part of Jeffers' credo
is less significant here than the clear expression of the appropriate material for
poetry—the relationships between people and the space around them. It would
certainly be impossible, for instance, to achieve a transformation of profane space
if one does not really see and feel the objects in that space. Careful attention to
the object is the first specific step in seeing inside, perceiving the energy and the
spirit. In many of his other poems, Jeffers is constantly at work on the creation
and discovery of sacred space.

 Another poet who is also conscious of the search for sacred relationships
with space is William Stafford. In many of his poems, earth, air, water, trees,
wind, and other features of space predominate. These are not simply natural
materials to be understood in a literal fashion, but are also intended to tran-
scend the literal facts. In that stance, Stafford is conscious of the poet's similarity to the mythopoetic predecessors in the West who not only saw ravens
as birds, but who went far beyond the literal in establishing qualitative facts
about the human spirit with Raven. This vision of space as metaphor moves
the poet close to the sacralization of space because it assures a vision that looks
beyond the physical facts, beyond active subjugation required by an inherited

mythos. Stafford's attention to the necessity of sacralizing space is clearly stated in many parts of his poems:

> Love the earth like a mole,
> fur-near. Near sighted
> hold close the clods,
> their fine print headlines.
> Pat them with soft hands
>
> from "Starting with Little Things"

> Great is Earth our home.
> Great is the sky.
> And great are weeds in the fields.
> We celebrate earth and air
> as we sing in the wind.
>
> from "Weeds"

> One way to find your place is like
> the rain, a million requests
> for lodging, one that wins, finds
> your cheek. . .
>
> from "Bring the North"

Stafford's search for sacred space has led him to a unity with things around him. Through image and statement he responds poetically to space rather than in an aggressive, exploitative way. Although he is conscious of profane space and traditionally profane objects like weeds, he calls frequently for a new mythos of "Be, be," instead of "Do, do." In this act of claiming "we are all gestures the world makes," space is sacralized through that solitary encounter between poet and object.

These illustrations of particular poets who have sought out some means to sacralize the space around them could go on for some time with only slight repetitions. Each poet seems to have perceived the necessity of this transformation in a different sense. For instance, Vi Gale's poem "High Desert" in *Clearwater*, shows that the act of naming is a means to sacrality: "the voice that drums/this landscape back as mirror or mirage,/that names this highest homeland, is our own." *Naming*, often in catalogues, is one of the means of sacralization in the poetry of David Wagoner also, as can be seen in "Guide to Dungeness Spit." Many of the poems of Richard Hugo suggest a profound consciousness of profane space that only sometimes can be transformed. The recent Idaho poems of Vern Rutsala suggest a specific return to and investigation of the aura of sacred space around one's home or birthplace. These varied postures still come together, however, on one specific detail: profane space must be transformed. If enough unacknowledged legislators of reality make this transformation their concern, something will happen.

In fact, wilderness areas were undoubtedly transformed from profane to sacred space in precisely this fashion. Out of the settled landscape that now surrounds them, wilderness areas are qualitatively different. Writers, priests, poets, lawyers, and magicians (scientists) have all been intensely involved in this struggle to declare such areas sacred. From Emerson and Thoreau to Aldo Leopold and John Muir to Wallace Stegner and Bernard DeVoto to Edward Abbey and Gary Snyder, the American imagination under frontier profane space conditions has been at work transforming profane space into sacred space. Almost without exception, the mythos for this change has been a hybrid of deism and transcendentalism in which natural objects were either divine revelations of divine truth or manifestations of divine mystery. In wilderness, the destructive excesses of the mountain man are no longer allowed to his modern and preserved counterpart—the backpacker. Although Hells Canyon was clearly disputed territory, it certainly has at least two agreed-upon public meanings. It will endure beyond any individual. That people do not remain in it shows how clearly it has become an interesting paradox of sacred profane space. It is through this process of orientation in the West, which meant destruction by the Genesis mythos, that this vision of sacred space emerged.

V.

I believe that Americans came to the West as a people in search of a home, yet they were followed by the ominous cloud that declared that the world was not sacred and that it was not our home. The presence of profane space created by the Genesis mythos has forced writers and poets to respond since literature is, in many ways, a function of space. If the initial responses to profane space were either destruction or rejection, it is now clear that writers are in search of a means to sacralize the territory. Some have yearned for the "free trapper's" Eden and seen the tragedy of a life which takes no responsibilities for sacralizing space. Others have sought the means to transformation in the indigenous mythology, poetry, and folklore. Still others have faced profane space alone and come out, in a sense, as mythological poets who have achieved a sense of unity between themselves and the space around them. This mythological function for poets and writers who have grown up in the West or who claimed the territory is, I believe, going to be seen more and more frequently as we all continue to search for ways to be at home in a space we never thought would have to be home. (Usually, we have moved on; there is always more land, isn't there?) I propose that Western writers and poets sensed the inadequacy of the Genesis mythos which removed God and humans from the cosmos and which declared no ethical stance for the conquerors toward space, and that those writers and poets have begun to declare a new mythos that will sacralize the territory before it is destroyed.

If the voices of writers like Jeffers, Stafford, Abbey, Stegner, Snyder, and Waters are heard, their search for sacred space will become the headwaters for a future in both literature and society. Such a new mythos will continue to search out and articulate the means to sacrality; it will not be "nature poetry" or "nature writing" in the conventional sense that "nature" is an object separate from human beings. Instead, it will express the unity and sacrality of all life, a poetry which will allow us to be at home and allow our lives to continue. Perhaps when Wallace Stevens said that the great poems of Heaven and Hell had been written, but the great poems of Earth remained to be written, he foreshadowed all I have said. If Stevens is right, we may be near the beginning of wisdom.

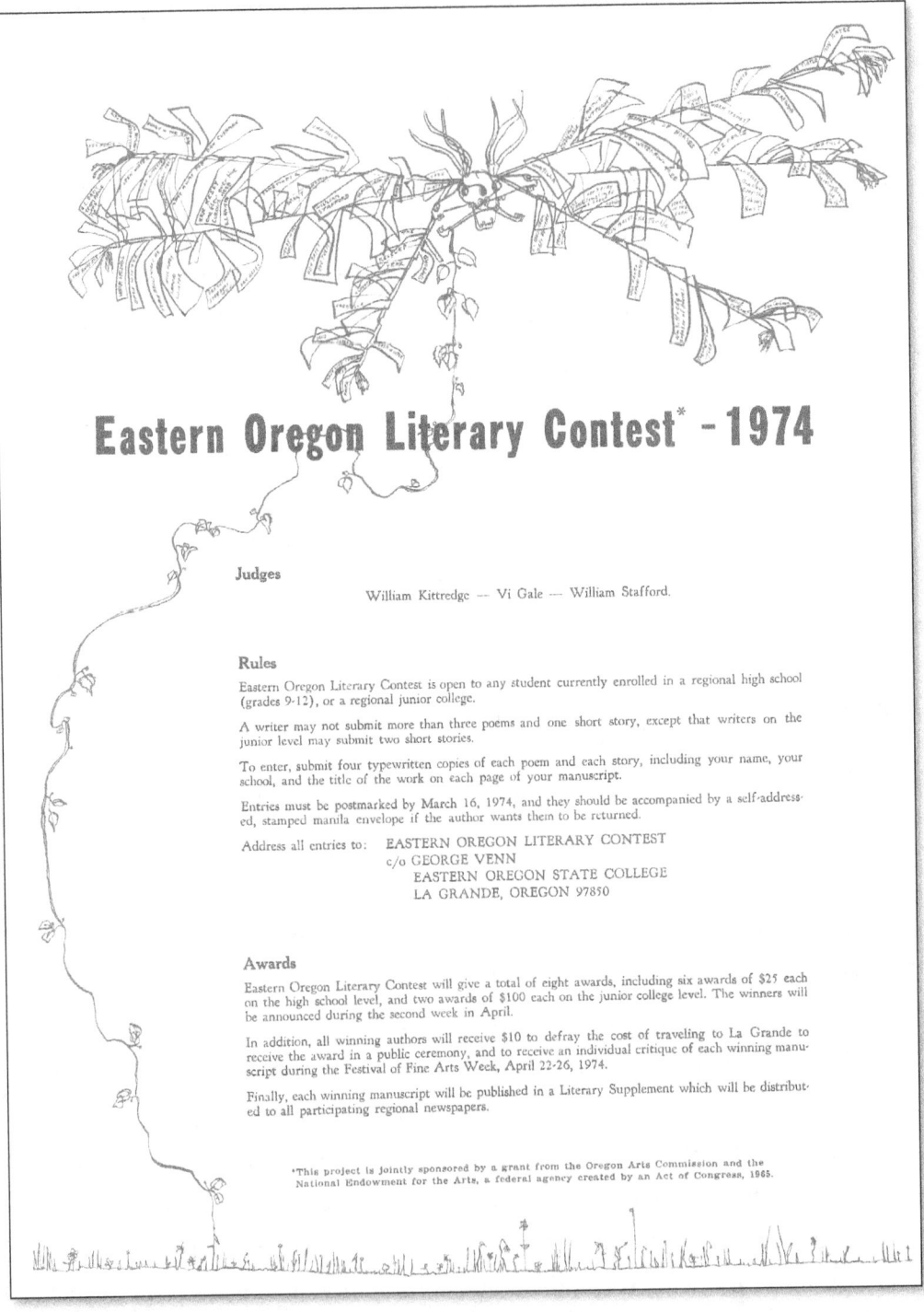

Eastern Oregon Literary Contest* - 1974

Judges

William Kittredge — Vi Gale — William Stafford.

Rules

Eastern Oregon Literary Contest is open to any student currently enrolled in a regional high school (grades 9-12), or a regional junior college.

A writer may not submit more than three poems and one short story, except that writers on the junior level may submit two short stories.

To enter, submit four typewritten copies of each poem and each story, including your name, your school, and the title of the work on each page of your manuscript.

Entries must be postmarked by March 16, 1974, and they should be accompanied by a self-addressed, stamped manila envelope if the author wants them to be returned.

Address all entries to: EASTERN OREGON LITERARY CONTEST
c/o GEORGE VENN
EASTERN OREGON STATE COLLEGE
LA GRANDE, OREGON 97850

Awards

Eastern Oregon Literary Contest will give a total of eight awards, including six awards of $25 each on the high school level, and two awards of $100 each on the junior college level. The winners will be announced during the second week in April.

In addition, all winning authors will receive $10 to defray the cost of traveling to La Grande to receive the award in a public ceremony, and to receive an individual critique of each winning manuscript during the Festival of Fine Arts Week, April 22-26, 1974.

Finally, each winning manuscript will be published in a Literary Supplement which will be distributed to all participating regional newspapers.

*This project is jointly sponsored by a grant from the Oregon Arts Commission and the National Endowment for the Arts, a federal agency created by an Act of Congress, 1965.

"Poster: Eastern Oregon Literary Contest 1974." *From 1972 to 1974, George Venn proposed and directed an annual literary awards contest for college and high school students living east of the Oregon Cascades. Funded by the Oregon Arts Commission and supported by regional newspapers, the award-winning manuscripts were chosen by William Kittredge, Vi Gale, and William Stafford. (See p. 362)*

Preface to

THE LITERATURE OF EASTERN OREGON

After Louie Attebery introduced me to Pacific Northwest regional literature in 1965 at The College of Idaho, I realized in 1973 that I still had only general knowledge of writing and writers in the sub-region east of the Oregon Cascades. So, in February of that same year, seeking to discover more of that literature, I designed the following questionnaire and mailed it to forty two regional librarians:

Section I. [Please list your holdings] in twelve categories: Diaries, Poetry, Novels and Short Stories, Folklorists, Biographies, Histories, Autobiographies, American Indian Literature, Informal Histories.

Section II. Who are the most important authors who've written about Eastern Oregon?

Section III. Do the books with the largest circulation in your library include regional writers, and do they include writers like Louis L'Amour, Max Brand, Luke Short and Zane Grey?

Section IV. Are your readers as familiar with regional authors and their work as they are with authors outside the region?

Section V. Do you believe that Western American history and literature deserve more serious attention?

A majority of librarians responded. With assistance from the Division of Continuing Education, I compiled and analyzed the causes of regional neglect and remedies for that neglect of serious literature, and presented the following lecture to a large and appreciative Baker [not yet Baker City] crowd in April. To follow through, I mailed a copy of the lecture and the informal 14-page bibliography to everyone.

Sources: Oregon Division of Continuing Education & Baker Contemporary Lectures, Baker Public Library, Baker, OR: 2 April 1973; Left: logo by Ian Gatley, 1972.

THE LITERATURE OF EASTERN OREGON:
A BAKER CITY ADDRESS

When I first proposed this lecture, a colleague of mine immediately told me that there was no literature of Eastern Oregon. When I explained that I intended to use the word "literature" in the most general sense, he was slightly relieved. When I further explained that I wanted to make an inventory of writing by people in Eastern Oregon and about life here, he began to smile. He thought he could trust me not to upset him, one of those strange qualities which one admires more in posts than in men.

Like most people who live here, he believed that we were still conquering the west. We should still be a frontier or pioneer society in which our major concerns would obviously be our crops and gardens, our cattle and horses, logs and lumber. The idea that we had a developing literature which deserved attention simply didn't occur to him. As "Bunchgrassers" removed and isolated from the virtues of civilization in the Willamette Valley (such as polluted air, water, and overcrowded cities), it would only be pretentious for us to write poetry or fiction, history or autobiography. Whatever we produced east of the Cascades would be remembered more in board feet or bushels, not poetic feet and chapters. Somewhere, I suspect he subscribed to the notion that serious writing only comes from cities and urban people rather than from remote and rural people or that good writing can only come from the past after the writers are held safely under tombstones. If he knew that Eastern Oregon has a list of writers numbering more than a hundred, that a tradition of writing here continues to thrive, and that we are not simply dumb country cousins of the "Webfeet," I think he would be surprised and slightly worried.

I further suspect that he would not be alone in his surprise. The majority of students from Eastern Oregon have never heard of Joaquin Miller, H. L. Davis, Reub Long, or William Kittredge. They will be so familiar with the 20 lines of Shakespeare they once memorized in high school that they have forgotten them. They might know several poems by Longfellow or Tennyson, or a novel like *Hot Rod* or *A Separate Peace*. But if you ask them about the poetry of Paul Tracy or H. L. Davis, or about *Honey in the Horn* or *Owyhee Horizons*, they're often dumbfounded that such writers and books even exist. If I move the questioning outside the narrow realm of students, success is slightly better. Most people outside of schools have seen or read something by Reub Long or R. A. Jackman, and many people know the work of Bill Gulick and Giles French. But according to a recent survey of librarians in Eastern Oregon, which I made with the assistance of Mrs. Winnifred Oesterling and the Division of Continuing Education, it would be safe to say that even the majority of readers in Eastern Oregon are more familiar with writers outside the region and the life of President Nixon than they are with writers on the other side of the Wallowas or with their own lives.

That we give more attention to writers and writing from other places is not unusual and should be expected for a variety of good reasons too numerous to discuss here. And there was a time as recent as sixty or seventy years ago when very little was written about Eastern Oregon which could be found in print. You could have read the poetry of Ella Higginson or C. E. S. Wood. You could have perused the writing of G. W. Kennedy, an early Methodist minister who rode all over eastern Oregon, then recorded that life in *The Pioneer Campfires* (1914). Louise G. Stephens wrote *Letters from an Oregon Ranch* in 1905, and Charles Sternberg published his *Life of a Fossil Hunter* in 1909, describing his expedition to the Oregon desert in 1877. And if you were interested, there would have been hundreds of pioneer diaries and journals in old trunks in attics, and more official records in places like the War Department in Washington, Hudson's Bay Co. annals in London, and so on. But by and large, there simply wasn't much printed about Eastern Oregon that was available to a large public.

In such a time before the rise of serious literature in the trans-Mississippi west, we had no alternative but to read novels and poems, histories and biographies which came to us from London, Paris, New York, or some other large urban center. But we have lived here nearly 150 years now, and in that time, we have created a sizable and significant collection of books which we can no longer afford to ignore because we are finally realizing that the West is a distinctive region and that its culture deserves more honest attention than we see on television. We do not live in a world of black hats and white hats and saloon girls with hearts of gold or hearts of coal. We live in an area which is finally gathering the strands of a cultural tradition and a cultural identity different from both the East and the South, and it is time, I believe, to give that developing culture our attention. Even in the survey of librarians, nearly 75% of them agree that western history and literature deserve more honest attention.

. . .

Such a focusing of attention might begin by looking briefly at three specific causes of our general neglect of regional traditions in Eastern Oregon. The first of these causes can be most clearly seen in the experience of some of our regional writers and artists. Consider Joaquin Miller. In 1864 he moved to Canyon City, became judge of Grant County, made two trips to Portland to have his books printed at his own expense. But it was not until Miller went to London and published *Songs of the Sierras* in 1871 that he gained limited recognition among the residents of Oregon. He revisited Canyon City in 1907 and wrote one of the more interesting pieces of travel writing in our literature, *A Royal Highway of the World,* which describes a stagecoach trip from Canyon City to Burns. Or consider the experiences of H. L. Davis. It was not until he was "discovered" by H. L. Mencken, a Baltimore publisher of *The American Mercury,* that Davis began to write prose which eventually brought him both a national reputation and the Pulitzer Prize in 1935 for his novel on the settlement of Eastern Oregon, *Honey in the Horn*. Or consider the experience of Betty Feves, the potter and ceramicist from Pendleton who couldn't sell anything in Pendleton until after she had won both national and international prizes. Only then was she named "Woman of the Year" in Round Up city, and only then could she begin to sell a few pots in a local store.

Recently I was talking with Don Gray, a painter who currently lives in Union. He told me that he sends most of his vendible paintings to galleries in Portland or Seattle, and that his work is relatively unknown in the region east of the Cascades. In all four of these individual artists, you can see that ancient problem so well-stated in biblical maxim: "The prophet is without honor in his own country." For some inexplicable reason, some outsiders must praise regional artists before their own people will claim them. Often, people around artists will never venture the praise they might deserve. Instead, we remember that so and so lived just across the street in that old house, or we remember he had bad breath, long hair, drank too much, or that he was on the football team at Halfway.

Why we don't recognize and cultivate the talented among us is not a question I can investigate here, and I might also add that this is not a phenomenon unique to Eastern Oregon. It happens all over America. I only hope to identify this ancient and invidious human foible as one of the causes behind our neglect of regional writers and artists. The consequences of such an attitude are many. Joaquin Miller moved to California, traveled to England, lived on the East Coast, always looking for an appreciative audience. H. L. Davis applied for and received a Guggenheim Grant and moved to Mexico where he wrote *Honey in the Horn*. Ben Hiatt, poet and publisher of the *Grande Ronde Review*, moved to San Francisco. Like the "Brain Drain" of several years ago, we can see a veritable exodus of talent from the region by men and women who can help us understand how we feel about ourselves and the land, but who leave because no one seems to be interested in their work.

Another consequence of this attitude which disparages anything local and praises anything distant is that we are about to lose a vast and important heritage from the four native American tribes in Eastern Oregon and our own pioneer tradition. Around us in all of the small towns, out on old homesteads, in nursing homes, on the reservations, the old pioneers who settled the country and the tribal elders who watched that invasion are all dying. They take to their graves invaluable stories of pioneer life, of old Indian traditions, ways of thinking and acting we will never be able to retrieve. For example, the last speaker of the Cayuse language died several years ago and there is no one who can speak it now even though it was once the language of the people who ruled the Blue Mountains from the Palouse to the John Day. And how much of our own pioneer tradition have we lost in the same way because we simply didn't think something around us was as important as the latest innovation in hats.

Recently I was told by a man who works for the state highway department that during lunch one day beside a road he found a heap of trash. In it, he discovered letters written in 1864 and a diary from the same year. Sensing their value, he put them in a shoe box and took them to someone he knew would preserve them. Even in my own family, the contents of my uncle's desk were dumped into a barrel when he died, including diaries, letters, and business documents from about 1900 to 1956. Luckily, I found the barrel out in the barn after the desk was sold. All of this, of course, is intended to illustrate that if we continue to ignore what is around us, we can only pass on to our children a world in which the past has been blown away like topsoil in an east wind. I should also add that this concern is shared by many of the librarians in Eastern Oregon. Over and over in the questionnaires, I find these kinds of statements: "Pioneer stories need to be preserved and recorded before it is too late." "I think we could be more aware of our early history and the people who settled in the West. Arlington has many old timers here and they are passing away so history will be the only source left, soon." Without an interest in what is immediately around us, the past, upon which we erect the present and the future, will be lost.

• • •

A second cause of our neglect of regional literature in Eastern Oregon can best be seen in the singular fact that, according to the librarian's questionnaires, Zane Grey, and writers like Louis L'Amour, Max Brand, Luke Short, are probably the most popular writers of fiction in Eastern Oregon today. That such writers hold our imagination in thrall for page after page is certainly testimony for the strong appeal of the western formula. But what readers in the region don't seem to understand is that, by and large, such writers essentially descend from a group of eastern hack writers who discovered in the 1830s that the western formula would sell literally thousands of books. With utter disregard for what was happening in the west and often with profound ignorance of the lives of western people, they began to write the wildest blood and thunder, hair-raising, shoot-em-up fiction which satisfied the desire of the hungry eastern readership for excitement. It should further be understood that almost without exception, the hacks were more interested in profit than they were in telling or finding out the truth about human experience west of the Mississippi. The way to make a profit was, of course, to appeal to the public's desire for fast action, lots of killing, rescues of damsels in distress, skulking Indians, huge sinful villains and virtuous albino heroes, the white hats and the black hats who still ride hard on the T.V. screen today. None of the tedium, the struggle, the hardship of everyday life for men, women or children on the frontier or on the Oregon Trail was ever presented for very long because they would, of course, bore the eastern reader.

This desire to make the west far more razzle-dazzle than it ever was can be seen even better through a comparison of A. B. Guthrie's Pulitzer Prize novel, *The Way West*, with the film version of his story shot in the Three Sisters area. When the producers of the film found that letting wagons down steep hills with cordon and block fastened to a huge ponderosa simply wasn't exciting enough, they invented an impossible and fantastic derrick which would lower Conestoga wagons over the edge of a 500 foot cliff. Guthrie's careful historical research was replaced by something which would sell because it was more wild and exciting.

Not only has this distortion been practiced on people who came through this valley, but it has also been worked on the lives of mountain men and cowboys so extensively that even the old cowboys themselves cannot recognize their portrayal in fiction or on movies. For example, most authentic cowboy autobiographers like Andy Adams and Charlie Siringo say that the life of the cowboy was often so boring that he had to resort to memorizing labels on cans, then having contests to see who could recite the most labels. Kit Carson himself became thoroughly embarrassed when he found a novel in the wreckage of a wagon which described some impossible rescue of a helpless damsel with 1,000 Sioux on his tail. Essentially, a wild west was created for readers that never did exist, but because it sold books, it prospered and continues to thrive through the hack western novel and the T.V. or Hollywood western. Such portrayals packed with derring-do have actually become the models for western life, and continue to attract thousands of readers not only in Eastern Oregon but throughout the world.

Imagine the consternation and the uproar then, when a first generation Oregonian named H. L. Davis, who had lived most of his life in Antelope, The Dalles, and Yoncalla, came to the forefront of American literature in 1935 with a novel about the settlement of Eastern Oregon, a novel not based on myth or illusions of a wild west, but on direct personal experience. The reception of *Honey in the Horn* was tempestuous, to say the least. And his other writing about Eastern Oregon has been equally controversial here because it looks a little too closely at what we are, because it slices through too many of the illusions we hold about our experience.

I hope you can see from the persistence of such writing that myths about the west are probably more powerful than western reality. Certainly it can be said that we have been treated to outright fabrication for so long in western literature that we don't believe anything honest can be written about it any more. I sense that we would rather be entertained by a false portrayal of the life of the cowboy than be provoked by a close look at his character. We would rather continue to believe that all Indians are villains creeping up on the camp for a massacre, or riding around the wagons like howling savages, rather than accept them as human beings with all of the human qualities which we call civilized. We would rather continue to believe that the west is wild and woolly, that we are great conquerors in the tradition of Manifest Destiny, rather than accept another vision which sees the west as dusty and hot, as more inclined to dwarf us with its mountains and vastness than to impress us with our ability to subdue the natural world. Faced with those alternatives, it is not difficult to understand why Zane Grey is still far more popular than H. L. Davis, and why we continue to neglect our own literature.

* * *

A third cause of our neglect of our own writers was alluded to in the opening of the lecture, namely, that we seem to equate cultural achievement only with large populations crowded into cities or with some past civilization like Elizabethan England or Renaissance Italy. In short, we tend to believe that everything great or important comes either from the past or from some other country or state. In rural and remote areas, there seems to be a pervasive sense of cultural inferiority which consistently manifests itself in various ways. Many people in Eastern Oregon leave for what they believe to be some more important place as soon as they graduate from high school. And many students come to Eastern Oregon University for one year only to discover that "nothing's going on here, there's nothing to do here," by which I guess they mean there aren't as many stores or cars or lights. I assume they think Portland is an important place.

This same attitude pervades entertainment. I have observed that it is far more acceptable to drive to Portland to the opera than it is to drive to Weiser for the Old Time Fiddler's Contest. And we seem to believe we are better people if we can dress in the latest styles from the large cities. The same can also be said about literature. Many people read *Love Story* or *Jonathan Livingston Seagull* because they saw someone talk about it on television, while a book of poems like *Owyhee Horizons* by Paul Tracy, a plumber who once lived in Baker County, probably didn't sell over 500 copies, and most of those to libraries. We tend to believe that nothing is going on here. We feel backward, we feel behind. We keep a constant eye on the coast or on television to see what's happening there so we will know what to think, read, or wear next. In such a monkey-see, monkey-do atmosphere, local culture in Eastern Oregon can only go knocking from door to door looking for handouts, and little more.

This sense of inferiority in remote and rural areas, which have not been so completely blessed with the virtues of civilization that they can still see the mountains through the air, has disasterous consequences. Life here and in areas like Eastern Oregon becomes a servile imitation of life in large cities, even though we have many more alternatives, more space, fewer people, cleaner air, and fewer polluted streams. Anything which might have distinguished one region from another tends to be minimized, and in most of our towns today you can find the sticky fingers of mass culture. Cities in Eastern Oregon are Portlands in the egg with one wasteland of a main street, a freeway zooming by, a slum in the bud. Most of us watch the same T. V. programs, hear the same songs on the radio, read the same best-sellers and generally make our lives imperfect copies of lives everywhere else.

In many ways, a similar sense of uniformity is fostered by the schools. Most children grow up reading school books in which Daddy drives up to the suburban house in his big car, parks next to a huge green lawn, gets out of the car in a nice dark suit and white shirt, and goes inside to read the evening newspaper. Imagine the child of a wheat farmer in Helix, Oregon, reading such a book in the second grade, then looking at her father when he rattles in on the tractor after rodweeding summer fallow all day with a tailwind. Dressed in overalls and a straw hat with gray dust so thick in his beard, he looks like a ghost. And he's too damn tired to read the paper. And maybe he shouts at the dog or cusses the wind a little, then starts to sing some profane folk song. What is that child going to think? The same basic problem of standardization in mass culture is prevalent even in high school reading where students will be very fortunate indeed if they read anything about life west of the Mississippi or west of the Rockies during their entire high school careers. On a suggested reading list for high school students you will find few if any books which deal with human experience and landscape in rural or remote areas like Eastern Oregon.

A student of mine last quarter saw this problem very clearly in the material she was sent by a national church group for flannel graph lessons in Sunday School. She taught the children for several Sundays using material she was sent in which people all lived in urban houses with urban problems, and she told the stories too. And she got fed up with it, as she told me, and decided to adapt the stories to the environment and problems the children knew and understood. She put in barns and a loafing shed and alfalfa and barb wire and pines and the Wallowa River, and eventually, she started to write her own stories and discontinued her subscription to the national magazine. I hope you can see here the consequences of a sense of cultural inferiority in areas like Eastern Oregon. While fiction writers were at one time captivating an audience with distortions of the wild wild west, we now have mass literature, mass entertainment, mass-produced teachers trained to go anywhere, all of which serve to minimize any regional diversity.

To this point, I have suggested that there are at least three causes behind our neglect of regional literature in Eastern Oregon and in the west. Let me summa-

rize them here before I continue with what I hope will be sufficient antidotes for such a situation. First, I stated that in the past, local writers and artists have simply not enjoyed local public support for their work until they have first migrated to some other larger city and established a reputation there. Secondly, the popular fiction of writers like Zane Grey, who often created a wild wild west without historical precedent made it nearly impossible for an honest and authentic western writer like H. L. Davis to gain an appreciative audience. *Honey in the Horn* does not reinforce all of those illusions about a wild and perpetually exciting west, but rather shows an accurate and not always pleasant picture of pioneer life. Given a choice between Davis and Grey, the majority of readers today tend to chose Grey. The third cause behind our neglect of our own regional traditions can best be stated by saying that we tend to believe everything great or important comes either from the past or from some other place. In rural and remote areas like Eastern Oregon, there seems to be a pervasive sense of cultural inferiority which manifests itself in various aberrant ways. The city of Elgin must redecorate itself in a Swiss decor, call the Wallowa Mountains the Alps of Oregon. It is not enough to be Elgin. Elgin must be a little Swiss village before we find it interesting. From stories I hear about Elgin, there is little need to import a European identity.

. . .

If it is true that the unexamined life is not worth living, and if it is also true that we have neglected the literature which springs from our local experience and which examines our lives, what can be done to counteract those three causes I have listed? What can we do about a group of writers and a literature which are without honor in their own territory? What can we do about the illusory, mythic west? What can we do about that sense of cultural inferiority which seems to be so prevalent in rural and remote areas? I am not sure I can supply answers to subdue this three-headed Sasquatch which I've just identified as roaming Eastern Oregon, and perhaps no one else can supply those answers either. But having come this far, I feel obligated to propose some course of action. Without that, I would feel only like the chronic complainer we all know who can see what is lacking, but who is not sufficiently imaginative to propose some solutions.

How does anyone set out to encourage the citizenry of Eastern Oregon to cultivate the work of artists in the region? Certainly there must be ways in which we can encourage this kind of local attention. I note the presence of an art gallery here in Baker which is already working to create a local audience for painting. Without searching beyond the Cascades, such a local effort in painting can be found in many small communities. The Eastern Oregon Literary Contest and Supplement, which last year attracted nearly 150 entries from the 65 high schools and 3 junior colleges in the region, is working in the same direction in literature. We circulated good regional literature to a readership of nearly 80,000 people last spring through the generosity and cooperation of the National Endowment for the Arts, the Oregon Arts Commission, and regional newspaper editors and publishers. And in the creative writing program at Eastern Oregon University, we continue to encourage students to discover what they know and understand. *(See p. 350)*

Even with this kind of effort, groups of poets or other writers do not seem to be gathering in a fashion in Eastern Oregon like they gather under the auspices of the Oregon State Poetry Association on the other side of the Cascades. And perhaps that is good. Perhaps more organizations are not what we need most. I think the only way we are going to cultivate our own tradition is by first finding out what those traditions have been. I think that what we lack is knowledge, not desire. Is it true that if we simply had access to local Indian myths like "The Monster in Wallowa Lake" or "Beaver and the Grande Ronde River," we would be more interested? Would we read diaries and journals of early explorers and pioneers who crossed the Oregon Trail if we could find them in print? Would we read E. S. McComas's *Journal of Travel* if we knew it described early life in the Baker area? Would readers be attracted to Isaac Hiatt's *Thirty-one Years in Baker County*, Loretta Field's *The Powder River of Eastern Oregon*, or Paul Tracy's *Owyhee Horizons* if they simply knew they were available? I have no clear and easy answer to these questions, but I can say, on the basis of the librarian's questionnaire, that many people in Eastern Oregon are interested in reading such books. Even your local librarian says that "people are hungry for information about their area. Anyone who writes travel, history, biography, poetry, picture books, botany, and yes, even cook books, becomes important. This material is very much in demand." And I can assure you that such sentiments dominate the librarians' understanding of the reading public. On the strength of such a response, it is possible to say that the most effective way to cultivate artists and writers around us is simply to make a more concerted effort to find out who they were and what they did. I can assure you that until I spent considerable time in preliminary research and reading, I had no clear knowledge myself about what had been written here.

In addition to simply informing ourselves and continuing local efforts like the art gallery, we could also insist on the teaching of some regional literature in the schools, even though such a proposal would probably meet with serious resistance from the traditional English teacher who, like an interchangeable part, is trained to go anywhere in the United States. We could insist that county courts hire professional local historians at the same salary they hire road engineers. We could start programs in local literature at libraries and encourage local writers to speak and discuss their work with interested people. We could encourage grade schools to participate in the Poets-in-the-Schools program in Oregon which is now concentrated almost exclusively in the Willamette Valley. Cities could hire poets to write verse for public occasions and ceremonies. It is almost too easy to say that if we spent as much time thinking of ways to turn our energy and our vision here on ourselves, things could only improve for regional writers, their books, and regional culture.

The second question of how to encourage the citizens of Eastern Oregon to see through the clichés and stereotypes of the blood-and-thunder shoot-em-up black-hat-white-hat Hollywood hackwriter nonsense is more difficult. In many ways, we seem to believe that what a group of eastern hacks and Hollywood script writers invented in their offices and studios is what life is really like here, and once we believe that, it is both difficult and painful to divest ourselves of our desire for a wild wild west of perpetual romance and endless excitement, so topheavy with guns and horses that it often makes us laugh.

There are two antidotes that come to mind as partial remedies for this particular problem as it appears in Eastern Oregon. The first is to read as many of the formal and informal histories of the region as you can find in your library, and I can assure you that there are many nights of interesting reading ahead if you track down these books. In the questionnaires returned by the librarians, I have a preliminary count of 20 odd biographies, 10 autobiographies, 40 odd informal histories, and at least that many more formal histories. That's nearly 110 books, a good start for anyone! I suggest history and authentic personal documents for the same reason that biblical translators invariably go back to the original Hebrew documents when they translate the Old Testament into English. The only way to avoid foolish errors and illusions or treasured misconceptions passed on by other translators is to ferret out as many original sources as you can find in the dusty back rooms. Even though you may not find a historical perspective in diaries by people who passed through this valley, you will gain a more authentic idea about their experience from their writing than you will ever gain from "Wagon Train."

The second antidote I would recommend to counteract the blood-and-thunder stereotypes of television and pulp westerns is serious western literature by writers who are committed to rendering the "highest kind of justice to the visible universe," writers who seek the truth and make their appeal rather than writers who only seek to entertain or to sell another thousand copies with an exciting cover and shallow characters. In Eastern Oregon, I am not familiar with many writers whose literary integrity I am confident is not dedicated to mere sales. For Oregon Trail reading, I would suggest Francis Parkman's *The Oregon Trail* and A. B. Guthrie's *The Way West*. For the settlement period I would recommend H. L. Davis' *Honey in the Horn, The Winds of Morning, Team Bells Woke Me,* and all of his poetry. The work of Nard Jones also can take a stance here with Davis. And in the modern period, I am only familiar with the work of William Kittredge. From the librarians' questionnaire, I have harvested the names of many other writers with whom I am not familiar such as Wayne Overholser, Glenn Vernam, Ernest Haycox, Robert Ormond Case, Dwight Bennett, Ray Tracy, Maria Goffin, Honoré Morrow, and many others including poets which will be listed in the bibliography. It should be understood that I do not place all of those writers with whom I am unfamiliar in the category of hacks, for certainly that would be a gross injustice. But because of limitations on time and background, I can only speak for those three or four I have mentioned.

If we move outside Eastern Oregon in our search for the serious writer in the west, we meet with many who have grown up here as first generation writers who are not out selling their heritage for profit. Such a list would include Vardis Fisher, Frank Waters, Walter Van Tilburg Clark, Wallace Stegner, A. B. Guthrie, Archie Binns, Ken Kesey, Fredrick Manfred, Richard Hugo, Don Berry, and many others. A complete bibliography of those writers could be found quite easily in the new quarterly *Western American Literature* published at Colorado State University. Of course, we could also increase our chances of escaping the wild wild west by simply shutting off the T. V. once in a while. Not only would the west be quieter, it might also have a chance to mature without the illusions superimposed on it by the east and Hollywood.

The third question—"How can we counteract this pervasive sense of cultural inferiority in rural and remote areas?" is probably the most difficult question of the three. As is true with most difficult questions, there are no easy answers. I think we must ultimately resort to history to demonstrate that there is simply no justification for the idea that to be rural, remote, and agricultural means that our art must be inferior or that our writers will be deficient. Instead of sending all our talented students off to Eugene or Portland or San Francisco or New York, let us remind them that all art is essentially local. It springs from a knowledge and an encounter with specific facts in the universe which we find immediately around us or which we find in ourselves. That two of the most highly praised writers in the history of modern literature—James Joyce and William Faulkner—both wrote their entire lives about areas no larger than Baker County should be ample evidence for the incredulous. Immediately, I am tempted to spin out a longer list of names to persuade the cynics that you can live on the rim of the Malheur Desert and be as good a writer as you can in Portland, but I think I will spare you that today.

In addition to insisting that all art is essentially local, we should also remind ourselves and our artists that excellence does not require huge populations, that there is no equation which says that to be great you must go to New York or

London or Paris. Athenian culture, which we admire so much for its incredible accomplishments in poetry, philosophy, architecture, and drama, is a classic example of such a principle. There were not as many people living in Athens during its era of high accomplishments as there are living in Baker and Union counties today. American Indian cultures are even more startling in this respect when we consider that a tribe of 5,000 people or less could generate a culture replete with myths, legends, customs, religion, and language, in an area that, in many cases, was also no larger than Baker County.

If we can believe that being rural and remote does not doom us, and if we can also believe that huge populations do not guarantee excellence in art, then perhaps we can lay the third head of this monster down. What I hope has been most obvious throughout these remarks is the necessity of paying our best and closest attention to what is around us. By looking carefully at our nascent literature, perhaps we can make the future of Eastern Oregon possible. Think of it: if everyone read all of those books, if all of those writers (spiritual pioneers) came back to towns and schools, if all of the westerns were turned off and the paperback hacks turned out to pasture on cheatgrass, if we returned to those original sources, if we saw that there is nothing superior in size or cities, something would happen. It might not be what we expect, but I can assure you it would be exciting.

CHAPTER 25 | Historical Fiction (1971)

Preface to

ELIZABETH GURLEY FLYNN: BRINGING DOWN MISSOULA

During Spring, 1970, while completing my MFA in short fiction at the University of Montana, I enrolled in a Western history course with Dr. David Emmons. Searching for a research topic, I came to a dramatic sentence in David Lavender's *Land of Giants* about Elizabeth Gurley Flynn and the 1908 [*sic*] Missoula free speech fight—a dramatic event right on the streets where I lived. Trusting Lavender's date, I wasted a week searching local newspapers and found nothing, so I shifted to 1909 and found everything to make a good story. So began my first regional research: reading Montana newspaper microfilm, studying Syndicalist movement histories, discovering Flynn's autobiography, uncovering dusty Missoula City Council minutes, and interviewing a retired Northern Pacific Railroad brakeman. Giving my paper an "A," Emmons suggested I send the paper to Vivian Paladin, then editor at *Montana the Magazine of Western History*. She offered me $100 and said revise—30 pages had to be tightened to 15—and she was right. After 1971 publication in *Montana, The Magazine of Western History,* a 1972 history of Missoula (Koelbel) heavily plagiarized my original article without credit, but the more I learned about the IWW and Flynn, the more I knew I had to revise my more objective original to better suggest Flynn's obscured personal life, so the originating facts enriched by extensive further research evolved into my first historical fiction.

Sources: *Montana, The Magazine of Western History.* 21.4 (Fall, 1971): 18-30; Photos: portrait of E.G. Flynn (1911) courtesy of Tamiment Library/Robert F. Wagner Labor Archives, New York University; Jack Jones (ca 1921) courtesy of Newberry Library, Chicago. For other photos and credits see text or Chapter 25 "Notes."

ELIZABETH GURLEY FLYNN: BRINGING DOWN MISSOULA

SEPTEMBER, 1909

Into the golden valley—clear, cloudless, high blue—an afternoon train whistles from the west, the plume of steam and smoke dissipating as the Northern Pacific chuffs into Missoula from Spokane. Brakes squealing on steel. A young woman with grey-blue eyes and jet-black hair deboards at the Missoula depot—its gold-yellow Chinese bricks used as ballast in ships hauling Chinese coolie labor across the Pacific. As she steps down, blasts of steam hiss and explode from the undercarriages. No fanfare. No warning. No sign saying, "This 19-year old orator and revolutionary, this girl who grew up in the slums of South Bronx in New York and in Manchester, New Hampshire, this girl named Elizabeth Gurley Flynn, will bring Missoula, Montana, to its civic knees in two weeks." Flaming red tie, black dress, white spotless collar, oval face, broad clear forehead, mischievous eyes—another eastern dreamer come west—like Narcissa, like Abigail, like many more—to act out a civilizing dream.

As she steps down from the train, Jack Archibald Jones, a Minnesota miner, her 32-year old husband, bulls his way out of the crowd. Black suit, white shirt, short cravat, he greets her with a too-eager embrace. He is blue-eyed, short, a block of mine-hardened muscle. The first western miner and labor organizer Flynn met, he proposed to Flynn when she was seventeen during a tour of Minnesota's Mesabi Iron Range in 1907—her first journey west. Both Flynn and Jones are agents of the Industrial Workers of the World (IWW) founded four years ago by Big Bill Heywood. Twenty hobo brigadiers from the West went to Chicago to get Heywood elected as their president. Radical stepchild of the Butte-based

Western Federation of Miners (WFM), the IWW is militant, class-conscious, revolutionary. Heywood hired Flynn to organize One Big Union in the west—a plot against the giant of industrial capitalism.

Frank Little, a half-breed miner, picks up her suitcases—one heavy with song-sheets and pamphlets, one light with clothing. As the husband and wife greet each other, Little walks away toward the street, then lingers apart discreetly—like a big brother on a date. Black-haired, brown, furious, quiet, Little belongs to the Butte WFM, the most powerful, largest labor union in the west. Since 1893, the WFM has been working to improve miners' lives and mine conditions. For hard rock miners like Frank Little, a hearse waits at the mine head—every day.

Flynn holds herself back from Jack Jones—her belly heavy and four months pregnant now. After her first pregnancy ended in miscarriage in Chicago, their boss, Vincent St. John, had apparently separated them—sent Jones to Missoula in the fall of 1908 to prepare the way for Flynn's appearance there. Now, reuniting, there is cool distance between them. Worried about another miscarriage, Jones wants Flynn to settle down now, to become a wife and mother, to give up her wild life of traveling, agitating, writing, speaking, organizing, marching, drinking. Flynn doesn't want to settle down. She's come to resent Jack Jones' efforts to domesticate her. She doesn't love him, finds him boring, but will not tell him this for another year. Besides, other men—a lot of other men—interest her.

Three of them start walking south down the echoing boardwalks of Higgins Avenue. Flynn is studying the Garden City, Gate of the Golden West, studying the dirt street crisscrossed with wheel ruts from buggies, wagons, carriages, buckboards, surreys. By the station, she sees the loitering, rouge-faced prostitutes in front of their cribs along the tracks. "Who runs the cribs?" she asks Jones. "The mayor, I think, or some city bosses," he says. She sees her husband—furtive, protective, older—his clothes too tight, his face flushed with heat, his neck thick, big hard hands. Two men on horseback whip their mounts into a race down the dirt street. Flynn, Little, and Jones pass new brick hotels with perfect facades, saloons with open doors and glistening bars. They walk through the cool sour-sweet odor of beer wafting out the open doors. "Twenty nine saloons between the railroad and the river," Frank Little says. "They like to keep the stiffs drunk

here," says Jones. "Harder to organize them that way," says Little. He smiles at
Flynn. Frank Little is lithe, quiet, alert—like a hunting cougar. Banks bustle
with black suited, black-hatted men. Women in gaudy colored hats ride by. The
rattle of carriages, thud of freight wagons of boxed fruit and sacked grain, jos-
tling buckboards, sweating draft horses, the sharp stench of horse manure, men
shouting, harness, hames, collars, lines slapping everywhere, drunks asleep in the
dirt, young men in overalls panhandling for bread. Fine dust boils up, then drifts
away. Gold afternoon sun bakes the rutted dirt street. A red Winston car stops
before a frightened horse. Ahead, Flynn can see the turrets, awnings, and brick
facades of new multi-storied buildings in the business district. Electric poles
bleached by sun line the street like crosses.

Already, she is questioning Jones: How big's the city jail? How many police?
How violent? Who's mayor? What kind of budget for prosecution, prisoner
meals, crowd control, mass arrest?

At an intersection, Flynn stops, looks back: a tawny grass mountain slopes
down behind the depot—a horizon half mountain and half sky. She loves the
west, the clear air, warm days, cool nights. No fall rains have come to the wide
valley. Summer drought burns on. To the south, a fire on Mt. Lolo spills a blue
haze into the Bitterroot Valley. The three of them walk together, Flynn between
the two men, all their shared idealism concealed by their common clothes. This
raven-haired, blue-eyed woman is Irish, but no one can see she is fearless. Before
she quit her New York City high school, she had made her first public speech in
1908 denouncing the status of women under capitalism. She's already been arrested for public speech-making. The dream she has come to articulate in Missoula is
also taboo—an American dream of economic justice for the underclass, a dream
for men who believe they live in a classless society. No way to see her packing this
idea of one of the first free speech fights in the West down that boardwalk.

So why Flynn? Why Missoula? Why 1909? Since its founding in 1893, the
WFM had been challenged all over the west by finks, federal troops, the press, the
law, and mine-owners' mercenaries. Some men, such as Bill Heywood, believed in
new and more radical tactics, in more effective force—any force to achieve social
change. By 1909, the IWW had learned that men who organized workers were

sure to be beaten or killed. That violence destroyed men's morale. Someone had to organize the thousands of poor, working, migratory men, someone who could not be clubbed or shot, someone who might wake up the loggers, miners, farm workers, fruit pickers to the dream of a better life. Labor needed an invulnerable messenger to carry a dangerous message. They needed eloquence, courage, commitment. Police wouldn't dare club or shoot a 19-year-old woman. Beautiful young, articulate, and pregnant, Flynn's message of class consciousness, civil liberty, and social reform was sure to be heard.

As they walk, Flynn learns that her husband has not done much. He's found a cabin for them out by the Bitterroot River. He's found exploitation—three employment agencies on Higgins Avenue. Perfect, she thinks, grateful for an easy target of decadence and fraud. That attack will draw men to her larger cause—the union to organize. That is Flynn's charge from IWW headquarters in Chicago. Unite the hungry, angry, itinerant working men against those who exploit them. Use the streets. Speak publicly against injustice. Give capitalism hell. Make human exploitation difficult. Test the constitutional protection of free speech. Be arrested. Persuade men to follow you. Fill the jails. Make the system feed you. Pack the courtrooms. Demand individual jury trials. Overload the system. Draw public attention! That is Flynn's problem now: Jones has not attracted many new men to the IWW. Is there something too genteel, too complacent about Missoula? Flynn wonders if the Gem of the Mountains has no Irish men, no men with a sense of outrage, of justice? She needs them now.

Can she flood the Missoula courts and jails? She doesn't know. When she calls, will the men she's addressed in Kalispell and Spokane rally to her cry? Will the miners who welcomed her in June in Butte hop a side-door Pullman or ride the rods to Missoula? How many men will she need? Will enough of them come? Will they be beaten, shot? Will the Pinkertons come? What about the Sixth Infantry, U.S. Army, stationed at Fort Missoula? They will side with the city—no allies there. Flynn has to subdue a city of 12,000. Surprise will be on her side—at the beginning—but police violence will also work against her. Middle-class self-interest and respectability is on her side—that Horatio Alger belief in economic justice—but middle-class greed, apathy, fear, silence, propriety, censorship, and cowardice are all against her. She has Joe Hill's songs—hymn parodies easy to learn—and she has copies of the *Industrial Worker* newspaper to distribute. Will the local press be against her? Will passion sustain her? Will idealism enslave and blind her? And what about this man beside her—this estranged muscular block of a husband she no longer loves? Her baby? Her health? She has previously miscarried. This is her second pregnancy.

"What about the AF of L?" she asks Jones. "Are they with us?" Jones points the direction of the new courthouse under construction. The old courthouse has been moved and sits on timbers and cribbing.

"Refused to let us use their hall," Jones replied.

"Did they say why?" she asked.

"We're too radical," he said.

"That's nothing new," she said. "Are they organizing here?"

"I haven't seen much," Jones said.

"Pretty useless bunch, if you ask me, "she said. "In the last depression, the AF of L let four million workers go down the road without a fight. Where's the justice in that?"

"Craft unions like to be cozy with the bosses, "said Frank Little.

"They just beg like spaniels for minor change," Jones said

"That's what makes us different, what makes them nervous," Flynn said. "The IWW stands for revolution—any way we get that done is fine."

"That's why they're afraid of us," Jones said.

"What about a base of operations?" Flynn asks. This is a critical detail. Jones has found that cabin for them—a place to cook, eat, and sleep—but she also needs a place close to the business district, close to the major crossroads for traffic, commerce, workers. Without that central place, her voice cannot launch the fight or shelter an audience. She has the voice. Her audience will be mostly young working men without women. That's why the whores are everywhere. Missoula calls them "secretaries" and "soiled doves." Will she will carry the crowd? With the crowd, can she can bring Missoula down?

At the Harnois Theater, 200 block on East Main, they go in. Jones has found this place—a new dry basement—told Uncle Charlie Harnois' manager that his wife was going to be giving lectures. The manager doesn't think twice about renting to her. Harmless girl, he thinks. Good-looking, well-spoken, bold, but she seems harmless enough. Some sadness in her eyes, heavy curving brows, a hard, uncompromising mouth. Flynn pays him cash—all the better. Under the Harnois she is close enough to everything—employment agencies within earshot on Higgins, jails close, trains a few blocks, business district two blocks, Chamber of Commerce next door—sweet situational ironies. Flynn is theatrical, idealistic, subversive—an underground woman. What better spot? Money for rent?—the IWW saw to that. With the cabin for personal refuge and retreat, she now has a downtown base of operations. To Charlie Harnois, she's a minor issue. He's just filled all 924 seats of his new theater upstairs on opening night, made a killing on his first show. Renting out the basement? Frosting on his cake.

"Where's the Starvation Army?" she asks Jones. Through the open basement door, she hears the wavering music begin—drums, trumpets, tambourines, accordion, and raggle taggle choir beginning to sing. She grins at Jack Jones, takes his hand. Laughing, they start walking toward the hymn sound of "In the Sweet By and By." Frank Little stays behind at the Harnois, guards the luggage. He thinks the couple want to be alone. The preaching has not begun. The Salvation Army street evangelist knows where the loggers, mill-hands, fruit pickers have to pass. Standing with Jones at the corner of Higgins and Front, she studies the new facades rising on all sides as the music of heaven bounces off the bricks of the earthly First National Bank, the Hammond Building, the Florence Hotel, the Mercantile:

> There's a land that is fairer than day,
> and by faith we can see it afar
> For the Father waits over the way
> to prepare us a dwelling place there.
>
> In the sweet by and by
> we will meet on that beautiful shore
> in the sweet by and by
> we will meet on that beautiful shore.

She studies the dirt street and boardwalks leading south to the river, the black steel bridgework seeming to start across the cold, blue Clark Fork, then stop— mid-air. Higgins and Front is the crossroads—with shelter from the river wind. Working stiffs have to cross the river here to reach South Missoula, to reach the Harper and Baird logging camp on O'Brien Creek, the Bitterroot wheat fields and orchards. Bars, whorehouses, dives, flophouses line Front Street east and west from Higgins Avenue. This is where she wants to speak—the place where the bindlestiffs and working poor will intersect with the red brick center of respectability—biggest bank, biggest hotel, biggest general store, major office building—all with new colloquial facades, classic windows, neat capitals, perfectly balanced fenestration. Poor men will gather here. Important men must pass through here. Flynn has found her place.

They walk out on the makeshift Higgins Avenue bridge and stop, stare down into the slow-swirling blue river, then look eastward—up the Clark Fork into the mouth of Hellgate Canyon. As the river flows west—cold, deep, powerful—the temporary wood bridge trembles beneath them. Cool east wind cuts through Flynn's thin black clothes.

"What happened?" Flynn asks. She shivers, wraps her arms around herself.

"The flood washed the steel center spans right out."

"Is this all they can do?" she asked. She points at the seeming flimsy wood pilings.

"It's just temporary," Jones says.

"It's like the Hudson," she says.

"For a while, they thought it might take the whole town," Jones says.

"Clean the place up in a hurry, eh?" she smiles.

"We cross here to get to our cabin," Jones said. Flynn does not respond.

. . .

SEPTEMBER 27, 1909

Early afternoon. Soft gold light. Boiling dust. Standing on their home-made platform of barrels and boxes at Higgins and Front, Flynn, Little, and Jones attract a crowd of men on foot, men in black hats, mackinaws, and black overalls,

some in sweat-stained vests and suspenders, some in wool shirts, muddy hobnail boots. Flynn, Little, and Jones are singing "The Preacher and the Slave," that parody of the "Sweet By and By:"

> *Long haired preachers come out every night*
> *just to tell us what's wrong and what's right*
> *but when asked about something to eat*
> *they can only this message repeat:*
>
> *you will eat by and by*
> *in that beautiful land beyond the sky*
> *work and pray, live on hay*
> *you'll get pie in the sky by and by.*

The crowd of men laugh, catcall. What a lark—jeering the pious majority! The Salvation Army is absent now, but these men know the sacred version. The idea of an impotent and too other-worldly idealism hits them like a sledge between the eyes. Bars begin to empty. Their voices echo and rebound off the brick facades. The singers are surrounded by the skulking pride and hidden self-pity of young single men, immigrant men, itinerant men, off-the-farm men, out-of-work men, westering men, some of the 78,000 men who had applied for but not been granted land when the Flathead Reservation was opened up for settlement in August. This Irish girl—red tie, black skirt, white blouse, hair gleaming in the light—she makes men stop, listen, laugh. Some begin to hope. "Sing for your pie in the sky," she calls before the chorus, and some of the men sing while others abhor the satiric sacrilege and turn away. Jones, Little, and Flynn choose a parody of "Revive Us Again" for energy and humor, "Hallelujah, I'm a Bum:"

> *I went to the boss to draw my payroll.*
> *He figured me out nine dollars in the hole.*
> *Hal-le-lu-jah, I'm a bum, hal-le-lu-jah, bum again.*
> *Hal-le-lu-jah, give us a handout to revive us again.*
>
> *Oh, how can we work like other men do,*
> *how can we work when there's no work to do?*
> *Hal-le-lu-jah, I'm a bum, hal-le-lu-jah, bum again.*
> *Hal-le-lu-jah, give us a handout to revive us again.*

Once the singing draws her crowd, Jack Jones introduces Flynn's speech and she begins to attack: "Fellow workers, the working class and the employing class have nothing in common. There can be no peace so long as hunger and want are found among millions of the working people and the few, who make up the employing class, have all the good things of life. Now who can tell this Irish girl why a logger has to pay just to get a job from O.K. Employment Agency? Who can tell me why the man pulling green chain gets fired the first day on the job at Western Lumber? Is Bonner, Hammond and Eddy in cahoots with the owner of the agency? You bet they are. Is Big Blackfoot in cahoots with the owner of the agency? You men know what I mean. How many of you've been fired after your first wages were paid by one of those outfits? How many of you still had to pay that employment agency crook his fee? I see men nodding all over. Well, workers of America, that's a rotten trick to play on men who've done the hard work, the dirty work of this country since the covered wagons came. This girl's here to see that stop—once and for all. They're cheats and crooks and here's one Irish girl who's not afraid to say so right here and now. The Industrial Workers of the World are here to expose their corruption and we can't be stopped. We're going to stand up here and make it hot for those damn employment agencies until they change their ways. A man should get a fair shake." She shakes her fist. A crowd has gathered now. Her voice rises over the audience with her outrage. She is fearless, articulate, coherent. She will eventually be considered the equal of William Jennings Bryan and Billy Sunday. In a later strike, one of her speeches will cause 25,000 garment workers to walk off the job. She sees sash windows sliding up in the Florence Hotel across the street, people leaning out the windows to listen. "I agitate a listener. I know how to get the power out of my diaphragm instead of my vocal cords, and I'm happy to be free to give capitalism hell," she would say later.

"Socialists. Radicals. A woman." The news blows like fine inexorable street dust into windows, mouths, nostrils, doors. Employment agency owners bolt for city hall and the police. Mayor Andrew Logan, a blacksmith, swaggers out of his City Carriage and Wagon to see for himself, then merchants and the mayor withdraw to the edges of the crowd to watch. Burly, blue-uniformed police officers and Police Chief Jacob Vealey surround the platform. More men crowd forward.

"The bulls are here now. Sure to be a fight," one drunk hobo says and falls flat on his face in the dirt, his whisky bottle half empty spilling out.

Flynn continues. "And where was the damned AF of L when you were hungry in '96?" The crowd grows and the streets slow down. "And why do the bosses hire these Pinkertons and Redburns and get these bulls out here to shut an Irish girl up and shed our blood?" Horse drawn buckboards, buggies, stop at the back of the crowd. Their drivers stand up and crane their necks. Men in black clothes crush together. "And why is it legal for scabs to take your jobs? You're the men who built the Northern Pacific. You're the men who move the dirt, drive the tunnels, lay the steel. You're the men who pick the prunes, knock the apples, punch the headers, cut the timber, grease the chutes, set the chokers, heave the cants, skin the horses, herd the sheep." With every clause, she brandishes her fist in the air. Men push forward, stand with upturned faces, listen transfixed by this messenger from the blind goddess of justice.

When she asks if they are tired of being gouged, they roar "Yes," and when she asks if they love their starvation wages, they roar "No," and when she asks if they want to do something about it, they roared "Yes" and she lays out the IWW plan—one big union, one single union all over the world, one union the bosses can't break with scabs or troops, one union the bosses can't beat with capital or liquor or bribes, one union they can't shoot or beat to death with henchmen and mercenaries—a union for all the working men and solidarity forever among us all. "You aren't wage slaves. Lincoln freed the slaves. You shouldn't be gouged by crooks or those confounded employment agencies." She points a terrifying finger at the Higgins Avenue storefronts where she can see their sheepish owners listening and she denounces them again. Their owners withdraw and lock their doors. She moves on to larger targets. "And how many of you got a piece of that new Indian land? About 81,000 people wanted that land and only 3,000 got any. Where's the justice in that now, I ask you?"

Missoula has heard nothing like this before—a voice for justice shouting in the streets.

As Flynn's attack goes on, the crowd jams the intersection to the bridge. When the Salvation Army band and choir appear before the First National

Bank in their black and red pseudo-military uniforms, she heckles them for filling the wage slaves full of holy hop just so they'll forget they are wage slaves. She calls them the Starvation Army and a local old madcap—Crazy Briggs—prances and wildly preaches to the facade of the First National Bank about repentance. The crowd laughs at the jokes of the raven-haired girl. They sing "Preacher and the Slave" again and the Salvation Army is shocked and silent. The Christians have not heard themselves satirized in song before. Flynn sounds like that tent evangelist who came to town and fleeced everyone by telling them the world was coming to an end, but she doesn't want everyone to be saved in some other world. She wants this world to be changed. She wants those rich bosses to confess their greed, repent, start spreading salvation on the earth by sharing more of their wealth.

In the middle of her speech, Flynn sees soldiers in dress blues—campaign hats, leather gloves, white neckerchiefs—working their way around the back of the crowd. She heckles them and points: "There's the biggest drones in America," she calls out, "eating high off the hog while the working class starves. These are the blue-coated bastards who went up to Arlee in '92 just to push the poor men in Coxey's Army around. These are the men who attack unarmed miners at Cripple Creek," she shouts at them. "And why did you use your guns to kill strikers in the Coeur d'Alene? And why beat up strikers in the bull pens you build for the capitalists? You're a bunch of over-fed, bored, lily-livered bullies."

As Flynn speaks, the soldiers push like a blue splitting wedge toward the front of the crowd. "Here come the capitalist dogs," she says. "Now, you watch them violate the Constitution of the United States and try to shut an Irish girl up. Does anyone have a Constitution here? Give it to the fattest one when he gets here, see if he can read, or if he just learned to bite." She rails on them for killing whatever they don't understand, for being governmental pawns against working men.

Jacob Vealey, the chief of police, sees a riot coming. Standing next to Flynn's platform with his officers, Vealey signals his men to lift their night sticks, push the crowd back, and form a fence between the approaching soldiers and the flimsy IWW platform. More sash windows in the surrounding buildings are sliding upward now, more people hang their heads out, stare down into the crowd before the woman. The corporal and his men push their way through—flushed, big-necked, angry. "And now look here—the brave bullies are after more innocent blood," Flynn shouts over the crowd. "And coming to attack a pregnant woman now, are ye? What big brave boys you are. Your mothers should have taught you better manners." The crowd roars with laughter. The soldiers have a bloody nose or two in mind, maybe a few split lips and loose teeth, maybe a few stars spread around among the whole damn foul-mouthed bunch of them and chuck the god-damn anarchists in the river.

"Back off now, boys," says Vealey when they reach his cordon. "I don't want trouble started here and neither does your captain." Vealey stares down the red-faced huffing officer at the front of the column.

"She insulted us," the corporal complains.

"The lady's got a right to her opinions," Vealey says, "and if you want to file a complaint, come along to the station," then he turns to Flynn, Little, and Jones. "You three better pipe down now and lay off the boys in blue."

"Anarchists," a soldier shouts, "anarchists don't deserve your protection."

Vealey picks up his admonition to the IWW trio again: "You had the crowd on your side before you attacked these soldiers. Better come down now and let sleeping dogs lie," he says.

"They're dangerous," Flynn says. "I don't care if I say it to their faces. We have constitutional rights in this country. We're not going to be shut up. We'll be back at 5:00 then." Flynn, Jones, and Little come down off the platform and pass out literature among the crowd—just like the Salvation Army would pass evangelical tracts. The soldiers head south, cross the river. The men disperse into the Front Street and Higgins Avenue bars, speakeasies, brothels, honky-tonks, Chinese joints—anywhere they can sit, eat, smoke, drink, talk, and rest.

When Little and Jones and Flynn stand up before the Hammond Building again at 5:00 p.m., four police mount the platform with clubs drawn. "The men are under arrest for disturbing the peace," Jacob Vealey announces, "but the woman will be allowed to go." The crowd is immediately silent now. Flynn comes down, but she fears what is coming. Violence may have been inevitable now. Sooner or later, Frank Little and Jack Jones will resist. They have already agreed. The IWW code—anything goes—requires that they not submit easily. The crowd starts to yell like a prizefight mob now. Frank Little reads the Bill of Rights, his fists clenched to the paper, his face a shadowy fury. Burly Jack Jones stands dark, thick-necked, hunched shoulders passive and squared off as blind Goliath. Flynn turns away as Little shouts out the Bill of Rights and curses the god damn bulls who hate the Constitution and she hears Jones explode like a wounded bear charging out of brush and screaming at the overfed sons a bitches who are no friend of the working man. She hears the scuffle and scream and crack of the clubs breaking bone as her men are bloodied, beaten, and dragged away.

Her back is turned. She can't bear the sight of blood.

She is passing out red cards, newspapers, pamphlets to the hands from the Bitterroot, brown, work-hardened hands of men who are picking tons of ripe apples, pears, plums; to the hands from the Blackfoot, Seeley, Swan, work-hardened by days, years, lives on axes, peaveys, canthooks, crosscut saws; to the calloused hands from the Bonner mills, the empty hands of the unemployed. More men come to her now. In the soft reddish aura of dusk, she recruits them for the next round, her shoes marking the dirt street. She tells men to join her union, to help an Irish girl fight. She's young, charismatic, sexy. She wants their help. They follow her.

Everything as planned—so far. Missoula doesn't see her strategy of civil disobedience—she knows. Overnight, a killing frost comes down. In the morning sun, vegetable gardens are suddenly filled with blackened wilted leaves.

The next afternoon, Flynn stands again before the Hammond Building at Higgins and Front. Chief Vealey has ten uniformed officers around her now. Outside the ring of police, hobo workers surround her. She sends a Bitterroot logger from O'Brien Creek on the platform to read the Declaration of Independence. Would that stop them? Vealey's men drag the logger down and arrest him. From the new district office of the U.S. Forest Service, H. L. Tucker watches the crowd, the police, the raven-haired woman on the boardwalk. He is listening now. His window is open. When the logger is dragged down, Tucker explodes. He runs down the stairs of the Hammond Building, bursts out onto the boardwalk, and speaks to Flynn. "Go, go," Flynn tells him and puts the Declaration of Independence in his hands. At least there is one man of conscience in Missoula, and a federal employee too. She needs spontaneous, powerful men, men who act out their feelings, men she can inspire. Tucker jumps on the platform and continues to read the Declaration of Independence until he is also brought down and arrested. She has two more men stand up to read. Two more men arrested.

SEPTEMBER 30, 1909

Thursday morning. Imagine Flynn standing outside the Missoula City Hall. She studies the white team of fire horses—sleek, powerful, Mustang-headed geldings feeding in their nosebags. Under the horse stalls in whitewashed basement cells, Jack Jones, Frank Little, H. L. Tucker, and George Applebee lie on crude bunks. Jones and Little are bloodied, broken-boned, wounded. A boy has brought her news from Tucker and Applebee. Sheriff Sherman has beaten Jones again. No doctor has been sent to them. Flynn wants to reassure them—some-how—but there are police everywhere.

Standing there before the classically-balanced brick facade of City Hall, she studies its illusion of colloquial calm, its two eyebrow windows, its Greek golden mean, its perfectly centered doors, perfectly proportioned windows. The basement jail is invisible to her. A dark hawk circles over the hills to the north—a high shadow in the morning light. She regrets falling in love with Jones. Two years ago, he seemed the right man—a professional revolutionary, a comrade in the cause of organizing miners, but after her first baby was born dead, after the winter in Chicago, she feels immense distance and near indifference. She thinks only of the union to be organized, this city to be defeated, and she has sacrificed whatever marriage they had to that cause. Pleasures might come later—whatever they were. Did she believe in pleasures anymore? Ideas seem to be capturing her. In her uterus, the new baby makes a half turn. The stable boys take the nosebags from the white fire horses and lead them one by one from their stalls. She can see the cracks in the plank floor, imagines her men in their cells, the horse urine drizzling down on her men. She will have to wait. This is not the time to show compassion.

Judge Harry Small sits black-robed, white-haired, and reads aloud: "You are charged with holding meetings on the public streets in violation of city or-

dinances. It is alleged that these men, assisted by one woman, occupied prominent positions on platforms constructed on boxes and barrels from which they
addressed the general public and they are said to have hurled uncomplimentary
remarks at passersby who failed to respond to their entreaties to stop and listen to their pleas for public recognition. The members of the Salvation Army
and of Uncle Sam's army were assailed in the most bitter terms... How do you
plead?" Judge Small asks, then examines the four unshaven men who stand before him in irons.

They are all dressed in boots, mackinaws, and overalls—except for the Forest
Service man—who wears braces, a vest, green slacks, and a rumpled white shirt.
Why would a federal employee be mixed up with these bums? Chains clank. Prisoners shift their weight. A huge purple bruise and an eye swollen shut on one
man's face. Another man's eyes wander—unfocused, glazed, crazed. He sways and
nearly falls face down. They are all straw-covered and unwashed. One looks part
Indian—Frank Little's face wounded and dark with hatred or is it pain?

"Not guilty," one says eagerly. Flynn sits and watches with reporters.

"On what grounds?" Judge Small demands.

"The Salvation Army made more noise than we did, your honor."

"Irrelevant. The police charges clearly state that you yourselves were loud, un-
ruly, provocative, and a danger to the peace."

"But their band and preacher were the loudest thing for four or five blocks in
any direction. We could barely hear ourselves."

"Irrelevant." Judge Small hits his gavel on the table before him. "I find you all
guilty of disturbing the peace and hereby sentence you to 15 days in the county
jail or you may pay a $10.00 fine. I will further give you men the option of a sus-
pended sentence if you will promise to refrain from making public speeches."

"We would rather go to jail," Applebee says.

"Jail it is, my boys," Small replies. "Case closed." His tiny gavel comes down.

Flynn watches the four men led away in chains. She feels that she has been
convicted with them, but she also knows that Missoula police will hesitate to
arrest a woman four months pregnant. Flynn walks immediately to the Western
Union office.

Though she seems an isolate, she is not in this alone. During the spring and summer of 1909, Flynn has lived and spoken in Butte, Kalispell, Spokane—industrializing regional cities all within a few hours by train. At Western Union, she sends telegrams to Butte and to Spokane, and the latter will immediately publish her full page, front-page call for help in the *Industrial Worker*—with this ending:

> *Are you game?*
> *Are you afraid?*
> *Do you love the police?*
> *Have you been robbed, skinned, grafted on?*
> *If so, then go to Missoula and defy the Police,*
> *the courts, and the people who live off the wages*
> *of prostitution.*

Walking back to the Harnois Theater, she doesn't think of Jack Jones, but only of the fighting speech to come. She has to inspire these Missoula men to keep up their sacrifices until reinforcements come.

By 5:00 p.m., another crowd of men waits for her at the dirt and brick intersection where poverty meets propriety. She sees Jacob Vealey and his blue police force standing by the platform. She has four men ready now—Montana loggers in tin pants, pinetop shirts, hobnail boots. Clifford Hughes climbs onto the boxes and barrels and begins, "Fellow workers and friends," and the blue policemen take him down, and Louis Miller climbs up and begins to read the Constitution and he is taken down and Peter Brown climbs up and opens his mouth and he is taken down, and John Clifford climbs up and starts to read the Bill of Rights and they take him down. These men know her strategy now—pack the city jails. Like a queen bee filling a hive, she now has eight men in cells.

Are more men coming to her now? How long would they take? All weekend? She is at their mercy now. She suddenly feels vulnerable, alone, afraid. How many men will she have by Sunday? It is Thursday now, September 30, 1909. She will have to wait. If she has the men, Sunday will be a good day to provoke the final confrontation. With thirteen churches, Missoula will not like a Sunday disruption. Timing will be on her side. She retreats to the Harnois Theater to sleep. One of her molars aches. Her jaw feels swollen, inflamed.

OCTOBER 1, 1909

On Friday morning, Clifford, Hughes, Miller, and Brown are released from the City Jail and come back to her basement headquarters. They've been treated just like drunks—intoxicated by speech. No release for ringleaders Jones, Little, Tucker, and Applebee. They have been shunted to the county hoosegow. How big is it?—she has to know. No one knows for sure. It's up on cribbing and looks small. Well, damn the luck. Together, Flynn and the men plan the afternoon arrests. She tells the men about the telegrams, the army of bindlestiffs on the way from Spokane and Butte. The men wash their hands, drink boiling coffee from their clean tin cans, eat meat and cheese sandwiches slabbed with homemade bread and butter. There is a bag of raw onions to gnaw. They roll cigarettes and light their pipes. Talk ranges around the circle—rats in jail, horse urine through the ceiling planks, friendly railroad bull in the Missoula yards. They're lucky. They're close. They're conspirators. She listens to their talk like a new missionary might listen to her new converts in some tribe.

At 4:30, they walk quixotic for Higgins and Front street again. In late, long-shadowed light, the tower of the First National Bank shines like a copper-jacketed bullet. Her men climb their boxes and barrels and begin singing. Vealey and his force immediately surround her platform. They are waiting for her again. They let the singing go on for a while. As the boisterous crowd gathers, Flynn sells pamphlets, memberships, red cards. She needs petty cash. Her men open their mouths and begin their speeches. Horse-drawn buggies and wagons cease their jangle and drivers listen. One by one, the blue-uniformed police take the speakers down from the platform, but this time the crowd will not open. The men surround the platform. The police cannot walk their prisoners the block and a half to jail. She has a stalemate on Front and Higgins.

"Hitch a team to the hose wagon and roll it down here," Mayor Andrew Logan shouts to Albert May, the Fire Chief. Police Chief Vealey himself mounts the IWW platform and someone immediately shouts, "Disturbing the peace, disturbing the peace." Vealey lifts his arms above his helmeted head for silence, then shouts, "I am warning you all. Disperse immediately or you will be washed. "Disturbing the peace," someone shouts. The crowd roars and begins to chant,

"Arrest the bull, arrest the bull." Vealey waits five minutes. The white fire horses pull the hosewagon to the river. The crowd does not move. These damn hoboes are daring him. Authority will have to act or be mocked. Vealey sees Albert May is ready. He has two men on the nozzle. Vealey gives the signal. The fire nozzle hisses air. The hose begins to writhe and swell. Suddenly freezing river water stings the air like cold hard silver. Wet men shouting, cursing, shoving at each other, wet frightened horses bolting and wagons tipping over on muddied men screaming, wet slick hair and dresses of whores, wet aprons over the heads of storekeepers and bartenders—everyone in pain, panic, mud, flight. Eventually, Clifford, Hughes, Miller, and Brown are led down the mud ruts street to the same jail to spend the night again.

These four men make a repeat performance. This buys her time.

The press—who seem to have carefully censored all violence so far—follow Flynn everywhere now. Reporters from the *Butte Sentinel*, the *Daily Missoulian*, and the *Anaconda Standard* go to court with her the next morning. Flynn and the IWW are news. This time, Flynn coaches her men—refuse to plead in police court and demand a jury trial. This is more expensive. Due process cannot be denied. The press will report everything. She must remove the protective isolation from Missoula now. Silence, secrets, and fear will defeat her— she knows. All Montana and Washington have to hear, Coeur d'Alene District miners have to hear, Butte miners have to hear—Gurley Flynn is in Missoula and she's in trouble now.

OCTOBER 2, 1909

Saturday night, the jury convicts Clifford, Hughes, Miller, and Brown—just as Judge Small had the night before. When Judge Small sentences them to fifteen days in the county jail, the four men cheer him and begin to sing. The judge looks dumbfounded. "Order, order," he shouts and brings his gavel down.

While her men are on trial that evening, Flynn herself mounts the barrels and boxes beneath the Hammond Building again. In eerie white light from the Salvation Army's carbide flares, she speaks to the crowd briefly and the police just listen. Several hundred men chant "Girley, Girley, Girley," as she speaks—

even her middle name, a homophone, helps her cause. It is more than she can say for "Vealey" and "Small." She speaks until dark, then walks to the Harnois basement again.

She is never alone now. Homeless, farmless, immigrant, migrant, harvest hands, timber beasts, miners, muckers, teamsters, apple knockers, loggers, mill-hands—men come to her. She is heroic Liberty, revolution, hope, change. She is the possibility of prosperity, respectability, power. Some will ride the rails south when the weather turns cold. Some will show up drunk or get fired. Some will be cheated and fired for protesting too loudly. They are mostly hungry, gaunt, young. They are men whose American Horatio Alger illusions of wealth or ease have been forever stripped from them. In fact, these are the first migrant workers in the west, and they are mostly white. They hold stiff cold hands out to the stove, drink coffee from their tin cans, eat sandwiches and raw onions, get warm, then walk back to the jungle fires outside of town along the tracks to sleep. At the Harnois,

Elizabeth Gurley Flynn (center) with F. W. Flynn (man on right), and other Butte Federation of Miners, 1909.   Photo: Iron In Her Soul, Helen Camp, 1995

Flynn sees her comrades from Spokane drift in. It is Saturday night. She has a full basement now. Will this be enough? She isn't sure. As she rests and listens, she feels her baby push and turn inside her. She feels heavy, tired, exhilarated. All the new faces change everything. Maybe there is a chance to beat greed now. Maybe. Late, she retreats to the cabin on the Bitterroot.

OCTOBER 3, 1909

Sunday, more men speak, more men arrested: H. Mattson, Sam Tobin, B.C. Stork, A. Roe, A. Johnson, G. E. Boyd, Joe Marsh, G. E. Bailey—all eight from Spokane. Maybe she will win in spite of Missoula? Her message has shown its potency. Now, she will test the messenger—herself. How far will Vealey and Logan and Small let her go? She doesn't know.

On Sunday night, she walks surrounded by new men to Higgins and Front and mounts the platform. Burning torches wash the crowd's faces with smoky waves of red and black shadows. She teaches them a song that parodies the hymn, "Power in the Blood." A few men from Spokane join in, men she had met at the IWW hall where she spoke earlier that summer:

> *There is power, power*
> *In a band of working men*
> *When they stand hand in hand,*
> *That's a power, power*
> *That must rule in every land...*

After she leads her song, Chief Vealey speaks to her from the street in front of the platform. "You're under arrest now, Mrs. Jones," he says, "so please come quietly." He is a retired Northern Pacific engineer, but he looks like a bulldog to her, a bulldog of public order which—to her—means public silence, the great threat to justice, democracy, poverty, integrity everywhere. Reporters crowd forward to listen now.

She does not resist. Disobedience is sufficiently articulate.

Vealey helps her down, and he leads her off to the county jail through the cat-calling crowd. Five reporters follow now. A pregnant girl had been arrested—"an arch disturber, organizer, and leader of the Industrial Workers of the World," writes one. "A woman of unquestionable courage when engaged in the work of her organization," writes another. "She gave her name as Mrs. J. A. Jones," reports a third, "and stated that the IWW could not be suppressed and that the work would be carried on as outlined even if ten men are jailed every day." Irrepressible woman. While being booked into the jail, she still speaks to the press. The charge against her: inciting the members of her organization in their tirades and activities against the public order.

There is no women's jail. All the other jail cells are full now. Chief Vealey shows her to the witness room in the county jail where Mrs. Vealey provides her a cot, a basin, water pitcher, towel, and slop jar. Mrs. Vealey stays with her long enough to learn of her condition and learns that she had previously miscarried. Flynn asks for a dentist to extract her tooth. She is in pain, jaw swollen now. The Chief will send a dentist in the morning. They lock the messenger in.

Alone on her cot in the witness room, Flynn stares out at the far cold stars. She has coarse wool blankets, but there is no heat. Lying there, she thinks she might be losing the fight, but then hears the men start singing in the jail. They are so loud—the sound comes through the walls. She smiles to herself in the dark. The message cannot be contained. She is tired. The inflamed molar aches. She cannot sleep.

OCTOBER 4, 1909

Monday morning, the papers deliver more narrow columns of bad news to Missoula—100 more IWW men are coming from Seattle; 100 more are coming from Portland; twenty five more men from Spokane left on the train last night; thirty more men left Spokane this morning. In Butte, the Western Federation of Miners writes and publishes a public denunciation of Missoula police violence in the *Butte Miner*. While reporters—like all writers—sometimes fail the truth, word-of-mouth news about beaten, broken, bloodied men travels quickly. The same denunciation will appear Wednesday in the *Daily Missoulian*.

The raven-haired woman filled with speech may be more than they have anticipated. Missoula may regret its error. Missoula realizes that they may have underestimated Flynn, but still Missoula does not know how to respond. They spend Monday thinking and talking. Someone monitors the newspaper office.

Someone telegraphs Spokane police. Someone rides horseback out to the Missoula jungle and sees the brush filling up with hoboes—more poor men than Missoula has seen since the Flathead land rush.

OCTOBER 5, 1909

On Tuesday afternoon, Flynn walks from her cell to her trial—police court on the second floor of city hall. With all the reporters present, with her powers, strategies, and condition now more completely known, Judge Small dismisses her case immediately and without comment. No one writes anything. What journalist would dare report that Missoula has arrested a pregnant 19-year old New Yorker who is about to bring them to their knees? What kind of city is this? Flynn seems invulnerable to law. Victorian decorum prevents anyone saying she is pregnant. As this dreamer walks free out the door of city hall, Jacob Vealey and Harry Small stare in wonder and anger. They wish the new courthouse and jail were finished. They wish the old ones were larger. Her men are singing in the cells now. They are loud. They draw a crowd to the jail now. Surrounded by more men, she starts a song and walks back to the Harnois Theater basement and disappears.

The war that Flynn has started, however, advances around her. Her friend from Spokane, Edith Frenette, has arrived. Just before dinner, Frenette and twenty men from Spokane go marching as to war. At Higgins and Front, twenty new men stand up to speak and the Missoula police take twenty men down. Mrs. Frenette waits, then she herself mounts the platform and she is also brought down. They begin to sing "Solidarity Forever," and they march gladly to jail.

As the noisy crowd follows the singing Wobblies down Higgins Avenue, woodsmoke rolls down roofs and fogs the cold October streets. In the darkness, a rock flies out of the crowd and hits one of the policemen on the arm. No one can see who has thrown it. Like most allegations of Wobbly violence, no one knows if a Wobbly actually committed it. When Edith Frenette and her men arrive at the jail, the Wobblies in the cells begin to sing their organizing hymn to the tune of the "Marseillaise" and Frenette sings with them as she disappears indoors—locked in the same witness room that Flynn herself had slept in the night before.

Civic collapse is just offstage.

Mayor Andrew Logan, the stout blacksmith, no longer appears as a city government representative. No record explicitly explains his absence, but he seems to be implicated in the corrupt employment agencies, the whorehouses, the violence against Jones and Little. The city is now represented by Acting Mayor H. T. Wilkinson, an alderman from the Third Ward. Missoula has already hired six more police and has paid for a Saturday night jury trial. Missoula has to hire another man to help the treasurer and clerk at $100 per month. Missoula police are still arresting everyone who stands up to speak, but worse yet, the Apple Show is coming when Missoula streets should be bustling with settlers, Indians, workers and their families from the Bitterroot, the Swan, the Blackfoot, the Flathead—all the outlying valley folks always come to town with money to spend. Crops are mostly in. It is like Harvest Home. Cash registers should be ringing all over town. Central business district merchants now complain that the IWW meetings have and will obstruct the streets and interfere with Apple Show business.

The worst of it? That Flynn woman is still running around free. She has packed the jails with 43 hungry men whose meals are costing Missoula serious money. In the city jail, the prisoners sing in their cells, make speeches, chant slogans in chorus, and their hullabaloo is so loud that guests in the Missoula Hotel and Judge Small in his courtroom complain. All of the prisoners must move to the county jail. And the Wobblies prisoners now refuse to leave the county jail when the doors are opened before breakfast. They demand food.

OCTOBER 6, 1909

Only one local man breaks solidarity—call him a university sociologist. He is married and has been arrested. When the jail doors swing open before breakfast, he leaves to explain to his wife where he has been all night. When he returns at 8:30, the Missoula crowd stands watching him. Embarrassed, dumbfounded, he stands outside the locked jail doors looking in.

"Whatta you want, fella?" the policeman on duty asks.

"I must be allowed back in," the professor says.

"Why's that?"

"They'll assume I'm a coward."

"Not a chance."

"But I've studied deviance all my life."

"You're out, now you stay out," the policeman says. The Missoula crowd laughs, and the sociologist slinks away—red-faced—to the new university across the river.

OCTOBER 7, 1909

H. T. Wilkinson can see that Missoula is being overrun. As Acting Mayor, he has to try something different now—anything to get this woman and her rabble rousers out of town. Thursday morning, he tests Andrew Vealey with a compromise: see if Flynn will agree to just stop speaking in the central business district—they can speak anywhere else in the city as long as they don't disrupt traffic and pedestrians.

Chief Vealey walks to the Harnois Theater basement to see the Flynn woman—who is surrounded by a crowd of new men now—more than 30 have rolled in by side door Pullman since yesterday. Vealey is no longer dumbfounded. He presents the acting mayor's compromise, Flynn tells him that she will get an answer for him quickly, and he goes out. From the boardwalk, he hears a loud roaring "No" and a louder "Yes" and several rounds of applause. Flynn's raven hair, white oval face, blue eyes flash through the open door. Andrew Vealey looks down to her from the sidewalk. He sees her swollen jaw has subsided some. The infected molar is gone now.

"The men insist on speaking wherever they chose," she says.

"But what about the rights of our citizens?" Vealey asks.

"We're protecting their constitutional right to free speech," she says. She beams a broad smile. "See you tonight, Chief."

Missoula wants an easy truce, but the Irish girl will not give it to them—not yet. She senses the elation of victory and she knows what victory means: news will go out that speaking on the public streets is legal. She needs that precedent, that affirmation of civil liberty. Nothing can be allowed to mute that message now. All spring and summer she has been preparing for this moment. Now, cities all over the West will hear that resistance to the IWW and free speech is impossible. The right to organize the union rests on the success of this Missoula precedent.

At 4:00 p.m., the Wobbly crowd marches up East Main singing and Flynn marches at their center. Wobblies sing down Main to Higgins and fill the street. All traffic stops. The crowd turns up Higgins to Front, and 35 poor men stand up to read the Constitution or the Declaration of Independence, and Missoula takes thirty five poor men down and marches them away—singing—to jail, bed, board, and trial. Flynn cheers her men on, but does not mount the stage herself now.

That evening, Chief Vealey begins the capitulation. He tells the *Anaconda Standard* that everything has changed: "We will file charges against these men arrested tonight and their trials will settle the question as to whether or not the ordinance under which we're working can be enforced."

Thursday night. Is this over? There are seventy eight men in jail for reading the Constitution or the Bill of Rights or the Declaration of Independence on the streets. Is seventy eight men enough to persuade Missoula that something needs to change? Tomorrow, the crisis will come, the crisis that Elizabeth Gurley Flynn, aka Mrs. J. A. Jones, aka "Girley" Flynn has been trying to provoke since that day—three weeks ago?—she descended from the Northern Pacific train.

OCTOBER 8, 1909

In Police Court the next morning, the city attorney files complaints against thirty speakers of the IWW for attempting to speak and hold meetings in the business section of the city. Of the thirty, twenty five plead not guilty, and the remaining five refuse to plead one way or the other, declaring they do not have to plead anything, but demand separate jury trials. She watches as they are all released on their own recognizance until 2:00 p.m. tomorrow, when Judge Small promises to set their cases for trial. Perhaps the issue of constitutional law will actually be addressed? Somehow, she doubts it. She is winning because she is costing the city money it does not have, and because her men are costing the business district its respectable tranquility. There seems to be no legal or constitutional issue here, no, this is just pragmatist against revolutionary.

By Friday noon, she has gone back to the Harnois Theater basement again. The men cheer when she comes in. The celebrating has begun. A huge black kettle of beef mulligan simmers on the stove. Fresh coffee boils in a gallon can. There are loaves of stale bread. There is whiskey. She tells them to be ready for tonight. It might not be over yet. One man hawks, spits, begins to sing "My Wild Irish Rose" and several men add harmony and bass. Flynn smiles and lies down on a makeshift cot to rest.

When the City Council meets that night, they allow only one reporter from the *Butte Miner* in the room. Defeat is not going to be made more public than absolutely necessary. Mayor Wilkinson explains that Missoula is tired of fighting, that the police want resolution now, that acceptance would be the best course of action. The City Council agrees.

Let them all go.

There will be no trial.

The IWW can make public addresses anywhere—so long as they don't block the streets. The boardwalks are wide enough. That should work.

The news goes immediately to Flynn.

She has won.

The public street is her forum.

There is hope, she says. Silence has not won.

That evening, the IWW speakers stand on their boxes and barrels beneath the Hammond Building. The crowds gather to listen again as the Wobblies rail against the bosses, gougers, cheaters, exploiters and the Wobblies tell them how one big union all over the world is the only way to make any difference and that working men have to stick together if they want any control over their own lives and, as the police listen, reporters write down that the Wobblies will make a free speech fight in *any* city that doesn't allow them to exercise their constitutional right. They will win again. Justice and truth are on their side. Fear, silence, propriety, greed—Flynn and her men have overcome them all.

In the dusk, the police herd the crowd from Higgins onto the boardwalks and down West Front. Traffic over the river goes on smoothly now over the trembling bridge. No more arrests. After the sunset burns the brick facades, turrets, and towers around them into temporary gold, the subsiding light around them goes gray, dims blue. Cold wind off the river chills their hands and faces. For the last time, Flynn walks with the men to the Harnois basement where there is fire, food, whiskey, celebration.

With all the charges dropped, men from the jails began to come to the Harnois basement. They are greeted with loud jubilant cheering until H. L. Tucker and George Applebee carry the beaten Jack Jones into the room. There is a sudden silence. Two other men carry the broken Frank Little. The new men see their bloodied, swollen, and broken faces and swollen discolored hands. "Get a doctor," Flynn orders. A man runs out. The murmur of outrage quells the sense of celebration. They try to keep their voices low now out of respect.

They watch Flynn walk quietly to Jack Jones, kneel beside his cot, caress his face, speak softly to him. A man soaks his handkerchief in cold water and lays it on Jones' forehead, another does the same for Little. Flynn returns to the front and addresses the men crowding around her: "This is war, you men must know. In America, you have no right that is not exercised—and no American knows what exercising such rights will take, and no one knows which of us will have to bear the price of proving such rights exist, and no one knows who will escape with a minor wound, who with a major sacrifice." Out of the night, the doctor comes in, examines Jones and Little where they lie on cots at the back of the room, and begins treating them. Flynn goes back to see them. They are swathed in new white bandages now and the doctor, who is preparing a cast for Jones' right hand, gives Jones morphine. She kneels and touches Jones' arm, then stands up and talks softly with the doctor. She feels distant and impersonal sympathy for the brutalized Jones. His bloody sobbing and swearing take over the room, but gradually the morphine slurs his speech into mumbling and drool. Someone promises revenge on Sheriff Graham—the talk of martyrs and retribution circles in the room like a curling snake of smoke. "When he's well enough, take him to the cabin," Flynn instructs H. L. Tucker—one of the faithful locals.

OCTOBER 9, 1909

Riding west through Frenchtown on the Northern Pacific the next morning, Flynn hears the loud rhythmic whack of steel wheels on each jointed rail. She sees how October frost has blackened the Missoula gardens along the tracks, how tamarack are going gold, how early snow has brushed Mt. Lolo's sloping ridge. Her swollen jaw is subsiding. With her tongue, she can feel the cavity where her molar is missing now. The place is raw and tender, but the taste of blood is gone. Heading for Spokane and the next free speech fight on that lucid frozen October morning, how could she know that her Missoula triumph may have been both tragic and delusory?

Several years later, H. L. Tucker, the Forest Service employee who spontaneously joined her Missoula cause, would die when his plane crashed into San Francisco Bay while he was dropping "Hands Off Russia" leaflets for the IWW.

In 1917, Frank Little would be lynched by a mob in Butte, and his body would hang from a bridge too long.

Flynn's hasty marriage to Jack Jones would end in Missoula. When she was arrested and tried three times during the next free speech fight in Spokane, Jones did not go to see her or assist her. He stayed in Missoula, his wounds probably still healing. When the Spokane free speech fight was over in early 1910, Flynn took the train alone to New York for the remainder of her pregnancy. They divorced in 1920—well after Flynn had been living with the great love of her life, Carlo Tresca.

Their only son, Fred Flynn, whom she carried *en utero* through both Missoula and Spokane free speech fights, would die in March 29, 1940—age 29. In the 1920s, Fred had told her that he "never understood why she had him when she did not have time to raise him." She never recovered from that negligence and guilt.

Jack Jones would become the owner of Chicago's Dill Pickle Club—a freethinker's paradise. He would die the same year as his son.

The Missoula victory would also mislead the organizing IWW vanguard. While Flynn had brought down the Garden City, that success would be nearly impossible to repeat. When she tried to use her Missoula tactics in Spokane, the larger city responded with more police, more money, more space. Spokane turned an empty unheated schoolhouse into a prison and kept up the arrests of street speakers until 1,200 men were jailed. The imprisoned Wobblies tried a hunger strike and even that did not work as expected. Spokane had no Apple Show coming. Spokane had more violent police. For months, there were riots and beatings.

Before speaking in Spokane, Flynn would chain herself to light posts with padlocks—Houdini-like—to make it difficult to immediately carry her away. The police would have to cut her out of her chains as she spoke. By those standards, Missoula had been a larking, Chief Vealey a country gentleman, Higgins and Main a Sunday picnic.

In the next ten years of IWW strikes, the one rock and cold water that had been thrown around in Missoula would become bullets, clubs, bloodshed, and death in Everett, Centralia, San Diego. The singing hallelujah bums and the Big Rock Candy Mountain dream that triumphed in Missoula was eventually smashed into coffins, prisons, broken bones, strikes, smithereens—for innumerable reasons—and by 1917, the IWW was under federal indictment and effectively metamorphosed into radical northwest legend, memory, song. Subsequently, Flynn led some famous strikes, fell in love with Carlo Tresca, founded the American Civil Liberties Union, and in 1936, she joined and became a leader of the American Communist Party. In 1952, she was tried and convicted of subversion and espionage under the Smith Act, and served 28 months in a Federal prison. From 1961–1964, she chaired the American Communist Party. She died in Moscow in September, 1964.

Preface to

RICHARD HUGO AT EASTERN OREGON UNIVERSITY: AN INTERVIEW WITH RONALD H. BAYES

In Fall, 1970, a new M.F.A. from the University of Montana where I'd studied poetry and fiction writing with Madeline DeFrees, Richard Hugo, William Kittredge, and Earl Ganz, I'd been hired by Eastern Oregon University (EOU) to teach writing and literature. That first year in La Grande I became the impresario for Ars Poetica, a campus-based, professional literary outpost and the only active literary reading venue east of the Oregon Cascades. Launched in 1961 with the advocacy of poet Ronald H. Bayes and inspired by the San Francisco Beat movement, Ars Poetica initially showcased campus writers, musicians, and artists but gradually attracted readings by major Northwest poets: in 1964, Portland poets Kenneth Hanson, Vern Rutsala, and Vi Gale, Montana poet Warren Carrier, and Washington poet Madeline DeFrees (then Sister Mary Gilbert). In January, 1965, Ed Dorn drove over from Idaho; in June Richard Hugo drove down from Montana; in October, Robert Creeley drove up from California after the Berkeley Poetry Conference. Fast forward to fall, 1983: after Richard Hugo's memorial reading, I discovered Bayes' 1965 taped interview with Hugo. Listening, I found Hugo's comments historic and enlightening, especially those on his fellow poets in *Five Poets of the Pacific Northwest*. Eventually, I sent the transcribed text to Ripley Schemm (1923–2012) for editing and permission, which she granted with one condition: delete Hugo's criticism of William Stafford flooding the mails with his poems. Like the Hugo House founded in Seattle in 1996 to honor Hugo's legacy, Ars Poetica continues today to create opportunities for writers in the region—a distinguished literary venue for over fifty years.

Sources: *Oregon East* 1950-1985: 92-98; Photos: Richard Hugo ca 1983 courtesy Mansfield Library Archives and Special Collections, University of Montana, and courtesy of Jennifer Schemm; Ronald H. Bayes (below) ca 1965 courtesy Pierce Library, Eastern Oregon University Special Collections.

RICHARD HUGO AT EASTERN OREGON UNIVERSITY: A 1965 INTERVIEW WITH RON BAYES

Ron Bayes: Dick, you have something to say about linguistic or verbal rights. Could you comment on this?

Dick Hugo: Yes. I was talking about what I call the private ownership of certain words. There are certain poets who do this. They use words that are so peculiarly theirs that you can't use them without sounding like you're imitating that particular poet. Also, these same poets have the same relationships to words that they have to the world, that is to say, there are certain places they emotionally own—certain scenes, sometimes certain birds, or certain kinds of fish. Yeats, you might say, owned the word *mackerel*. He owned the word *gyre,* and he owned *permed.* These are odd words. I was saying that there are certain poets who are obsessive and I look for the student who has obsessions because that's the one I'm most able to help because this is the kind of sensibility that I think I have.

I don't mean to say this is the only kind of poet there is: there are very good public poets such as Auden. People such as Auden use words at their dictionary value. As you read the words, they mean no more to Auden than they mean to you. With the so-called private poets that I've been talking about, Hopkins and Yeats—Dylan Thomas, to some extent perhaps—you always had the feeling that something is going on between the poet and the poem that you recognize you will never understand. This mystery tends to be a force that preserves the integrity of the poem. Now, the poem might mean more to the reader than it means to the poet. The point is that it meant something to the poet that the reader recognizes is there, but doesn't understand or comprehend. I think this goes on in certain Rouault paintings.

Bayes: Creeley has this quality for me. I don't know if it's identifiable as readily.

Hugo: It is not identifiable for me with Creeley's poetry, but his sensibility is so much different from mine that I never quite get on his wave length. I appreciate Creeley most for the odd line breaks he makes. I see a kind of magic going on, that kind of magic print can do on a page. Sometimes it works for Creeley. But Creeley's obsessions tend more away from images, places, and events—experience—and toward a kind of way of saying things. I think he's obsessed with having a method of saying things and it's a slightly different problem with him than what I'm talking about. I tend more to talk more from the standpoint of the Symbolist and Imagist. But this is true: there is something rather obsessive about Creeley. I don't get it—quite.

Bayes: There's a sense of the secret.

Hugo: That's right, there's a sense of the secret idea Creeley has built up in his mind of a personality he is playing at the time. All poets, of course, are childish and do things like this and there's nothing wrong with it. In fact, the best poets admit to being childish.

Bayes: It's an extension of mask then, isn't it?

Hugo: Yes, that's right, an extension of the idea of mask, but I never quite get on the wavelength with Creeley, so I'm not sure I'm on very firm ground talking about him. I've heard him read and I like to hear him read very much, a very charming public reader.

Bayes: Could you comment briefly on some of the styles in *Five Poets of the Pacific Northwest?*

Hugo: Far and away the most careful—some people would say *brittle,* but I would resent this—poet of the bunch would be Ken Hanson. Ken Hanson carves poems almost out of rock. He is not flashy on the surface and, therefore, he's perhaps the least well-known of the five poets and, in some ways, the least widely read. Also, Ken happens to be rather modest and has never made any effort to have a book published, whereas all the other poets in the anthology have had books published. Ken goes to pinpointing things in a very exact way so that they cannot be argued with at the moment they're said. This is his reason for being attracted to Chinese poetry: very brief statement so accurate that you are simply arrested at the moment. It does not have to be profound. Hanson usually doesn't go in for great profundity, although he himself can be very profound. I prefer his poems where he does get profound, such as "San Miguel," but he has always tended toward this other kind of poem, this very simple lyric. He's an extremely good craftsman and the kind of poet which all of the poets respect a great deal.

Bayes: I never thought of the two poems in juxtaposition before just this minute. I like the "Haircut on Poseidon Street" so very much; the wit is charming. It just made me think just now of Warren Carrier's "Marimba Player."

Hugo: Well, Ken, of course, is a very witty fellow. He has a terrific sense of humor and that shows up in his poems too. Carolyn Kizer is perhaps the roughest poet of any of us, that is to say, her poems sprawl. It seems to me they don't always sound the way she thinks they sound. Sometimes they sound better than she thinks, and sometimes they sound worse. Her main virtue as a poet is that she gets a tremendous amount of personal pain into the poem, a lot more than people seem to realize. She takes many more chances than any other woman poet I know of. Quite often, she has been far too melodramatic in a poem and falls on her face. But this I appreciate. I like to see people take big chances and not make it because when they do make it, there's a wonderful thing. I think that "Tying One On In Vienna," for example, is a really excellent poem.

Stafford, of course, is the best known of any of the poets in the anthology and rightfully so. He has been writing longer and he's written many many beautiful poems. His way of working is just the opposite of Hanson's. Ken will spend months and months, in fact, I know of one poem he spent 15

years on that only has about 16 lines in it, whereas Stafford works two hours every morning from 4 to 6 a.m., finishes about five poems a week, does not rewrite any of them, and simply has the mails flooded with them all the time. Bill always talks about strategies too. This is kind of a mystery, but Bill sets you up one way and then pulls the rug out from under you in the poem. He will go as close as he can to sentimentality, for example, and when you think he's going to slop over, suddenly, he is very hard-headed in a surprising and very swift...

Bayes: His title poem in *Traveling Through The Dark* is a marvelous example.

Hugo: That's right, it's a perfect example of it. You think the guy is going to really slop over and he doesn't at all; he's always fooling you. "Thinking for Berky" in *Traveling Through The Dark* is a great poem. Stafford has the kind of mind I admire very much. Going back to this obsessive thing I was talking about, obsessive poets tend to be country people. When they grew up as children, they didn't see very much—only a few people and just a few things—so that everything they saw took on a tremendous identity in their minds. This is a sensibility I also look for. I don't care too much for the urban poets although I recognize their value, but they don't move me the way people like Stafford move me. Mark Twain had the same kind of mind. Huck Finn takes on tremendous identity in your mind because Huck had identity in Twain's. A lot of this comes from not seeing very much when you're young. What you do experience then becomes extremely important and this becomes a habit of mind and you go through life seeing people in all of their identity. Stafford has this quality in his poem "Thinking for Berky." The girl has so much identity in Stafford's mind that she takes on identity in yours and also you know that she, in that poem, means something to Stafford that she will never quite mean to you. So he's a perfect example of what I was talking about.

Dave Wagoner is accused of being slick, at times, and I think that this is a little unfair to Dave. There is no doubt that Dave has written perhaps a bit too much for his own good considering how young he is. But he's really come on the last few years and written some beautiful poems. "Free" in has last book, "Plumage," "Out For A Night," and "A Guide to Dungeness Spit" are beautiful poems.

Bayes: "The Dungeness" poem is fairly recent?

Hugo: Yes, it is. It's a recent poem. Dave has matured very much as a poet. Dave has a good ear and he tends to work rather conventionally. He can write different ways. Stafford and I write for our own voices very definitely and remain rather unilateral in style. Dave is more facile and can write in different styles. His problem is, if it is a problem, that he never has had much of a voice of his own, and until he found ways of inventing mouths through which to speak—if you will—the poems never really came on. But you see in "Guide to Dungeness Spit," he invents the character of the guy doing the speaking and the character of the girl doing the listening. It's as if a very mature man were talking to a very subnormal adult woman. That is the stance that keeps the poem suspended.

Bayes: That harks back a little bit to what you said a moment ago on the rural basis providing platform or spring board. I recall that Dave said in Portland something about his being urban.

Hugo: Yes, he came from Hammond, Indiana, which is really a suburb of Chicago. In fact, John Dillinger was killed something like five miles from David Wagoner's home. So Dave has been through a bit. Dave does a lot of different kinds of writing. He's writing a very interesting play. His last novel I read is a gem; it's a real delight called *The Escape Artist*.

Bayes: He has how many novels?

Hugo: Dave has published four novels, three books of poems, and he is working on a play now on the Ford Foundation Grant. He's a very prolific writer. He even works harder than Bill. Dave writes something like five hours a day, and he's always at it, and he's really come on the last few years. Dave's my old fishing buddy and I've always wished him the best. I've been pleased with him the last few years. His writing is really coming out, getting better and better. In fact he's had three good poems published during the last few months in *Saturday Review*. One of them, called "Osprey's Nest," will be in his next collection.

Bayes: This is Robin Skelton's second or third year as a west coaster, isn't it?

Hugo: Yes, I own three of Robin Skelton's books. He comes from the north country in England over near the North Sea. I can't remember the name of the town. He's a pretty hard-nosed guy and, as a lot of north country Englanders are, kind of a tinge of the Norse in them. He taught at the University of Manchester for many years.

I know that when I first met him was kind of accidental. He came to visit Victoria, and Carolyn brought him down to the house and we had dinner for them. He told me, "I've written a review of your book for the *Times Literary Supplement* and I had some harsh criticisms to make and I hope you don't mind." I said, "Well, you can't mind when you have a book published. You're on the block and you just have to take it." Well, anyway, the review came out and he almost had nothing harsh to say. He had me on the hook for the main weakness of the book, mentioned it briefly, then gave me a terrific review. In fact, it was the best review on the book I had. This is how I first met Robin.

He mentioned at the time that Manchester as a city was a dreary place to live, that the air was heavily polluted. I remember him saying, "It isn't pleasant to hear your children cough all winter." Well, then he got his chance and he's been out about two years at the University of Victoria. He's had about 17-18 books published—not only books of his own. I think he did a couple anthologies such as this. I think he did one called *Six Irish Poets* and then he did another one. I can't remember it. He's a little hard to keep up with. He's quite energetic.

Bayes: I was remembering the mention of the review. I think they referred to Earle Birney as an anti-poet or something and Birney's kidding him a bit down in Eugene.

Hugo: Yes, well, he's been very hard on Earle. Earle, of course, is considered one of the two best poets in Canada by most Canadian literary people—he and Irving Layton. Of course, Canada is even more provincial than Missoula or La Grande. When he first came, he saw statements in newspapers saying that Earle Birney had a major reputation in England, and he immediately wrote letters to people and told them this just simply wasn't so—nobody in England ever heard of Earle Birney. So he was kind of harsh, but it wasn't Earle's fault. These are things Canadians say about their poets, and so it's a very nice place to be a poet. You can be very major there. Earle is actually a very good poet. He's written six or seven just beautiful poems. But that's the sort of thing Robin does—he's very combative. His own poetry is a bit more like mine than any of the others. It's a lot of poetry of scene, or location.

Bayes: This is Earle Birney?

Hugo: No, Robin Skelton. And quite lyrical, but he has the same problem a lot of English poets have. I've talked to him about it. The tradition is so well-established in England that they can't get it off their backs, that is to say, they're always writing *literature* there, and it's a hard thing to shake. In America, our tradition is rather diffuse and not easily identifiable. After all, when you have these poets in the 20th century—Pound, Eliot, William Carlos Williams, Wallace Stevens, E. E. Cummings—it's rather diffuse tradition. The real problem with American poets is just the opposite. The English poet knows how to write a poem before he's got one to write. The American learns how only when he's writing it. Both systems have their disadvantages. I think theirs is a worse one than ours because at least for all the pain one has to go through, we are creative, whereas they're constantly trying to get away from what is already nature to them and this is a pretty hard thing to do. They hear the language a bit more conventionally than we do. In fact, in America there is nothing to revolt against. This is why everytime a person comes along who says, "Well, we've got to break down the old establishment and get on with something new," and so forth—there is no old establishment. The problem in America is that the American poet is perfectly free to write any way he wants

to. This is his problem. Now all he has to do is write a good poem, but that's very difficult because it's much easier to be a rebel than it is an artist.

I think this is what gave the Beat movement its impetus. It was primarily a show business movement and not a movement of poetry. All of a sudden, we've got a new way of writing and so forth and so on. Well, I don't think the way that the Beats were writing was any different than what Kenneth Patchen was doing 30 years ago or what E. E. Cummings was doing throughout the time of World War I—a poetry of anger, a poetry of hostility, poetry telling people to go shove it. This really had all been done. This was nothing new. What happened was the little magazines had gotten somewhat sterile. You couldn't get a poem published without having six Greek references in it. But this didn't stop any real poet from writing his poems. I think that all this attack on Eliot was a little ill-founded. Eliot did not have the literary power Karl Shapiro credits him with. If he had, Dylan Thomas, Wallace Stevens—a lot of people—never would've gotten their poems published and never would've written their poems—had he been that all-fired powerful. But good poets just go on and write their own poems anyway.

Bayes: Shapiro's recent public attitudes have been, seems to me, so bitter as to remind one of Hillyer's attacks on Pound.

Hugo: Yes, I remember Hillyer's attacks. It may be true. I don't know whether Shapiro's trying to say, "I want to be a part of literature too and T. S. Eliot won't let me" or just what's behind it because some of his arguments make no sense to me. I just don't credit Eliot with having the literary power that Shapiro says he had. He didn't stop any other I know of from writing his poems. If Shapiro is not a good poet, I don't know his poetry well enough to say, chances are it is not T. S. Eliot's fault.

Bayes: Well, I suppose we'd better wrap up this chat, Dick. Thank you very much.

Hugo: Well, thank you for having me, Ron, and I hope to come back real soon.

Bayes: Good.

ARS POETICA ARCHIVE:
RECORDS OF READINGS BY WRITERS, POETS, FACULTY, AND STUDENTS AT EASTERN OREGON UNIVERSITY
1961-1988*

1961
EOU Faculty & Students (**Bob Pfifer, Ron Bayes, Gordon Clarke, Alvin Kaiser**): February 3, 1961
(Ron Bayes is impresario 1961-1966)

1962
EOU Faculty (**Ron Bayes, Alvin Kaiser, Leonard Kimbrell, Mervin Rummels**): February 9, 1962
EOU Faculty & Students (**John Ford, Don Johnson, Fred Park, LeRoy Mobley, Gaylen Sears, Sarah Stein, Jack Evans, Ron Bayes, JoAnne Slatton**): March 9, 1962
Joseph Ferguson & Fredric Franklyn: November 8, 1962
EOU Faculty & Students (**Gordon Clarke, Richard Hiatt, Werner Bruecher, Miriam Hielman, Vern Partlow, Mona Searles, Alvin Kaiser**): December 7, 1962

1963
EOU Faculty & Students (**twelve readers unidentified**): February 15, 1963
William Stafford, Gena Ford, Eddie Case: April 13, 1963
EOU Faculty (**Ron Bayes, Audrey Snodgrass, Mary Davison, Gordon Clarke, Werner Bruecher, and Alvin Kaiser**): October 18, 1963

1964
Helen Luster, Roger Seeman, and EOU Students (**Terry Moser, Joe Lucas, Cheryl Domschot, Ben Hiatt, Mel Buffington, Deanna Talbott, John Gibson, Kathy Edvalson, Nick Smith**): January 31, 1964
Ken Hanson, Vern Rutsala, Vi Gale, Arthur Boggs: April 25, 1964
Blu Mundy, Jack Rye, Gordon Clarke, Alvin Kaiser: October 17, 1964
Warren Carrier, Sister Mary Gilbert, Jack Gilbert: November 20, 1964

1965
Edward Dorn: January 22, 1965
Helen Luster & EOU Students (**Lynn Blickenstaff, Sherry Hutchinson, Sam Miller, Constantine Stathos, Bobby Watson, Mel Buffington, Rodney Barker, Jan Kepley**): April 17, 1965
Richard Hugo: June 30, 1965
Robert Creeley: October 9, 1965
Helen Luster, Ron Bayes, John Evans, Sally Stein: December 3, 1965

1966
EOU & Central Washington College Students (**Rob Miller, Joanna Meldrum, Tom Kendall, Kay Kinney, Don Nickles, Mike Lamoreaux, John Holfer**): January 29, 1966
John Woods: March 6, 1966
Rolfe Humphries, Carolyn Kizer, William Stafford: April 23, 1966
Kenneth Hanson & Richard Hugo: November 4, 1966
(Ron Bayes in Japan 1966-1967. Robert Selby becomes impresario)

1967
EOU Students & Faculty (**Rob Miller, Nancy Baker, Bob Becker, Robert Selby, Dennis Carter, Kay Kinney, Sam Miller**): February 11, 1967

1967 *(cont.)*
Robert Duncan (discussion by **Robert Selby & Bill Dodd**) & Three Interviews (**Charles Quaintance, Floyd Hill, Paul Rosenthal**): March 11, 1967
Knute Skinner & John Logan: April 18, 1967
Vi Gale & Ralph Salisbury: October 28, 1967
(Ron Bayes returns)
Paul Engle: November 27, 1967

1968
EOU Faculty (**Al Kaiser, Gordon Clark, Ron Bayes**): January 18, 1968
Howard McCord & Jonathan Williams: February 3, 1968
EOU Faculty (**Sarah Stein, John Evans, Andrew Anderson, Johannes Spronk, Werner Bruecher**): February 16, 1968
Robert Peterson & Basil Bunting: April 19, 1968
Keith Wilson & Drummond Hadley: May 4, 1968
(last reading by Ron Bayes)
Richard Hugo: November 16, 1968
(Herb Gottfried becomes impresario)

1969
Fred Candelaria & Gena Ford: May 2, 1969

1970
James DenBoer: February 12, 1970
(last reading by Herb Gottfried)
Paul Zimmer: December 7, 1970
(George Venn becomes impresario)

1971
Ken Kesey: April 13, 1971
Dannie Abse: April 16, 1971
Anthony Hecht: Fall, 1971

1972
Charles Simic: February 7, 1972
John Haislip: April 29, 1972
Barre Toelken Concert: May 12, 1972

1973
Sandra McPherson: February 12, 1973
William Stafford: April 27, 1973
Henry Carlile: October 29, 1973

1974
Diane Wakoski: January 28, 1974
Primus St. John: February, 1974
James McAuley: April 26, 1974
Gary Snyder: November 14, 1974

1975
John Haines: February 10, 1975
Rob Miller, John Bush, Mel Buffington, David Memmott: April 14, 1975
Bill Ransom and **Sam Hamill**: December 1, 1975

1976
Chad Walsh: March 12, 1976
Dean Phelps: April 19, 1976
Barre Toelken & Twilo Scofield Concert: May 23-24, 1976
Vern Rutsala: November 8, 1976

1977
James Crowell: May 23, 1977
Robert Hoeft & Grey Elliot: May 23, 1977
Sandra McPherson & Henry Carlile: October 17, 1977

1978
Jon Silkin: May 8, 1978
Kim Stafford: May 13, 1978

1979
Come Out of the Brush Invitational: March 18, 1979
Jim Heynen: April 18, 1979
Karen Swenson: October 29, 1979

1980
Ron Bayes: April 16, 1980
William Pitt Root: November 15, 1980

1981
William Stafford: April 7, 1981
George Venn: May 27, 1981
Beth Bentley: October 26, 1981
(George Venn in China. Tom Madden becomes impresario)

1982
Gino Sky: February 8, 1982
(by Tom Madden)
Belle Randall: April 14, 1982
(by Tom Madden)
Richard Hugo Memorial: November 2, 1982
(George Venn returns)
Mark Halperin: November 29, 1982

1983
Kenneth Hanson: March 7, 1983
Carolyn Kizer: April 4, 1983
Tom Madden & Brad La Fran: May 2, 1983
Gary Miranda: December 5, 1983

1984
Carol Jane Bangs: February 27, 1984
Carolyne Wright: November 5, 1984

1985
Craig Lesley-GV Interview: May 5-6, 1985
(by Pat McNamer)
Ursula Le Guin: May 24, 1985
Civ Cedering: November 13, 1985

1986
EOU Student Short Fiction: March 17, 1986
John Keeble: June 2, 1986
Paul Merchant: November 24, 1986
(by Mark Shadle)
EOU Student Poetry: December 8, 1986

1987
Peter Sears, Kim Stafford, Primus St. John, Ingrid Wendt: May 9, 1987
Garrett Hongo: November 9, 1987

1988
Czeslaw Milosz: April 27, 1988
(Last reading by George Venn)

1989
David Axelrod & Jodi Varon become impresarios and continue into the present—another 25 years of readings.

*revised edition 5/12/14. Indices to the entire Ars Poetica Archive housed in Pierce Library may be read on-line at http://library.eou.edu/collections/. Click on "Other."

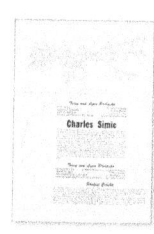
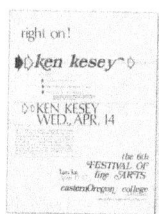

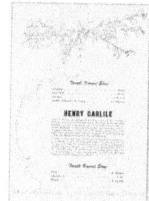
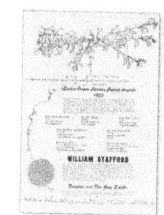

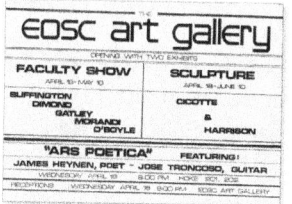

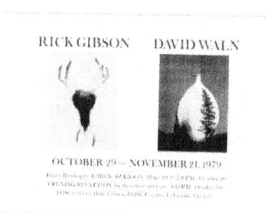

NOTES AND SOURCES
(for photo credits, please see "Permissions and Credits")

Chapter 1. Beaver and the Grande Ronde River
BOOKS
Nez Perce Tribe. "Beaver and the Grande Ronde River." *Indian Legends of the Pacific Northwest*. Ella Clark(ed). Berkeley: U. of California 1953. The 2002 speech uses a somewhat revised version of the published text. Reprinted by permission.

Chapter 2. Where the Crooked River Rises
BOOKS
Waterston, Ellen. *Where the Crooked River Rises...*Corvalllis: OSU Press, 2010.
_____ *Then There Was No Mountain: A Parallel Odyssey of a Mother and Daughter through Addiction*. Taylor Trade Publishing, 2003.
_____ *I Am Madagascar*. La Grande: Ice River Press, 2004.
_____ *Between Desert Seasons*. La Grande: Wordcraft of Oregon, 2008.

Chapter 3. They Also Served...
BOOKS/MANUSCRIPTS/LETTERS
NOTES (APA):
1. Fred Hill, unpublished interviews with George Venn, 2004-2007.
2. See Feb. 25, 1945 letter/photo in the following pages. For an account of his friendship with White, see Fred Hill, "When I Knew Minor White." *History of Photography*, 16: 2 (Summer, 1992): 147-151. For the larger picture of White, the WPA Art Center, and La Grande, see George Venn, "Rider in the Wilderness: Minor White in La Grande 1940-41." *Calapooya Literary Review* 2 (Spring, 2004): 21-26. Both pieces include photographs by both photographers.
3. From Fred Hill, "Memories of Military." Unpublished 1-page typescript given to his children to introduce his Christmas gift in 1994. The gift was Robert P. Nichols and Katherine Sams Wiley, *The Strafin' Saints: The 71ˢᵗ Tactical Reconnaissance Group Memories of their Service in the Pacific Theater 1943-1945*. The book includes thirty six black-and-white photos by Hill and from the Fred Hill Collection— all in the author's possession.
4. Roy Stanley, *World War II Photo Intelligence*. (New York: Scribners, 1981): 2.

5. On Oregonians in World War II, see John R. Elting, *GI—World War II Commemoration*: "Costs, Casualties and Other Data." no date. Gordon Dodds, *The American Northwest: A History of Oregon and Washington*. (Arlington Heights, IL: Forum Press, 1986): 262; Laura Mosher, fax to author, United States Military Academy, March 28, 2007; *United States Army in World War II: The Army Ground Forces*. (Washington, D.C.: Department of the Army, 1947):169.

6. In a 2004 inventory of his World War II archive, Hill gave this three-part description: "Fred Hill to Martha Simonson Hill Letters(1943-1945)." 315 original texts—handwritten and typed—with original envelopes, enclosures, etc.; "U.S. Army/Fred Hill Photo Collection." 40(+−) images by anonymous Army photographers in four sets of photographs: (a) bombed Manila; (b) the 503rd paratroop drop on Corregidor; (c) "Grab shots" by aerial photographers; (d) aircraft nose art; "Fred Hill Personal Photo Collection." Taken by both Fred Hill and his squadron photographers during 1943-1945 while in the United States, on board four different ships, and at Army and civilian sites in New Guinea, Netherlands East Indies, The Philippines, and the Ryukyu Islands. This collection contains 300 black-and-white prints, 600 black-and-white negatives, and 700-800 35 mm color slides. These estimates do not include pre-1943 photos, 8mm movies, Army propaganda leaflets in Japanese, and other artifacts.

7. For Hill's published black-and-white photographs, see John W. Casey, *Warriors Without Weapons: Triumph of the Tech Reps.* (Corvallis, OR: Premiere Editions, 2004), 44, 87; Evelyn Whitfield, *Three Year Picnic: An American Woman's Life Inside Japanese Prison Camps in The Phillippines During WW II*. (Corvallis, OR: Premiere Editions, 1999 and 2002), 69 and 106; Hampton Sides, *Ghost Soldiers*. (New York: Doubleday, 2001), 4, 118-119; Michael John Claringbould, *Forty of the Fifth: The Life, Times and Demise of Forty U.S. Fifth Air Force Aircraft*. (Kingston, Australia: Aerothentic Publications, 1999), 23, 27, 84, 88, 94; Robert J. Martin, ed., *Fifth Air Force*. (Paducah, KY: Turner Publishing, 1994), 17, 23, 172, 173, 174; Robert P. Nichols and Katherine Sams Wiley, *The Strafin' Saints: The 71st Tactical Reconnaissance Group Memories of their Service in the Pacific Theater 1943-1945.* (Houston, TX: privately published, 1994), 322-346; Claire Phillips and Myron B. Goldsmith, *Manila Espionage*. (Portland, OR: Binford and Morts, 1947), 26-155. For coverage of Hill's work in a permanent collection, see Dick Mason, "Local Photographer's Images Preserve Airborne Legacy: Fred Hill's Work on Permanent Display at Tillamook Air Museum." *The Observer* (La Grande), May 19, 1999, 3. Hill has also regularly supplied prints to numerous veterans and their families, a service he still provides for a fee to anyone who contacts him.

8. Fred Hill, "A Different Memoir of World War II." (typescript of illustrated speech delivered to Union County Historical Society, La Grande, Oregon , November 9, 2002: 1-5.

9. Using commercial 35 mm film sent by friends, family, and Martha, Hill also took over 700 color slides during his tour of duty. For his published color photographs, see Jeffrey Ethell, Warren M. Bodie, and Bob Boyd, *WW II Pacific War Eagles: China/Pacific Aerial Conflict in Original Color*. (Front Royal, VA: Widewing

Publications, 1997), 124-129, 133-136, 145, 157, 204; Mike Beno, ed., *At Ease.* (Greendale, WI: Reiman Publications, 1996), 29, 146; Jeffrey Ethell, *The Victory Era in Color.* (Greendale, WI: Reiman Publications, 1994),130-133; Chuck Yeager and Clarence Anderson, *There Once Was A War.* (New York and London: Penguin, 1995), 51, 126, 175, 211; Jeffrey L. Ethell and David C. Isby, *G.I Victory.* (London and Mechanicsburg, PA: Greenhill Books, 1995), 125, 127, 129, 130, 136, 140; Jeffrey L. Ethell, *WW II War Eagles: Global Air War in Original Color.* (Hiawassee, GA: Widewing Publications, 1995), 185.

10. This and the following paragraph are based on Hill's thirty eight letters sent to Martha from Mindoro between January 7 and April 4, 1945.

Chapter 4. Literature of the Northwest Symposium
Periodicals

Findlay, John. M. "Something In The Soil...*Pacific Northwest Quarterly* 97-4 (2006):179-189.

Chapter 5. Soldier to Advocate
Books and Periodicals
Notes to "Prologue" (APA)

1. Sherry Smith. *The View from Officer's Row.* (Tuscon: U. of Arizona, 1990), 136.

2. Robert Hamburger. *Two Rooms: The Life of Charles Erskine Scott Wood.* (Lincoln and London: U. of Nebraska Press, 1998), 24. This is the only current biography of Wood.

3. Edwin Bingham. *Charles Erskine Scott Wood.* (Boise: Boise State Univ. Press, 1990), 12. This monograph is the only contemporary literary study of Wood's writing.

4. Hamburger, 16-31.

5. Hamburger, 9.

6. William Faulkner, "Speech of Acceptance upon the award of the Nobel Prize for Literature," in *The Faulkner Reader.* (New York: Random House, 1943), 3.

7. C. E. S. Wood Collection, Carton 28, Cylinder A-1 Transcript, 2. Huntington Library, San Marino, California.

8. Hamburger, 1.

9. Bingham, 12.

10. C. E. S. Wood Collection, Carton 28, Cylinder A-1 Transcript, 1.

11. Wood's commanding officer is Captain Robert Pollock, Twenty-first Infantry. For further references see July 5, July 22, and "Accounts Pages" at the end of diary. Hamburger, 6.

12. Gordon Dodds, *The American Northwest.* (Arlington Heights, Ill: Forum Press, 1986), 159; Charles Erskine Scott Wood, *The Poet in the Desert.* (New York: Vanguard, 1929). See Bingham, pp. 13-14 for a detailed use of Wood's unpublished journal from this march.

13. "Wood Diary," C. E. S. Wood Collection, WD Box 29 (4), 10 July 1928.

14. Hamburger, 33.

15. Doug Halsey, National Park Service, Fort Vancouver, Interview by author, 29 August, 2001.

16. C. E. S. Wood, letter to General Howard, 19 March 1883. Oliver Otis Howard Papers, Bowdoin College Library.

17. Howard Papers, dates cited.

18. Hamburger, 33.

19. Hamburger, 35.

20. C. E. S. Wood Collection, Carton 21, Wax Cylinder Transcript, 1.

21. Wood Diary," C. E. S. Wood Collection, WD Box 29 (4), 10 July 1928.

22. The original is housed in the C. E. S. Wood Collection, Huntington Library, San Marino, California, and is published here by permission. It was given to the Huntington sometime after 1947 by Wood's second wife, the poet Sara Bard Field. Cataloged with the title "Diary [kept in Alaska and] on the Nez Perce campaign." Box 26 (1).

23. C. E. S. Wood, letter to General Howard, 16 May 1877. Oliver Otis Howard Papers, Bowdoin College Library.

24. This journey—self-censored for his sexual encounter admitted years later—took shape as Wood's article, "Among the Thlinkits in Alaska." *Century Monthly* 24 (July 1882): 323-39. Rpt. *Wood Works*. eds Edwin Bingham and Tim Barnes (Corvallis: Oregon State Univ. Press, 1997), 43-63. For the sexual encounter, see Hamburger, 39.

25. Hamburger, 41.

26. Bruce Hampton, *Children of Grace*. (New York: Henry Holt, 1994), 42; Major Henry Clay Wood, *Status of Young Joseph and His Band of Nez Perce Indians...* (Portland: Oregon: Assistant Adjutant General's Office of Headquarters Department of Columbia, 1876).

27. Except as noted, all quotes in this paragraph are from Alvin Josephy, *The Nez Perce Indians and the Opening of the Pacific Northwest*. (New Haven: Yale Univ. Press, 1965), 386-442.

28. To decode Erskine's shorthand, I've done the following: (1) standardized spelling and mechanics; (2) added [in brackets] month and place names, Army campsites, and captions; (3) added paragraphs to longer passages; (4) noted indecipherable words with [illegible], and arbitrary choices with [lost? last?]. When Erskine underlined, I use [Wood's emphasis]. All of Erskine's post-war additions in ink—dates, overstrikes, additions, marginalia, interlineations—are enclosed in {+ italics}, as is his one major 1878 revision. All of Erskine's deletions are enclosed in {–italics} .

29. For these terms' sources, definitions, and history, see Steven E. Kagle, *American Diary Literature: 1620-1799*. (Boston: Twayne, 1979), 142; Steven E. Kagle, *Early Nineteenth Century Diary Literature*. (Boston: Twayne, 1986), 104.

30. Bingham, 12; Hamburger notes that "[These] fragments...from his Sitka journal suggest that he [Wood] wished to produce...a humorous anecdotal account of frontier life, its roguish characters, and colorful speech" in the manner of Bret Harte and Mark Twain. 37. They may also reflect his brother Max's earlier advice:

write "little sketches... of some of the funnier ports..., [with] a little mirth, a little love, and a good deal of fiction."

31. C. E. S. Wood Collection, WD Box 6 (7)
32. C. E. S. Wood to McWhorter, 12 March 1941, cited in *Hear Me, My Chiefs.* (Caldwell: Caxton, 1952), 260.

Notes to "Epilogue"

127. Brown, 208.
128. According to General Howard, Wilkinson's 'gallant services' at Clearwater [on July 11 and 12] resulted in a promotion to...brevet major. In 1878, his unprovoked slaughter of noncombatant Palouse Indian men, women, and children near Wallula caused Wilkinson to apply "for an eight-month leave of absence in order to look for a new career" as founder of the Forest Grove Indian School, an institution dedicated to forced assimilation that caused the deaths of many Native American students. See Cary C. Collins, "The Broken Crucible of Assimilation," *Oregon Historical Quarterly*, Winter 2000), 470.
129. Sean Monahan, <smonahan@bowdoin.edu>, "General Howard's Hands," 8 June 2001, personal email (8 June 2001).
130. Wood Collection, WD Box 6 (7).
131. In Fee, Wood identified an "official journal which I kept as adjutant in the field." (335) In his unpublished autobiography, Wood stated that "I had to keep an accurate set of books that would make history but as when the campaign was over, he [Howard] carried the books off with him...." (Wood Collection, Carton 28-Cylinder A-1). Cited in Note 105, this "Adjutant Journal" may be the document deposited in the Huntington Library titled *Journal of Expedition against Hostile Nez Perce Indians from Lewiston I.T. to Henry Lake, I.T.* Attributed to Wood, the journal's authorship is dubious—at best: the handwriting—except for the title page—is not Wood's and appears to be copied; the first page carries the disclaimer, "Following memorandum taken from jacket diary of Captain M. C. Wilkinson, A.D.E., July 10, 1877." Throughout the text, Wood is referred to infrequently and always in third person. Wood may or may not have dictated this record, but he clearly did not write this text. While Howard attributes such a journal to Wood and quotes from that text throughout his *Nez Perce Joseph* (1881), Wood's original "Adjutant Journal" may have been lost or remain in private hands. An intensive search of archives during this writing did not discover it.
132. [C. E. S. Wood,] "General Howard's Battle With the Nez Perces Indians, July 11; Sketches by an Officer of General Howard's Staff," and "Pictures of the Day," *The Daily Graphic*, 3 August 1877, 1, 233; [C. E. S. Wood,] "Scenes of General Howard's Campaign Against the Nez Perce Indians; from Sketches by an Officer in the Field," and "Pictures of the Day," *The Daily Graphic*, 16 August 1877, 1; [C. E. S. Wood, "General Howard's Campaign Against the Nez Perces Indians; Position of the Camp on August 20 when the Horses Were Stampeded by the Indians," and "Pictures of the Day," *The Daily Graphic*, 8 September 1877, 1; W. [C. E. S. Wood], "A Fight at Break of Day," 27 August 1877, *The Daily Graphic*, 366. Wood's artistic

process—self-described—was simple: taking his pad and pencil, he would find the right place, sit down, and rapidly sketch the subject, then later, he would refine and finish the drawing in pen and black ink. Wood to McWhorter, 3 January 1942, McWhorter Collection, Holland Library.

133. Charles E. S. Wood, "General Field Orders No. 6," *Supplementary Report (Non-Treaty Nez Perces Campaign) of Brigadier-General O. O. Howard, Brevet Major-General U.S. Army, Commanding Depart of the Columbia* (Portland: Assistant Adjutant General's Office, Department of the Columbia, 1878), 619. At the end of the 1879 reprint of this text in the Wood Collection, Wood wrote, "I am afraid I am responsible for this document—except the "Under God." CESW."

134. To track Wood's 1877 leaked versions and revisions of the "Chief Joseph Surrender Speech," begin with *Bismark Tri-Weekly Tribune*, 26 October 1877; *The Inter Ocean* (Chicago), 9 November 1877, 2; *New York Times*, 16 November 1877, 1; *National Tribune* (Washington DC), 16 November 1877; *Harper's Weekly*, 17 November 1877, 906; *Portland Daily Standard*, 4 December 1877. Note: some of these anonymous leaks were probably accomplished with the name and collaboration of Thomas Sutherland. To track Wood's "Surrender Narratives" defending Howard, begin with "The Pursuit and Battle. Semi-Official Report of a Staff Officer." *Chicago Tribune*, 10 October 1877; "The Captive Chief," *San Francisco Chronicle*, 1 November 1877; "To Editor Daily Standard," *Daily Standard* (Portland), 4 November 1877. Note: the last story was ghostwritten as Sutherland. To track Wood's secret mission as Howard's envoy to President Hayes, see C. E. S. Wood to General Howard, 16 November 1877, Howard Papers.

135. After General Howard's death in 1909, Wood became more critical of Army conduct, published his disagreements with General Howard, and described his military service as follows: "in my youth, I, stupid, fought/wearing the livery of that thing the State/Whose might is by the richest bought/a bully which protects the great." "Testament," cited in Bingham, 41. Once—late in his life and off the official record—he referred to Howard as "my ignorant superior officer." Wood Autobiography, Carton 28, Wax Cylinder A-1 Transcript, Huntington Library.

136. C. E. S. Wood, "Captives of Joseph's Band Coming Into Miles' Camp; Closing Scenes of General Howard's Campaign Against the Nez Perces Indians: Sketches by an Officer of General Howard's Staff." *The Daily Graphic* 3 November 1877,1. At the age of ninety two and nearly blind, Wood told McWhorter, "The sketches I made...were of the Indian camp which consisted of dug-outs in the hill...and I also made sketches of some horses in the hollow beneath the camp and of some figures of Indians, above the camp near the top of the hill." (Wood to McWhorter, 3 January 1942, McWhorter Papers) A photocopy of one drawing—without place or date—was included in Wood's papers at the Huntington where I identified it in 1999.

137. Tim Barnes, "Beyond the Bear Paw Mountains: Charles Erskine Scott Wood's Literary Campaign for Freedom," *Sweet Reason* 5 (1986): 16.

138. Sherry Smith, *The View from Officer's Row.* (Tuscon: Univ. of Arizona, 1990), 136.

139. Bingham and Barnes, 224.

140. Charles Erskine Scott Wood, *The Poet in the Desert*. (Portland: F. W. Baltes, 1915), 103.

141. Wood, *Poet* (1915), 101.

142. Sara Bard Field, ed. *Collected Poems of Charles Erskine Scott Wood*. (New York: Vanguard, 1949), 267. (Note: this collection reprints the 1918 version.)

143. Wood, *Collected Poems*, 267-269.

144. Charles Erskine Scott Wood, *The Poet in the Desert* (New York: Vanguard Press, 1929), 134-140.

145. "Ballads of the Nez Perce War." C. E. S. Wood Collection, WD Box 8 (16), Huntington Library.

146. "Ballads of the Nez Perce War." C. E. S. Wood Collection, WD Box 8 (16), Huntington Library.

147. Wood to C. J. Brosnan, 7 January 1918, Special Collections, Univ. of Idaho Library, 4.

148. Barnes, 12.

149. "I took it for my own benefit as a literary item." Wood to McWhorter, 31 January 1936, McWhorter Collection, Washington State Univ. Library. This statement was also reprinted in various newspapers after Wood's death in 1944.

150. For two of Wood's early "verbatim transcript" claims, see *Harper's Weekly* 17 November 1877, 906 and *Report of the Secretary of War 1877-78*, 1: 630. For a more recent and incomplete evaluation of that claim, see Haruo Aoki, "Chief Joseph's Words." *Idaho Yesterdays* 33 (1989): 16-21.

151. McWhorter, *Hear Me*, 260-261.

152. Brown, *Flight*, 161.

153. Jerome Greene, "Appendix B: Two Army Shootings at the Salmon River, June 30 and July 7, 1877." Unpublished manuscript; Jerome Greene, <Jerry_Greene@ nps.gov> "The Night of June 30, 1877?," 8 March 2004, personal email (8 March 2004). See July 6 entry and notes for the second shooting.

154. Mary Rose, *C. E. S. Wood and Chief Joseph: Brothers in the American West*. (Vancouver, WA: Celebrate Freedom Exhibition, 1991; Leverett Richards, "Vancouver Exhibits Look at Indian Wars," *The Oregonian*, 3 October, 1991.

155. See David Michael Liberty, "It's Never Too Late to Give Away a Horse," *Oregon Historical Quarterly*, 105, No. 1. (2004): 96-107.

156. Mary Christina Wood, "The Gift," 5. Wood File, Clark County Historical Museum, Vancouver, WA.

157. Rick Bella, "Nez Perce Ceremony Emphasizes Forgiveness, *The Sunday Oregonian*, 23 April 2000, 3M-C9.

158. Greene, 389, N.46.

159. Sherry L. Smith, "Reimagining the Indian," *Pacific Northwest Quarterly*, 87.3 (1996): 151.

Chapter 6. **Rider in the Wilderness**
BOOKS

White, Minor. *Mirrors, Messages and Manifestations*. New York: Aperture, 1969.

PERIODICALS/PRESS

Hill, Fred. "When I Knew Minor White." *History of Photography* 16.2 (1992): 147-151.

Bradley, Isabel Kane. "Minor in La Grande, 1940-1941." *Aperture* 95 (Summer 1984): 26-27.

The [La Grande] *Observer*. Extensive Articles and Coverage, 1939, 1940, 1941.

The Beacon. Eastern Oregon College. Extensive Coverage, 1939, 1940, 1941.

La Grande Council Minutes, 6 December 1939—25 February 1942.

INTERVIEWS

McKenzie, Glen. Personal Interview. 6 May 2004.

Bunnell, Peter. Letter to George Venn. 23 May 1985.

Brownton, Gerda. Personal interview. 4 May 1985.

Hill, Fred. Personal interview. 12 May 2004.

Turner, John. Personal interview. 14 May 2004.

Venn, George. Letter to Peter Bunnell. 7 May 1985.

Bunnell, Peter. Personal interview. 5 April 2004.

Chapter 7. *Down in My Heart* by William Stafford

BOOKS/PERIODICALS

Stafford, William. *Down in My Heart: Peace Witness in War Time* by William Stafford. Corvallis: Oregon State University Press, Corvallis, 1998. Northwest Reprint Series.

Johnson, David. "The Shadow of Camp Walport. *Varieties of Hope*. Gordon Dodds, ed. *Oregon Literature Series,* George Venn, ed. Corvallis: OSU Press, 1993.

Coffield, Glen. "Crossing Hawthorne Bridge." *From Here We Speak*, Ingrid Wendt and Primus St. John, eds. *Oregon Literature Series*, George Venn, ed. Corvallis: OSU Press, 1994.

Wilson, Adrian. "All War Stinks to High Heaven: A C.O's Diary from World War II." *Talking on Paper*, Shannon Applegate and Terence O'Donnell, eds. *Oregon Literature Series,* George Venn, ed. Corvallis: OSU Press, 1994

Chapter 8. Chief Joseph's 'Surrender Speech' as Literary Text

BOOKS

Aoki, Harou. *Nez Perce Texts*. Berkeley: U. of California Press, 1979.

Barnes, Tim and Bingham, Edwin, eds. *Wood Works: the Life and Writings of Charles Erskine Scott Wood*. Corvallis: Oregon State U. Press, 1997.

Beal, Merrill D. *I Will Fight No More Forever*. Seattle: U of Washington Press, 1963.

Brown, Mark H. *The Flight of the Nez Perce*. New York: Putnam, 1967.

Bingham, Edwin. *Charles Erskine Scott Wood*. Boise: Boise UP, 1990.

Fee, Chester Anders. *Chief Joseph*.... New York: Wilson-Erickson, 1936.

Field, Sara Bard, ed. *Collected Poems of Charles Erskine Scott Wood*. New York: Vanguard, 1949.

Hampton, Bruce. *Children of Grace*. New York: Henry Holt, 1994.

Haines, Francis. *Red Eagles of the Northwest*. Portland: Scholastic Press, 1939.

Howard, Oliver O. *Nez Perce Joseph*. Boston: Lee and Shepard, 1881.

Josephy, Alvin. *The Nez Perce and the Opening of the Pacific Northwest*. New Haven and London: Yale U. Press, 1965.

Josephy, Alvin. M. "The American Indian and Freedom of Religion..." in *The Changing Pacific Northwest*. eds. David Stratton and George A. Frykman. Pullman, WA: Washington State U. Press, 1987.

Lavender, David. *Let Me Be Free*. New York, Harper Collins, 1992.

McWhorter, Lucullus. *Yellow Wolf*. Caldwell: Caxton Printers, 1940.

_____ *Hear Me, My Chiefs*. Caldwell: Caxton Printers, 1952.

Miles, Nelson A. *Personal Recollections and Observations of General Nelson A. Miles*. New York: Werner, 1896.

Ramsey, Jarold. *Coyote Was Going There*. Seattle: U. of Washington Press, 1979.

Vanderwerth, W. C. *Indian Oratory*. New York: Ballantine, 1971.

Wood, Charles Erskine Scott. *A Book of Tales*. Portland, OR: The Attic Press, 1901.

_____ *The Poet in the Desert*. Reprint. New York: Vanguard, 1929.

NEWSPAPERS

Chicago Times
Chicago Tribune
New York Graphic
Bismark Tri-Weekly Tribune

PERIODICALS

Aoki, Haruo. "Chief Joseph's Words." *Idaho Yesterdays* 33 (1989): 16-21.

Brown, Mark. "The Joseph Myth." *Montana, The Magazine of Western History* Jan. (1972): 2-17.

Bingham, Edwin. "Oregon's Romantic Rebels: John Reed and Charles Erskine Scott Wood." *Pacific Northwest Quarterly* 50 (1959): 77-90.

Joseph, Chief. "An Indian's View of Indian Affairs." *North American Review* 128 (1879): 421-433.

Wells, Merle W. "The Nez Perce and Their War." *Pacific Northwest Quarterly*. Jan.(1964): 37.

Wood, Charles Erskine Scott. "Private Journal, 1878." *Oregon Historical Quarterly*, March, (1969): 5-38.

_____. "Chief Joseph, the Nez Perce." *Century Magazine* 6 (May, 1884): 135-42.

_____. "Famous Indians: Portraits of Some Indian Chiefs." *Century Magazine* (July, 1893): 439.

LETTERS

Wood, C. E. S. Letter to Lucullus Virgil McWhorter. 31 January 1936.

Wood, C. E. S. Letter to John Rea. 3 November 1930.

Barnes, Tim. Letter to George Venn. 4 November 1996.

GOVERNMENT DOCUMENTS

Report of the Secretary of War, 1876-77. U.S. 45th Congress 2nd Session House of Representatives Document 1, Part 2, Vol. 1, "Supplementary Report. Non Treaty Nez Perce Campaign." National Archives.

Chapter 9. **William Stafford in Northwest Literature**
BOOKS/ARTICLES

Broughton, Irv. "A Symposium on Northwest Poetry." *Mill Mountain Review* 2.1 (1975): 6-17.

Clark, Suzanne. "Bernard Malamud as the Western Other." *Oregon English Journal* 13:1. (Spring, 1991): 24-27.

Fiedler, Leslie. *Being Busted.* New York: Stein and Day, 1969.

Hugo, Richard. *The Triggering Town....* New York: Norton, 1979.

Kizer, Carolyn. Hugo/Stafford Anecdote as told to George Venn, La Grande, OR, 1983.

Malamud, Bernard. *A New Life.* New York: Farrar, Straus, and Cudahy, 1961.

Putnam, Ann. " 'Wine of Wyoming' and Hemingway's Hidden West." *Western American Literature* XXII (Spring, 1987): 17-32.

Seager, Allen. *The Glass House: The Life of Theodore Roethke.* New York: McGraw-Hill, 1968.

Roethke, Theodore. *The Collected Poems of Theodore Roethke.* Garden City: Doubleday, 1966.

Stafford, William and Richard Hugo. "The Third Time the World Happens." *Northwest Review* 13: 3 (1973): 46.

Stafford, William. *Writing the Australian Crawl.* Ann Arbor: U. of Michigan Press, 1978.

Chapter 10. StoryLines Northwest (**NEH & ALA**)
BOOKS

Jaeger, Lowell. *Northwest Series Discussion Guide.* ALA and NEH, 1997.

FAXES/LETTERS

Venn, George. Letter to Paul Zalis. 7 January 1995.

Zalis, Paul. Letter to George Venn. 20 December 1995.

Venn, George. Letter to Paul Zalis. 26 June 1996.

Robertson, Deb. Letter to George Venn. 11 September 1996

Brandehoff, Susan. Letter to George Venn. 31 December 1996.

Venn, George. Letter to American Library Association. 1 January 1997.

Jaeger, Lowell. Letter to George Venn. 6 January 1997.

Venn, George. Letter to Lowell Jaeger. 27 January 1997.

BROADCASTS/RECORDINGS

StoryLines Northwest: Cassettes 1-13. National Endowment for the Humanities & American Library Association, June, 1997. Broadcasts Fall, 1997.

Venn, George Interview. *"Honey in the Horn—H. L. Davis."* National Public Radio, Northwest Stations. Missoula, Montana 19 October 1997.

DOCUMENTS
ALA Grants submitted to NEH for *StoryLines America: A Radio/Library Partnership Exploring Our Regional Literature.* 1996 & 1997.
Robertson, Deb, ALA project director to NEH and George Venn. "Final Report GL-21414-96" 5 June 1998.

Chapter 11. Editing an Invisible Literature: *The Oregon Literature Series*
BOOKS

Abbot, Dorothy. *Mississippi Writers: Recollections of Childhood and Youth.* Jackson, MI: U. Press of Mississippi, 1985.

Applebee, Arthur. *Tradition and Reform in the Teaching of English: a History.* Urbana, IL: NCTE, 1974.

Applegate, Shannon and O'Donnell, Terence, eds. *Talking on Paper: An Anthology of Oregon Letters and Diaries.* Corvallis: Oregon State U. Press, 1994.

Appleman, Deborah, et al. *Braided Lives: An Anthology of Multicultural American Writing.* St. Paul, MN: Minnesota Humanities Commission/Minnesota Council of Teachers of English, 1991.

Ardinger, Rick. *Where The Morning Light's Still Blue.* Moscow, ID: U. of Idaho Press, 1994.

Attebery, Louie. *Idaho Folklife: Homesteads to Headstones.* Salt Lake and Boise: U. of Utah/Idaho Historical Society Presses, 1985.

Beckham, Stephen Dow, ed. *Many Faces: An Anthology of Oregon Autobiography.* Corvallis: Oregon State U. Press, 1993.

Bevis, William. *Ten Tough Trips.* Seattle/London: U. of Washington Press, 1990.

Bingham, Edwin and Love, Glen. *Northwest Perspectives: Essays on the Culture of the Pacific Northwest.* Seattle/London: U. of Washington Press, 1979.

Dodds, Gordon, ed. *Varieties of Hope: An Anthology of Oregon Prose.* Corvallis: Oregon State U. Press, 1993.

Fischer, Jeff, ed. *Maine Speaks.* Brunswick, ME: Maine Writers and Publishers Alliance/Maine Council for English Language Arts, 1989.

Jones, Suzi, and Ramsey, Jarold, eds. *The Stories We Tell: An Anthology of Oregon Folk Literature.* Corvallis: Oregon State U Press, 1994.

Kittredge, William and Smith, Annick, eds. *The Last Best Place: A Montana Anthology.* Helena, MT: The Montana Historical Society Press, 1988.

Lee, W. Storrs. *Washington State: A Literary Chronicle.* New York: Funk and Wagnalls, 1969.

Love, Glen, ed. *The World Begins Here: An Anthology of Oregon Short Fiction.* Corvallis, Oregon State U. Press, 1993.

Lutwack, Leonard. *The Role of Place in Literature.* Syracuse, NY: Syracuse U. Press, 1984.

Maguire, James H. *The Literature of Idaho: An Anthology.* Boise : Boise State U. Press, 1986.

McFarland, Ron and Studebaker, William, eds. *Idaho's Poetry: A Centennial Anthology*. Moscow: U of Idaho Press, 1988.

O'Connell, Nicholas, ed. *At The Field's End: Interviews with Twenty Pacific Northwest Writers*. Seattle, WA: Madrona Press, 1987.

Robbins, William, Frank, Robert, et al. *Regionalism and the Pacific Northwest*. Corvallis: Oregon State U. Press, 1983.

Runciman, Lex and Sher, Steven. Northwest Variety: *Personal Essays by Fourteen Regional Authors*. Corvallis, OR: Arrowood Books, 1987.

Sorrells, Rosalie. *Way Out In Idaho*. Lewiston, ID. Confluence Press, 1992.

Wendt, Ingrid and St. John, Primus, eds. *From Here We Speak*: An Anthology of Oregon *Poetry*. Corvallis: Oregon State U. Press, 1995.

ARTICLES

Flanagan, Anna. "NCTE Affiliates Find Work on Anthologies Demanding, Rewarding," *The Council Chronicle* (Sept 1994): 9.

Jones, Suzi. "Regionalization: A Rhetorical Strategy," *Journal of the Folklore Institute* 13.1 (1976): 105-120.

UNPUBLISHED SOURCES

Gaffney, Deb. Anecdote. ca 1995-96

Snider, Michael. Advanced Research English 410, Eastern Oregon University, Fall, 1984.

Olsen, James Warren. *The Nature of Literature Anthologies Used in the Teaching of High School English 1917-1957*. Unpublished Phd dissertation, U. of Wisconsin, 1969.

Chapter 12. Remembering Wallace Stegner

BOOKS

Stegner, Wallace. *The Sound of Mountain Water*. Doubleday, 1969.

Venn, George. *Marking the Magic Circle*. Corvallis: OSU Press 1987

Stegner, Wallace. *Wolf Willow....* Viking: 1962.

RECORDINGS

Stegner, Wallace. "Graduation Address." Utah State University. Personal Cassette Recording. Logan, Utah, 3 June 1972.

A Tribute to Wallace Stegner. Videotape. University of Portland, Schoenfeldt Distinguished Writers Series, 10 October 1993. 105 min.

LETTERS

Venn, George. Letter to Wallace Stegner. (Reading list from "Daily Bulletin." La Grande: Eastern Oregon College, 8 March 1971.)

Stegner, Wallace. Letter to George Venn. 17 January 1971.

Alexander, Jo. Letter to Wallace Stegner. 24 October 1986.

Stegner, Wallace. Letter to George Venn. 15 November 1986.

Venn, George. Letter to Wallace Stegner. 17 November 1986.

Stegner, Wallace. Letter to George Venn. 28 November 1986.

Daniel, John. Letters to George Venn: 3 September 1993; 4 September 1993; 18 August 1993.

Schoenfeldt, Arthur. Letter to George Venn. 11 October 1993.

Venn, George. Letter to Arthur Schoenfeldt. 16 October 1993.

Doyle, Brian. Letter to George Venn. 12 October 1993.

Chapter 13. Dialogue At Wallowa Lake
BOOKS/PERIODICALS

Anon. *Fishtrap Gathering 1990:* Agenda.

Writer's Northwest Handbook 1989-1993. Eds. Dennis/Linny Stovall. Hillsboro, OR: Media Weavers.

Writers Northwest 1983-1993 (tabloid). Media Weavers. Hillsboro, OR: 75,000 circulation.

"Fishtrap Gathering Reels in Eastern Publishers." *Arts East* 5.4, 1988:1.

LETTERS

Stovall, Linny. Letter to George Venn. 30 July 1990.

Venn, George. Letter to Dennis and Linny Stovall. 1 December 1990.

Stovall, Linny. Letter to George Venn. 4 December 1990.

Chapter 14. *Yellow* (Anne Pitkin) *All That Comes to Light* (Lisa Steinman)
BOOKS

Pitkin, Anne. *Yellow*. Corvallis: Arrowood Books, 1989.

Steinman, Lisa. *All That Comes to Light.* Corvallis: Arrowood Books, 1989.

LETTERS

Brunvand, Dana. Letter to George Venn. 17 July 1989.

Brunvand, Dana. "Style Sheet for Reviews." *Western American Literature*. Undated.

Venn, George. Letter to Dana Brunvand. 17 September 1989.

Brunvand, Dana. Letter to George Venn. 20 September 1989.

Chapter 15. Ursula Le Guin At Eastern Oregon University
BOOKS

Le Guin, Ursula. *The Lathe of Heaven.* Charles Scribner's Sons, 1971.

Le Guin, Ursula. *Always Coming Home.* New York: Harper and Row, 1985.

Le Guin, Ursula. *The Left Hand of Darkness.* New York: Ace Books, 1969.

Spivak, Charlotte. *Ursula Le Guin.* Boston: Twayne, 1984.

Cummins, Elizabeth. *Understanding Ursula Le Guin.* Columbia: U. South Carolina Press, 1990.

LETTERS

Le Guin, Ursula. Letter to George Venn. 4 November 1985.

Le Guin, Ursula. Letter to George Venn. 31 May 1985.

Vatter, Barbara. Letter to George Venn. 6 June 1985.

RECORDING

Le Guin, Ursula. "Fiction Reading & Interview." Special Collections, Pierce Library. Ars Poetica Archive tape recordings #62 & 63.

Chapter 16. Nard Jones, Weston, and *Oregon Detour*
BOOKS

Cook, Jean. *Washington Authors.* Seattle: Washington State Library, 1936

Jones, Nard. *Oregon Detour.* New York: Payson and Clarke, 1930

_____*The Petlands.* New York: Brewer, Warren and Putnam, 1931.

_____ *Wheat Women.* New York: Duffield and Green, 1933

_____*All Six Were Lovers.* New York: Dodd, Mead, 1934.

_____*West, Young Man* (or *Young Pioneer*). Portland: Metro. Press, 1937.

_____*The Case of the Hanging Lady.* New York: Dodd, Mead, 1941.

_____*Swift Flows the River.* New York: Dodd, Mead, 1941.

_____*Scarlet Petticoat.* New York: Dodd, Mead, 1941.

_____*Still to the West.* New York: Dodd, Mead , 1946.

_____*Evergreen Land.* New York: Dodd, Mead, 1947.

_____*The Island.* New York: William Sloan Associate, 1948.

_____*I'll Take What's Mine.* New York: Gold Medal Originals, 1955.

_____*Ride The Dark Storm.* New York: Gold Medal Originals, 1955.

_____*Driver's Seat.* New York: Doubleday, 1956.

_____ *The Great Command.* Boston: Little, Brown, 1959.

_____*The Pacific Northwest.* New York: Doubleday, 1963.

_____*Seattle.* New York: Doubleday, 1972.

Meinig, Donald. *The Great Columbia Plain.* Seattle: U. of Washington Press, 1968.

Powers, Alfred. *History of Oregon Literature.* Portland, OR: Metropolitan Press, 1935.

Strelow, Michael, ed. *An Anthology of Northwest Writing.* Eugene: Northwest Rev., 1979.

Turnbull, George S. *History of Oregon Newspapers.* Portland: Binfords and Mort, 1939.

Warfel, Harry R. *American Novelists of Today.* New York: American Book, 1951.

PERIODICALS/NEWSPAPERS

Alexander, Jo. "Reprinting Northwest Americana." *The Burnside Reader* Powell's City of Books & Miriam Sontz, Summer (1992): 15-22.

Davis, H. L. and Stevens, James. *Status Rerum: A Manifesto, Upon the Present Condition of Northwestern Literature.* The Dalles, Oregon: privately printed, 1927.

Pollard, Lancaster. "The Pacific Northwest: A Regional Study." *Oregon Historical Quarterly*, LII September, 1951.

Jones, Nard. *Weston Leader.* Columns 1920-1930. Clark Wood, ed.

Merriam, Harold G., Ed. *The Frontier.* 11 November 1930.

Blue Moon. Whitman College Literary Annual, 1922-26.

INTERVIEWS (UNPUBLISHED)

These individuals kindly granted me interviews between March and August, 1981: Blair Jones, Audrey Jones Baker, Debbie Jones, Anne Mynar Jones, Darcy Dauble,

Margaret Sutherland, Frank McCorkle, Kathleen McCullough, Jack Beathe, Walter Rayborn, Russell McCollister, Jim and Audrey Lieullen, Wilma Reynaud, Thelma Gentry, Vernon O'Harra, George Gottfried, Otis Gould, Jean Kirk, Hugh and Florence Gilliland, Jack Hass, the W. E. VanWinkles, Stella Gordon, Chester Maxey, Robert Polzin, Larry Dodds, Wayne O'Harra, Ruby Kirk, Frank Greer, Claude Price, Attras McCorkle, Jennebel Vincent, Sheldon Delph, Herb Culley, Mrs. Clayson Adams, Mr. Barnett, Jean Vincent, Warner McCorkle.

Note: most of the biographical evidence in the essay and nearly all of the pre- and post-publication history of the novel come from these interviews.

Letters/Documents (unpublished)

William Rose Benet, Assistant Editor of *Saturday Review* and Editorial Advisor to Payson and Clark to Nard Jones. New York, April 1, 1929.

Cassell, Dave. Letter to George Venn.

Renken, Valerie. Untitled Nard Jones Report, Eastern Oregon University, 1978.

Sutherland, Margaret. Letter to George Venn.

Wood, Clark. Letter to Nard Jones. 16 April 1930.

Circulation Records, 1930-1959, Umatilla County Library and Weston Branch Library.

Oregon Detour Scrapbook, Jones Family Papers, Seattle, WA.

Venn, George. Personal Papers. *Eastern Oregon Librarians' Survey.* 1973.

Chapter 17. John Haislip and *Seal Rock*

Books/Periodicals

Haislip, John. *Seal Rock.* Selma, Indiana: The Barnwood Press, 1986.

_____ *Not Every Year.* Seattle: U. of Washington, 1971.

_____ "Seal Rock." *American Poets In 1976.* William Heyen, ed: Indianapolis: Bobbs-Merrill, 1976: 72-89.

_____ "The Example of Theodore Roethke." *Northwest Review* 14.3, 1975: 14-20.

Rock, John. Cover painting: "Oregon Coast–Fog Lifting."

Letters

Witte, John. Letter to George Venn. 23 February 1987

Venn, George. Letter to John Witte. 13 April 1987.

Witte, John. Letter to George Venn. 20 April 1987.

Chapter 18. *Marking the Magic Circle*

Books

Tuan, Yi-Fu. *Topofilia.* Prentice-Hall, 1974.

Gould, Peter and Rodney White. *Mental Maps.* Penguin, 1974.

Bachelard, Gaston. *The Poetics of Space.* Orion, 1964.

Ardrey, Robert. *The Territorial Imperative* (1st). Dell, 1971.

Emerson, Ralph Waldo. *Essays, First Series.* "Circles." 1841.

Eliade, Mircea. *The Sacred and the Profane...*Harcourt Brace, 1959.

"Early Morning: Washington 12 Toward Ohanapecosh." *Off The Main Road*. Portland: Prescott St. Press, 1978: 42-43.
"Larch in Fall." *Marking The Magic Circle*. Corvallis: OSU Press, 1987: 11.
"From Half-Dead Grass." *Marking The Magic Circle*: 14-15.

PERIODICALS

"Winter Sailor." *Portland Review* 27.2 (1981): 86.
"My Mother Is This White Wind Cleaning." *Poetry Northwest* 22.2 (1981): 21.
"Voice From Another Wilderness." *Poetry Northwest* 21.1 (1980): 53.

LETTER

Attebery, Louie. Letter to President David Gilbert. 6 March 1984.

Chapter 19. *Northwest Variety: Personal Essays by 14 Regional Authors*

BOOKS/ARTICLES

Love, Glen and Edwin Bingham, eds. *Northwest Perspectives*. Seattle/Eugene: U. Of Washington Press, 1979.
Robbins, William, Robert J. Frank, Richard E. Ross, eds. *Regionalism and the Pacific Northwest*. Corvallis: OSU Press, 1983.
Robbins, Tom. "Why I Live Where I Live." *Esquire*, Oct. 1980.
Dialogues With Northwest Writers. Eugene: Northwest Review Books 20. 2-3, 1982.
Carlson, Roy. Ed. *Contemporary Northwest Writing*. Corvallis: OSU Press, 1979.
Haislip, John. "Seal Rock." *American Poets in 1976*. William Heyen, ed. Indianapolis: Bobbs-Merrill (1976): 72-89
O'Connell, Nicholas, ed. *At The Field's End: Interviews with 20 Pacific Northwest Writers*. Seattle: Madrona Publishers, 1987.
Venn, George. Review of *At The Field's End: Interviews with 20 Pacific Northwest Writers*, by Nicholas O'Connell. *Publishing Northwest* 6.3 (1988): 13. (1987): 13.
Friedman, Jane & T. Sisk, eds. *The Northwest Review of Books*. Seattle: J & T Pub., 1985

LETTERS

Walsh, Frank. Letter to George Venn. 8 August 1985.
Arrowood Books. Letter to Reviewers (George Venn). March, 1987.
Venn, George. Letter to Lex Runciman. 31 March 1987.
Runciman, Lex and Steve Sher. Solicitation Letter to 30 Northwest Writers. March 1986.
Runciman, Lex. Letter to George Venn. 4 April 1987.

Chapter 20. **The Paradox of Ai Qing**

NOTES TO ESSAY:

1. Beijing Library Editorial Group, trans. by Daisy Rothgery, *Ai Qing on Poetry* (Beijing: Beijing Library, 1981), pp. 24-28. Also, Prof. Lu provided other sources, though the period between 1958 and 1978 was generally omitted in all Chinese materials available to me in China.

2. D. W. Fokkema, *Literary Doctrine in China and Soviet Influence, 1956-1960* (The Hague: Mouton and Co., 1965): 13.

3. Fokkema, pp. 3-11. 1 have added the titles.

4. Ai Qing, *Shih lun,* trans. Julia C. Lin in *Modern Chinese Poetry An Introduction* (Seattle: University of Washington Press, 1972): 187. It should be noted that Lin's review of the poet is not wholly reliable, since it fails to recognize the significance of Ai Qing's opposition to the Yenan prescription.

5. Fokkema, p. 61.

6. Fokkema, pp. 168-172.

7. Ai Qing, "Author's Preface," trans. Pen Wenlan and E. C. Eoyang in *Selected Poems of Ai Qing* (Bloomington and Beijing: Indiana U. Press and Foreign Languages Press, 1982): 11-12.

8. See the poem "Fish Fossil" for the poet's treatment of his exile and return.

9. This designation was rescinded by the Party in 1961 when Ai Qing was restored to full membership.

10. Ai Qing, "Chronology," trans. E. C. Eoyang in *Selected Poems of Ai Qing* (Bloomington and Beijing: Indiana U. Press and Foreign Languages Press, 1982): 217.

11. The information in this paragraph was synthesized from multiple sources, including an interview with the poet by the author in Beijing in July, 1982. Some of this description is also deduced from other statements by the poet.

NOTES TO TRANSLATIONS:

FISH FOSSIL

This poem was written after the fall of the Gang of Four when Ai Qing was again allowed to return to Beijing. Actual date of composition is 1977. The poem describes metaphorically the causes and effect of his twenty years of exile from literary life, during which he was allowed to write but not to publish.

line 16: *petrified, petrified,* not repeated in the original, is doubled here for ambiguity and rhythmic integrity of the line.

line 28: *candlefish* is a species of smelt burned for light by certain American Indian tribes on the northwest coast.

HAIL

Written during his exile in Xinjiang, this poem describes public destruction created by the hail of warring street gangs during the civil war which is usually called the Cultural Revolution. The diction is more formal in Chinese.

PERSIAN CHRYSANTHEMUMS

The title refers to an uncommon variety of this flower commonly found in the city of Yenan, the communist capital during the Anti-Japanese War. The flower is used here as an image of spreading revolutionary seed to the city of Daqing, Heilongjiang Province in northeast China, the largest oil-producing city in China today.

line 9: *Yenan* refers to the years 1935-49 when the city was used as the communist capital.

line 10: caves refers to cave dwellings commonly found in northwest China which were inhabited by both revolutionary leaders and common people. The place names refer to districts where different leaders lived.

BURNING THE WASTELAND GRASS

In 1957, Ai Qing was banished to Xinjiang Province in northeast China. The Bei Da Huang area close to the Chinese-Soviet border became his home in exile for nineteen years. Written in 1958 but unpublished until 1980, this poem describes a frontier scene in that border region.

lines 3-4: the original order of' these lines in Chinese is inverted in English for emphasis.

line 6: *gone for glory,* literally translated, would have been the Chinese idiom, *beyond the ninth heaven.* While it is tempting to use such English idioms as *beyond the highest heaven* or *on cloud nine,* neither of them is accurate diction in this context, which requires the spectacle of wildfire to be praised.

line 14: *trembling lives* in Chinese is the noun catalog *of jackals, wolves, foxes, rabbits.* Metonymy compresses the line and keeps it rhythmically unified in English.

THE LOST YEARS

Written in 1978 during a visit to Harbin, this poem was prepared for an audience who gathered to hear Ai Qing speak about his twenty years of suffering in exile and silence. Instead of making a speech, he wrote this poem and read it. During our 1982 interview, he said he preferred this poem to many others in the book. "That time was gone forever," he said, "and the poem should be sad."

line 11: lost years is isolated here for emphasis and tension in English

line 13: loess is a buff to yellowish brown loamy soil found in North China and believed to be chiefly deposited by wind. This word is used here for ground because it is homophonic with loss.

lines 18-19: see "Fish Fossil" where the poet further develops this image as a self-portrait

Chapter 21. Carolyn Kizer at Cannon Beach, 1981... with Tim Barnes

BOOKS

Skelton, Robin, ed. *Five Poets of the Pacific Northwest.* Seattle: U of Washington, 1964.

Kizer, Carolyn. *The Ungrateful Garden.* Bloomington: Indiana U. Press, 1961.

Barnes, Tim and Edwin Bingham. *Wood Works: The Life and Writings of Charles Erskine Scott Wood.* Corvallis: OSU Press, 1997.

Williams, C. K. *With Ignorance.* New York: Houghton Mifflin, 1977.

Rich, Adrienne. *A Dream of a Common Language.* New York: Norton, 1977.

Barnes, Tim. *Of Almonds and Angels.* Skookum's Tongue Press, 2007.

Barnes, Tim. *Definitions for a Lost Language.* Skookum's Tongue Press, 2010.

Barnes, Tim. *Everyone Out Here Knows: A Big Foot Tale*. Arnica Creative Services, 2014. (A children's book illustrated by Angelina Marino-Heidel and based on a poem by William Stafford).

PERIODICALS

Kizer, Carolyn. "Poetry: the School of the Pacific Northwest." *The New Republic*. July 1956:

Kizer, Carolyn. *Poetry Northwest,* ed. Seattle:U of Washington, 1960.

LETTERS

Venn, George. Letter to Carolyn Kizer. 28 August 1998.

Kizer, Carolyn. Letter to George Venn. 11 September 1998.

Kizer, Carolyn. "Vita." August, 1998: 2 pp.

Kizer, Carolyn. Letter to George Venn. 4 January 1984.

RECORDINGS

Kizer, Carolyn. "Ars Poetica Reading." Tape #55. La Grande: Eastern Oregon University 4 April 1983: 60 minutes.

Kizer, Carolyn, Rolfe Humphries, William Stafford: "Ars Poetica Reading." Tape #19. La Grande: Eastern Oregon University. 23 April 1966: 60 minutes.

Chapter 22. **Northwest Poetry and the Land**

LETTERS

Attebery, Brian. Letter to George Venn. 20 January 1980.

Attebery, Brian. Letter to George Venn. 5 March 1980.

Stafford, William. Letter to George Venn. 21 January 1980.

Stafford, Kim. Letter to George Venn. 1 February 1980.

UNPUBLISHED MANUSCRIPT

Balakian, Peter. "Poetry of the Northwest: Aspects of Achievement." The College of Idaho, Caldwell: 6 January 1980: 7 pages.

Chapter 23. **The Search for Sacred Space in Western American Literature**

LETTERS

Trelawny, Victor. Letter to George Venn. 18 December 1975

Trelawny, Victor. Letter to George Venn. 16 June 1976

BOOKS

Feldman, Susan. *The Story Telling Stone*. New York: Dell, 1973.

Eliade, Mircea. *The Sacred and the Profane*. New York: Harcourt Brace, 1959.

Rothenberg, Jerome, ed. *Technicians of the Sacred*. New York: Doubleday, 1969.

Nash, Roderick. *Wilderness and the American Mind*. New Haven, Conn: Yale, 1967.

Berger, Peter, et al. *The Homeless Mind*. New York: Random House, 1974.

Stone, Christopher D. *Should Trees Have Standing*. Los Altos, CA: Wm. Kaufmann, 1974.

Barbour, Ian G. *Western Man and Environmental Ethics*. Boston: Addison Wesley, 1973

Guthrie, A. B. *The Big Sky*. Sentry Edition. Boston: Houghton Mifflin, 1965.

Fisher, Vardis. *Mountain Man*. New York: William Morrow, 1965.

Elder, Fredrick. *Crisis In Eden*. Nashville: Abingdon, 1970.
Stegner, Wallace. *The Sound of Mountain Water*. New York: Doubleday, 1969.
Hanson, Kenneth. *The Uncorrected World*. Middletown: Wesleyan, 1973.
Skelton, Robin, ed. *Five Poets of the Pacific Northwest*. Seattle: U. of Washington, 1964.
Smith, Henry Nash. *Virgin Land*. New York: Random House, 1950.
Fiedler, Leslie. *An End to Innocence*. Boston: Beacon, 1948.
Leopold, Aldo. *A Sand County Almanac*. Oxford: Oxford University Press, 1966.
Waters, Frank. *The Dust Within the Rock*. New York: Farrar and Rinehart, 1940.
Snyder, Gary. *Earth House Hold*. New York: New Directions, 1969.
Craven, Margaret. *I Heard The Owl Call My Name*. New York: Doubleday, 1973.
Jeffers, Robinson. *Selected Poems*. New York: Knopf and Random House, 1963.
Cather, Willa. *My Antonia*. Boston: Houghton Mifflin, 1954.
Stafford, William. *Someday Maybe*. New York: Harper and Row, 1973.
Gale, Vi. *Clearwater*. Chicago: Swallow Press, 1974.
Williams, William Carlos. *In The American Grain*. New York: New Directions, 1956.
Shepard, Paul. *Man in the Landscape*. New York: Ballantine, 1967.
Clough, Wilson O. *The Necessary Earth*. Austin: U. Of Texas Press, 1964.

PERIODICALS

"Western American Literature, 1966-1976." Logan, UT: Western Literature Assn.

Chapter 24. The Literature of Eastern Oregon
LETTERS

Venn, George. Letters and Questionnaires to 42 Eastern Oregon Librarians. 23 February 1973.

_____ "The Literature of Eastern Oregon Questionnaire, Sections I.-V. Instructions:"
Twenty Five Public Librarians. Completed Questionnaires Returned to George Venn. Feb/ March, 1973.

PUBLICATIONS

"The Literature of Eastern Oregon: A Truncated Bibliography." La Grande: Eastern Oregon College, Oregon Division of Continuing Education, Spring, 1973: 1-11 (alphabetized non-fiction), 11-14 (alphabetized fiction and poetry.)
Note: librarians did not submit their listings in MLA format. Copy of all originals are archived.

Chapter 25. Elizabeth Gurley Flynn: Bringing Down Missoula
BOOKS

Adamic, Louis. *Dynamite: The Story of Class Violence in America*. New York: Doubleday, 1935.
Baxandall, Rosalyn Fraad. *Words on Fire*. New Brunswick: Rutgers U., 1987.
Brissenden, P. F. *The I.W.W. A Study of American Syndicalism*. New York: Columbia U., 1919.
Camp, Helen C. *Iron in Her Soul*. Pullman: WSU Press, 1995.
Flynn, Elizabeth Gurley. *I Speak My Own Piece*. New York: Masses/Mainstream, 1955.
_____*The Rebel Girl: An Autobiography*. New York: Intern. Publishers, 1973.
Foner, Philip S. *History of the Labor Movement in the United States, Vol IV*. New York: International Publishers, 1965.

Koelbel, Lenora. *Missoula The Way It Was*. Missoula: Gateway Printing, 1972.

Kornbluh, Joyce, ed. *Rebel Voices....* Ann Arbor: U of Michigan Press, 1964.

Lavender, David. *Land of Giants*. New York: Doubleday, 1956.

Limerick, Patricia. *The Legacy of Conquest*. New York: Norton, 1987.

Polk, R. L. *Missoula and Hamilton Directory*. Missoula, MT: Missoulian, 1909.

Renshaw, Patrick. *The Wobblies....* New York: Doubleday, 1967.

Stevens, James. *Big Jim Turner*. Garden City, NY: Doubleday, 1948.

Venn, George. "At the Foul Line." *Oregon East* 26 (1995): 93-106.

NEWSPAPERS

The Anaconda Standard, Anaconda, Montana

The Butte Miner, Butte, Montana

The Industrial Worker, Spokane, Washington

The Daily Missoulian, Missoula, Montana

PAMPHLETS

Anonymous, *Missoula—The Garden City*. Missoula, MT: Missoulian Print, 1909.

Missoula County Trades and Labor Council. *A Graphic Story of Organized Labor in Missoula County, 1896-1946*. Missoula, MT: Missoulian, 1946.

UNPUBLISHED SOURCES

Evans, Robert Emlyn. *The Enactment of Legislation Designed to Suppress the Industrial Workers of the World*. Missoula, MT: University of Montana, 1941.

Missoula City Council Minutes, 1909.

INTERVIEW

Forrest Warwick, retired employee of Northern Pacific Railroad, an eyewitness to the events in 1909. Spring, 1970, Missoula, Montana.

Chapter 26. Richard Hugo with Ronald Bayes...

PUBLICATIONS

"Hugo, Richard." Interview with Ron Bayes. *Oregon East 1950–1985*. (1985): 92-98.

Anon. "Northwest Poet Here Wednesday." *The Observer*. La Grande, OR. 29 June 1965: 5.

RECORDINGS

"Hanson, Kenneth & Richard Hugo. "Ars Poetica Reading." Pierce Library Recording #20. La Grande: Eastern Oregon College: 4 November 1966.

"Hugo, Richard. "Ars Poetica Reading." Pierce Library Recording #? La Grande: Eastern Oregon College, 16 November 1968

LETTERS

Venn, George. Letter to Ripley Schemm. 1984.

Schemm, Ripley. Letter to George Venn. 1984.

NOTES AND SOURCES

PERMISSIONS AND CREDITS

Cover
  "Mask 2" (watercolor) by Stephani Stephenson, 1984.

Chapter 1. Beaver and the Grande Ronde River
  TEXT: by permission of U California Press and "My Last Address." *RondeDance* 1.1
    (2006): 9-11.
  IMAGE: "Beaver's Meanders." Aerial of Lower Grande Ronde River. Snake River and
    Joseph Creek confluences at the top. Credit: Dave Jensen, 25 April 2008.
    By permission of Dave Jensen Photography

Chapter 2. Where the Crooked River Rises
  TEXT: reprinted courtesy of the author and *Oregon Historical Quarterly* Vol. 112,
    No. 2 , (Summer 2011): 268-269.
  IMAGES: reprinted by permission of Ellen Waterston

Chapter 3. They Also Served...
  TEXT: reprinted courtesy of the author and *Oregon Historical Quarterly* 108.2 (2007):
    294-316.
  IMAGES: all images reprinted courtesy of Fred Hill

Chapter 4. Literature of the Northwest Symposium
  TEXT: reprinted courtesy of the author and *Northwest Review* 45-3 (2007): 30-35.
  IMAGE: John Witte photo courtesy of John Witte

Chapter 5. Soldier to Advocate
  TEXT: reprinted courtesy of the author and *Oregon Historical Quarterly* 106.1 (2005):
    34-75.
  IMAGES: courtesy of the Huntington Library

Chapter 6. Rider in the Wilderness
  TEXT: reprinted courtesy of the author and *Calapooya Literary Review* 2 (2004):
    21-26.

IMAGES (two photos by Fred Hill):
"Minor White Reconnoiter, High Valley, 1940."
_____ "WPA Art Center Administrator & Instructor."
IMAGES (courtesy Fred Hill Collection):
White, Minor. "Eagle Cap Boulder."
Hill, Etha. "After An Exchange of Bad Puns."
DOCUMENTS (courtesy Fred Hill Collection):
Anon: "Class Schedule, Art Center, 1940."
_____ Letter, Minor White to Etha Hill, 21 March 1945

Chapter 7. Down in My Heart by William Stafford
TEXT: reprinted courtesy of the author and *Oregon Historical Quarterly* 100.3 (1999): 339-342.
IMAGES: William Stafford photo courtesy of Lewis & Clark College Watzek Library Archives and Special Collections

Chapter 8. Chief Joseph's 'Surrender Speech' as Literary Text
TEXT: reprinted courtesy of the author and *Oregon English Journal* 20 (1998): 69-73 and Rpt. http://www.ochcom.org/pdf/Wood-Venn.pdf.
IMAGES: reprinted from *Soldier to Advocate* (2006) and permission of Huntington Library; "Negotiating the Surrender" Sketch from "Grace Howard Gray Scrapbook." OHS Spectator No. 3, Summer 2000, p. 5. Reprinted courtesy of Oregon Historical Society.

Chapter 9. William Stafford in Northwest Literature
TEXT: reprinted from *Oregon English Journal* 19.1 (1997): 16-17.
IMAGES: Leslie Fiedler (1973) by permission of Archives and Special Collections, Mansfield Library, University of Montana. Theodore Roethke (1952) by University of Washington Libraries, Special Collections, Portrait Collection, Negative WW 18784; William Stafford (1960?) photo courtesy of Lewis & Clark College Watzek Library Archives and Special Collections; Bernard Malamud(1958) photo from Harriet's Collection, OSU Libraries Special Collections & Archives Research Center, HC3273

Chapter 10. StoryLines Northwest (NEH & ALA)
TEXT AND DOCUMENTS: reprinted courtesy of the American Library Association
IMAGES: Lowell Jaeger and Paul Zalis in KUFM studio photo courtesy of Paul Zalis

Chapter 11. Editing an Invisible Literature: *The Oregon Literature Series*
TEXT: reprinted courtesy of the author and the videotape transcript
IMAGES: "OLS Editors." courtesy of Pat Scott, Portland State University, 27 August 1990; Governor Barbara Roberts Presentation photo 12/9/94 courtesy of OSU; OLS Covers courtesy of OSU Press

Chapter 12. Remembering Wallace Stegner
TEXT: transcribed by the author from *A Tribute to Wallace Stegner*. Videotape.
University of Portland, Schoenfeldt Distinguished Writers Series, 10 October
1993. 105 min.
IMAGES: Wallace Stegner photo courtesy of Merrill-Cazier Library, Utah State
University, Special Collections and Archives; "Stegner Memorial Speakers"
courtesy University of Portland

Chapter 13. Dialogue At Wallowa Lake
TEXT: reprinted courtesy of the author and *Writers Northwest Handbook* (4th) (1991):
12-13.
IMAGES: *Fishtrap 1988* courtesy of Fishtrap/OPB; Dennis and Linny Stovall and
Writers Northwest Handbook(4th) courtesy of Media Weavers publishers Dennis
and Linny Stovall

Chapter 14. Yellow (Anne Pitkin) *All That Comes to Light* (Lisa Steinman)
TEXT: reprinted courtesy *Western American Literature* 25.1 (1990): 53-56.
IMAGES: author photos courtesy of Anne Pitkin and Lisa Steinman; Steinman cover
by Chi Meredith; Pitkin cover anon; both covers courtesy of Arrowood Books
publisher Lex Runciman

Chapter 15. Ursula Le Guin At Eastern Oregon University
TEXT: reprinted courtesy of *Oregon East* 19. (1988): 37-50, and Ursula Le Guin.
IMAGE: Lisa Kroeber photo courtesy Ars Poetica Archive, Special Collections,
Pierce Library, Eastern Oregon University

Chapter 16. Nard Jones, Weston, and *Oregon Detour*
TEXT: reprinted courtesy of the author from *Oregon Detour* by Nard Jones. Corvallis:
OSU Press, Northwest Reprint Series (1990)
IMAGES: Nard Jones (ca 1926) courtesy Penrose Library Archives, Whitman
College; Nard Jones' residence, Weston, Oregon (ca 1993) courtesy Jan Boles
Photography

Chapter 17. John Haislip and *Seal Rock*
TEXT: reprinted courtesy of the author and *Northwest Review* 25.2 (1987): 157-160.
IMAGES: John Haislip photo by William Stafford courtesy of Lewis & Clark
College Watzek Library Archives and Special Collections; book cover courtesy
of John Rock

Chapter 18. Marking the Magic Circle
TEXT: reprinted courtesy of the author from *Marking the Magic Circle* (1987)
IMAGES: photo courtesy Jo Alexander; Grande Ronde Valley and River Meanders
from Mt. Harris courtesy Dave Jensen Photography

Chapter 19. Northwest Variety: Personal Essays by 14 Regional Authors
TEXT: reprinted courtesy of the author and *Publishing Northwest* 5.5 (Sept/Oct 1987): 1-2.
IMAGES: cover by Carol Williams reprinted courtesy of Lex Runciman, Publisher, Arrowood Books; Lex Runciman photo courtesy of Lex Runciman; Steve Sher photo by Ann Sanfedele, courtesy of Plutzik Goldwasser Family Foundation, copyright steven.sher.poetry@gmail.com

Chapter 20. The Paradox of Ai Qing
TEXT: reprinted courtesy of the author and *Northwest Review* (Fall, 1984): 107-115.
IMAGES: photo courtesy George Venn Collection, 1982. "Fish Fossil" drawing and cover of *Songs* for *Coming Home* (Sichuan People's Press, 1980) courtesy of Ai Qing.

Chapter 21. Carolyn Kizer at Cannon Beach, 1981... with Tim Barnes
TEXT: reprinted courtesy Tim Barnes and *Oregon East* 15. (1984): 41-50.
IMAGES: Tim Barnes photo courtesy Ilka Kuznick; Carolyn Kizer photo courtesy Thomas Victor; William Stafford photo: "Carolyn Kizer and W. S. Merwin, NCTE Conference, New Orleans, 1966." Courtesy of Lewis & Clark College Watzek Library Archives and Special Collections.

Chapter 22. Northwest Poetry and the Land
TEXT: reprinted courtesy Brian Attebery and *Oregon East,* (1986): 33-42.
IMAGES: William Stafford, Kim Stafford, George Venn, Ann Copeland, Peter Balakian, Brian Attebery, Jennifer Attebery photos by William Stafford courtesy of Lewis & Clark College Watzek Library Archives and Special Collections; Madeline DeFrees by permission of Archives and Special Collections, Mansfield Library, University of Montana; Richard Hugo photo courtesy of Jennifer Schemm.

Chapter 23. The Search for Sacred Space in Western American Literature
TEXT: reprinted courtesy *Portland Review* 22. (1976): 6-19.
IMAGES: Manuel Izquierdo calligraphy reprinted courtesy of archives, Portland State University; Primus St. John photo courtesy Ars Poetica Archive, Special Collections, Pierce Library, Eastern Oregon University

Chapter 24. The Literature of Eastern Oregon
TEXT: reprinted courtesy of the author and Oregon Division of Continuing Education, 1973
IMAGE: Ian Gatley poster logo courtesy of Ars Poetica Archive, Special Collections, Pierce Library, Eastern Oregon University

Chapter 25. Elizabeth Gurley Flynn: Bringing Down Missoula
TEXT: reprinted courtesy of the author and *Montana...*21.4 (Fall, 1971): 18-30.

IMAGES:

(1) Portrait of E. G. Flynn item 12, 1911; Elizabeth Gurley Flynn Photographs; PHOTOS 018; box 1; folder 1; Tamiment Library/Robert F. Wagner Labor Archives, New York University.

(2) Jack Jones photo courtesy of Newberry Library, Chicago: "Dill Picklers in Costume: Barbary Coast Costume Ball." Bx.4 (oversize) Fl.278, ca 1921-1927: selected, cropped, enlarged.

(3) "E. G. Flynn with Butte Miners,1909. "from *Iron in Her Soul* by Helen Camp. Pullman, Wash: WSU Press. 1995. eBook. (AN 21749) photo gallery as photo #9. The caption identifies the man on the left as F. W. Flynn, Butte Federation of Miners.

Chapter 26. Richard Hugo with Ronald Bayes...

TEXT: reprinted by permission of the editor and *Oregon East 1950-1985*: 92-98.

IMAGES: Richard Hugo by permission of Jennifer Schemm; Ronald H. Bayes by permission of Special Collections, Pierce Library, Eastern Oregon University; Ars Poetica posters courtesy the author.

PERMISSIONS AND CREDITS

Photo by: Stephani Stephenson

GEORGE VENN

Poet, writer, literary historian, editor, linguist, and educator, George Venn (1943) is an eclectic, complex, and distinguished figure in western American literature. As one university press editor described him, "Venn's blend of creativity and scholarship is unique...." Venn recently enhanced that description in the 2005 *Contemporary Authors*: "Politics: Independent. Religion: Ecumenist; mystic; no literalistic ethnocentric orthodoxy; everything universal." His distinguished and eclectic literary practice is best affirmed by *MARKING THE MAGIC CIRCLE* (1987), a collection of fiction, poetry, essays, translations, and Jan Boles photographs. In 1988, this book won a silver medal from Literary Arts; in 2005, the same book was selected by the Oregon Cultural Heritage Commission as one of the 100 best Oregon books in the two centuries.

As a poet and fiction writer, George Venn studied at The College of Idaho, at City Literary Institute, London, and at the University of Montana. In the 1970s he won a Breadloaf scholarship and studied briefly with the novelist John Williams. In 1980, his poem "Forgive Us..." from *OFF THE MAIN ROAD* won a Pushcart Prize.

When he received the 1995 Andres Berger Award, The Oregonian described him as "One of the best-known and most respected poets in the state." His 1999 collection *WEST OF PARADISE* was a finalist for an Oregon Book Award. His poems and stories have been widely published in regional periodicals and anthologized in seventeen different state, regional, and national collections, most recently in *Teaching with Fire: Poetry that Sustains the Courage to Teach*. His work has been included in the national Poetry in Motion program, carved in stone at the New Oregon Zoo, and featured in the Ron Finne film "Tamanawis Illahee." Three different composers have set his lyrics to music for concert performances across the Pacific Northwest.

As a writer and literary historian, Venn studied with folklorist Louie Attebery at The College of Idaho and with graduate faculty at the University of Montana. His sixty articles, essays, and reviews have appeared in thirty-two different periodicals, and his prose has been anthologized in nine different collections, most recently in *World Views and the American West*. Reviewing his third book, critic Glen Love wrote that George Venn is "one of the foremost serious regionalists in the Northwest...." In 1992, editor Jo Alexander wrote that Venn's essay, "Nard Jones, Weston, and *Oregon Detour*," inspired Oregon State University Press to begin what became the "Northwest Reprint Series." In his 2003 study, *On Sacred Ground: The Spirit of Place in Pacific Northwest Literature*, Nicholas O'Connell wrote that Venn's essay, "Continuity in Northwest Literature," broke new ground by "suggesting that the landscape might serve as the focal point for a distinctive regional literature."

As an editor and critic, Venn has reviewed manuscripts for federal agencies, university presses, literary magazines, and small presses. In the 1970s he edited the *Eastern Oregon Literary Supplement*, a regional annual with a circulation of 60,000. In the 1980s, he edited and published interviews with Ursula Le Guin, Carolyn Kizer, and Richard Hugo. In 1986, his edited Chinese folktale appeared in *Folklore India*. He has served on the editorial boards of the *Oregon Historical Quarterly*, *Oregon East Magazine*, and *Northwest Folklore*. From 1989–1994, he served as General Editor of the 2,300-page *Oregon Literature Series*. For that six-volume project, declared by NEA a national model and awarded an Exemplary Programs grant, Venn received the Stewart Holbrook Award for "outstanding contributions to Oregon's literary life."

In 1995, the National Council of Teachers of English also recognized the project with a Multicultural Publishing Award.

As an educator and linguist, Venn first taught English-as-a-Second Language (ESL) as an undergraduate while studying Spanish at universities in Ecuador and Spain. After completing his M.F.A., he joined the English faculty at Eastern Oregon University where he taught courses in writing, ESL, American Literature, Literature of the West, Northwest, and Native American Literature. He also served as director of the EOU Creative Writing program; director of the ESL Program; instructor in the German-Oregon international exchange program; advisor to *Oregon East*, the EOU student literary journal. On four occasions between 1970 and 1988, Venn was nationally recognized by CCLM when *Oregon East* placed in the top twenty collegiate literary magazines in the United States. In 1981–82, while teaching at Changsha Railway University in China, he collaboratively translated poems by the exiled modernist Ai Qing. From 2001–2003, he served as President of the Oregon Council of Teachers of English. On retiring as professor of English and Writer-in-Residence, he received the Distinguished Teaching Award.

For more information, please see *Contemporary Authors* 231 (2005) and www.georgevenn.com

www.ingramcontent.com/pod-product-compliance
Lightning Source LLC
Chambersburg PA
CBHW081132020726